March 81 - $7 95

Hope Is an Open Door

JOURNEYS IN FAITH

Creative Dislocation—The Movement of Grace,
Robert McAfee Brown

Speech, Silence, Action! The Cycle of Faith,
Virginia Ramey Mollenkott

By Way of Response,
Martin E. Marty

Hope Is an Open Door

Mary Luke Tobin, S.L.

Journeys in Faith
Robert A. Raines, Editor

ABINGDON
Nashville

HOPE IS AN OPEN DOOR

Copyright © 1981 by Abingdon

Library of Congress Cataloging in Publication Data

TOBIN, LUKE, 1908–
Hope is an open door.
(Journeys in faith)
Bibliography: p.
1. Tobin, Luke, 1908–   2. Nuns—United States—Biography.
3. Church and social problems—Catholic Church.I. Title. II. Series.
BX4705.T6722A33   271'.9   80-21414

ISBN 0-687-17410-4

Scripture quotations noted RSV are from the Revised Standard Version of the Bible, copyrighted 1946, 1952, © 1971, 1973 by the Division of Christian Education of the National Council of the Churches of Christ in the U.S.A. and are used by permission.

Other Scripture quotations are some of the author's favorite lines, taken from a variety of translations.

MANUFACTURED BY THE PARTHENON PRESS AT
NASHVILLE, TENNESSEE, UNITED STATES OF AMERICA

There is a wise madness in these walls.
                    —Thomas Merton,
                Loretto and Gethsemani

To the Loretto community
            gratefully
for wise madness
. . . in the past
. . . in the present
. . . and expected in the
    future

Acknowledgments

I wish to express my deepest gratitude to Cecily Jones, S.L., for her immeasurable help, both editorial and technical.

I also extend special thanks to other members of the Loretto community—to Mary Schaldenbrand, Jane Marie Richardson, and Marie Francis Kenoyer—for very substantial and helpful suggestions.

There are others who deserve thanks and gratitude, especially Helen Sanders, Mary Frances Lottes, Deborah Pearson, and Ann Patrick Ware, all of the Loretto community; and Dorothy Wagner of Church Women United.

Acknowledgment is made also to The Thomas Merton Legacy Trust, for permission to use material excerpted from the Merton tapes, now housed in the Merton Collection at Bellarmine Library, Louisville, Kentucky.

Contents

Editor's Foreword

People within and outside the church today are engaged in a profound revisioning of the faith journey. Wanting to honor our own heritage and to be nourished by our roots, we also want to discern the signs of the Kingdom now, and to move into the 1980s with a lean, biblical, ecumenical, and human, faith perspective.

The Journeys in Faith series is offered to facilitate this revisioning of faith. Reflecting on the social justice openings of the 1960s and the inward searching of the 1970s, these books articulate a fresh integration of the faith journey for the years ahead. They are personal and social. Authors have been invited to share what has been happening to them in their faith and life in recent years and then to focus on issues that have become primary for them in this time.

We believe that these lucidly written books will be used widely by study groups in congregations, seminaries, colleges, renewal centers, orders, and denominations, as well as for personal study and reflection.

Our distinguished authors embody a diversity of experience and perspective, which will provide many points of identification and enrichment for readers. As we enter into the pilgrimages shared in these books, we will find resonance, encouragement, and insight for a fresh appropriation of our faith toward personal and social transformation.

When Pope John XXIII opened the Vatican windows in 1962, permitting the breezes of the Spirit to sweep through the Roman Catholic Church, many doors swung open as well. And through one of them walked Sister Mary Luke Tobin. A member of the Sisters of Loretto for more than fifty years, and its president at the time, she was one of the fifteen women in world Catholicism invited to be auditors at the Vatican Council. Relationships with Catholic leaders across the world, and also with world Protestant leaders who were present as observers, opened doors for ecumenical work and witness in the decades ahead.

Mary Luke Tobin gives us, in this book, a fascinating inside interpretation of the changes in church (especially Roman Catholic) and society over the last twenty years. Protestants and other readers, as well as Catholics, will find their understanding of the struggle for change in church attitudes and policies deepened. Though Tobin is disappointed today in the slow pace of creative change, she embodies and articulates abiding confidence that the purposes of the Spirit are at work, even in frustration and setback, and will eventually prevail.

Her commitment to peace and justice in the world and to justice and freedom in the church permeates these pages. A principle resounding throughout is her insistence upon the priority of persons over institutions—whether the institution is a coal company or a Vatican structure. The deep and nourishing support of the Loretto community in her years of prophetic social witness reminds us of the importance of such supportive community for all of us and raises questions as to how we can find, create, and sustain it. Her personal friendship with Thomas Merton over several years provides delightful, loving, and humorous snapshots of his life and work. As a member of the Church Women United national staff for several years, she showed herself a truly ecumenical person, woman, sister, and religious Christian. Her large loyalty to God aligns her, with appropriate reverence, to her other loyalties. We are moved, as we watch Sister Mary Luke involve herself in civil disobedience, political action, shareholder resolutions, lawsuits—all in prayerful pursuit of the open door of gospel hope. Espousing a church of liberation and resistance in the 1980s, she herself is an open door of hope. One never knows about sainthood to come, but *humanhood now* is marvelously manifest in Mary Luke Tobin. Readers beware: Doors of hope within you and around you may begin to swing open!

Robert A. Raines

Introduction:
The Gospel Christ
Is the Door

The heart of Christian faith, the gospel of Jesus Christ, endures on its own, I believe, in any century—for it has ever-renewing resources within it. "Re-visioning" the faith as it encounters the reality of societal and church changes therefore becomes a necessary task, required by the inexhaustible riches of the Word.

Here I will be reflecting on the story of the way faith meets the reality of a rapidly changing culture within the church, the world, and one religious community. This gospel faith, which for me has proved itself both steadfast and dynamic during the many critical changes of the last twenty years, affords the underlying theme of this account.

My own experiences in the faith revisioning process appear in this story as the figure of so many doors—opening into new areas, making accessible new levels of understanding. These doors have invited me forward; and I have entered, sometimes eager, sometimes apprehensive, but always grateful afterward for what they have disclosed.

For me, the gospel Christ is THE DOOR, opening the way to a future where the possibilities of newer aspirations may be realized for the individual; for the community, both religious and secular; and for the wider world.

Each door I have walked through has led to a revisioning of the faith in a new time. And all these new widenings of the horizon have clarified my faith and enabled me to see how the passage of time within our current history, rather than restricting or constricting gospel vision, has revealed its capacity for expansion.

Doors opening onto new perspectives, then, is the image I have chosen for exploring, in the light of faith, some key elements of my life in the past twenty years: attendance as an auditor at Vatican Council II, including initiation into an ongoing ecumenical dialog; participation in the developments in the Loretto community during those years; acquaintance with Thomas Merton and his insights; activity in social-justice movements, especially at the time of the Vietnam war; and finally, involvement in the present struggles with problems of economic imbalance, the subordination of women, and the nuclear threat.

I am convinced that even though the twenty-first century presents enormous challenges to our world, a door of hope is opened by the One who tells us that God's kingdom is to be found in justice, mercy, and the making of peace.

I have a unique vantage point as a member of the Roman Catholic religious community, Sisters of Loretto, which has been especially involved with the changes of this period. Although my perceptions of the recent decades are seen through that particular lens, my observations of change in no way undercut the profound experience of the lived-out faith and love that I have shared in a Roman Catholic religious community and that has enriched me for more than fifty years. Furthermore, I see relationships between the community's development and that of the church as a whole, for as Christians and as members of religious communities, we all are part of our society and of its religious consciousness.

I have become aware during these last twenty years of a movement away from an earlier religious milieu—a milieu characterized, I would say, by a mentality that was, in varying degrees, individualistic, legalistic, and parochial—toward a contemporary religious scene with characteristics I would describe as person-oriented, participatory, more widely inclusive, and struggling toward justice both at home and abroad.

More explicitly, these new values include the importance of the human being—his or her experience, freedom, and responsibility for development of personal potential; the importance of sharing interpersonal relationships; and the importance of participation in decisions that affect one's own life and future. Alongside these understandings there emerges a further insight: All persons, especially the deprived and oppressed, have a right to the justice that empowers them to share a more human life, wherever they live in the world. These values provide a common thread, appearing and reappearing at various stages in the account of my faith revisioning.

Has the faith experience of Catholics in general moved from a spirituality largely characterized by individualistic morality and piety, to a spirituality that embraces concern for social justice as a constitutive element? For some it has. This book is an attempt to share my views of this movement as I have observed and experienced it.

As I reflect on the specific persons, events, and communities of this time, I hope the reader will experience something of my excitement as each new door offers its own epiphany.

1.
The Door of Church Reform: Vatican Council II

And when they arrived, they gathered the church together and declared all that God had done with them, and how he had opened a door of faith to the Gentiles.

Acts 14:27 RSV

God continually has opened doors of faith to the church throughout its history. Our age is no exception, and Pope John XXIII was, I believe, the courageous instrument of God for a new day in the Roman Catholic Church. From 1962 until 1965, the ecumenical council known as Vatican II was in progress. I recall the January day in 1959 when the world was informed that John had called all the bishops to Rome to help renew and update the church. I was overjoyed and greeted all the harbingers of this unusual event with delight.

At the opening of the council in October 1962, the atmosphere was charged with expectant excitement generated by hopes for such renewal. The press was

active in seeking out every sign that old structures were
giving way to new; and Xavier Rynne's articles in *The New
Yorker,* focusing on the contests between conservatives
and liberals among the council fathers (the bishops of
Vatican II), were read eagerly by council-watchers.

We who were members of religious communities were
aware that a new era was upon us. Belgian Cardinal
Suenens had stunned the still highly structured religious
communities with his *Nun in the World.* Nuns, he had
written, were too separated from the present currents of
life that are moving among the people of the world and
should be acting as "animators" for groups of men and
women whose everyday lives need evangelization. Some
found his work a door for new ministries for religious;
others saw it as an opening to secularism and disintegra-
tion.

At the end of the second session of the council, in 1963,
the same cardinal questioned the composition of the
Vatican assembly by asking why the fathers were
deliberating about "the Church," with half its members
unrepresented. Inevitably, Suenens' speech forced the
council fathers to confront more than a rhetorical
question. Were women in fact to be consulted in any way
by those who were deliberating on the status and future
of their church?

In August 1964, I was elected president of the
Conference of Major Superiors of Women, an association made up of the heads of religious congregations of
women (often called orders) in the United States. This
group had been working since the 1950s to effect the
renewal and adaptation called for by some farsighted
leaders of the Sacred Congregation of Religious, that
official body in Rome that "accredits" religious orders.
But it is not likely that the leaders of the well-organized

and cooperative corps of United States religious superiors had any conception of the incredibly far-reaching effects that the Vatican changes were to have on their lives and on the lives of the members of their communities.

En Route to Rome

The major superiors were sufficiently interested in the council, however, for members of their executive committee to suggest that I proceed to Rome during the forthcoming third session, to learn what I could, from my place on the periphery of the action, about the exciting developments occurring daily at Vatican II. Cardinal Suenens had urged women religious to be present at the other meetings that were going on in addition to the formal sessions, in order to exercise some influence, perhaps by their visibility and the evidence of their interest. In any case, in late September 1964, I set out for Rome.

One evening during the voyage across the Atlantic, I received a telephone call from a reporter for the *New York Times*. "How do you feel about your invitation to attend Vatican II as one of the fifteen women who have just been invited?"

I stammered that I knew nothing of such an invitation. But the reporter assured me that word had come from the Vatican just that morning, indicating that invitations were on the way. To me the news was thrilling! To realize that the church was taking the question of Cardinal Suenens seriously, even in a small way, lifted my heart. This door, swinging open to admit fifteen women from different parts of the Roman Catholic world, represented an unexpected sign of hope. It signaled at least a minimal awareness of the questions women were asking and some recognition of their secondary status in the church. True, fifteen women among twenty-five hundred bishops was hardly a "quota," but it was a beginning.

The ship could not move fast enough for me to reach Italy, but soon I arrived in Rome, where I stepped as quickly as possible across the threshold of Saint Peter's into the impressive convocation. For the first time, television and radio had made the event of a universal council of all the bishops of the Roman Catholic Church a center of attention in the world.

When I was first interviewed by the layman who was a sort of major domo in charge of auditors, he indicated that women had been invited in order to participate in those sessions "which would be of interest to them." At that point, I said that indeed, I was interested in whatever the bishops were discussing. I made a mental note that I would never miss a session; I now know that all the other women made the same note. And it soon was taken for granted that we would attend every day.

I received a formal identification card and presently met the other fourteen women who were sharing the auditors' status with me. Eight of us were women religious—principally leaders of conferences in our own countries. The other seven were laywomen, also selected because of some leadership role. We occupied a tribune, or loge, one of the four facing the high altar of Saint Peter's. Opposite us on the other side of the altar were the "Protestant observers." They observed; we audited; none of us spoke.

All the speeches were in Latin; but some generous clerics who had accompanied their bishops as *periti,* or experts, offered to assist us in translating the addresses as they were given.

Work on Planning Commissions

My role at the council, however, was not to be entirely passive. Three women auditors were invited to be full participants in the planning commissions for the preparation of documents—one on the church in the modern world and one on the laity. Mère Guillaume, a French nun, and I were from the group of religious; Rosemary Goldie, an Australian laywoman already active in a world laity council, was the third.

From the beginning of the council, I was convinced that members of religious orders and laywomen need to work together in the church. I can see now that our alliance foreshadowed a development of women's groups in the following years.

I was elated when I discovered that Mère Guillaume, head of the forty-five-thousand-member Daughters of Charity, and I, even across language barriers, were very much of one mind regarding needed changes in the church. She was a strong and courageous leader, whose untimely death shortly afterward was a great misfortune. I had looked to her as an ally in many of the difficulties I sensed were ahead of us in the renewal of religious life.

I watched with keen interest as developing interventions and disputations unfolded—as cardinals and bishops voiced their opinions and finally voted for or against the sixteen council documents. The work of the council basically concerned the identity, role, and mission of the Roman Catholic Church; the relation of the church to the world; and the relation of the church to other religions. Most of the major documents of the council dealt with aspects of these issues.

The first document to be approved was that on the liturgy. As one who has had a longtime interest in use of

the vernacular for the Mass, and in more flexibility in the
liturgy, I was delighted at the development of the
document and at its approbation, following a lengthy
discussion. Wisely, those who prepared the format for
each day frequently called on the Uniate churches of the
Eastern Catholic rite (those related to Rome rather than
to the Patriarchs) to provide the approved but varied
liturgical Mass rites. We auditors, including the laymen,
were the only participants in the daily Communion, since
presumably each bishop had celebrated his own Mass
earlier. I was happy and awed to be receiving Communion under both species, bread and wine, at these
sometimes strange and even exotic ceremonies. Most of
us never before had witnessed the colorful rites of
Eastern Catholics. Visible proof that the church was able
to sustain its universal worship and teaching amid varied
customs certainly helped the bishops to come to terms
with a more flexible liturgy—a liturgy, for example, as
the Ethiopian rite celebrated it, with bongo drums and
strange-sounding wailing prayers.

Inclusiveness—A Gospel Value

Through experiences such as these I began to realize
that an ever-more inclusive theory and practice were
indeed dimensions of the gospel. This perception lay at
the heart of many of the changes that needed to be made,
I believed, and through the door opened for me by the
council, this discovery was to be a criterion for much of
the remainder of my life.

The bishops had taken a serious step during the first
session of the council by insisting that an early chapter of
the document on the church should be titled "The
People of God." By emphasizing that the people are
indeed the church and that all leadership positions have

their origin among the people, the council fathers had swung open a vast door for wider participation of all. Of course, the results of such a decision are still in process; but for every parish council that exists in name only, there is another that is struggling for its rightful share in the decision-making processes of the parish. The incorporation of this resolution into a long tradition of highly stratified leadership will ask unflagging toil of the hardiest. Those in power move out of it reluctantly, if at all. To translate the ideal of collegiality into the practice of participation will require years of commitment. But the decision of the bishops in their first great act set a precedent that was not to be reversed.

Looking at the question of the church in the modern world, the council set to work to shorten the distance between church leadership and the people who are the church. If it is true that "the joys and the hopes, the griefs and the anxieties of the [people] of this age, especially those who are poor or in any way afflicted, these too are the joys and hopes, the griefs and anxieties of the followers of Christ," as the document *The Church in the Modern World* states,[1] then deep concern for the human condition must be a distinguishing mark of every Christian.

Problems of Humankind: Disarmament and Other

The problems of humankind are vast indeed, and the bishops could deal with only a few. Thomas Merton, our neighbor and consultant, had alerted me to his great concern about any statements the bishops might make on war or disarmament, so I was keenly interested in listening to the discussion of that subject. Every step taken to "outlaw war" was encouraging. "It is our clear duty, then, to strain every muscle as we work for the time when all war can be completely outlawed by international consent."[2]

However, those of us hoping for greater condemnation of the arms race and nuclear weaponry were disappointed. A much stronger statement has since been made by the Vatican. "The arms race is to be condemned unreservedly. Even when motivated by a concern for legitimate defense, it is, in fact, a danger . . . an injustice . . . a theft . . . a mistake . . . wrong . . . a folly."[3] Pope Paul VI also said, "Let those shameful weapons be banned. . . . Let us pray that this murderous device [the atomic weapon] does not kill peace while seeking it."[4]

From the frequent meetings of the commission on the church in the modern world, during the closing session of the council, I recall two episodes in particular that enabled me to rejoice that there was an ear listening to the problems of humankind. One day after an eloquent speech by a lay commission member about the problems caused by the church's directives about birth control, Cardinal Leger of Canada suggested some wording that found its way into the council document: "No one but the spouses themselves may determine how many children a couple will have."[5]

At another time, Père Yves Congar, an outstanding Dominican theologian, was working on a reference to women, which would be incorporated into the document. Struggling to praise and honor them, Père Congar had devised a somewhat flowery sentence to extol women's contributions to the church. After he had read it to the commission members, he noted little enthusiasm on the part of the three women among them. Looking at Rosemary Goldie, he asked, "Do you not like my complimentary sentence about women, Rosemary?"

After a moment's hesitation, Rosemary replied with

simple dignity, "Père Congar, you may omit all the pedestals and incense. Just state that women wish to be treated as the full human persons in the church that we all believe they are, and that will be enough for us." I do not think that Père Congar understood why we were not enthusiastic about his efforts. But until Rosemary's answer is heard fully in the church, the same lack of enthusiasm for any church statements about women will continue.

Ecumenical Developments

Even before the council, I had become interested in the ecumenical movement, so it was thrilling for me to see the church progressing on this front. Although fifteen years later there is still much foot-dragging in this area, some hopeful steps were taken at Vatican II. The Pope prayed publicly in a vesper service with the Protestant observers; and in view of the long years of separation, this was a welcome event. Bilateral dialogues between Protestant churches and the Catholic Church were set up, and not only have such commissions continued but they have quietly overcome much misunderstanding and have arrived at new agreements in the course of their progress. However, official leadership in both Catholic and Protestant churches has been very slow to implement these recommendations.

One striking example of such reluctance relates to inter-Communion. After more than ten years of official theological dialogue—after agreements have been reached on the nature, centrality, and meaning of the Eucharist—we still have not arrived at the point where we may freely share the Lord's Supper. Granted that there was need for an official theological consensus, why do we wait so long for these decisions to be put into practice? My growing recognition that ever-greater inclusion is an imperative of the gospel leads me to impatience at the slowness of this implementation. Surely Christians who have agreed on the basic understanding of the Eucharist should be sharing Communion at their various liturgies. I am afraid that such long delays only contribute to a growing indifference to Christian ecumenism.

It was a delightful experience to become acquainted with the many outstanding Protestant leaders who were present at Vatican II, especially those from the United States. Methodist Albert Outler, Douglas Horton of the United Church of Christ, and Presbyterian Robert McAfee Brown were among those I enjoyed meeting. I did not suspect at that time how profoundly some of us would share activities in coming years.

Religious Life

One of the council documents treated religious life in the church and strongly affirmed the keystone on which that life is built. "Since the fundamental norm of the religious life is a following of Christ as proposed by the Gospel, such is to be regarded by all communities as their supreme law."[6] I was happy that this statement was central to the document, since any more ecclesiastical or time-conditioned phrase would have been a betrayal.

I also was delighted to read a section that affirmed the need for a commitment to social justice among those who have chosen the life of the religious community. "Communities should promote among their members a suitable awareness of contemporary human conditions and of the needs of the church. For if their members can combine the burning zeal of an apostle with wise judgments, made in the light of faith, concerning the circumstances of the modern world, they will be able to come to the aid of [people] more effectively."[7] I was becoming increasingly sensitive to the relationship between social justice and the luminous example and actions of Jesus in the Gospels. It seemed to me then that this statement would encourage social concern among those in religious life, as a result of their reflections on Scripture.

But one of the disappointments of Vatican II was that the document on religious life was largely so uncreative and reflected a reluctance to launch us into wider perspectives. Little in that document really suggested any changes as an outcome of the major currents I saw moving through the council—greater inclusiveness; participation; awareness of personal and communal responsibility, leading to involvement with the problems of the world; a broader ecumenism.

I realize now that the lack of positive directions from the council in this respect was not wholly a disadvantage for us as religious communities. Far from it. We discovered before long that the responsibility to develop these wider perspectives could be carried out only by our own creativity—by our own best efforts and energies—spurred on by new hope in the Spirit's presence among us and around us. In the next chapter, I will comment more specifically as to the effects of Vatican II on religious communities.

My invitation to be an auditor at Vatican II had opened a door onto the ever-widening vistas that this council of the Catholic Church was revealing, not only in regard to the possibilities of religious communities, but also onto all areas of a faith-related life.

Basic Themes

As one document after another was voted upon and became part of the history of a council of many surprises, the same basic themes were reflected: the church as the people of God; the primary importance and dignity of the individual person; the responsibility of that person for his or her participation and decision-making within the total community; a listening to the griefs and anxieties of the world's people; the practice of inclusiveness; and the extension of the boundaries of the church to include all Christians and also those of other world faiths. It is hard to remember now that, for the first time, communities of Protestant Christians were acknowledged as "churches" by Vatican II. Many of the old barriers indeed had fallen.

The establishment of special relationships with Jews was inaugurated, and structures were recommended for that purpose. Attention was called to Paul's statement in Romans, "the irrevocable call of God to the Jewish people." There was insistence that all texts be purged of any anti-Semitic tones and that dialogue with Jews be continued. The document calling for these changes, *The Relationship of the Church to Non-Christian Religions,* reads,

Since the spiritual patrimony common to Christians and Jews is thus so great, this sacred synod wishes to foster and recommend that mutual understanding and respect which is the fruit above all of biblical and theological studies, and of . . . dialogues. . . . Moreover, mindful of the common patrimony with the Jews, and motivated by the Gospel's spiritual love and by no political considerations, the Church deplores the hatred, persecutions, and displays of anti-Semitism directed against the Jews at any time and from any source.[8]

This deploring, of course, will not suffice unless action is taken. The eradication of anti-Semitism necessarily will

be a continuing task, so deep-seated are its seeds in
Christian history.

Modern racial anti-Semitism [writes Rosemary Ruether] is a
continuation and a transformation of the medieval tradition of
theological and economic scapegoating of the Jews. [But her
thought suggests that] the fulfillment of the divine promises is
not simply behind us as an event completed in the past but
ahead of us as a horizon of redemption that judges our present
shortcomings and calls us toward the renewal of life. Here the
longing of Christians joins the longing of Jews for God's
ultimate victory in the pacification of [humankind].[9]

And there were further themes of renewal that
developed into documents. This new look at "the signs of
the times" (as Pope John had called the updating of the
church) included concern for human culture; marriage
and the family; life in its economic, political, and social
dimensions; the bonds between the family of nations;
and peace. Each of these areas was presented in relation
to the ideals proclaimed by Christ in the Gospels.

Women in Church and Society

The very presence of women in and around the
council hall called to consciousness the issues that women
were facing. My own widening concern for the problems
of liberation included that of women; and even at that
stage I hoped fervently that there would be recognition
of the need to eliminate the discrimination experienced
by women and a determination to do something positive
about it. I became increasingly aware of the second-class
status that women were assumed to hold in the church.

But I took courage from the few evidences of concern
that I saw. After all, if the church was willing to state a

position for women's equality publicly, I felt we had at
least a glimmer of hope.

Two statements within the council documents speak
out clearly against discrimination. In the document *The
Church in the Modern World,* we see, "With respect to the
fundamental rights of the person, every type of
discrimination . . . based on sex . . . is to be overcome and
eradicated as contrary to God's intent."[10] That statement
is the strongest imperative for the rights of women that
appears in church documents. Although it is a negative
statement, it reveals the continuing injustice by acknowledging the need for a corrective.

Also, in the *Constitution on the Church,* we read,

. . . The chosen People of God is one: "one Lord, one faith,
one baptism" (Eph. 4:5). As members, they share a common
dignity from their rebirth in Christ. They have the same filial
grace and the same vocation to perfection. They possess in
common one salvation, one hope, and one undivided charity.
Hence, there is in Christ and in the Church no inequality on
the basis of race or nationality, social condition or sex, because
"there is neither Jew nor Greek; there is neither slave nor free
person; there is neither male nor female. For you are all one in
Christ Jesus" (Gal. 3:28).[11]

On the last day of the council, a great outdoor Mass was
celebrated in front of Saint Peter's. At its conclusion, part
of the program involved the presentation of certificates
of honor to distinguished persons in various categories.
Four philosophers, for example, were so honored; they
walked across the platform and received from the hands
of the Pope some special insignia of recognition. Then
four literati, four musicians, and so on, were singled out
for praise. Finally, four women walked across the stage.

And the announcer proclaimed that "women should be honored for their contribution to the church."

I turned to my nearest neighbor in the bleachers, Father Godfrey Diekmann, and said, "But women are not a *category* in the church. They should not be honored as women more than men should be honored as men. Men *and* women are the church, aren't they?"

Father Godfrey looked at me and said, "You're right, Sister; you women need to help us see this."

Unfortunately that insensitive state of affairs regarding women in the church still obtains. Godfrey Diekmann was one of the persons who even then realized that the treatment of women and the attitude toward them were unfair. Today I am grateful for many thoughtful biblical scholars—persons like Phyllis Trible in the Protestant tradition, and also the members of the Catholic Biblical Commission—who see the treatment of women in the church not only as unfair, but as unbiblical and unchristian. The open door that revealed to me the enormous discrepancy between Christian faith and practice, in the area of women in church and society, has only opened wider as I have become more conscious daily of the need to work ceaselessly for the goal of the equality of all persons.

Follow-Up

During the third and fourth sessions of the council, I was present every day until the conclusion, in December 1965. Follow-up meetings took me back to Rome on two separate occasions the next year, as plans evolved for implementing the decisions regarding women religious. These meetings set the stage for the wide experimentation which the Pope authorized for all religious communities in 1966. However, renewal was not to be easily achieved.

The stress and tensions of those times were so great because there were no maps to follow, and differences of opinion between the Vatican officials and the council leaders were quite evident. I saw that the possibilities opened up by the council revealed opportunities for a new way of living the gospel in contact with a needy world. The greater freedom, flexibility, experimentation, and new "apostolic" ventures were exciting to me. I was ready to put it all into practice at once. Therefore I was perplexed and dismayed when I discovered that the authorities at the Vatican were not equally enthusiastic about our plans for "the renewal and adaptation in the religious life" that had been called for. The imperatives for the new, fresh vision were so compelling that I could not understand why some of the Vatican authorities were so reluctant.

I remember one or two interviews with the head of the Sacred Congregation of Religious, Cardinal Antoniutti, who was chagrined and alarmed at my readiness to carry the new initiatives into actual practice. The preponderant influence at the council was moving in the direction of greater flexibility and experimentation, however, and the Cardinal could hardly prevent the openness to the wider engagement with the world that the documents advocated. Some quotations from council texts should be sufficient to illustrate this direction. "The human race has passed from a rather static concept of reality to a more dynamic, evolutionary one." "Authentic freedom is an exceptional sign of the divine image within [humans]." "Faithful to the Gospel and benefiting from its resources, united with every [one] who loves and practices justice, Christians have shouldered a gigantic task demanding fulfillment in this world." Religious are urged by the Spirit, states one text, "to reflect seriously and actively so as to discover how their institute could and should be adapted ever more perfectly to the continuously changing circumstances of their own times."[12] Quotations like these are numerous in the documents. To me they made the directions of the council quite clear.

Because I was representing the sisters of the United States, I met with Cardinal Antoniutti on a few occasions. I tried to convey to him the concern of the leaders of our religious communities for these developments. At our formal meeting, those women had expressed to me their desire to have a part in the decision making that affected their lives, either by a deliberative vote or in a consultative manner.

I understand something of the cardinal's fear that the innovations might get out of hand. There were and still are many persons in the church who decry the changes of Vatican II. So I attribute his caution to those fears. In any case, the frustration of that period was painful to me. It was certainly not easy to find myself in opposition to the cardinal, but I felt that the changes were in solid accord with the leadership of the council. Friction was inevitable because our perspectives on changes in religious life were so different: Static and dynamic forces were in conflict. I remember leaving the cardinal after our meetings with tears in my eyes and disappointment in my heart. I felt a growing concern that we American religious, in particular, were facing an uphill struggle, as indeed we were.

And yet, although I did not know it then, better circumstances were in the making. At the conclusion of the council, new structures were set up to permit the very innovations the documents had recommended. A decree issued in 1966 directed broad experiments, which provided the opportunity for communities to decide on their own steps to renewal.

My last meeting with Cardinal Antoniutti took place in Rome after the council, only a short time before his death. We exchanged greetings, and he said to me seriously, "I want you to know, Sister, that what I did in regard to the innovations in religious life, I did for the good of the church."

I appreciated that acknowledgment and responded, "I, too, Your Eminence. What I have done to encourage these new developments in religious life, I believe I have done for the good of the church."

We parted in a friendly manner—two persons expressing their love for the church in two very different ways.

A Wave of Euphoria

I returned from the council on the crest of a wave of euphoria. What a season for change was with us! In retrospect, I am glad for the euphoria; it generated courage and impelled me and those working with me here in the United States to become the change agents for a renewed religious life in the church. Often we were to find ourselves caught between strong currents of reaction that pulled backward toward more traditional and safer landmarks and other equally strong trends pushing forward toward the unknown, with little reference to the significance of the past. While I felt keenly the pain experienced by those of more conservative outlook, whose past experiences had ill-prepared them for change, I had a deep sense of the rightness of the movement forward and a readiness to work for the new values, in spite of the inevitable cost.

Because I was open to the ecumenical ventures blossoming in this country, I was frequently invited to share platforms with Protestant and Jewish speakers and to engage in many social-justice efforts that emerged from Judaeo-Christian roots. Although it is true that lagging and fearful leadership at the decision-making levels in the churches has put the brakes on ecumenical progress, there are numerous persons committed to the work of manifesting the oneness of truth and love.

When Pope John XXIII called the ecumenical council, he had clearly stated, "We Christians have been separated for too long. Let us study how to bring about Christian unity. It is for the Catholic Church to lead in this matter." Doors opened by such glorious faith as his, unafraid and ever helpful, call us forward—never backward into fear.

Although the impetus given the church by John XXIII was not enough to carry forward the full implementation of the grand designs of the council, there is no limiting or predicting the influence of that brave spirit in the church. Nor is there any limiting or predicting the influence of the many brave spirits who even today are struggling to bring to reality the visions of the council. Those Catholics who trust that the Spirit of Christ was moving through Vatican II find in this faith their best hope for a Christian and, indeed, for a human, unity.

I think we can say that, although so much remains to be done to implement the council's initiatives, the seeds sown are taking root and growing. We may be like the man in the Gospel story who, after sowing the seeds, went about his business, and one day was surprised at their great growth.

An Assessment

First, I would like to list some developments since the council that I consider healthy and hopeful. A more flexible liturgy has taken root almost everywhere. Not only has the transfer to the vernacular, or everyday language, been successfully effected, but new methods of fuller participation, such as liturgical dance, mime, audiovisual aids, and such, have met a growing acceptance.

Another sign of development is the wider incorporation of lay people, both women and men, in pastoral ministry. In the relatively small parish where I often worship, I was surprised to hear the pastor invite the congregation to a reception for the "340 persons engaged in pastoral ministry in this parish." This includes readers at the liturgy, Communion ministers, teachers, visitors to the sick, and so on. Unthinkable, twenty years ago! Furthermore, reports from ministers tell us that this pastoral experience results in much satisfaction and joy. Thus it seems safe to predict that this innovation will continue and grow.

I have mentioned parish councils involving collegial decision making. Occasionally, even at the diocesan level, such councils exist. Someday we may have a national pastoral council that is truly collegial! As women become more fully incorporated into decision making and as they participate as ministers in the church, constructive changes will undoubtedly occur. The thinking and experience of women are sorely needed if there is to be an alive and creative church. In particular, the entire area of sexual morality is incomplete, to the extent that the insights of women have not been included.

In addition to parish councils, peace and justice

commissions have been instituted at diocesan and sometimes at local levels. The leadership of these committees, from my experience, is usually alert to issues of
justice in our society. Further, participation in such
efforts is often ecumenical and is expected to be
increasingly so.

Religious education has incorporated the teachings of
Vatican II, as is evidenced in most of the textbooks now
in use. Seminary professors include, of course, the overly
cautious, as well as those who have moved along with the
biblical and theological views encouraged by Vatican II.
No doubt it will take some years before we see the results
of teachings in many areas, but the new texts are bearing
fruit, as is apparent already in many improved Sunday
homilies.

These hopeful signs indicate to me an era of
ever-broadening change, impossible without such a
gathering as the Vatican Council—that assembly of all
the bishops, which spoke as the universal voice of the
church.

For me, indeed, Vatican II opened a door on an
inspiring ideal—so inspiring that I am dissatisfied with
present progress, when there is so far to go.

For example, consider what is implied in a major
declaration of the council—"The people are the church."[13]
This statement comprises a number of goals: respect
for all persons (regardless of race, sex, or nationality),
openness to their gifts and development, opportunity
for them to share in making the decisions that affect
their lives, ecumenism, and recognition of the equality
of men and women in the church. That expression seems
to me to capture the fundamental spirit of Vatican II.
But as yet, the path leading from the standards set

forth to their implementation is largely untrod.

Is there, on the part of church leaders, a fear of loss of security—loss of role—in effecting change?

One hardly can be unaware today of a disaffection apparent among many sensitive, intelligent persons who have been loyal to the church, but who are dismayed at the discrepancy between the council statements and their implementation.

Nearly twenty years after my experience at Vatican II, I am more and more convinced that there is grave need for the leadership of the church, which wisely opened the doors for the Vatican Council, to facilitate ways for the people truly to be the church. And I believe this is possible. I can speak with such confidence because I have experienced, in my own community of Loretto, the movement from hierarchical to collegial positions and operations, and I can testify that the transition works. Leaders' willingness to risk, based on trust in the talents and goodness of the people, is the indispensable condition for pressing forward for this change.

And we are not without examples in the church itself. In Latin America, for instance, the bishops have given formal endorsement to the small groups called *communidades de base* that gather, often with lay leadership, to analyze their situation in the light of the gospel, with a view toward improving their condition.

Official leadership is, of course, necessary for unity, continuity, and doctrine in the church, but when the authorities recognize that arbitrary rule is superfluous and that resources abound among the people, they will encourage new leaders to emerge. Thus they will endow the church with fresh creativity.

My own criterion for knowing that "summer is nigh"

will be met when the people concerned about their own problems and those of the world feel free to dissent from, dialogue with, and even challenge, church leadership. Then a community of faith and justice can propose to others what they themselves profess: "The rulers of this world lord it over their people, but not you. You shall be among them as those who serve" (Luke 22:25-27).

The Future

How then is the future viewed, from the vantage point of one who attended Vatican II?

I have spoken of my hope for leadership that will accept the advocacy of collegiality, but I am left with nagging questions. Will the current Pope, with his strong support of hierarchical authority, be able to move toward the very collegiality he advocates? He has said that there can be no turning back from the decisions made at Vatican II. Will his growing experience and his exposure to other cultures moderate his views on the participation of church communities in decision making? Will his pastoral compassion keep pace with his sense of the necessity for governing?

Creative theologians and thinkers such as Edward Schillebeeckx, Karl Rahner, and Hans Küng are gifts to the church in this postconciliar time. Their thinking and probing, built on earlier theologians, is the kind of reflection on "faith seeking understanding" that we all sorely need. I hope that regrettable prohibitions, such as those on Hans Küng and the humiliating questioning of Schillebeeckx, will not continue in our church. Rather than mistrust and suspicion, I hope that trust in, and gratitude for, those thinkers who have demonstrated their love for the church will prevail. There is so much truth to learn.

I, too, do not really believe that there can be any turning backward. The growth I referred to earlier—in parishes, in wider participation in ministries, as well as in a more creative pastoral education and practice—springs from the seeds sown at Vatican II. They are continuing to bear fruit, and I believe coming decades will strongly affirm this development; but we need to take the long view.

An example of a long view occurs to me here. The third session of the council ended on a somewhat discouraging note: The document on religious liberty had been voted down! Although there was to be one more session, I was depressed at this turn of events. I remember that on the last day of the session, Sister Jane Marie Richardson and I were walking along a street near the Tiber with Paulist Father Thomas Stransky, a friend and a council expert, on our way to lunch. After expressing my disappointment, I asked him what he thought.

I have often recalled his answer. "Future history will not ask whether the document on religious liberty was passed in 1964 or 1965. I believe it will pass at the final session, and there's plenty of evidence for thinking that. The important thing is that it *will* pass."

He was right. And I believe that the currents of change set in motion by the council will indeed proceed, in spite of temporary setbacks.

Finally, Vatican II stimulated in me a desire to see a renewed church of creative people—a church faithful to Jesus' description of authority and thus true to its own roots. I am grateful for that far-reaching and provocative faith experience. "The first sign of Christian hope," says Paul Ricoeur, "is to believe that something can always be done in every situation. When the Gospel says that the Church has the promise of eternal life, this means that the message of truth and love can take root at any period of history."[14]

To me, it seems that the event of Vatican II was a special epiphany of hope for the church in our time. The council was a door opened wide—too wide to be closed.

2
The Door of Belonging: The Loretto Community

Behold, I have set before you an open door, which no one is able to shut; I know that you have but little power, and yet you have kept my word and have not denied my name.

Revelation 3:8 RSV

In the fall of 1979, the Sisters of Loretto initiated a law suit against the Blue Diamond Coal Company. The action came about because of the company's refusal to list the Loretto community as "shareholders of record." Conscious of the company's record of abuses in regard to pollution, environment, health and safety regulations, and labor relations, a coalition of concerned persons and groups in Appalachia sought a way to correct these wrongs. The Loretto community, along with several other groups, purchased shares of Blue Diamond stock, in an effort to bring the number of shareholders up to that point at which the company would be forced to accept Securities and Exchange Commission regulation.

But the company refused to acknowledge the sisters as shareholders, leaving them no choice but to bring suit. At this writing, the suit is still not settled.

The case made news immediately, and a flurry of articles and interviews appeared. What made the story so newsworthy was that the challenge to corporate power and practices came from Roman Catholic sisters, whose stereotype had been one of conformity and of support of establishment power.

In response to announcement of the suit, officials of the Blue Diamond Coal Company had this to say. "It is difficult for the management of the company to understand how the vocation of the good sisters leads them" to involvements such as these.

What *is* the "vocation of the good sisters," and what *does* it lead them to? I would like to answer this question in the context of my own community, the Sisters of Loretto, a Roman Catholic order founded in the United States in 1812. But first, let us look at what is known in the Catholic Church as "religious life."

"The sisters"—members of religious communities of women—are rather well-known phenomena in the United States. Most Americans are aware of these groups of women in our society, who usually have dedicated themselves to teaching, nursing, and social work. They have been seen as fitting an expected pattern of service to the church. For the most part, they have worn a distinctive "habit" and have lived a somewhat secluded life.

Within the last fifteen years, however, this accepted stereotype has changed. Most religious sisters today do not wear a specified habit. They mingle responsibly and freely with colleagues, co-workers, and parishioners, and are engaged in a wide variety of occupations which, although they may include teaching and nursing, are far from being limited to those professions. And not only in professional life, but in personal life as well, their concern about the value and potential of persons leads them to want a part in decision making. Now there is a fresh sense of this desire for full personhood for all, not only in society, but also in the church. The importance of being change agents has been recognized.

In this chapter, I will be looking at some of these rapid and unpredicted changes in religious life, which are reflective of our society and culture as a whole, their causes, and their influence upon a related faith perspective.

The term "religious life," as used currently in Catholic language and practice, refers to that special category of persons, either men or women, who have chosen to join a religious community which has or which seeks official church approval. The "accrediting agency" for such approval is the Sacred Congregation of Religious, in Rome. Throughout the history of the church, such groups have been founded and have flourished according to the needs they served. Their members live in community, according to the evangelical counsels of poverty, chastity, and obedience, which traditionally have offered a single-minded style of life, devoted to the mission of the church.

As it developed in the United States in the nineteenth century, religious life took on some unique characteristics. Customarily, religious communities, or congregations, engaged in work that assisted the missionaries and pioneers. They strengthened the faith implanted on the frontier by establishing schools, hospitals, and institutions, for care of the people from infancy to old age. Usually, though not exclusively, these forms of charity were carried out by groups of women. They were intent on being of service to the church community wherever they lived and worked.

Such works demanded a life-style suited to institutions, which developed increasingly complex and controlled structures. If these institutions were to operate effectively, those who staffed them were required to adhere rather strictly to assigned and well-regulated duties.

To enable decision making, as well as to choose officers for the congregation, elected delegates met at a "general chapter" every six years. But the decisions made by them, mostly minor in character, did not alter the life-pattern substantially. For, emanating from Rome, canon law determined most major decisions—as for example, who would be admitted to membership; or the length of the novitiate, or training period. In fact, regulations issued by the body of delegates of a particular order were not only limited in scope but also tended to result in minute prescriptions for daily living, such as the hours of rising or retiring.

There is no question that the work of religious communities served the Roman Catholic community well, and even, in a limited way, other communities in the United States. The lives of religious women, disciplined and earnest, made a contribution to the growth of the church in America. But in all institutions, a cycle of renewal, growth, and inevitably, stagnation, unrolls. Religious life is no exception. Although one rightly may rejoice at the example of the dedicated lives of generations of devoted nuns, one must regret the escalating rigidity of the institutional structures, which permitted little or no deviation for individual or community innovation or creativity, especially in regard to ecumenical or world communities. Authority was highly centralized—benevolent but firm.

My own life in the community developed within such a pattern. I had grown up in Denver, Colorado, where I first met the Sisters of Loretto. My father's involvement in his Nevada gold mine and my parents' concern that my brother and I have good educations, dictated that we travel between Colorado and Goldfield, Nevada, with some frequency. I spent several summers of my early life in Nevada and California, although our home was actually in Denver. Like most gold mines, ours had its heyday and its decline; we were not unfamiliar with financial uncertainty.

I'm glad that we were educated primarily in Denver because there my keen interest in literature was cultivated by some excellent teachers in good public schools. When quite young, I developed a love for ballet, which later led me to seek training with the Russian ballet master, Alexander Kosloff. I became an assistant to the Denver ballet teacher, Helen McDonald Robinson, who was also a fine early mentor. Finally, during my first two years of college, I conducted my own ballet school.

Between the end of high school and the beginning of college, I had made a definite decision to "enter the convent." At that time, a door that I had never noticed before opened to me: life in a Catholic religious community. Personal response to the Word of God by entering "religious life," as that concept is understood in the Catholic tradition, became very attractive. That summer, I knew with certainty that this step was one I wanted to take.

My family was not enthusiastic about my chosen course, different from that of most young women. But they did not oppose it. They counseled me to wait a year or two to be sure it was what I wanted. I did so. But after I had attended college for two years, they were convinced that I was firm in my intentions, and I left with their good will. So I went to Loretto, a large rolling farm area in the Kentucky hills, to begin the two-year initiation process of becoming a Sister of Loretto.

Other novices who came to the order were as green about the life as I. We soon discovered that the strict discipline and silence were easier to tolerate when all marched along together and that the joys of "break days" and recreation helped build a certain esprit. Prayer periods during the day were frequent; work was arduous and thorough. Then suddenly, after several months at the novitiate, I remember realizing one day, while we were working away in the laundry, that it was indeed "our" laundry and not "theirs" that we were doing. Community was setting in.

Having proved to our superiors that we were serious about the life we were embracing, we were allowed to make our profession at a formal ceremony, where we pronounced religious vows. After that event, we were launched into "life on the missions," living in convents and teaching in the schools staffed by the order. Life in those days was—or so we thought—predictable.

The goals of education and religious life that prevailed in the Roman Catholic communities were set largely by the aspiration to extend and improve Catholic schools and to carry on the fairly unchanging tradition of our religious orders. Community leaders set their sights on quality education for teachers and students, and gradually they achieved their goal of higher education for all members.

Spirituality in our religious community developed within a regular daily schedule of devotions. "Vocal" prayers were said in common, based more on an individualistic than on a world-directed piety. There were, however, no limitations placed on aspirations toward a more advanced personal prayer life; we knew we were in a great tradition of saints and mystics.

There was a high sense of morale in the Roman Catholic Church, especially during the 1940s and 1950s. Young women in large numbers (compared to the past) began to crowd novice ranks. Our Catholic enthusiasm, not to say triumphalism, during this period seemed justified by our expanding numbers.

But something new was happening. A door marked "change" was quietly opening to a much wider vision of the church and of religious life. Even as it invited us across the threshold, it intimated an uncompromising, unequivocal demand for wide-ranging and painful readjustments. There were signs in the church and in religious communities of almost imperceptibly developing new faith viewpoints.

Even before the Vatican Council, fresh insights into the church as community, openness to new directions in biblical studies, a more participatory liturgy, and a developing ecumenical movement were appearing. A sense of the importance of social justice and its interdependence with these new movements was finding its way into the lives of women religious, and religious communities began to incorporate some of these ideas. As early as 1952, a conference for religious superiors in the United States had been set up through the initiative of Pope Pius XII's leadership. This sense of a changing climate was perceptibly increasing in the 1950s and early 1960s.

I, for one, welcomed these new trends gratefully. The call to a more participatory liturgy appealed to me. I had attended the first meeting of the Liturgical Conference in Chicago in 1940. I hoped for a richer and more profound exposé of Scripture, and found my own prayer life enormously enriched by the writings that followed Rome's encouragement of scriptural scholarhip in 1944. Although I am not a professional theologian, my interest in these writings was keen, and my understanding was growing.

I was reading books by serious and probing Catholic theologians such as Karl Rahner and Edward Schillebeeckx, who, with others, were preparing the ground for this new Catholic thinking. As I was trying to put my own thoughts into focus at Vatican II, I found an enormous stimulus in meeting these theologians and later, in sharing what I had learned with the leadership group in the community back home. One afternoon Sister Jane Marie and I talked with Schillebeeckx about his insights into the renewal of religious life. "Most of all," he said, "our religious houses should be sunny and smiling places." I recalled the tone and mood of that suggestion in many later moments of difficulty.

During those years I was serving as president of the Loretto community, and with other forward-looking companions, I was engaged in the exciting task of discovering how our religious community could align itself with a church opening up to the insights of Vatican II. In answer to that challenge, I was constantly analyzing our community's own situation in light of the dramatic new scenarios for change that were being drafted from ideas set forth by the new Catholic thinkers.

It was an exhilarating time, but also a time when it was necessary to break with a settled and more circumscribed style of living. Life not only in the religious community, but also in the church, was never to be so simple again. On the contrary, a constant "re-visioning" of faith was to be the mode for the coming years.

My own community had experienced some of this revisioning through the influx of ideas brought to our community leadership by our members who had studied in theological schools of recognized quality in both Europe and the United States. We were being readied, unconsciously, for a new way of living the religious life, and Vatican II was to swing wider open that door, which was not going to close.

What were some of the specific changes? Although it is difficult to attempt a summary, I can suggest some highlights. A first insight had to do with the importance of a new way of setting value on the human person, within the context of faith and the world. Recent psychological, sociological, and philosophical insights had influenced this concept. That perception led to an emphasis on the priority of persons over institutions, the value of each person's full participation in decisions affecting her and, flowing from this, each person's responsibility to seek justice in the world. I owe my own education in the relationship between psychological insights and theology to a Canadian theologian-psychologist, Noël Mailloux, whose vast wisdom and knowledge opened my mind and heart to much new understanding.

Further, as each individual deepened in her self-appreciation and played a greater part in decision making, the community itself became better able to hear and to respond to the call for justice within a faith dimension. Experiences such as Vietnam and Selma made the gospel of Jesus of Nazareth more imperative—more pertinent.

The three years from 1964 to 1967 were years of unceasing search and arduous work for the Loretto community, as we attempted to bring ourselves into accord with those subtle and not so subtle changes in church and world. This evolution was an education, not only for me, but for other members of the community as well.

The meeting of the 1964 "chapter of affairs" had set us as a community firmly on this path of responsible change. We began the process by involving community members in committees and task forces, which would look at all aspects of our lives. Plans for the 1964 policy-making assembly included community group discussions, which for us was a new practice. In a structured and set pattern for community living, such involvement rarely had been envisioned as part of the decision-making process. The theological task force struggled to create a strong framework for our lives—one that would take cognizance of the developments in theology and the growing awareness of the church's view of itself as it developed in Vatican II.

It required speed and intensity to match our ideas and practices to the vision of the future we had barely glimpsed. Things were happening fast in church and world. We were creating new models according to the new vision, but the community itself was not totally ready for this new vision. Our problem was finding ways to accomplish our goal, in the absence of time for more measured progress. Although I was heartened by the new models taking shape before us, I was also apprehensive because of the lack of time for the community's assimilation of the new.

"Aren't we going too fast?" I was asked by one senior member of the community. In my heart I was deeply sympathetic toward her anxiety.

But I could answer only, "I don't think we can pace it." It seemed to me that designing structures to fit the new needs was an immediate task. It would take all our resourcefulness. If we had hesitated, we would not have been able to complete the task of renewal that was urging us swiftly and steadily forward. Since it was hard for those of us in leadership positions, it was understandably much harder for those who had not spent long hours thinking through the process of shifting responsibility from outside regulation to self-determination. We struggled with one another's viewpoints, trying to conserve the deepest roots of our tradition and at the same time support among ourselves the impulse toward the responsibility for personal decision making.

This new vision of religious life was sharpened by explicit directions from the Vatican Council. In the special document from the Pope mentioned in the previous chapter, communities were urged to revise their own constitutions and customs so that they might fit into the new patterns. The document pointed out that "no one but the religious community itself should effect the changes to be made."[1] These words were warmly welcomed by those of us who were working closely together in leadership roles in the Loretto community, as well as by a remarkably far-sighted group of elected delegates.

This call from the Pope, implementing the council's decrees, asked communities to hold special meetings for this total revision. We were to set up experiments that would make possible the renewal of religious life as a lived response to the evangelical counsels—the traditional counsels of poverty, chastity, and obedience—and a ministry consonant with "the signs of the times." Everything could be questioned and changed, if the community so decided, except that which had to do with "the nature and purpose" of the congregation. Hence, customs in regard to habits, prayer schedules, work choices, could now be reevaluated and reassessed.

Our leadership group at Loretto immediately followed that welcome directive by convening a special representative chapter of the congregation at the earliest possible opportunity—in the summer of 1967. In preparation, we had worked out our own tentative constitution. Wisely, I believe, we had called this document guidelines, so that it would be flexible enough for future changes, rather than "fixed in concrete." The theological task force's work was then drawn up, and Sister Jane Marie Richardson brought ideas and texts together. *I Am the Way: Guidelines of the Sisters of Loretto* was the simple, creative, and classical work she forged.

The development of the document reveals, I believe, that commitment to God through "unceasing conversion to Jesus Christ" is the underlying current of the faith-life of the religious. It undergirds the motivation of service to neighbor. Some quotations from this text will illustrate this development in three specific areas: (1) Faith exists as the heart of this particular life choice. This faith affirms the individual person, as created and loved by God, and therefore supports the development of her potential gifts; (2) An understanding of relationships flows from this fundamental faith, embracing individuals and community; and (3) The community comes to hear and act on the prophetic word calling for justice.

1. Faith in God's Love

Gift, Decision, and Trust

To believe firmly in God's love requires the ability to receive a gift, to make a decision, and to trust human beings—oneself and others.[2]

This statement, I believe, in its spare and simple prose, points out the central qualities at the heart of the faith-life of the Christian community. To live as one who receives everything as a *gift*, is itself a definition of faith.

Maturity is often defined as the ability to weigh *decisions* and to take action accordingly. The Gospel urges us to stand on our own feet, relying on God, in trust: "The one who listens to my words and obeys them . . . is like one who, in building a house, dug deep and laid the foundation on rock" (Luke 6:47-48). There is never force. The Word is always an invitation; always evokes a free response.

The ingenious blending of belief in God's love, with *trust* of human beings, provokes a more inclusive notion of the underlying unity of God and person. The guidelines put this succinctly: "We profess unshakeable reliance upon God and human reliance upon one another."

It was a growing experience for us in community to realize that trusting ourselves was of a piece with trusting others. Had we all not taken the radical step of commitment, and could we not then be assumed to share common ideals? Of course; and so we tested new ways of encouraging each person to make her own decisions rather than being controlled by external rules.

I had to grow into this trust myself, and I really believe that we came to understand this only by our common living it out. But we needed long conversations to support one another as we assimilated our newer understandings and took the risk of "letting go" of our more restrictive practices.

I shared the complete text of the guidelines with Thomas Merton. After reading it, he commented, "This is really a very Christian document—an excellent piece of theology on the religious life."

One sentence in the guidelines caught his eye—it supports the whole import of Christian gift, decision, and trust. "Our lives as dedicated Christian women are meaningful to the extent that we cooperate, through unceasing conversion and self-donation, in the life-giving mission of Jesus Christ, who acts in history through human initiative." These and other lines illustrate the new visioning of faith, which is more dynamic, less restrictive, and more open to dialogue with the world than previous rules had been.

The guidelines seem to capture the importance and meaning of conversion to Jesus Christ: It is a continuing process, not a once-and-for-all action; a repeated turning toward the light, not a completed movement; an ongoing choice, not a time-conditioned commitment.

The guidelines throw light on the perennial richness of the evangelical counsels, revealing their potential for the changing times.

On Poverty (Shared Goods)

What we need to sustain us, in the present and future, becomes a corporate responsibility. We seek the delicate balance between being naïve and being preoccupied about goods of all kind.

How does the religious community deal with material goods? We pool resources, share assets, tailor needs. Pooling resources—sharing financial assets and liabilities—can be a risky venture, but it also can be a liberating one. Living without overconcern demands the not-too-much and the not-too-little.

On Chastity (Consecrated Celibacy)

The love of Christ which prompts our choice and directs our affections is experienced in us as a personal mystery, something which is its own reason for being.

To live a life of celibacy, as is traditional in Catholic religious orders, demands constancy in love and generosity. We have come to realize that recognizing our own sexuality is part of our wholeness as full human persons—as women—and that such recognition enables us to extend our love to others with greater warmth and insight.

The authenticity of our celibacy is manifested in our dedicated ministry. Without a whole gift of ourselves to others, celibacy easily degenerates into sterility; and with it, we testify to the fulness of life to be found in Christ and one another.

On Authority (Obedience)

Radical obedience is the continuing effort to become what God calls us to be. We promise to accept this task and to animate one another in fulfilling it.

In one way, the keystone of the religious life, as indeed that of the Christian life, is expressed in the simple yet profound terms of this article. The community around us helps us, animating us to search for what God calls us to be. To understand this fundamental meaning of obedience required a shift of viewpoint. Of course, we always had believed in "God's call through the Word expressed in Scripture and tradition." But the new emphasis required that we see God's will also in the people and events of the world around us. New decisions were needed for each new day. For me, this was both freeing and more demanding. It required a listening to the growing insights of the community, both near and far, as well as the assessing of my own responsibility for helping create a more human world.

2. Person and Community

The quality of trust is the *sine qua non* of a Christian community traveling along experimental paths today. For the person is constituted both by relatedness to God and by relatedness to others. Mutual trust emphasizes not only the dignity and value of persons and their incredible potential, but also their relationships to others. The guidelines continue to underline this point.

On Consideration for One Another

It is the love of Christ which has brought us together. It is he who nourishes our affection for one another, without which we cannot live and grow. Human affection is also dependent upon self-revelation. We therefore accept the serious and lasting obligation to speak with each other, to listen to each other, and so to be modified in thought and act. Let us be prompt, sensitive, and attentive to one another.

Perhaps no sentence in the guidelines has fostered community relations more than this counsel—that we accept the serious responsibility for communication with one another, and its resultant modification. We have been challenged by this one sentence again and again, both in personal contacts and in wider group decision making. Community provides the climate for a network of relationships and friendships. The personal links, in turn, nourish the spirit of human community, providing support and energy.

It is true that the task is continuous. The laughter and sunshine of life together is one part of a pattern, which also includes accepting differences and dealing with

misunderstandings. It is never easy to live with the
contradictions inherent in the clash of different personalities. I know that I have grown in maturity through the
correctives to selfishness that a common life provides.
Years together not only make us acutely aware of one
another's shortcomings, but also deepen our loyalty. We
are a family. The gatherings of friends at our ceremonies
of commitment and our jubilee celebrations, as well as at
our farewells at the time of death, are among the riches
we enjoy together.

Telling the stories of the past has become a favorite
community activity. The younger members delight in
hearing of the doughty women who outwitted the pastor
or accomplished racial integration in the schools.
Traditions are built in this way. Today's sisters, living and
working with the poor, or confronting corporations, or
teaching conflict resolution to preschool and older
children, or promoting full ministry for women in the
church, are weaving their stories into the tapestry of the
future.

3. Movement Toward Justice

Finally, the guidelines illumine the further impulse
toward justice at home and abroad. Sentences from the
guidelines reveal in a few words how the movement
toward justice flows from the gospel.

On Meeting Human Needs

Community in this present time is for mission. If we have come
together, it is in order that, rejoicing in and strengthened by
our mutual love, we may continually go forth to meet our
farther neighbors in their human needs and aspirations. . . .
The basic desire to be united in love with Christ and with all
people underlies the creation of this particular community of
faith. Membership in this congregation is an attempt to work

toward the full realization of human community by building something of it concretely here and now.

In company with others, the community member is urged by the basic constitution of her religious life to set about enhancing and fostering human community, wherever and in whatever ways she can. The tensions, strains, contradictions, and divisions in the world community are her challenges. But in order that such a task be not too overwhelming, she is invited to the daily work of creating community among her nearer neighbors. The ideal set forth in the gospel is her vision.

On Promoting Understanding

Therefore, let nothing in our lives cut us off from other human beings. Rather, may everything about us, our words and works and manner of living, promote understanding and harmony among ourselves and others. . . . To be such a power of reconciliation demands that we deeply respect diversity of being and diversity of gifts. It further demands that we collaborate with all those, whoever they may be, who seek to break down barriers between people and to build up human communion.

I have thought of this statement many times while working with groups and with other individuals, as we coalesce in common cause. Ecumenical cooperation provides the climate for breaking down barriers. I will cite some illustrations of this collaboration in the chapters ahead.

I have quoted freely from the guidelines to show how they point constantly to obedience to the gospel—the gospel that calls us to the demanding work of breaking down those barriers of injustice that prevent the building up of human community.

Our renewal process thus opened new doors of awareness that prepared us for confronting the violence of war and racism escalating in the mid-1960s. We had no choice but to address ourselves to the social-justice positions and activities of members of the group, and of the group itself, when it acted as a corporate entity.

Some Sisters of Loretto were involved in the march at Selma; but in the early 1960s, the community as a whole was uncertain about these actions. Some members were proud and jubilant; others were suspicious of an action they did not understand. Time was needed to assimilate such unusual activities, so acceptance was cautious, though steady.

The Vietnam war period was another occasion for growth and new insights. Individual sisters began to be involved with groups seeking to express their concern over social injustices. As the magnitude of human suffering increased, so did our awareness.

In 1967, for the first time, through its elected delegates, the community chose to take a corporate stand against the Vietnam war by joining Negotiation Now, a national call to action. That decision gave the needed affirmation and basis for further group-action statements, as well as for individual action.

When some sisters joined groups practicing civil disobedience in antiwar demonstrations, the assembly delegates realized they needed to reckon with the uneasiness of many in the community. In 1968, the delegates worked out a statement of support: "The courage of a Sister of Loretto to act on her Christian conviction deserves the support of her sisters. A common application of the gospel to any public issue may never be reached by us, but respect for another's integrity and conscience is a value that we affirm and pledge ourselves to preserve."

From that date until the present, the strong stand of the community through corporate statements has provided a solid reference for evaluation and confirmation for every kind of action for social justice, such as nonviolent direct action (including civil disobedience), participation in rallies, membership in national and international groups, educational efforts for peace, and so on.

By 1973, the community had become quite conscious of its need to look at its investment policies; in the following year, an investment committee was established, and membership in the Interfaith Center for Corporate Responsibility, a national organization, resulted. In 1979, the assembly of the Loretto community, with approximately three hundred participants, arrived at a significant statement on the nuclear danger. Both these actions will be described in more detail in the final chapter.

This sequence of decisions was made possible only by cohesion and support within the group. I think it may be assumed that all seven hundred fifty members of the community, understandably, had not been convinced that risk taking and controversial stands were good or necessary for members of a religious congregation. Because the direction in which we were moving seemed so right to me, it was painful to realize that some in the community held a different opinion. I must say, however, that I always felt that the leadership of the community—I and others—received strong affirmation. Coming home to a group that was eager and elated about the movements I was engaged in provided the tangible support that energized me to "go ahead."

One of the most powerful influences in my own faith development has been this readiness for support that the Loretto community has provided. The horizons opened up to me by entering the door of the Loretto community have provided a credible and supportive base for action as well as an indispensable source of new vision.

Crossing the thresholds of the many doors of renewal that opened as a result of the first involved challenge and risk. I believe that as a community we have found the risks well worth taking. Again and again in the 1970s and early 1980s, those of us who had been in leadership positions during the previous decade saw this development of persons and communities as a rewarding and life-affirming growth. The variety of opportunities open to and accepted by many in the community was unexpected, but reaffirmed our early convictions and strengthened our hope for the future.

As those new insights awakened the Loretto community, how did we move from reflection to action?

—We risked when we relinquished ownership and control of most of our own schools, but the resultant flexibility made possible wider choices of work, more suited to the talents and desires of each person. It also became clear that a community less concerned with the problems of institutional survival would be more free to be concerned about the issues of global survival.

A dramatic example, because unprecedented, of this kind of transaction occurred when the Loretto community transferred its ownership and control of Webster College to a lay board. This event could not have taken place when it did, and our insights might have been delayed, had it not been for the talent and ability of Jacqueline Grennan Wexler, then president of the college, and the wisdom of Sister Helen Sanders, the St. Louis representative of the order. Fortunately, the excellent administration and board at the college in the years since 1967 have affirmed the viability of this venture. It was not an easy move to make, and again we could not pace the steps to a smooth resolution of the event. Many sisters committed to professional education have remained at the college, so that their choices, too, have been affirmed.

—We risked when we extended the boundaries of community to include as "co-members" a growing number of persons—male, female, married, unmarried, Protestant, Catholic—who, though not vowed members, yet wish to share our values and ideals. But inclusion of these co-members has enriched the community with a diversity that has widened our horizons and also has given those persons a new experience of community.

—We risked when we encouraged open choice of community living groups, but the joys and difficulties of living out close interpersonal relationships in community now reflect more authentically the human reality that the gospel underscores. A sister chooses those with whom she lives. These might include a needy relative or a co-member. Or she may need the space and time made available by living alone.

—We risked when we arranged for more flexible financial planning by individuals and communities in the common practice of total sharing, but the reliance placed upon such a process has resulted in the ability to make financial and other resources available not only to one another, but far more widely, in response to the critical needs of neighbors near and far.

The personal responsibility for simple living, in accordance with the guidelines, has had a variety of applications. Some members have elected to live directly with the poor; a few have founded or live in Catholic

Worker houses. Some have taken up service that helps the poor directly. In addition, it is crucial that some among us dedicate our work to systemic change, in an effort to discover and correct the economic and social roots of inequity.

—We risked when we included an ever-wider participation in leadership roles within the community, but the development of the potential of each person's gifts enriched the total community with new creativity as we moved into broader engagement in world problems.

Progressing into such a totally new way of life presumed, above all, a high degree of trust on the part of both the designers of the policy and those who implemented it. Fortunately, Loretto designers and implementers felt that such trust was present, and that feeling has proved to be justified. In no better way could we have been energized for action.

How does one connect this community evolvement with the faith-source emphasized by the guidelines? The link is reflection and action motivated by Scripture. By centering our vision on the treasure of the Gospels, out of which one draws both new and old, the community pursues its daily reflections on the life, words, and actions of Jesus as paradigms for the twentieth and twenty-first centuries. The Beatitudes and works of mercy are continuing signposts for a much wider variety of Christian choices in the contemporary world.

The preceding analysis of risk indicates one element of the evolution of religious life. Some contrasts and comparisons may demonstrate a further development.

—Although institutions of learning remain necessary and viable locales for one's professional choices, and many sisters are involved in such institutions, others have looked toward new ways of educational involvement, such as pastoral education or peace and justice movements.

—Although the large traditional convent, where many sisters live a more structured existence under one roof, still remains an option for some, others have chosen to live in small communities, in groups of two or three, or even in some cases, alone. Working out the patterns of daily life—prayer together, the sharing of household tasks and conversation, the give and take of differing personalities in a close living-situation—has been a learning experience for these loosely structured groups. It has enabled these sisters to be more available to a neighborhood, more aware of the needs of ordinary citizens, and more directly involved in forming groups to act for justice at home and abroad.

—Although prayer continues to be the indispensable bedrock for the living-out of Christian life, its forms may vary. Common prayer may follow the style of formal recitation of the office or of informal reflection on texts from Scripture or from other sources. Personal prayer also enjoys a multitude of expressions, varying as widely as do the individuals who seek this contact with God through whatever practice is most congenial to them.

—Although prayer is an essential ingredient in the life of the woman religious, it generally has been integrated into the professional life of the "active" religious, leaving the choice of full-time prayer to "contemplatives." Today, however, some in active orders, including Loretto, have chosen a life of full-time prayer, living alone or in communities where a simple contemplative life-style prevails.

—Although action for social justice that flows from the imperatives of the gospel has many modes of implementation, all members are learning to respect the choices of others. Some elect to teach social responsibility and others elect to support it, but all try to embody such principles in their personal lives. Some have chosen to express their concern in more publicly involved ways, such as in confrontative rallies and demonstrations and by joining coalitions for wider political action in the struggle for justice. Some have felt that only examples of nonviolent civil disobedience will draw attention to critical problems that are otherwise unnoticed in an apathetic society, and they have been willing to be arrested in those causes.

—Although structures of community government have been reduced in number and set up more simply, new modes of developing common ideals and practices are continuing. While delegates to annual assemblies are charged with a few central decisions, more and more decision making takes place by consensus, even when this process involves hundreds of members. Some decisions that formerly were effected centrally are now made locally, or even individually.

When I say that the door that swung open will not close, I am thinking that the future, whatever it brings, is open to the completely new experience that is encountered when persons and communities, conscious of a greater responsibility for individual and group choice, accept the challenge to relate the events of the times to the gospel and to the justice mandated by it.

Let us return to the question of the coal company official. "How does the vocation of the sisters involve them in action" for the support of mining safety (or of any other such matter)? Perhaps he may best be answered by some final words from the Loretto guidelines.

The spirit of the poor proclaimed by the beatitudes demands more than our generosity and detachment. It does demand these. But it also demands a sharing in the struggles of the world against all the evil afflicting our sisters and brothers everywhere.

3.
The Door of Prophetic Friendship: Thomas Merton

And pray for us also, that God may open to us a door for the word, to declare the mystery of Christ.

Colossians 4:3 RSV

When the big oak door at Loretto swung open to admit the monk, Thomas Merton, to our home, a new affirmation and extension of my widened faith perspectives entered with him. Who in the American Catholic Church, and increasingly in Protestant churches, had not heard of this gifted writer who set aside a promising literary career to enter a strict and obscure contemplative monastery in Kentucky? I had read his poetry and books eagerly since 1948, but I never had expected to meet him.

My acquaintance with Thomas Merton came about when he was seeking an opportunity for his friend, Daniel Walsh, to give some occasional lectures in the Kentucky rural area. I remember the bright October day in 1959, when Merton, wearing his white monk's habit, and Dan Walsh, jaunty in his Irish hat, swung up the walk between the tall oaks at our motherhouse. Of course we were ready and eager to provide an opportunity for Dan Walsh to give philosophy lectures to our novices! As I led the two men down the hall to my office, I remember the novices peeking over the banister to catch a glimpse of the great man. That day opened another door for me—nine years of friendship and neighborly contact with the Christian poet-mystic whose writings have been so attractive to so many.

Merton's autobiography, *The Seven Storey Mountain,* tells how he found his way to Gethsemani and became a Trappist monk. And since writing was encouraged by his superiors, he had found more and more opportunity for that ever-congenial task.

His Writing

Merton's first published volume was a book of poems, which appeared in the early 1940s. His autobiography was an immediate bestseller and has gone through several editions. *Seeds of Contemplation,* a description of contemplative prayer, appeared soon, followed by *Thoughts in Solitude* and *The Silent Life.*

The following books include those I believe to be his most significant volumes. After 1965, although he was still rooted in the contemplative life of a monk, his works ranged over a wide area. *No Man Is an Island* spoke of relationships of the Christian to others; *Conjectures of a Guilty Bystander* reflects the monk as he confronts the turmoil and chaos of our present age; *Faith and Violence* grew out of thoughts on racism and war.

Merton's books of poetry include *Emblems of a Season of Fury* and *Original Child Bomb,* a prose-poem on the bombing of Hiroshima. *The Collected Poems of Thomas Merton,* published in 1977, contains all his published and most of his previously unpublished poetry. *The Way of Chuang Tzu,* a translation of a great Taoist's writings, was Merton's favorite among his own books. As his writing career developed, a change in style and subject matter may be detected: As he became older and more experienced, he was more wary of writing glibly or expansively on the subject of "the spiritual life" or "God."

Merton wrote quickly, intensely, and spent little time on revisions. He was uncannily keen to catch the deeper significance of passing world events and was eager to write his views and impressions. This style accounts for a certain unevenness but also expresses a sense of immediacy.

The reader of Merton's work becomes aware of his constant use of paradox, employed to express the contradictions in his own life and in the times—indeed, in all life. Parker Palmer said,

Thomas Merton has helped me understand that the way we respond to contradiction is pivotal to our spiritual lives. . . . There is a way to respond beyond choosing either this pole or that. Let us call it "living the contradictions." Here we refuse to flee from tension but allow that tension to occupy the center of our lives. And why would anyone walk this difficult path? Because by doing so we may receive one of the great gifts of the spiritual life—*the transformation of contradiction into paradox.*[1]

Contacts with Merton and His Thought

There were occasions when Merton stopped at Loretto, and there were other times when I drove the twelve miles to Gethsemani to consult with him about our then-developing renewal program. Sometimes we asked him to talk to the novices; sometimes, to the older sisters;

and sometimes, to those of us who were responsible for charting our course of renewal. He came when he could, and although he always protected his solitude and his seclusion, he and we enjoyed those occasional conversational exchanges. It is difficult to choose examples from his talks and our casual discussions; however, to give some sense of the flavor and direction of his thought, I would like to cite some selections from his conversations, tapes, and related writings.

Prayer

Early in the 1960s, I asked Merton to speak to our novices about prayer. In part, he said,

I think I could give you one general principle that goes for the whole of life. Watch out for impractical ideals. Because the impractical ideal is the kind that you work out in your head first, *a priori*, as the philosophers say. You work it out before and then you apply it to reality and you try to force reality to fit the ideal. You say reality has to be this way because this is the way it says in the book. And then when reality doesn't fit the ideal, you start fighting reality.

Don't let your prayer be a fight against reality. And the first reality you've got is yourself, and that's where prayer begins. It begins with you and you don't have to go from you to God, because God is in you. All you've got to do is to stay where you are. You don't have to get out of this earthly being which you are and climb Jacob's ladder and get way up in the heavens where God is, because if you do that, you'll never pray. You couldn't pray.

You have to look out for two extremes: on the one hand, an impractical idealism, and on the other hand, a kind of passive realism. The impractical idealism is the kind that says, "I've worked it out beforehand and that's the way it's got to be." On the other hand, the wrong kind of realism says, "Well, this is the way it is, what can you do?"—and just does nothing.

Both those views are basically pagan and both are basically static—that is to say, they never get anywhere. In between, there is another view, which is the Christian view: In the reality which I have and am now, there is a possibility for growth which God has put there.[2]

At the center of Merton's thought was the search for God—the careful search for God's will in the events of his life. Earnestly and unceasingly, through the sometimes turbulent course of his existence, his eyes were fixed on the ascent to wisdom. He yearned constantly for conscious union with God, the mystic's primary calling. Well acquainted with all the great mystics of the Christian tradition, he became increasingly well informed about the spiritual masters of other traditions, never ceasing to integrate their original insights into his own thoroughly Christian identity.

In one of Merton's last reflections, he insisted,

Prayer should lead us to wholeness, an all-around acceptance of ourselves and the world as it is, our religious life as it is, and other people as they are. Prayer is the great way of getting ourselves opened up to this acceptance. . . . Prayer is the flowering of our inmost freedom in response to the word of God. Prayer is the communion of our freedom with the ultimate freedom of God's infinite Spirit . . . which knows no limits or no obstacles.[3]

Racism

In his writings of the early 1960s, Merton spoke out often against the evil of racism. He had been moved by some of the great black leaders and had the unusual ability to understand their consciousness of injustice. Eldridge Cleaver wrote about Merton.

At that time I had a chance to read Thomas Merton's autobiography. Despite my rejection of Merton's theistic world view, I could not keep him out of the room. He shouldered his way through the door. Welcome, Brother Merton. I give him a bear hug. Most impressive of all to me was Merton's description of New York's black ghetto—Harlem. I used to keep his passage in mind when delivering lectures to other prisoners. Whenever I felt myself softening, relaxing, I had only to read that passage to become once more a rigid flame of indignation. I vibrate sympathetically to any protest against tyranny.[4]

Merton had looked forward to meeting Martin Luther King, and the two men had set a date for King to visit Gethsemani. They never met, however—King's tragic death occurred just two weeks before that date.

On one of the tapes Merton gave me in 1966, there is an intriguing episode that reveals much about his awareness of a new black consciousness. Alone in his hermitage, Merton decided to experiment with a meditation accompanied by a jazz recording. He taped this scintillating "dialogue" between the jazz player Jimmy Smith and the hermit Merton, carried on in the darkness of the Kentucky woods.

Merton begins, "While it's night, we're going to try an experimental meditation against a background of some jazz, and think in terms of what's going on in Louisville tonight, maybe. There have been riots in Louisville the last two or three days. . . . Now, the subject of this meditation is, Who You Identify with. . . . Outside, the moon is full; it's very quiet here. In other parts of the world, people are being killed. . . . Let's see what it sounds like."

As Jimmy Smith's fingers run up and down the keyboard, Merton's own empathetic words are synchronized with the musician's performance. As Jimmy Smith sings, "I'm a rootsie-tootsie man," Merton cries, "That's it, man! I'm with you and with your people. . . . This organ says something. I pray for your race, man. If you get a choice in the world today, you want to be with these people."

When Jimmy says, "Don't mess with me," Merton reflects, "Here I sit with all the wheels turning, and I'm listening to you, man. The moon's shining and the wheels are turning, yeah. Well, I'm against the white backlash, man; this means something. . . . If you understand what it means, you understand the future."[5]

Merton addressed himself to the topic of racism in more public methods of communicating, of course. Many of his articles and books of the 1960s make it clear that he understood, better than most whites, the oppressions and angers of black people.

I recall his suggestion that I read *The Autobiography of Malcolm X,* which had moved him deeply. In his review of this book, Merton stated that he was most impressed by the way Malcolm outgrew his early race hatred, especially after his visit to Mecca.

Not only was his Islamic faith clarified, but he experienced an extraordinary sense of community, of [solidarity] with other pilgrims from all parts of the world, including many who were white. He saw that it was not a simple question of black angels and white devils in the cities of the United States, but of the formerly colonial, under-developed world, filled with black, white, yellow, red, brown and mestizo populations (in other words the majority of the human race), against a highly developed affluent technological society which cannot really help the others in their struggle for liberation because it needs them to remain in a state of economic and political tutelage.[6]

Vietnam War

Merton saw the often-hidden roots of economic and social injustice as the principal causes of war. Since by the mid-1960s, the United States was becoming increasingly involved in the struggle in Vietnam, Merton began to write more and more about our participation in that war. In an essay called "Taking Sides on Vietnam," he wrote,

In my opinion the exorbitant U.S. war effort in Vietnam cannot be explained or justified by the reasons that are officially given ("to prevent South Vietnam from being overrun by Communism from the North"). The game of escalation continues to be more and more aggressive. Why is the U.S. anxious to maintain such huge military bases in South East Asia? Are these necessary for the "defense" of South Vietnam?[7]

I read most of Merton's articles on peace in mimeographed form, and I also shared the mimeographed volume of *Cold War Letters* which Merton distributed to his friends. Gordon Zahn has done us a great service by putting all Merton's writings about peace into a single volume.[8]

Merton's writings against war were very sobering, but certainly not inflammatory. Nevertheless, as Zahn states, persons in ecclesiastical and political power were able to influence Merton's superiors to have him silenced. He had refused to go along with what he regarded as the great illusion that the United States was a paragon of virtue, the lover of peace, and always right, while the communists were the embodiment of everything evil and base. The national fixation on this kind of oversimplified dichotomy could lead only to an anticommunism that was vicious, self-righteous, and rooted in rationalization rather than in reason. Merton perceived such a stance as leading to an inflated, arrogant, and ultimately death-dealing patriotism. What was needed, he wrote, was "moderation, rationality, and above all, a firm reliance on our strengths: constitutional processes of government, respect for the rights we want to defend, rational discussion, freedom of opinion, and a deep loyalty to our inherited ideals."[9]

Although Merton had been forbidden to publish these "peace" writings, he continued his efforts by mimeographing or by writing on the backs of envelopes. I recall his saying at the time, "Imagine, I have been forbidden to write on the subject of peace!" and a large advance check was returned to his publisher. Later, more permissive superiors and, of course, the impact on the church of Pope John XXIII, freed him from these restraints.

His discerning reflections about the Vietnam war are well put in the following words.

Therefore when I take a side in this question, it is not the side of the United States and it is not the side of Communism. Peking, Washington, Saigon, and Hanoi want the war to go on. I am on the side of the people who are being burned, cut to pieces, tortured, held as hostages, gassed, ruined, destroyed. They are the victims of both sides. To take sides with massive power is to take sides against the innocent. The side I take is then the side of the people who are sick of war and want peace in order to rebuild their country.

Once this has been said, it must be admitted that the American policy of escalation is what makes peace and order impossible in Vietnam. As long as bombings continue in North Vietnam, as long as rumors of an invasion of North Vietnam continue to grow, it is useless to expect an end to the horrors and inhumanities of the war. Resistance and counter-escalation are the obvious result.[10]

On Madness

The events of the 1960s grew more and more ominous. In Merton's writings of that period one can see that he was required by the profound reflections of his contemplative life to help others gain an understanding of the evils that he saw menacing the times. There began to appear in his writings a conviction that a sort of madness infected our society and that our awareness was essential to our avoidance of its effects. He saw this madness in the social evils of racism and the war in Vietnam, but especially in the threat of nuclear war. I would like to share some of his perceptions of the evidence of that madness.

In 1962, when the community of Loretto celebrated its sesquicentennial, Merton offered to write an essay in honor of the occasion. The theme that he used in presenting this reflection was the similarity between the founders of Loretto and those of Gethsemani. Rugged and brave pioneers, they had faced the hardships of the Kentucky wilderness with equal courage. Merton wrote, "We are not only neighbors in a valley that is still lonely, but we are equally children of exile and of revolution."[11]

As I look back, I can see that he already sensed a need to take a stand in opposition to the evils abroad in our world. Although Vatican II was turning the attention of the church to the need to be in tune with, and attentive to, all peoples of the world, there was another way in which we must oppose false values. Merton wrote about that stand in *Loretto and Gethsemani*.

There is something about Gethsemani that has nothing to communicate to multitudes; and I find it also at Loretto. It is a secret that reveals itself only partially even to those who live for a long time in our valley.

I suppose I will give scandal if I say it is a quiet mixture of wisdom and madness, a triumph of hope over despair. But we have both descended from ancestors who died accomplishing the impossible. Or rather from people who accepted as perfectly normal the incongruity and solitude which are the lot of the pioneer. Now we are safer than they, richer, more comfortable, better cared for, secure. But when I say there is madness in the old walls of our houses, I mean a wise madness that still, for all the public approval we have received from "the world," persists in a half ironic suspicion that all is not well with the world, and that we cannot be altogether part of it. This I know is the thing I must not say. We are of course engagés. We are in the world of our time, no doubt about that. We are in it to save it. Yet we still have to save ourselves from it, for unless we have a foothold that is not of the world, we will go down with it, and drag no one to safety.[12]

The "wise madness" that Merton admired among the early founders of both Gethsemani and Loretto is one of the paradoxes he employed to affirm his growing sense of a destructive trend in our twentieth-century world. He believed, however, in the profoundly Christian need to resist the oppressions and terror of a racist and war-minded society. His thoughts came through to me quite specifically in a tape he gave me in the summer of 1967. In it he spoke of his deep interest in Michel Foucault's book *On Madness and Civilization,* and he commented on Foucault's theme and on his method.

The book is important because it nowhere preaches anything. Rather, it lets the material speak for itself; and the rich material is concerned with the developing viewpoints about madness from the middle ages to the nineteenth century. Foucault allows the physicians and psychologists and sociologists (if you can call them that) of medieval times to speak for themselves without comment. And what appears is a bizarre collection of myths and semi-legendary views of madness. We see together on one hand the derangement of the mad, and on the other, the derangement of the sane, presented as parts of a single whole; they are complementary realities. The approach on the part of the doctors was an attempt to push madness away; to close, lock it up as a wholly wrong and unnatural thing.

We can see how we, too, are caught in the same structure of myths. We can look objectively at the complacent confidence with which the psychiatrists, say, of the seventeenth and eighteenth centuries, stood back and judged madness as if they themselves were perfectly sane. And then we can see how we do the same thing.[13]

In much of his writing in the 1960s, Merton reflects on the aberration, or madness, of modern times, as illustrated by the use of power; as evident in the astronomical increase of armaments as deterrents; or as associated with the risks to life and health from nuclear plants and operations—risks recorded every day in our newspapers.

Merton's plea for understanding the reality of this madness comes through to us quite clearly. Nowhere does he contrast madness and sanity more vividly than in the short essay, "A Devout Meditation in Memory of Adolf Eichmann."

One of the most disturbing facts that came out in the Eichmann trial was that a psychiatrist examined him and pronounced him *perfectly* sane. . . .

The sanity of Eichmann is disturbing. We equate sanity with a sense of justice, with humaneness, with prudence, with the capacity to love and understand other people. We rely on the sane people of the world to preserve it from barbarism, madness, destruction. And now it begins to dawn on us that it is precisely the *sane* ones who are most dangerous.

It is the sane ones, the well-adapted ones, who can without qualms and without nausea aim the missiles and press the buttons that will initiate the great festival of destruction that they, *the sane ones,* have prepared. . . .

The whole concept of sanity in a society where spiritual values have lost their meaning is itself meaningless. . . .

The ones who coolly estimate how many millions of victims can be considered expendable in a nuclear war, I presume they do all right with the Rorschach ink blots. . . .

I am beginning to realize that "sanity" is no longer a value or an end in itself. . . . If [modern people] were a little less sane, a little more doubtful, a little more aware of [our] absurdities and contradictions, perhaps there might be a possibility of [our] survival. But if [we are] sane, too sane . . . perhaps we must say that in a society like ours the worst insanity is to be totally without anxiety, totally "sane."[14]

Much of Merton's poetry also addresses itself to the kind of cruel and feverish insanity that has prevailed in our violent century. For example, *Original Child Bomb* gives a "rationalistic" description of the entire atomic destruction of Hiroshima, pointing out the religious terms used as code names in the operation—Trinity, papacy, and so on. The Cargo Cult poems, which appear in *Cables to the Ace,* as well as many of his last poems, give other examples.

Merton turned all his indignation into the devastating satire with which he wrote. His method of letting the material stand by itself is evident in "Rites for the Extrusion of a Leper." The poem needs little explanation, but allows us to draw our own conclusions from the inhuman treatment accorded to the afflicted or ostracized. Here again Merton is persuaded that our madness is revealed by our "rationalized" use of power. "We've got a fascinating picture of a society in which we have this really bizarre mosaic of madness and sanity, a kind of surrealistic picture of the whole thing," said Merton.[15]

His writing usually took the form of a "mosaic pattern," allowing spaces for afterthoughts or reflections and, even later, corrections—spaces between strongly put opinions. This allowed for a discontinuity as well as a cumulative development. It also was congenial to his bent for living with contradictions until they often could be seen as paradoxes.

The continuity between the horrors of World War II and the unimaginable holocaust of a nuclear war was expressed well in Merton's poem, "Chant to Be Used in Processions Around a Site with Furnaces." He puts words into the mouth of Hitler's Director of Furnaces, and horror is heightened by the matter-of-fact coldness of the account.

For putting them into a test fragrance I suggested an express elevator operated by the latest cylinder it was guaranteed

Their love was fully stopped by our perfected ovens but the love rings were salvaged

Thanks to the satisfaction of male inmates operating the heaters without need of compensation our guests were warmed

[Here Merton comes to a startling conclusion.]

You smile at my career but you would do as I did if you knew yourself and dared

In my day we worked hard we saw what we did our self-sacrifice was conscientious and complete our work was faultless and detailed

Do not think yourself better because you burn up friends and enemies with long-range missiles without ever seeing what you have done[16]

The Nuclear Peril

As early as 1962, Merton was writing about the nuclear dangers of our times. In his essay on the moral responsibility of Christians, he pointed out the error of allowing our decisions to be made for us—for instance, of abdicating our responsibility in the serious matter of nuclear war.

This brings us face to face with the greatest and most agonizing issue of our time. This issue is not merely nuclear war, not merely the possible destruction of the human race by a sudden explosion of violence. It is something more subtle and more demonic. If we continue to yield to theoretically irresistible determinism and to vague "historic forces" without striving to resist and control them, if we let these forces drive us to demonic activism in the realm of politics and technology, we face something more than the material evil of universal destruction. We face *moral responsibility for the destruction of civilization or even for global suicide*. Much more than that, we are going to find ourselves gradually moving into a situation in which we are practically compelled by the "logic of circumstances" deliberately *to choose the course that leads to destruction*.

The free choice of global self-destruction, made in desperation by the world's leaders and ratified by the consent and cooperation of their citizens, would be a moral evil second only to the crucifixion. The fact that such a choice might be made with the highest motives and the most urgent purpose would do nothing whatever to mitigate it. The fact that it might be made on a gamble, in the hope that some might escape, would never excuse it. After all, the purposes of Caiphas were, in his own eyes, perfectly noble. He thought it was necessary to let "one man die for the people."

Can we draw a line clearly, and say precisely when nuclear war becomes so dangerous that it is suicidal? If a war of missiles breaks out, we will have at the most thirty minutes to come to our momentous conclusions—even if we ever know what is happening at all. It seems to me that the time to form our conscience and to decide upon our course of action is *NOW*.[17]

Daniel Berrigan, reflecting on Merton's concern over the nuclear threat, has said:

In all his letters, he is haunted by the nuclear spectre, in days when few of us had begun to realize this cloud that was crossing the sun. For faith cannot be preserved if our reason goes under, and the church cannot survive if humanity is destroyed; that is to say, his definition of the destruction of humanity is acute. He wrote, "Our humanity is debased and mechanized, while we ourselves may remain on earth as the instrument of enormous and unidentified forces like those which press us today inexorably to the brink of cataclysm." He was not just focusing on the bomb; he was trying to talk about the spiritual implications of having, possessing, creating, researching, producing this nest egg of hell. . . .

It was not merely Merton's background and long spiritual journey in the world that prepared him for this; it was also and primarily his biblical sense of what was going on. From the Bible he was able to draw his images and resources which enabled him to speak the truth ahead of time. (There's a heavy price tag for that.) It was the fact that Merton was not only a converted child of the culture, but also a biblical person that kept him going, kept him fueled up. For him, suffering was not an imaginary concept, but reality.[18]

Merton's frequently appearing books and articles were a constant and sturdy support for my own evolution. I am thinking in particular of the essays in *Raids on the Unspeakable*, and later in *Faith in Violence*, published in the last year of his life. His articulation of a prophetic vision in these works was the vital and supportive rationale I needed to stiffen my own spine in the difficult confrontations of the late 1960s.

Renewal of Religious Life

Merton understood very well our efforts at Loretto for renewal as a religious community. He affirmed our new insights: the importance and dignity of the human person, openness to the spirit of the gospel as revealed in

the new and unexpected in the world, greater inclusiveness, removal of barriers between religious and other
persons, and readiness to serve the neighbor, both near
and far. He agreed with our efforts to create the more
flexible structures needed to implement these aspirations.

In the summer of 1967, when the Loretto guidelines
were prepared by Sister Jane Marie, I took a copy over to
Gethsemani and showed it to Merton. "Will you read it,"
I asked, "and tell me what you think of it?" He did so, and
within a week, we had in our possession a two-hour tape
of commentary.

Merton began by saying, "Yesterday Sister Luke and I
were talking about the religious life, its problems, and so
on, and thought it would be a good idea to make a tape . . .
for your general chapter. I'd like to talk over the very
excellent ideas in Sister Jane Marie's spiritual manifesto, so
to speak, which is really excellent—the best I have seen."

It is instructive that Merton spent at least half an hour
of the tape in commenting on the phrase *dedicated life*.

"The Congregation of the Sisters of Loretto, a dedicated
community of faith and service, exists to praise the Lord and to
minister to his people." The word *dedicated*. What is *dedicated*?
What does it mean to be dedicated? That is one of those words
full of ambiguities that we have to explore and understand
better.

A dedicated life—dedication is a trap. What does this mean to
say dedication is a trap? Dedication is a trap if everyone in the
dedicated life becomes completely controlled and completely
predictable. . . . If this is what the dedicated life is, and if it is
nothing but this, then it is a trap, and the sacrifice one makes in
entering it is the sacrifice of all possibility of real, spontaneous
love. That is the sacrifice of all possibility of growth, and it is
also really the sacrifice of all possible conversion.

We say *dedicated.* Rome says *dedicated,* and the Sacred Congregation says *dedicated,* and we don't all quite mean the same thing. What are the various possibilities in this word *dedicated?* Is the dedicated life a trap? That is the big question. Is the dedicated life cold storage? Is a dedicated woman one who has been placed in cold storage, who has been placed out of circulation, who has been removed from life, who has been frozen? That is what the dedicated life has meant and does mean to certain people—that it is the purpose of the religious community to keep people dedicated. They mean by this: to keep people in an ice box, to keep them out of contact with life.

If the dedicated life is a life of unceasing conversion, then it is not a trap. It is a freedom, and the freedom we seek in religious life is a freedom for seeking conversion, a self-donation, a renewed self-donation, the renewal of our gift. And this renewal of our gift is not simply a renewal of consent to being in a trap. It is new—it is not simply the reaffirmation, the reiteration of the old act of giving which you made in 1921, or something like that. It is a new act of self-donation here and now. Christ said he will make all things new, and perhaps now I have to give myself in a totally new way which I could not possibly have anticipated at the time of my profession, in a way which no one around here could have anticipated.[19]

Merton saw the religious community as a place of love and truth, where persons could come to redefine themselves in a situation that gives them space to detect the deceptive systems and false values prevailing in society. He continues on the same tape:

The religious life should provide trained and compassionate people living in a community where other people who are trapped by the falsity of a lying system, an inadequate system, may come and be led through discipline to a point of great hazard and difficulty, where they are forced to define themselves, and sweat blood doing it, and to die and rise again while doing it. To be concerned in their self-definition by the sympathy and understanding of others; thereafter to join with these others in freedom, in accepting social organization and discipline, but with total freedom and flexibility, not as an end in itself, not as an ultimate definition of their lives. And in this freedom to go on with the others to a creative, totally creative, self-definition of their own future, and of their community in its future; which means leaving everything wide open.

Applying this to you: It seems to me what you should be thinking is not how to close the future with definitions which you will henceforth live out, but how to keep the future completely open so that you will be able to liberate yourself and one another in an open community with the help of the Holy Spirit and with the help of your love for one another. And your love for one another should take a form, not simply of framing a definition and keeping each other in mind with the definition, but an undefined life, opened to the Spirit and moving freely with the Spirit, helping one another to stay open to the Spirit, reproving one another when you see one closing up against the Spirit (if you know what that is, and don't be too quick to assume that you know).[20]

The continual support that Merton gave to our search for renewal was expressed in a joyful last contact with him. In July of 1968, Merton had arranged to celebrate a Mass on the shore of the lake at Gethsemani with a small group of us from Loretto. It was a simple Mass—we were all learning new ways of celebrating the liturgy—and his homily emphasized the shared love commanded by the gospel. Afterward, at breakfast, with delightful simplicity, Merton expressed his joy at being permitted to travel to the East. None of us guessed at that moment that the trip would mean the end of his life's pilgrimage, for he died in Asia on December 10, 1968, the victim of accidental electrocution.

Identity

Merton quite often referred to death in his writings. In one of his talks to his own community, he expressed an idea which I think fits very well with a revisioning of the faith: He described a sense of freedom to come and go to the "center"—to the true, the inner self.

God is in our "center," and that center is all that is left when we die. Real freedom is to be able to come and go to that center. When we die, everything else is destroyed except that which is important, the true, inner self, the center. The only thing which is important is this inner reality, for God preserves it and is identified with it. Nobody can touch or hurt this center. We must be free to be in contact with this center. . . .We have to train ourselves to choose what will let this center operate. If you choose to handle everything that comes up so that you are in contact with this center, you will have freedom. . . . The reality which is the will of God can keep us in contact with this center at every moment. We must respond to it.[21]

I think often of some words Merton wrote much earlier.

In Louisville, at the corner of Fourth and Walnut, in the center of the shopping district, I was suddenly overwhelmed with the realization that I loved all those people, that they were mine and I theirs, that we could not be alien to one another even though we were total strangers. It was like waking from a dream of separateness, of spurious self-isolation in a special world, the world of renunciation and supposed holiness. . . .

Though "out of the world," we are in the same world as everybody else, the world of the bomb, the world of race hatred, the world of technology, the world of mass media, big business, revolution, and all the rest. . . . This sense of liberation from an illusory difference was such a relief and such a joy to me that I almost laughed out loud. . . . It is a glorious destiny to be a member of the human race, though it is a race dedicated to many absurdities and one which makes many terrible mistakes: Yet, with all that, God himself gloried in becoming a member of the human race. . . . I have the immense joy of being human, a member of a race in which God himself became incarnate. . . . And if only everybody could realize this! But it cannot be explained. There is no way of telling people that they are all walking around shining like the sun.[22]

This meaning of human identity—the union of self and others in God—seems to me to be the core of Merton's teaching. It expresses a further extension of my own continuing revisioning of the faith, for it invites us to an ever more all-embracing level, as well as to the deepest possible level, where all are united in one love.

It was encouraging to observe the integration of Merton's action for justice into his profound life of faith and with the expression of that faith in prayer. His own development records his coming to an acute awareness of the human reality, in which he saw not only "God alone," but also all people as glorious manifestations of God. Once this "vision" possessed him, he spared no effort or words in speaking out against social evil—especially against the oppressions of racism and war.

Even after 1965, when he had been permitted by his superiors to live as a hermit in a small cottage on the Gethsemani property, Merton continued to give lectures to the novices and to others in the monastery. In these later talks, he sometimes spoke of this integration of action and contemplation.

There is no contradiction between action and contemplation, when Christian activity is raised to the level of love. On that level, action and contemplation are fused into one entity by the love of God and our brothers and sisters. But for action to reach this level, prayer must be deep, powerful, and pure. God is the very ground of what we know, and our knowledge itself is his manifestation: Not that he is cause of all that is real, but that reality itself is his epiphany. God is never shown by the Bible, for example, merely as a *supplement* of human power and intelligence, but as the very ground and reality of that power. This is our greatest human dignity, our most essential power, the secret of our humanity.[23]

Merton had long been interested in the great Asian religions, particularly Zen Buddhism and Taoism. When he set out on his Asian journey in the fall of 1968, he sought to "drink from ancient sources of monastic vision and experience." He was drawn to the East by an attraction to the simpler ages in the world's history where "every aspect of life was seen in relation to the sacred."[24]

He believed that if the world is to be healed of its spiritual disorders that lead to material disasters, there must be a rapprochement between the East and the West, and especially between eastern and western religions; the church, he thought, should open itself to learning from the rich religious traditions of Asia. But Merton would have been the last to gloss over the theological differences between Christianity and the religions of Asia. For him, only Christianity looks to "the transcendent and personal center which is the risen Christ in whom all are fulfilled in one."[25] But he also knew and taught that love and truth converge in one God, approached by many different paths.

In December 1968, Merton realized that his experiences in Asia had borne the desired fruit: He had nothing more to seek there. In a moment of intense illumination, he sensed the culmination of his search. "All is understanding, all is compassion, all problems are resolved, and everything is clear simply because what matters is clear."[26]

It seems to me that one might say that Merton's death was timely. It was fitting that one who had faced so many questions in an ever-growing understanding of life should receive this final overflowing affirmation of his insights just a few days before the end.

In my faith revisioning, it was a privilege to share many of the probings and reflections of Thomas Merton, who was exploring the views from his own opening doors. To me he exemplifies the evolution from a more privatized spirituality to God-and-person-centered consciousness. Faced by the compelling events of the 1960s, he moved in both private and public expressions to a world-embracing attitude that was truly prophetic.

4.
The Door of Social Justice: Vietnam and After

But I will stay in Ephesus until Pentecost, for a wide door for effective work has opened to me, and there are many adversaries.
I Corinthians 16:8-9 RSV

My own reflections on the Scriptures during the late 1960s and early 1970s gave me a valuable insight into the relationship of the gospel to our present times. I recall a question that arose during my own meditation. Why was Jesus condemned to death? After all, he was one who went about doing good. As I pondered the Gospel accounts, I was struck by the fact that in several texts, when the enemies of Jesus had plotted among themselves to seek his death, they did so immediately following one of the episodes of his healing or liberating on the sabbath.

It seemed to me that there was a close connection. I believe that the actions of Jesus especially intend to show that it is important to value human needs above those of any institution, with its rules or regulations—even religious institutions. Those texts clarified my under-standing that the dignity of a human being with all his or her great potentialities, including the dimension of openness to the divine, was so important in the eyes of Jesus that he was willing to lay his life on the line to defend that conviction. This insight provided, I felt, a solid basis for taking actions—actions that should engage all Christians in similar struggles—for the enhancement of each human life and the human communities where life is lived out.

The example of Jesus, who chose such priorities of justice, seems to me to reveal a pattern for us all—particularly for those of us who live in powerful and affluent America.

But I came to these insights in my own prayer life only after the events and experiences of the 1960s had sharpened my awareness. At first I did not identify God's call with the need to open my eyes to the injustice and alienation of our times, and it would be misleading to pretend that I am not still struggling for the implemen-tation of this consciousness in my own life.

I had been captivated by Thomas Merton's poetic expressions describing prayer and his reflections on mysticism. I was surprised, then, and a little shocked, when he began to write less about personal prayer experience and more about the harsh realities of racism and war. He was clearly sensitive to the nuclear danger as early as 1961.

I also met Daniel Berrigan early in the 1960s, when he came to Loretto to give a talk. The imagery of his words and figures had always delighted me; thus I was eager for him to share his poetic insights into prayer. Again, I was disappointed during the hours he talked to us, since he spoke not of his poetry, but of the poverty and suffering of people in the South. He seemed interested only in recruiting young college people to give up their summers for volunteer work.

These disturbing developments obliged me to look farther than the familiar, and I was forced to bring my faith into confrontation with the cruelties of racism and war. I began to become more aware of the fact of social evil in my neighborhood and in my country. To involve myself as a responsible Christian and as a citizen with a voice, and to integrate these new insights into my own prayer life, became imperative.

As I became more active in issues of social justice, I began to understand more clearly the whole notion of social sin. My awareness of its implications deepened even further with my involvement in protests against the Vietnam war. Another door, which opened to me in 1970, led to a new discovery—that of my own and my nation's complicity in wartime decisions that resulted in great unnecessary suffering and death. That door opened as a result of a call I received from Tom Cornell, of the Catholic Peace Fellowship.

"Would you be willing to represent the Catholic Peace Fellowship on a fact-finding trip to Saigon in July?" he asked.

Three things helped shape my emerging consciousness of the war/peace issue and led me to say yes to his question, and to a role in peace advocacy: the statements of Vatican II; the increasingly vigorous resolutions of my own religious community; and the insights of Thomas Merton.

The Vatican II document, *The Church in the Modern World*, took a position against the arms race and urged the total banning of war: "The arms race is an utterly treacherous trap for humanity, and one which injures the poor to an intolerable degree. It is much to be feared that if this race persists, it will eventually spawn all the lethal ruin whose path it is now making ready."[1] I recall the struggles in the council commission over the problems of war and nuclear weaponry. There had been an expressed fear on the part of some bishops from the United States that speaking against armaments would weaken a stand against communism. But the statement in the document stood.

Back in the United States after the council meetings, I became gradually more sensitive to the war and to the military-buildup question. In 1967, the Sisters of Loretto declared their opposition to the escalating war in Vietnam and appealed to our government to begin negotiations to end it. This stand was reiterated by the Loretto community's general assembly (its legislative body) in succeeding years. In August 1971, for example, the assembly passed a resolution to request that President Nixon stop all military involvement in Southeast Asia by December 31, and withdraw support from the Saigon government. This call for withdrawal was repeated in 1972, when assembly delegates also condemned the continued bombing.

With my community's consistent stand for peace, and with its voice raised in dissent against U.S. policy in Vietnam, I felt an increasing responsibility to speak out in opposition to the war and to engage in antiwar activities. Therefore, the call inviting me to join the Vietnam trip on behalf of the Catholic Peace Fellowship came at a timely moment.

The Catholic Peace Fellowship had joined with the Fellowship of Reconciliation and the American Friends Service Committee to provide a chance for religious leaders to see at firsthand some of the realities of

Vietnam. I thought that this would be, as indeed it proved to be, a significant opportunity; and it was the occasion for personal contact with many Vietnamese whom I came to know briefly but affectionately in our short encounters.

The purpose of the eleven-member fact-finding team was to determine if peace initiatives existed in South Vietnam, and if they did, how they were expressed. From visits with many persons—lawyers, professors, farmers, publishers, groups of women, students, social workers, Buddhist monks, Catholic priests and others—we learned that while many peace desires existed, attempts to express them resulted in severe repression and some-times imprisonment and torture.

I was very moved by our conversations with the grassroots Vietnamese: women whose husbands or sons had been imprisoned or lost; students still bearing the scars from torture they had endured; Taoist monks at a floating "peace monastery," where they prayed for peace at least six hours a day, and where many conscientious objectors lived.

At the conclusion of our visit, we formed plans for a nonviolent walk to the American embassy to present a petition stating our objection to United States support for the Thieu government, of whose repressive acts we had gathered evidence. We assembled on a bright July day in front of the University of Saigon and were joined by thousands of students eager to participate with an American group that shared their own desires for an end to the war.

Our small band of eleven led the procession, with Ron Young of the American Friends Service Committee bearing aloft a huge white dove made of cotton batting. We led our singing followers down the Saigon streets,

while automobiles made way for us, and soldiers in
passing army jeeps gave us a peace sign. As we turned the
corner of one street and moved up another leading to the
embassy, we faced a grim line of Vietnamese soldiers,
guns lifted to shoulders, warning us against proceeding
farther.

It was formidable to advance in the face of those guns.
I did not realize they ejected only tear gas, and I
remember asking myself if indeed the students were to
be targets of real bullets. As we kept moving forward, the
tear gas was fired into our midst, dispersing us quickly.
Climbing over a motorcycle that blocked an alleyway, I
was assisted by the lithe and agile Episcopal bishop, Paul
Moore, who handed me a water-soaked handkerchief to
brush the tear gas from my eyes.

When we regrouped at our hotel afterward, we
discovered that about thirty students had been arrested.
We then called a press conference and declared that we
would not leave the city until the students had been
released. Ron Young and Don Luce, the able leaders who
had devised the demonstration, managed to obtain as
much good press coverage as possible from the episode.
The students were released that evening, and we flew
back to the United States the next day.

I remember one incident of particular poignancy
during the Vietnam trip. Two Catholic university
students visited me to ask about antiwar activities in the
United States. I can still see their searching brown eyes
and their quizzical expressions. "Don't the American
Catholic students understand our plight? Aren't they
aware of what we are going through? Why don't they
communicate with us and tell us that they are with us?"

I didn't know how to answer those students, but I felt
something of their dismay that there could not be better

understanding in a worldwide Christian family. What were the causes of such estrangement, and how could networks of solidarity be created? I am still wrestling with this dilemma, and it has urged me to a continual search for ways to promote greater understanding among co-religionists on opposite sides of a conflict.

The Saigon experience, with its firsthand contact with people so immediately affected by the war and by a repressive American-supported government, continued to sharpen my determination to work for peace. Many of my efforts were undertaken in conjunction with the Catholic Peace Fellowship, the Fellowship of Reconciliation, and Clergy and Laity Concerned.

Through all those activities, I was continually becoming more aware that there is all too little connection between our individual pieties and our responsibility for owning the acts of our government, which so easily programmed and promoted the vast bombing operations and attendant miseries in Vietnam. Never, I reflected, could faith be restricted to the narrow circle of personal piety alone.

I was happy to learn through our contacts in Saigon that there were indeed many antiwar people among the clergy there, especially among the Catholic priests, and that some editors and other professionals stood firmly against the war, doing what they could to combat it from within. I felt an immediate affinity with those people, especially with the priests and students who spoke to us earnestly about U.S. support of the Thieu regime.

It seems significant to me that during and after those years of the antiwar struggle, the community of non-violent protesters with whom I found myself largely associated were principally persons from the church and religious communities. Even today I find that it is those related to faith communities in some way who are the bulwark of many alliances for justice.

The ecumenical dimensions of all the meetings, conferences, and actions of that time were most evident. Again and again I found myself in the company of believing Protestants and Jews who held the same sustaining vision of the human person as the created image of God. My insights into this reality were deepened and enriched by my frequent contacts with many courageous Protestant and Jewish witnesses.

One of those active in the antiwar movement was Rabbi Abraham Heschel of the Jewish Theological Seminary in New York. I was challenged by his vision of the human person as the image of God, in words that served to deepen my own faith.

The prophet is one who is able to hold God and the human person in one thought, at one time, at all times. This is so great and so marvelous. It means that whatever I do to a person, I do to God. When I hurt a human being, I injure God. God has made human beings in his own image and likeness. Now, God is invisible. But to find God among us it is necessary to look only as far as the next human person. There is, I believe, a partnership of God and human beings. God needs our help. I would define a human being as a divine need. God is in need of men and women.[2]

Someone has remarked very truly that we often feel ourselves to be more of a community with those of a different religious tradition who embrace particular faith values with us, than with some in our own tradition who seem unaware of such values. In several episodes in the years between 1970 and 1975, I was with groups or pilgrimages that included some of those persons. I recall three particular occasions I shared with ecumenical friends during those years.

One way in which peace advocacy was exercised during the Vietnamese era was through challenging the war-connected activities of major corporations holding military contracts. A number of religious groups, through stockholders' proposals presented at annual corporation meetings, struggled to raise the consciousness of other stockholders, and of the public, to the complicity of big business in the destruction of Vietnam. Several times I was involved in visits to company executives in attempts at dialogue concerning their military production.

In late April of 1972, I led a prayer service at the stockholders' meeting of Honeywell, Inc., in St. Paul, Minnesota. Roman Catholic Bishop Walter J. Schoenherr, as well as other religious leaders, prayed and participated. Honeywell was one of the firms involved in producing antipersonnel weapons for use in Vietnam. These relatively small bombs, no larger than an orange, could be concealed easily, and when detonated, drove metal fragments into the flesh of their victims. Feeling that silence about these weapons was betrayal, we tried to convince the corporations making them, through visits, leaflets, and stockholder pressure, that they should cease their production of these inhuman weapons.

I recall that Reverend Richard Fernandez, who was coordinating this activity through Clergy and Laity Concerned, provided me with a plowshare, which I presented to the president of Honeywell at the close of the meeting. I was, of course, aware that this little symbolic exercise would be of no great avail; but we were all willing to use any statements or dramatizations that would expose the producers of our home heating devices and other useful goods as also being the makers of antipersonnel weapons.

It was increasingly evident to me that words and actions intended to persuade politicians to modify their stands were ineluctably connected with the gospel of love and life. Once this conviction had become clear, each decision to participate in an antiwar action did not need to be separately agonized over, but was a link in the chain of resistance and protest.

As part of an organized drive by Clergy and Laity Concerned to spur on Senate-House action, over one hundred religious leaders were lobbying on Capitol Hill one May day in 1972. When informed that there would be no antiwar legislation until after Nixon's visit to Moscow, we gathered in the rotunda for a prayer service. Again Rabbi Heschel was an inspiration. I recall that he meditated on peace in words similar to these.

The Vietnam war is the greatest religious issue of our times. For what does God demand of us primarily? Justice and compassion! What does he condemn above all? Murder—killing innocent people! How can I pray when I have on my conscience the awareness that I am co-responsible for the deaths of innocent people in Vietnam? In a free society, some are guilty; all are responsible.

William Sloane Coffin was leading the prayer service, assisted by others, including Robert McAfee Brown. To manifest our unity in opposition to the war, our group remained singing and praying in the rotunda after the closing hour. We were warned to leave, but we continued to pray and sing. Soon, of course, we were arrested and spent the night in a Washington jail.

Many other war protesters endured much more than I, in my few encounters with the law, but the happenings of that night and day were an invaluable object lesson. I understood, in a small but real way, some of the dehumanizing experiences of every jailed individual. I realized that the practices of thumb-printing, picture-taking, being marched around by wardens, as numbers, or as persons without names, have their effect in depersonalizing one.

The long night spent under a glaring light with three persons crowded into a concrete cell, with only one metal slab to be shared among us as a bed, was a harsh learning event. I am sure my sympathy since then for all prisoners, especially those sentenced to death row, has some of its roots in this small experience. When for any reason one is treated as a thing or as a number, the effect is more demeaning than one would believe. Again and again during those years, my conviction was reinforced that the faith of the followers of Christ requires speaking out loudly and clearly for the defense of human dignity.

In January 1973, I went to Europe on a peace pilgrimage of religious leaders to meet with officials of various European churches. The Christmas 1972 bombing of Hanoi had raised the question, What could the American religious community do to stop those massive bombing raids? It seemed that the activities and resources of the American religious community had not been sufficient and that we needed to seek help from the combined voices and actions of other nations. It was out of such concerns that a "mission of desperation" was assembled by a few American church leaders to meet the religious leaders in several European countries and to appeal for an international voice of conscience to help accomplish what we alone could not.

In that group were United Methodist Bishop James Armstrong, Rabbi Leonard Beerman, Harvey Cox, Episcopal Bishop Robert DeWitt, Robert McAfee Brown, and I. We really "represented" nobody but ourselves; ours was an *ad hoc* group. However, we believed ourselves to be faithful envoys of our religious bodies, since they all had taken strong official stands against the war.

In his assessment of the visit, Robert McAfee Brown commented that the broadening ecumenical perspective included not only Americans of different faiths, but also the shared concerns of the world religious community.

Whether we were talking to British, Dutch, German, or Vatican groups, we sensed at once that we had common moral concerns that transcended and even obliterated our national differences. In a time when our domestic religious voices seem so impotent, it is fortifying to discover that other voices can be added to ours. If we shored those voices up a bit, they shored ours up even more.[3]

Our visit reinforced my own belief that ecumenical action coming from a common Judaeo-Christian faith is far more forceful than action taken by a single religious body.

It was an exhausting trip. On Monday we met with the board of the British Council of Churches, chaired by the bishop of London. Tuesday we met in Amsterdam with some persons with political interests, including two members of the Parliament. Later that day we were in The Hague, attending a joint meeting of the executive committees of the Dutch Reformed Church and the Dutch Council of Churches. Still later that day we conferred with Cardinal Alfrink of the Netherlands. On

Wednesday we met in Bonn with Gustav Heinemann, president of the German Republic; then we went to talk with the Rhineland synod of the German Evangelical Church. That evening we met in Stuttgart with a member of Willy Brandt's cabinet. Thursday we spent two and a half hours at the Vatican, with staff members who were advisors to the Pope and officials in some of the pontifical commissions.

Among these visits, I remember especially the cordial and understanding interview in Rotterdam with Cardinal Alfrink, whom I had admired for his clear-sighted challenges at Vatican II. He listened to us intently and promised to act on our behalf. Just a few days earlier, he had sent a telegram to President Nixon, and he gave a copy to our group when we met with him. The telegram read, "Highly shocked by terrible inhuman military violence. I express solidarity stricken people Vietnam. Request urgently immediate ending bombing because of human reasons and to open better prospects peace by non-military means and by negotiations with all parties involved."

As we approached Germany, I was moved deeply as I heard Rabbi Beerman ask Harvey Cox, who was acting as our coordinator, to permit him to address the synod of the Evangelical Church of the Rhineland, which we planned to attend. Harvey Cox readily agreed. It was a poignant moment when we heard a Jew reflect, to an affirming audience, how difficult it had been for him even to enter Germany. He spoke strong words from his heart, warning us about the danger of placing power and nationalism above human beings. Rabbi Beerman had special reason to speak, for his temple in Los Angeles is named for the great Leo Baeck, a Berlin rabbi imprisoned by the Nazis. In pleading for a strong voice from the German church, he quoted from one of Baeck's writings. "Which is worse—the intolerance that commits outrages, or the indifference that observes outrages with an undisturbed conscience?" The synod provided us with another moment of tempered joy when we were introduced to Eberhard Bethge, the friend and biographer of Dietrich Bonhoeffer.

Another heartening event of this fast-paced pilgrimage was our visit in Stuttgart with Martin Niemoller. We all were genuinely impressed when we conversed with this man who had displayed so much courage in the dilemmas and anguish of the Germany of World War II. I recall that as we talked with him about the reluctance of German church people to speak about Vietnam because of a sense of guilt about World War II, he responded, "What I have made wrong in the past is no excuse not to act rightly in the present." We could not help reflecting on the courage required in such agonizing decisions.

In Rome, we met with the Pontifical Commission on Justice and Peace, as well as with spokesmen for various councils and convocations concerned with peace and education. Those groups expressed serious and genuine concern over the ravaging of Vietnam by the bombings and solicited from us any suggestions as to what the Vatican might do. In addition, they urged us to prepare a statement on the principle of proportionality as expressed by Harvey Cox. "Excessive power on the part of a stronger nation in its war with the weaker renders that war reprehensible from the Christian point of view." Although we did not see the Pope himself, we had carried with us a letter to present to him. It read in part, "We realize that a word of love spoken on behalf of the Vietnamese will necessarily be a word of judgment spoken against our own nation. And yet we ask for that word of love and judgment, for here the pastoral and prophetic roles coincide."

Back in the United States, a statement from our group was submitted to the Subcommittee on Europe of the House Committee on Foreign Affairs. At all times during these missions, we were constantly writing to the President and to Congress, urging the cessation of the bombing of Vietnam. Did such appeals and appearances further the cause of peace? There is little evidence that they did. However, one can only resort to the conviction that all antiwar efforts were useful in helping to bring about an end to the war.

Another ecumenical experience that involved me in social-justice issues was my work on the board and, later, on the national staff of Church Women United (CWU). In 1970, I became chairperson for citizen action on the CWU board—a position directly related to social-justice concerns. That work reinforced my conviction that CWU was willing to take stands indicating their commitment and readiness to risk, even if it meant loss of face. Church Women United had courageously broken down many racial barriers for middle-class women and had opened possibilities for wider racial integration.

When the board of managers met in Wichita, Kansas, in April 1971, we adopted a statement of "Concern for Our Continuing Involvement in Indochina." Excerpts from this resolution illustrate CWU's steady stand against the Vietnam conflict and our determination to heal the wounds of war.

As Christians, we are called to love all humankind. We must share the guilt for the killing and suffering of people, and for the destruction and defoliation of their lands which have been

inflicted by our nation. . . . Because we value life, we believe a
military solution to this war is neither possible nor desirable. . . . We call upon church women at once through every
means available to them to persuade our government to end
this war through complete and total United States withdrawal
by December 31, 1971, and to engage in those means that will
assist citizens in Indochina to build a real peace.[4]

It was at the Wichita ecumenical assembly that Church
Women United first met Sister To Thi Anh, a Catholic
sister from Vietnam, who spoke with quiet conviction of
her people's strong desire for peace. "For our part, we
choose life. . . . Everyone who is killed is someone's
beloved." Anh's association with CWU, her beautiful
embodiment of the unity of East and West, continued to
be an eloquent call to peacemaking in Vietnam.

I remember well a church woman who stood in the
sunlight at our peace demonstration in Wichita, while the
television cameras played on the crowd. I heard her say,
"This is my first peace demonstration. I'm here because I
believe in this. But I hope the folks back home don't see
me on TV!" That statement perhaps spells out the
courage and the commitment of many CWU people as
they moved toward a stronger stand against the war.

In January 1973, Margaret Shannon, executive
director for Church Women United, invited me to join
the national staff in New York as citizen-action director.
At that time, CWU's president was Claire Collins Harvey,
a gifted and committed black woman, whose witness to
the value of prayer and fasting was an integral part of her
life. The ensuing six years confirmed my growing appreciation for the potential effect when a broad religious
community works together against societal evils.

Church Women United enabled many women to move

farther in an ecumenical community than would have been possible in their sometimes narrower denominational settings. This was an additional support to my convictions about the strength provided by common faith motivations.

The link between the Vietnamese sister, To Thi Anh, whom I mentioned earlier, and Church Women United was further strengthened in the spring and summer of 1972. The Leadership Conference of Women Religious (LCWR) and CWU jointly sponsored a speaking tour, during which To Thi Anh met with many interfaith and women's groups across the country. As chairperson of the LCWR justice and peace commission, and because of my CWU role, I helped coordinate the arrangements for this tour with Virginia Baron, who was the able staff citizen-action director of CWU at that time.

Anh's message was always beautiful and serene, but touched with the sadness she continually felt for her people. She saw deeply into the problems of peace in Vietnam, and she believed in the importance of unity among the different religions in seeking that peace. She herself always impressed me as an integral embodiment of deep faith.

When Anh returned to Vietnam in late summer, having completed her doctoral studies, she opened the House of Peace, a center for reconciliation in Saigon. The purpose of the center was "to promote the capacity for cooperation among people." Church Women United helped purchase and furnish this lovely oasis, where many Saigon women, wearied by war's cruelties, found space for thinking, meditating, and strengthening themselves. Later, just after the Paris peace agreement was signed early in 1973, CWU saw that the House of Peace could be used in a concrete way to help with the

reconstruction of Vietnam. A special collection at the
World Day of Prayer that spring went to Anh's project, to
contribute to the reconciliation and rebuilding.

When I recall this initiative of Church Women United
to heal the wounds of war, I ask myself, Why did the U.S.
government not take such initiative? If the money
promised in the peace treaty had been remitted to
Vietnam, would we have had the terrible exodus of the
starving across Southeast Asia?

I heard from Anh in the spring of 1980. She was still
living in the House of Peace and teaching at the
university in what is now Ho Chi Minh City. She had
faced a difficult decision in 1975—whether to remain in
Saigon with her people or to accept the many invitations
she had received to come to the United States. Among
those who offered her hospitality was Carl Rogers, her
former professor in California. The tenuous thread of
communication reveals little about her present life. She
enjoys the faculty and students at the university, but
longs to continue contacts with her American friends.
Woman of peace that she is, Anh will have found a way of
reconciliation in the midst of the inevitable tensions and
hardships of her present situation.

Resourcing the citizen-action program for Church
Women United was the kind of work that enabled me to
be involved daily with social-justice issues. "Indeed a
wide door for effective work was opened to me." Three
activities in which I was engaged during those years were
surely open doors into broader opportunities for
effective understanding and action. Because of the
religious nature of CWU's goals, my own growing faith
insights were congenially integrated into activities
designed to help build a more human world.[5]

For example, the involvement of women in devising their own "people's platform" was a most fruitful project, with long-term consequences. In the people's platform, two thousand units of CWU throughout the country studied the needs within their own communities, and the parallels and extensions of these needs in a global setting.[6]

From the beginning, the people's platform's call for Christian concern for the poor inspired the efforts of unity. The program reflects the idea that food, shelter, health, education, work, justice, peace, and human rights are all necessary to the development of whole human beings and that the interrelatedness of these needs requires a comprehensive strategy for fulfillment. Hunger, health, education, and the environment have the highest priority in the platform. The community as a whole has a responsibility to guarantee to each of its members the right to adequate food, health care, education, and the enjoyment of natural resources.

The issue of justice—particularly the inequities of the criminal justice system—concerned the contributors to the people's platform. They recognized that unemployment, lack of education, and discrimination are often the root causes of crime. They questioned the structure of a system that reinforces those causes by penalizing most harshly the minorities, women, and the poor. While acknowledging the right of the community to be protected from crime and violence, the platform encourages the search for alternatives to incarceration for the purpose of facilitating rehabilitation.

Very relevant today is one issue addressed in the people's platform—peace and the military budget. The platform deplores "the role of the United States as the chief purveyor of armaments to the world, and suggests that channeling military funds into the areas of food and economic assistance would be much more effective and intelligent defense spending." Furthermore, the platform advocates "a strengthening of the United Nations as a vehicle for dealing with the causes of war and for building a viable system of international relationships based on economic justice."

Developing a program on human rights seemed a necessity in view of the growing violation of human rights and our awareness of such violations throughout the world. The need for this program became abundantly evident to me when I participated in the CWU trip to Asia in 1974. In the spring of that year, CWU sponsored a Christian "causeway" to Asia, in which forty-eight American women crossed the Pacific to meet and talk with Asian women related to CWU in various countries. Dorothy Wagner, of the CWU staff, designed the causeway. Her friendship with many international church women and the consequent faith exchanges enriched the trip. Conversations with the Asian women dealt with the problems of injustice and violence and explored the possibilities of new patterns of international living.

I would like to mention one of those women, whose face and voice remain in my memory and whose spirit is unforgettable. Oo Chung Lee is a Korean woman whose determination while under attack in the cause of human rights has been a symbol of courage for Church Women United. Apprehended and detained several times by the Korean CIA, this brave woman continued to confront the government for its abuses, such as allowing young women to be inducted into prostitution in the promotion of business projects in Korea. This she did with calm dignity. Asked how she could continue to speak out and incur possible reprisals, she replied, "It is necessary to take risks. Without risks, no growth and progress toward justice is possible."

I remember Oo Chung Lee's words to us in Japan at the conclusion of our meeting. "Don't be fearful about speaking out. Don't worry about us. We know what we have to do. We ask you to carry back to the United States the word that your government is supporting oppressive and exploitative Third World leaders like ours."

On that causeway, I was able to visit Vietnam again, and again I had the joy of sharing some time with To Thi Anh, in her simple and tasteful House of Peace.

I was very moved by the causeway experience (my group visited Thailand as well as Vietnam), especially when we observed the World Day of Prayer at Hiroshima. The sad experience of visiting Hiroshima will never leave me; the grim twisted ruins are stark reminders of the fatal tragedy. During the prayer service, one Japanese woman stood and bowed. "I apologize for my country's attack on the United States." What could one reply? In my heart at that moment, I knew words were inadequate. Human sinfulness involves us all. Have we really learned anything from the experience of Hiroshima? Denise Levertov, in one of her poems, puts that question to us in moving words.

> The shadow's voice
> cries out to us to cry out.
> Its nails dig
>   into our souls
>   to wake them:
> "Something" it ceaselessly
> repeats, its silence

a whisper, its whisper
a shriek . . .

". . . *something can yet*
be salvaged upon the earth:
try, try to survive,
try to redeem
the human vision
from cesspits where human hands
have thrown it, as I was thrown
from life into shadow . . ."[7]

On our return to Tokyo, we participated in a peace consultation held at the foot of Mt. Fuji. The causeway was a concrete example of the ability of women of different languages and cultures to work together for peace. However, it became clear that the Asian women of all the countries we visited had one urgent message for us Americans. "Ask your government to stop supporting the repressive regimes of Asia—Indochina, Korea, and the Philippines."

In 1977, we designed a consultation on human rights for an assembly at Purdue University, which included a meeting with international church women. The consultation opened with the reflection that the issue of human rights today is front-page news and that as Christian women, hearing the call of the oppressed, we have no choice but to look at world situations where those rights are being ignored.

In introducing the program, I noted that two distinct United Nations covenants (both outgrowths of the original UN Declaration of Human Rights, drawn up in 1948) provide the full range of human rights—both civil-political rights (Covenant I) and economic-social-cultural rights (Covenant II). I stressed that increasingly, in East and West, both civil-political and socioeconomic rights are closely linked in the new interdependent world situation. This is especially true in the Third World, where both sets of rights are frequently unmet or precarious. I was impressed that Pope John Paul II, in his 1979 visit to the United Nations, stressed the importance of these covenants. It seems incredible that as I write this chapter in 1980, the United States Senate has yet to ratify them.

Deepening these insights and directions, then, became the focus of the human-rights seminars in New York and in San Francisco the following year. Both seminars began with a talk by a young woman, Diana Huston, who had experienced the brutal action of a police state. Soon questions surfaced. How could this happen? Could it happen elsewhere? Here? Are we implicated? How do we look at this within a Christian context? How do we become involved in change?

Assisting in the seminars were Robert McAfee Brown and Sydney Brown, husband and wife. Sydney is an expert in studies of women and work, and her understanding of the neglected economic rights of women was heard and greatly appreciated by the group.

We explored, with Robert McAfee Brown, the theological implications of human rights and shared some of his findings, which insist that we see the issue of human rights as both human and Christian. Brown used documents, such as the UN declaration, to show that human-rights concerns are vital to many people other than Christians. Human dignity and the worth of the person, as well as the importance of structures, are central. Political freedom precedes (in liberation), but food, shelter, and health follow, as *rights*—not as privileges.

We reflected on liberation as the biblical basis for human rights: Exodus (freedom from slavery), Jeremiah 22 (to know God is to do justice), Isaiah 58 (the fast Yahweh asks is to do justice), Luke 4 (setting free the oppressed), and Matthew 25 (the *nations* will be accountable). The church must be the protagonist of the poor, the voice of the voiceless—but more, the one who fosters empowerment. One conclusion of our reflection was that the Sacraments themselves are the very signs of such empowerment and that all we really need to do is act with courage, relying on biblical promise.

Perhaps the following comment of a participant in one seminar well summarizes the attitude of all those who took part in the programs. "I hope to use whatever opportunities and gifts I may have to open myself to the issues of human rights in Christian perspective, so that I shall not be as an unopened book, filled with valuable information, but unable to give. I want above all to share the values gained from my fine experience."

During my years on the national staff of Church Women United, I found my own faith insights affirmed and valued by both staff and constituency. Our common biblical background proved to be a stronger basis for this support than any of us had expected.

For example, it seems to me that one illuminating biblical text for our motivation in the struggle for human rights—for better human conditions and for peace with justice—is found in Luke 4. In the synagogue of Nazareth, Jesus made the words of the prophet Isaiah his own. "He unrolled the scroll and found the place where it is written, 'The Spirit of the Lord is upon me, because he has chosen me to preach the Good News to the poor. He has sent me to proclaim liberty to the captives, and recovery of sight to the blind; to set free the oppressed, and announce the year when the Lord will save his people' " (Luke 4:17-19).

There is the drama of kairós, a special moment of grace, in the scene that ensued after Jesus rolled up the scroll, sat down, and began to speak to the people. "This passage of scripture has come true today, as you heard it being read" (Luke 4:20). With what majesty and joy Jesus spoke these words, and indeed the people were "well impressed with him" (Luke 4:22).

In this text we see the true unfolding of God's plan for his people, from the early days of the promise to Isaiah, until the embodiment of its fulfillment in Jesus. But as we know, Jesus had not long to savor this moment of prophecy fulfilled. He assumed at once the prophet's task of speaking to reality, no matter how difficult, and began to reveal to his opponents their own hardness of heart—their own failure to live up to the admonition of Isaiah. Pride-stung and angry, they burst into action, and he was driven from the town.

There is no way to evade the conclusion that the struggle to achieve the goal of the New Creation is never-ending. But neither is discouragement a reason to withdraw into passivity. The story of the life, death, and resurrection of Jesus is the one enduring hope for Christians. Scripture itself assures us that the promise is greater than all our fears.

"Behold, I have set before you an open door which no one is able to shut; I know that you have but little power and yet you have kept my word and have not denied my name" (Rev. 3:8). Is there not in this text a promise that

even those who have little power, but who have acted in
the hope of God's power, will find before them ever-open
doors?—doors to justice, which no one can prevent them
from entering—for they "have had faith in God's
promise."

5.
The Door of
Global Involvement:
Current Oppressions

And there I will give her her vineyards, and make the valley of Achor a door of hope.

Hosea 2:15 RSV

In the book of Hosea, the prophet laments Israel's unfaithfulness and the disasters that accompanied it. In the restoration that God will bring about, the Valley of Achor (the name means *misfortune*) will be transformed into a gateway of hope leading into a land of new promise. We are able to continue our struggle for, and with, those who seek liberation from human distress and oppression, only through the belief that the dark valley will become the door of hope offered by the gospel.

The list of oppressive situations in our world today is long, and few successes appear in the campaigns against them. Any observer of the current global scene could draw up his or her own list. My list, in 1980, includes the following: first, the economic distress of the poor,

117

exploited by the unjust practices of rich nations; second, the situation of women who, in rich or poor countries, are always the last and least on any ladder of equality—economic, social, political, or religious; third, an alarming increase in the arms race, with the risk of nuclear danger—even of nuclear holocaust.

Nor are these oppressive situations unrelated. At the root of all, there is the determination to maintain and protect the high standard of living enjoyed by the affluent nations. But since the resources of the earth are scarce and limited, the poor nations have all too little access to them—not even sufficient access to provide for human living conditions for most of their people. Competition for these resources on the part of rich nations, and resentment on the part of the poor nations, have produced fears and hostilities. The result has been a desperate arms race. Furthermore, in a military economy, women are those most likely to be affected by the disproportionate spending on arms, rather than on human services.

We hardly need more evidence that "valley of misfortune" is the proper name for our world with its present problems. The gap between rich and poor is widening, and in the process the problems listed above are exacerbated. But what does the work of transforming the valley entail?

The Christian faith, by speaking a prophetic word, counters the ideological claims so firmly entrenched in our consumer society. We live in a culture conditioned by that ideology, which comes dangerously close to idolatry. The technological accomplishments of our age have so impressed us that we have elevated them to become our universal norms for all success. Thus we have justified exploitation in the name of technological achievement, as illustrated by stories of Third World indebtedness for the tools of progress.

The function of faith is to proclaim the coming rule of God. Only response to the prophetic utterances of Scripture will shatter the idol and break the rationale by which we support injustice. Nor can we ignore a possible co-optation of faith, which may become so much a part of our culture that it can slide over, almost unnoticed, into becoming a support for our exploitative society. The work of translating a harsh reality into a New Creation becomes a difficult agenda. Where does one begin? One practical means toward this urgent task is working with others who are transforming "misfortune" into a gate of hope.

Early in my experience, I learned that many people who are also dedicated to justice had arrived at their conviction through motivations that are different from mine. Others reached their wholehearted commitment either from humanistic concerns or from religious convictions in Judaism, Buddhism, or some other faith. For me, meditation on the liberative actions of Jesus, who manifested in his life that he valued persons and their well-being above every other consideration, convinced me of the necessity to involve myself with the struggles of oppressed peoples. Such reflections had persuaded me to become active in the antiwar movement and have led me to where I find myself today—involved in various actions directed toward the three interrelated problems I have cited.

Need to Hear the Cry of the Poor

First among these problems that call for our present attention is the growing gap between the rich and the poor. It is certainly difficult to find means to engage oneself with the poor and struggling, when one is sociologically identified with middle-class America. This ongoing effort involves me at the present time in what I confess are only small ways to work for the transformation I have come to see as necessary in my own response to faith.

"How then will the cry of the poor find an echo in your lives?" asked Pope Paul VI. "That cry must first of all bar you from whatever would be a compromise with any form of social injustice."[1] To compromise with social injustice in our time would be to make peace with the various kinds of racism, sexism, classism, and oppressive forms of capitalism that operate in our society.

Michael Crosby, reflecting on the Pope's statement, reminds us that "our ministry, supported and reinforced by prayer, should be a true action-reflection model. It should stand in the world as a witness to God's great concerns: that the goods of the earth be distributed with equity toward all and that the image of God be manifested as fully as possible in every human being. The cry of the poor must be echoed in our lives."[2]

Similar sentiments, I have been glad to discover, are shared by a significant number of groups in our country that are engaged in activities for justice. For example, I am affiliated with some of the organizations working along these lines, such as NETWORK, Bread for the World, American Friends Service Committee, and Christians for Socialism.

NETWORK, originated by Catholic sisters, maintains national offices in Washington. It serves as a resource center for gathering and disseminating legislative information, and through the legislative process, it works to influence public policy toward a more just world.

NETWORK members aspire to be "active co-creators of a more just society."

Bread for the World also addresses the legislative process, especially in the area of world hunger. Its staff regularly lobbies in Washington on hunger issues and coordinates work in Congressional districts.

The American Friends Service Committee provides communications and staff services for peace and social action on national and international issues, including the problems of world hunger and the refugee situation.

Christians for Socialism is a national organization whose chief purpose is the study and discussion of alternative systems for social change.

Recently I have been especially involved in two other groups that work against the exploitation of the poor by the wealthy: Theology in the Americas and the corporate responsibility effort. The former concerns itself with the problems of the poor from a theological perspective. The latter addresses the condition of the exploited by challenging multinational corporations. I have chosen these two for lengthier discussion.

Addressing Economic Exploitation: Theology in the Americas

Liberation theology, originating in Latin America, caught the interest of many in the late 1960s and early 1970s. Describing the process of liberation theology, Gregory Baum writes, "The meaning of Christian faith and theology emerges in a community only as a reflection on their struggle and only through a clear analysis of the structure of their oppression. Engagement precedes reflection. In the words of Gustavo Gutierrez, 'Theology ... is always the reflection on the struggle for emancipation.' "[3]

One group in the United States which responds seriously to this theology, moved by its concern for the oppressed, is the Theology in the Americas movement. I became interested in this movement after meeting Sergio Torres and other liberation theologians through Sister Margaret Coakley. These contacts have led to several years of involvement in the activities of this significant group.

When the organization held its inaugural meeting in 1975, in Detroit, one realization soon became evident to the participants: North American Christians could not adopt, as their own, a theology that springs from Latin America. Caucuses of blacks, women, Hispanics, Native Americans, and others, especially in the United States, made this clear. Only through reflection on their own situations and on the social and economic factors that had created the present oppressive conditions in the United States, could North Americans develop their own theology. The groups that emerged from these caucuses at Detroit set themselves to the task of creating a Theology in the Americas. After reflecting on its own situation, each identity group planned to bring its insights to the others.

These theology task forces, or projects, as they came to be called, went through several evolutions, but by 1980 they were listed as: Black Project, Hispanic Project, Women's Project, Professional Theologians' Task Force, Alternative Theology Project, Labor and Church Dialog, Ecumenical Dialog, Native American Project, and Asian-American Project.

Each project has developed a series of important activities, with prospects for ongoing programs. In 1977, the Black Theology Project sponsored a significant conference in Atlanta. An Hispanic theology conference took place in San Antonio in 1978. The Women's Project produced "A Project of Women, Work, and the Economy," a slide show which graphically illustrated the condition of poor women in the United States. In 1979, the Native American Project sponsored a conference on survival.

Perhaps one can describe the development of Theology in the Americas up to the present by looking at some of the objectives of the 1980 conference: to discern the social and political *signs of the times* from the perspective of the exploited and excluded, who constitute the majority in North American society today; to assess the task of the *prophetic church* in challenging unjust ecclesiastical structures and practices that prohibit the carrying out of Christian mandates; to keep the *international dimension* as a priority in theology and to strengthen links with other liberation movements in which Christians participate throughout the world. Reflection on "visions of a new society" and "tasks of a prophetic church" was set as the theme of the 1980 conference. During that conference, a new structure developed. This structure, with multiracial and indigenous groups, and with women making up 50 percent of the representation, gives promise of mutual cooperation from all projects in the struggle against the economic oppressions in American society. Fragile as the new structure is, it bears within it a hope that rises from unity.

Addressing Economic Exploitation: Corporate Responsibility

In recent years, at three or four shareholders' meetings, I have presented resolutions asking for company social responsibility. At first this experience of confrontation was very difficult, but lately, I have found it easier because I am able to concentrate more on the educative possibilities of this kind of presentation. At least it is a chance for the shareholders to hear a point of view other than that of the corporation.

The corporate responsibility movement represents a ten-year effort on the part of American religious groups to examine their financial investments, in an effort to harmonize them more carefully and conscientiously with basic underlying theological beliefs. Churches and religious institutions are dependent on their financial holdings (both those received as gifts and those purchased) to maintain their existence and to provide for their members, as well as for the continuation of their mission. We have seen the rise of the corporate responsibility movement within the churches, as an attempt to raise important theological and ethical questions about corporate structures; to increase awareness of the impact of corporate practices and policies; and to point out the moral implications of corporate decision making, since corporations are among the most powerful institutions in the world today.

One of the ways I have become involved in this work has been through the Interfaith Center on Corporate Responsibility in New York. This Center had its beginning in 1967, when five Protestant denominations voted their combined $2.7 million in the Eastman Kodak Company, to demand the hiring of more unskilled blacks. Participation by other Protestant groups, as well as by Catholics, came later. The effort of churches and church institutions to examine their possessions—specifically, their investments—has brought religious communities into the arena of corporate social responsibility.

I mentioned that I was involved in challenging

military-related corporations during the antiwar movement. Now it has become increasingly important to look at multinational corporations as they contribute to the oppression of Third-World peoples. Corporate shareholder actions have included challenges related to equal employment opportunity and Affirmative Action, human rights, environmental concerns, military production and sales, agribusiness and world hunger, advertising and the media, health and product safety, investments in foreign countries, consumerism, and international political contributions.

In 1974, the Loretto community developed an investment committee, whose responsibility was to "deliberately use our investment power as a tool for realizing social justice both through the correction of social injustice and the promotion of projects of positive social value. Where and when to invest will be determined by the potential of realizing these objectives as well as by the economic wisdom of the investment."[4] Community action of this kind facilitates and supports undertakings such as the suit against the Blue Diamond Coal Company, referred to earlier.

Although the shares we hold as a community in any corporation are few and not high in value, the ability to present challenging resolutions to the corporations has had some effect. The chance to raise issues in the minds of shareholders through published resolutions and to speak in favor of resolutions on the floor at shareholders' meetings has considerable merit. Furthermore, the public challenging of corporations to disclose more information about their marketing practices, employment policies, and profits, has proved an effective instrument of change.

I recall, for example, that in 1977, Church Women

United and the Sisters of Loretto co-signed a resolution
to Mattel Toy Company shareholders, regarding the
company's unfair employment practices in Korea. Our
information had come from specific working women
whom we knew in that country. Mattel agreed to comply
with the provisions of our resolution and did take some
limited action. A similar success followed our challenge
to Gulf Oil. The company, replying to our request,
agreed to stop contributing to politicians in Korea. Small
but cheering results!

I attended a shareholders' meeting of Rockwell
International in 1979, to speak in favor of the Loretto
community's resolution asking Rockwell to set up a
committee to investigate the health and safety regulations at Rocky Flats, Colorado, where nuclear bomb
triggers are made. We know that at least some
shareholders heard us then, because we received more
than the necessary 3 percent of votes required in order to
re-present a resolution the following year, which indeed
we did.

Efforts to provide the poor with access to the resources
of the earth, whether by shareholder action, legislative
pressure, or other means, require commitment and
patience. Some success is needed to keep up one's
courage,and even though slight, it provides the élan for
further efforts.

Justice for Women

A second present concern for me is the oppressed
situation of women. Since women's subordination is
inseparable from all other exploitative conditions, I
believe this issue fits exceedingly well into a faith context.
Entering the struggle for bringing about a more just and
human world includes the effort to ally oneself with the

liberating attitudes proclaimed by the gospel. It is clear that by his teaching and action, Jesus demonstrated the truth: Each person is of value beyond price. In a world of unequal opportunities for women, helping to provide the chance for each one to develop her God-given gifts is an imperative for bringing about the coming of God's kingdom.

When I first met Christian feminists and read some of their writings, I began to realize that I, too, am a Christian feminist. Sexism, which perpetuates the subordinate status of women, has such deep roots in patriarchal systems and has been operating for so long in history, that I often find myself wondering if its eradication ever will be possible. As a Christian who views the liberating Christ as the model for transforming action, I do indeed see faith as necessarily engaging me in this struggle.

It is always painful to see anyone who claims the title "follower of Jesus" using the gospel message to justify actions that exclude women from areas of participation and decision making in the church. It seems to me that if one follows Jesus, one must embrace actions which free all oppressed people, women as well as men, from unjust and restrictive structures and policies. Although women have few opportunities to express their concern about discrimination publicly, it is heartening to witness the continuing actions of women who express dissent or who, like the Women's Ordination Conference, continue to call women together to study and reflect on their exclusion. (The Women's Ordination Conference was begun in 1976 as a study forum for those interested in furthering the ordination of women in the Roman Catholic Church and it now has a national office.)

The way my consciousness was raised by Vatican II,

concerning the oppressive situation of women, is pertinent here. At that time I came to see that church structures, especially in canon law, ratified the secondary status of women. I then realized that conferences of women religious, for example, needed to prepare themselves for a difficult struggle if they were to overcome this oppression.

It is interesting that women religious have both advantages and disadvantages in the struggle to overcome this oppression: disadvantages, in that they have not been included in the decision-making structure of the church; advantages, in that their invisibility in ecclesiastical bodies has left them free to develop creatively on their own. This creative work outside church structures can be only a half step toward ecclesiastical structures that will affirm full personhood for women and that a church true to its own statements on discrimination must implement.

As I have illustrated through my own community's experience, the variety of work choices for women religious today has inserted them into many forms of action for an improved world—a New Creation. I have shown also how the community has devised new structural forms and decision-making models.

Differences in life-style exist, of course, between women religious and laywomen, and these differences may create a certain distance between them. However, many such barriers have been removed through new models of work and prayer together, and even through joint living ventures.

Can it be that through their growing involvement in issues of social justice, women religious may contribute liberating insights to the entire church? Such possibilities may be in the making.

Rosemary Ruether, one of the relatively few lay theologians, spoke recently to an assembly of the Loretto community. Discussing the need for women to work for ordination in the Roman Catholic Church, she said that by ordination, women may be in a stronger position to call church officials to greater faithfulness to the gospel demand for justice and peace.

Again, in a reflection on Christian devotion to the Virgin Mary, Ruether quoted from Pope John Paul's speech in Mexico in 1979. "From Mary who in her Magnificat proclaims that salvation has to do with justice to the poor, there flows authentic commitment to the rest of humanity, our brothers and sisters, especially for the poorest and the most needy, and to the transformation of society."[5] Ruether commented:

The important point of Mary's faith is that through it God's liberating action can become effective in history, the liberating action which God has promised. . . . She is not merely an "advocate" or "agent" of God; she is herself the liberated Israel, the humiliated ones who have been lifted up, the hungry ones filled with good things. The language for this liberation in Luke is explicitly economic and political. The mighty are put down from their thrones; the rich are sent empty away.[6]

Ruether was thus able to reveal, through the traditionally loved symbols of the Catholic Church, a fresh understanding of the present. For example, Mary is often seen as representing the church. "Mary is the messianic people, who continues the liberating action of God in the world. The last becomes first, and the first last. A poor woman of despised race is the head of the church. Those who would enter the kingdom must line up behind her."[7]

Looking on the Magnificat in this way opened a new door for me. While this interpretation draws on the deep storehouse of Christian tradition, it also discloses new implications of faith related precisely to the events of current history.

At the same time I was becoming aware of the tasks of Christian feminism in the church, I was realizing more poignantly the plight of women in the world today. Through working with the Women's Project of Theology in the Americas, as well as with other women's groups seeking feminist goals, I came to understand even more clearly the inequalities experienced by women today. "Women in all human communities have had to struggle for life against odds and without the objective conditions which ground hope," stated the presentation of the Women's Project. "Women have drawn energy for the struggle out of the struggle itself, surviving by savoring and celebrating small victories."[8]

While on the staff of Church Women United, I helped organize a coalition called the Religious Committee for the Equal Rights Amendment (ERA), to assist in coordinating denominational task forces in their efforts for passage of the ERA. This action brought me in contact with many competent and committed Christian and Jewish women who represented their faith communities on this committee. But I also met some fearful women, who saw equality before the law—the objective of the ERA—to be in some way destructive of home and family. Some connected the ERA with abortion; others felt its passage would encourage women to seek jobs outside the home—this in spite of the fact that 30 to 40 percent of women who are heads of households have no choice but to work. Such apprehensions are not easily dispelled. I believe that, at their root, these fears imply that some women have accepted the judgment of inferiority.

In our efforts for equality, I believe it is crucial for Christians to recover a sense of the values of Jesus—that all persons are equal. Compounding the difficulty of working for feminist goals is the unfortunate reality that many women are not even aware of their subordination. I am convinced that only when women reach a greater consensus about the inequities they undergo, can the movement grow strong enough to change a sexist church and society.

Arms and the Nuclear Threat

The most urgent necessity of our time is not merely to prevent the destruction of the human race by nuclear war. Even if it should happen to be no longer possible to prevent the disaster (which God forbid), there is still a greater evil that can and must be prevented. It must be possible for every free person to refuse consent and deny cooperation in this greatest of crimes.[9]

Thomas Merton wrote this in 1962. Twenty years later, these words sound a note of prophecy to us. In view of the appalling escalation of nuclear arms on the part of the great powers, the warnings we have heard from scientists and social critics are even more ominous.

There are thousands of nuclear weapons in the world—enough to destroy everything several times over. The technology of weapon making already is so advanced that it may be said to precede, and even to determine, policy making. Thus the following quotation from James Schlesinger, former U.S. Secretary of Defense, illustrates the irreversible position that technological "improvements" or innovations seem to have forced us to take. "Under no circumstances could we

disavow the first use of nuclear weapons," said Schlesinger in 1975. "If one accepts the no-first-use doctrine,
one is accepting a self-denying ordinance that weakens
deterrence."[10]

Michael Clark, of New York City's Riverside Church,
has stated, "We are on the brink of developments which,
for the first time, will give the advantage to the side which
strikes first. This is the threshold we are approaching.
We have not yet taken the final steps. If we do so, it will be
extremely difficult, if not impossible, to pull back."[11]

I am convinced of the need for alliances, and here
especially, when confronting this escalation is so crucial,
we need solidarity with like-minded groups. One of these
groups is the American Friends Service Committee
(AFSC), which sponsors a program on disarmament and
concern for nuclear arms and power. In Colorado, the
AFSC has promoted several actions through the Rocky
Flats Disarmament/Conversion Project; these have sup-
plied for all of us an important base for protest against
the continuing production of nuclear weapons, with all
its attendant evils.

Nuclear power is a development about which there is
also well-founded anxiety. There is a growing realization
of the connection between nuclear armaments and
nuclear reactors, for nuclear energy presents us with
many of the same problems as do nuclear weapons—ra-
diation hazards, deadly waste products, accidents, high
costs. And the exportation of nuclear power plants to
other countries has meant the spread of nuclear weapons
as well.

One of the groups to which I belong, SANE (A
Citizens' Organization for a Sane World), promotes the
conversion of nuclear plants to the production of
constructive and useful products so badly needed today.

Such conversion would actually make possible a fuller employment than that presently provided by nuclear plants. Bringing together the energies of those who seek full employment with the determination of those so rightly concerned about nuclear dangers could indeed lead to a more hopeful solution to the crisis. Only by our combined efforts will the push for solar energy be successful.

In this crisis of a nuclear age, we again find underlying support in the awareness that the struggle for a humanity more severely threatened than ever before demands our full commitment to the gospel. It calls for our continued confidence in the sustaining character of the ever-renewing sources of our faith, aware that it is faith that calls us to justice. For me it means, in practice, a readiness to respond to each invitation for action against the nuclear threat and to join others in this common effort.

Once again I have been encouraged by the readiness of the Loretto community to face up to emerging issues. Aware of the nuclear crisis and its implications, the Loretto assembly worked out a position paper to reinforce the community's education and action in this area. The nuclear statement adopted by the assembly in August 1979 contains the following major points.

Rooted as we are in our Judaeo-Christian heritage, we view our opposition to nuclear weapons and nuclear energy as an urgent moral imperative. We recognize that the burden of leadership in this regard falls not only on concerned persons throughout the world but especially on the community of faith.

Moreover, at this point in history, recognizing the urgency of this problem, we wish to dedicate both personal and community efforts and resources in this direction through ongoing education and action. We realize that part of the struggle to disarm the world and create a clean, safe environment is to engage in a process of disarming ourselves of our sometimes violent and competitive behavior toward one another and toward our environment. Furthermore, we commit ourselves to press politically for the development of safe, alternative energy sources, especially renewable resources, to call for a moratorium on further development of nuclear power plants, to demand that our government take a moral stand on our use of energy as it affects future generations and international relations, to support SALT II as a minimal step toward arms limitation, and to urge the U.S. government to work toward global disarmament.[12]

It is significant that the assembly, including forty elected delegates and nearly three hundred other participants, arrived at the statement by consensus. The fact that the statement is owned by the entire community makes it much stronger.

Some presentations during the discussion reflected the moral issue involved in nuclear responsibility from a religious standpoint. For example, I read the statement from Thomas Merton cited earlier in this chapter. I also read a quotation from a speech by Dr. Joseph Weizenbaum to the 1979 World Council of Churches Conference on Faith, Science, and the Future. "Science is an extremely tiny keyhole through which the world may be viewed. What it reveals about the world is, to be sure, enormously important and of course useful. But science provides us no moral criteria for the behavior of scientists as scientists or as ordinary people."[13]

The guidance of moral criteria is needed, not only for scientists, but for all of us. Certainly it is true that the Loretto community was able to arrive at a consensus decision such as this only through serious, regular reflection on moral issues in the light of faith, and by the continuing experience of a supportive community. A year after the adoption of our statement, the community took another step in its efforts to work against the nuclear threat. The 1980 Loretto assembly established a committee of community members to work even more intensely in this struggle. In particular, the committee is promoting the passage of the mutual freeze proposal between the United States and the Soviet Union—a proposal to freeze all further testing, production, and deployment of nuclear weapons—as well as the continuing education of Loretto members and others about the nuclear dangers the world now faces and the involvement of greater numbers of community members in antinuclear movements. Through efforts such as these, we in the Loretto community have learned that growth in a faith context includes actions of many different types—some moderate, some radical—but all springing from serious concern for the world's threatened good.

Gateway of Hope

It may be naïve for those of us who are opposing the overpowering forces of the unequal distribution of wealth, women's oppression, the arms race, and the nuclear peril, to dream that our small efforts can do much to transform the Valley of Achor into a gateway of hope. But the power of hope is mighty, also, as the courageous spirit of the oppressed in many Third-World countries demonstrates.

Those of us who live in affluent countries and who have aspirations toward a more just world, but little experience of actual poverty and economic distress, need the example of prophets and saints, especially from the Third World, to give us courage to continue our work for justice. One of the most recent and illustrious of these was Archbishop Oscar Romero of El Salvador. The archbishop had taken a strong position against the ruling powers in his country who were repressing the landless poor. But his stand made many enemies; he was assassinated in March 1980, as he celebrated Mass in a hospital chapel in San Salvador. I feel both sorrow for his loss and joy for his courageous example, as I reflect on his martyrdom.

In one of his last sermons to his people, the archbishop said, "We need Christians who are active, critical; who analyze things; who don't accept everything; who know how to say *yes* to justice and *no* to injustice." Romero was such a Christian. He moved beyond speech to action; beyond security to risk; beyond fear to acceptance of death as the price of solidarity with his people. He called himself a man of hope, saying, "I have tried to sow hope, to maintain hope among the people. There is a liberating Christ who has the strength to save us. I try to give my people this hope. . . . If I am killed, I will rise in the Salvadoran people."

Hope is the very soul of biblical faith and the heart of Christian resurrection-faith. It is stronger and more enduring than the deepest dejection and discouragement. Because of such hope, and because of the people who bring it to us by their example, our work within a liberation context will be both life-giving and fruitful.

6.
The Door of Hope: A Meditation

"I am the door," Jesus said. In this metaphor I have found both mystery and invitation: The Door and the Speaker are one. The door invites in and beckons out. "I am the way." Those who listen to the words of Jesus—to the gospel in its dynamic richness—and who adopt the attitude of Jesus, will find light and direction for our century, or for any century.

Light for the journey falls across the threshold where Jesus, the witness, stands. The figure of Jesus as door, suggests to me several possibilities for meditation—the door as openness, as disclosure, as empowerment, and as invitation.

To appreciate *openness,* we must have experienced encouragement to try the new, to seek alternatives, to view fresh possibilities—as my experiences at Vatican II and with the Loretto community have exemplified. Openness indicates an attitude of willingness to risk, to trust.

The door as *disclosure:* Light and openness follow on

the readiness to "receive a gift." Gregory of Nyssa, in the early centuries of the church, wrote that grace, the gift of God, "gives us ever new eyes to look on ever new suns." It is true—the doors of the past, which opened onto their own special blessings, encourage us to open the doors of the present and the future.

The door as *empowerment:* "Enter by me and you will be saved. You will go in and out freely." And elsewhere, "All these works and greater shall you do." In this promise, no limits are set on the believer's achievements in Christ's name, since here empowerment is prophesied down through the centuries. It is the Spirit who is promised, and all things are possible to those who believe.

The door as *invitation:* Finally, we are invited to go through the door to an unknown destination—not only from day to day, from year to year, but to the end of our lives. The trust, confidence, and courage that enable us to go through the "little doors" and experience the "little deaths" of daily living, somehow rehearse us for the opening of that final door.

Thomas Merton, in his meditation "The Door," writes, "Christ said, 'I am the door.' The nailed door. The cross they nail shut with death."[1]

The mystery of the cross inevitably reaches into all our lives—we all have known its reality. The paradoxes of life/death, light/darkness, good/evil belong to everyone's experience. In placing our faith and hope in the witness of Jesus, we have declared our identification with his attitude: We must work for God's cause, the good of people, in spite of the suffering and defects that inevitably accompany this quest. But the resurrection promise of the Scriptures—the affirmation that Jesus lives—is greater than all our fears, and supports us in all our struggles.

Merton continues, "The resurrection: I am the opening, the showing, the revelation, the door of light, the light itself."[2]

We know that we do not go through the door alone, or first. First through the door into the Kingdom, says Jesus, will go the poor, the blind, the lame, the oppressed. But if we have accepted the invitation to accompany them by compassion, and to relieve their oppression by action, this door will welcome us also.

Notes

1. Vatican Council II

1. Walter M. Abbott, S.J., ed., *The Documents of Vatican II* (New York: America Press, 1966), pp. 199-200.
2. *Ibid.*, p. 295.
3. *Vatican Statement to the United Nations Ad Hoc Committee on the Review and Role of the U.N. in the Field of Disarmament* (May 1976).
4. "The Holy See and Disarmament," *The Pope Speaks*, vol. 22 (1977), p. 246.
5. Abbott, *Documents*, p. 254 (paraphrased).
6. *Ibid.*, p. 468.
7. *Ibid.*, pp. 468-69.
8. *Ibid.*, pp. 665-67.
9. Rosemary Ruether, "The History of Christian Theology and the Demonization of the Jews." This paper, fully developed in her book *Faith and Fratricide*, is cited in Gregory Baum, *The Social Imperative* (New York: Paulist Press, 1979), pp. 50-52. The second part of the passage cited is Baum's paraphrase of Ruether's thought.
10. Abbott, *Documents*, pp. 227-28.
11. *Ibid.*, p. 58.
12. *Ibid.*, pp. 204, 214, 307, 462, 468. The council document on religious life states, "The appropriate renewal of religious life involves two simultaneous processes: . . . (2) an adjustment of the community to the changed conditions of the times." The quotation in our text from the introduction to the document paraphrases this statement.
13. *Ibid.*, pp. 24-37. These pages contain the second chapter of the council document on the church titled "The People of God."

14. Paul Ricoeur, *Political and Social Essays* (Athens: Ohio University Press, 1974), p. 113.

2. The Loretto Community

1. Pope Paul VI, *Ecclesiam Suam* (September, 1966).
2. *I Am the Way: Guidelines* (Nerinx, Ky.: Sisters of Loretto, 1967). This and all other quotations from the Loretto community guidelines cited in this chapter are from this source.

3. Thomas Merton

1. Parker J. Palmer, *In the Belly of a Paradox: A Celebration of Contradictions in the Thought of Thomas Merton* (Wallingford, Pa: Pendle Hill Publications, 1979), p. 8.
2. Thoms Merton (Talk given at Loretto Motherhouse, Nerinx, Ky., 1963).
3. Merton (Lectures given at Gethsemani community c. 1960–1968).
4. Eldridge Cleaver, *Soul on Ice* (New York: Dell Publishing Co., 1968), p. 34.
5. Tape given to author by Merton (now in Merton Collection).
6. Thomas Merton, *Faith and Violence: Christian Teaching and Christian Practice* (Notre Dame, Ind.: Univeristy of Notre Dame Press, 1968), p. 187.
7. *Ibid.*, p. 109.
8. Gordon C. Zahn, ed., *Thomas Merton on Peace* (New York: McCall Publishing, 1971). This book is being republished in a revised edition, *The Nonviolent Alternative* (Farrar, Straus & Giroux, Noonday Press, 1980).
9. Merton, quoted in Zahn, "Original Child Monk: An Appreciation," *Merton on Peace*, p. xvii.
10. Merton, *Faith and Violence*, pp. 109-10.
11. Merton, *Loretto and Gethsemani* (Nerinx, Ky.: Loretto Motherhouse, 1962), p. 3.
12. *Ibid.*, p. 5.
13. Tape given to author by Merton (now in Merton Collection).
14. Merton, *Raids on the Unspeakable* (New York: New Directions Publishing Corp., 1964), pp. 45-49.
15. Tape given to author by Merton (now in Merton Collection).
16. Merton, "Chant to Be Used in Processions Around a Site with Furnaces," *Emblems of a Season of Fury* (New York: New Directions, 1961), pp. 46-47. From *The Collected Poems* of Thomas Merton. Copyright © 1963 by Thomas Merton. Reprinted by permission of New Directions. British Commonwealth rights granted by Laurence Pollinger Ltd.
17. Merton, "Peace: A Religious Responsibility," *Merton on Peace*, Zahn, pp. 123-25.
18. Daniel Berrigan (Talk given at formal opening of the Thomas Merton Center for Creative Exchange, Denver, Col., September, 1979).
19. Tape given to Loretto general chapter by Merton (now in Merton Collection).
20. *Ibid.*
21. Merton (Lectures given at Gethsemani community c. 1960–1968).

22. Merton, *Conjectures of a Guilty Bystander* (Garden City, N.Y.: Doubleday & Co., 1966), pp. 140-41.
23. Merton, *Opening the Bible* (London: Unwin Books, 1972), pp. 54-55.
24. The first phrase quoted in this paragraph is from Merton, *The Asian Journal* (New York: New Directions, 1975) p. xxiii. The second is cited in George Woodcock, *Thomas Merton, Monk and Poet* (New York: Farrar, Straus & Giroux, 1978), p. 159.
25. Woodcock, *Thomas Merton*, p. 156.
26. Merton, *The Asian Journal*, p. 235.

4. Vietnam and After

1. Abbott, *Documents*, p. 295.
2. "A Conversation with Dr. Abraham Joshua Heschel," typescript (New York: National Broadcasting Company, 1973), pp. 5, 9.
3. Robert McAfee Brown, "A 'Mission of Desperation,' " *The Christian Century* (February 14, 1973), p. 210.
4. Church Women United Board of Managers, "Minutes" (April 1971).
5. One of the excitements of working in this movement was being part of a team with Margaret Shannon, whose creative ideas sparked much of what happened in the national office.
6. See *Guidebook for People's Platform for a Global Society* (New York: Church Women United, 1975–1977).
7. Denise Levertov, "On the 32nd Anniversary of the Bombing of Hiroshima and Nagasaki," *Life in the Forest* (New York: New Directions, 1975), pp. 58-59. Copyright © 1977 by Denise Levertov. Reprinted by permission of New Directions.

5. Current Oppressions

1. *The Pope Speaks*, vol. 11 (1966), p. 115.
2. Michael H. Crosby, *Thy Will Be Done: Praying the Our Father as Subversive Activity* (Maryknoll, N.Y.: Orbis Books, 1977), p. 55.
3. Baum, *Social Imperative*, pp. 11-12.
4. Loretto General Assembly, "Proceedings" (August 1974).
5. Rosemary Ruether, "Is There a Liberation Mariology?" (Paper presented at Loretto General Assembly, August 1979).
6. *Ibid.*
7. *Ibid.*
8. Theology in the Americas Conference, "Women's Project Presentation" (1980).
9. Merton, "Peace: Christian Duties and Perspectives," *Merton on Peace*, Zahn, p. 18.
10. James Schlesinger, (Press conference, July 1, 1975), vol. 32, *Facts on File* (1976), p. 470.
11. Michael Clark, "The Riverside Church Disarmament Program," *Fellowship* (January-February 1980), p. 9.
12. Loretto General Assembly, "Proceedings" (August 1979).
13. Joseph Weizenbaum (Lecture given at World Council of Churches

Conference on Faith, Science, and the Future, Massachusetts Institute of Technology, July 1979). Dr. Weizenbaum is on the faculty at M.I.T.

6. A Meditation

1. Merton, *The Asian Journal,* p. 154.
2. *Ibid.,* pp. 154-55.

Damaged Parents

Norman A. Polansky
Mary Ann Chalmers,
Elizabeth Buttenwieser,
and David P. Williams

Damaged Parents

An Anatomy of
Child Neglect

The University of Chicago Press/Chicago and London

NORMAN A. POLANSKY is Regents' Professor of
Social Work at the University of Georgia; MARY
ANN CHALMERS is a doctoral student at the
University of Pennsylvania; ELIZABETH
BUTTENWIESER is a social worker at the Institute,
Pennsylvania Hospital, Philadelphia; DAVID P.
WILLIAMS is a doctoral student in the Depart-
ment of Counseling and Human Development
Services at the University of Georgia.

The University of Chicago Press, Chicago 60637
The University of Chicago Press, Ltd., London

©1981 by The University of Chicago
All rights reserved. Published 1981
Printed in the United States of America

85 84 83 82 81   5 4 3 2 1

Library of Congress Cataloging in Publication Data
Main entry under title:

Damaged parents, an anatomy of child neglect.

  Bibliography: p.
  Includes index.
    1. Child abuse—United States—Addresses,
essays, lectures.   2. Socially handicapped
children—United States—Addresses, essays, lectures.
3. Social work with the socially handicapped—
United States—Addresses, essays, lectures.
I. Polansky, Norman Alburt, 1918–
HV741.D35   362.7'044   80-22793
ISBN 0-226-67221-2

To Our Parents

Celia Kaplan Polansky
Joseph J. Polansky
Mary Chalmers
Charles W. Chalmers
Mary Jane Werthan
Albert Werthan
Kathryn Phillips Williams
Ivor Williams

Contents

Preface

This book contains the distillation of fifteen years of the study of child neglect. It seeks to answer a series of interlocking questions: What does neglect typically look like? How widespread a phenomenon is it? What sequelae does it leave on the personalities of the children? How costly are these sequelae for the rest of society? Who are the neglectful parents, and what forces in their lives have damaged their parenting? From what we now know about them, what principles may we infer about the tactics for their treatment, person by person and family by family? And where do we stand with respect to strategies for our large-scale programs?

A major study and several ancillary ones directed at these issues are reported here. We have also tried to integrate our own studies with other information that has seemed germane to the topic. Our need for more knowledge and for improved methods of treatment is, of course, enormous. For neglect is a massive social blight, and its intimate connection with mental illness, retardation, delinquency, and other causes of wasted lives means that if we were able to do more about this social problem, we could vastly magnify the leverage social workers have on a number of others.

I have been responsible for the writing of this book, as my contribution in the division of labor in our group. This has been my way of compensating my colleagues for the efforts and skills required in reaching the families in this study. It is also a way of thanking the Philadelphians who permitted us to enter their lives, and who shared their experiences with us for the sake of all others in similar positions.

The tasks of analysis, resynthesis, and conceptual formulation have been long. Understanding neglect calls into play everything one has learned as both behavioral scientist and clinician; working toward its alleviation requires our best efforts as caseworkers and social work administrators. Naturally this problem, which was at first so ineluctable and eventually so intricate, is intellectually engaging, but one cannot term this a book a labor of love, in the sense of something pleasurable. The children are too sad, their parents too lonely. In the end, one bears witness to what seems an unending series of crimes whose perpetrators have also been victims.

Our admiration, therefore, is very great for so many in the frontline casework positions who are constantly at work trying to help the families of neglect. Through this work, we have met a throng of fine social workers, practitioners and administrators of whom all the rest of us may be proud. So many of them have the warm shrewdness, the combination of love and practicality, the indignation leavened with humor that is in the best tradition of our field. Our greatest wish is that what we have reported will prove of help to them as they go about their work.

And one always hopes that research into any applied area will simultaneously contribute to the advance of more general theory. Hence, we have made bold to show how findings concerning neglect exemplify or elaborate our understanding of the human personality and of the general principles of social work practice.

In professions like ours, all integrations are temporary; there is much left undone, much more to uncover. Thus we are comforted even as we are adjured by one of the Jewish sayings of the fathers, "You are not required to complete the task, but neither are you permitted to relinquish it" (Pirke Avot, Mishnah IV: Nezikim 2:15–16).

It is a pleasure to acknowledge now the invaluable collaboration of others in this study. Dr. Armond Aserinsky, a wise and energetic clinician, took over our psychological testing at a time when it was experiencing difficulties. He performed much of the testing himself, and recruited and trained others as needed, earning our enduring admiration. Our consultant on design and the computer analysis of data was Dr. Samuel Snyder. His fine background in developmental psychology contributed valuable information as well as methodological expertise, and aided by John J. Norcini, he carried major responsibility for a long series of complicated computer analyses.

The logistical problems of an in-depth field study of 125 families required setting up something approaching a small, temporary social agency, with Mary Ann Chalmers also making use of her background in office management. The two fine project secretaries she recruited were Kathleen Corcoran, and her successor Karen Corcoran. A third Corcoran sister, Ann, helped out with baby-sitting while parents were being tested, and Denise Graham contributed to our clerical group. The study also benefited from the contributions of our two highly qualified case readers, Mrs. Trudy Dworkin Persky and Mrs. Myra Singer. It is fortunate when one can find insightful clinicians who will cheerfully submit themselves to the disciplines of instrument refinement and training toward reliability on case judgments.

Given the difficulties involved in reaching families showing signs of neglect, even with our offers of help, the task of recruiting them into research was formidable. Moreover our design required that each family also be known to some other agency in order to give us a sample "identified" as neglectful to contrast with a control. Thus the study could not have taken place at all without the intelligence and perspective of a group of agency administrators and staffs who were willing to refer families to us. Among these are Miss Charlotte Hamill, a great social worker, who offered us her shrewd and generous support from the beginning, and Mrs. Alice Whiting and the other staff members at the Delaware County Child Care Service, from which Miss Hamill has since retired as director. We also received generous and cordial support from a number of others whom it is a pleasure to mention, however briefly: Sister Marie Gaffney, Director of Social Services, Sister Mary Katherine, Administrator, and the staff of the Family Division, Catholic Social Services of Philadelphia; Mr. Joseph Taylor, Executive Director and the staff of the Association for Jewish Children of Philadelphia; Mr. Kavonzo Hyde, Director, and the staff of the Philadelphia Society to Protect Children; Mr. Ben Sprafkin, Director, Mr. Elliott Rubin, Associate Director, and the staff of the Jewish Family Service of Philadelphia; Mr. Joseph Wnukowski, former Commissioner, Mrs. Mary Smith, Assistant Director, Family Division, Mrs. Lily Lang, Supervisor, Protective Services Division of the Philadelphia Department of Public Welfare; Mrs. Olga Haggard, Director of Professional Services, and the staff of the Children and Family Service, Episcopal Community Services; Mr. Gerald Weissberg, Director, and the staff of the Kaiserman Branch of the Jewish Ys and Centers of Greater Philadelphia; Ms. Jackie Mondros, former Director, Harrowgate Community Center.

The research reported here was supported in part by Grant 90-

C-442 from the National Center for Child Abuse and Neglect, Administration for Children, Youth and Families of the Department of Health, Education, and Welfare to the University of Pennsylvania School of Social Work. We wish to thank Dean Louise Shoemaker, Dr. Richard Estes, and others at the School for their hospitality during the two years the project operated out of the School. The grant manager for this project was Mrs. Cecelia Sudia of the Children's Bureau. Grant managers of previous projects whose work is also incorporated here are Dr. Charles Gershenson, Children's Bureau, and Mrs. Virginia K. White, Community Services Administration. These fine professionals, each knowledgeable and highly motivated to help the children of this country, absolutely belie the stereotype of "Washington bureaucrats."

Any dedicated researcher who is also a member of a working faculty owes his colleagues of many years a very great debt for keeping school while he pursues his obsessions. Thus I want to express appreciation to Dean Charles A. Stewart, and to other old friends on the faculty at the University of Georgia School of Social Work, who have made my freedom possible. I also want to express my gratitude to our former Provost, S. William Pelletier, who with Dean Stewart provided the safety net of a leave of absence from my home setting so that a person with my medical history could dare adventure in Philadelphia.

This work could not have been written without the enthusiastic spirit and sturdy support of my wife, Nancy Finley Polansky. As always, my biggest debt is to her.

Norman A. Polansky

One

Is This Child Worth Salvaging?

There are ever increasing numbers of Americans who do not want to be parents. Many of them have children. There is a very large number of Americans unable to offer children the care essential to become competent and reasonably happy adults. Many of them also have children. When the level of parental care becomes dangerous to the child's survival or his future we call it marginal child care or outright child neglect.

Public Ignorance without Bliss

Most of us are unaware of child neglect even when we are witnessing it. Child abuse is so abhorrent we would prefer not to notice it, but its shock value brings it forcibly to attention. Neglect, however, is also unpleasant enough that we want to avoid noticing it, and it is a silent, insidious phenomenon, easily denied. Abuse rises to a bang and declines to a whimper, but the typical unchanging nature of neglect encourages us to ignore it. Even the decay of a family's standards is often imperceptible, like the aging of one's parents.

Neglect is a matter of things undone, of inaction compounded by indifference. Since it goes on at home, it is a very private sin. Seldom does it announce its presence in direct, unmistakable terms. We may infer it from the marks it leaves on children that are immediately visible, although it often remains unrecognized until we must deal with its effects on the personality of a damaged adult. One must be both willing to notice it and knowledgeable about its signs. It is little wonder that most of the public is unaware of poor child caring. Its ignorance is even greater as to how widespread the problem is. But this is not a blissful ignorance.

The public may not want to attend to child neglect, but it lives with the distortions of human personality that are left in its wake. The decline of ordinary civility in American cities is so bad that London seems like an oasis, but civility is scarcely the problem. One dreads a blackout due to power failure as much as anything because of the pillage that will follow it. Indeed, we can hardly afford a natural disaster. The day when we could stroll home alone in the night through an American city is growing ever more distant in memory. And the free-floating hostility, the lack of restraints against hurting fellow humans are not, as some suppose, confined largely to the neighborhoods of the poor and the minorities. Fraternity brothers vandalize their own houses. Knifings follow high school sports contests. Some of us can recall when being asked to chaperon a dance announced one's entrance into middle-age. Now, the thought that one could prevent a disaster is a tribute to one's manhood. America is becoming a barbarous country, with too many of the barbarians still living at home to blame their behavior on "outside influences."

In desperation, people turn to "law and order," so needful of safety that they are glad to sacrifice ancient principles of civil liberty and individual rights. Government is thought of as an expression of the personality traits most common among the governed. But the nature of government is just as often geared to compensate for elements of character *not* found in a high proportion of those making up the body politic. Will we stop at confining more and more of our barbarians permanently in prison? Or are we witnessing a prelude to authoritarianism in the largest democracy man has ever known? Neglected children, as we shall see, contribute more than their share to a dilemma all of us have to live with.

Most victims of child neglect survive and grow up, after a fashion. Thus as long as we do not prevent maltreatment of children, or offer specific repair to those subjected to it, we bear its costs in other areas. Neglect contributes to emotional illness, mental retardation, and a variety of physical handicaps. Less obviously but surely nonetheless, it tends to produce people whose ability to live independently is marginal, and who are really unable to work productively during much of their lives. As they carry out their efforts to help, social workers are fully aware that resources to support work depend not only on the public's values but also on its The economic drain produced by stunted lives, however, is of concern not only to social workers. With diminishing natural resources, we need everyone to contribute to our national strength. Sheer economics suggests that public ignorance of neglect is a luxury the nation can no longer afford.

Further, there is reason to believe that the central role of neglect in other social problems makes its treatment a highly strategic leverage for preventive work. So there is ample justification for going beyond recognizing the problem to making a national effort, as a matter of enlightened self-interest. But more than selfish reasons are involved. One would have to be inhuman to disregard the suffering prevalent in these families. Here is one such family, one of the hundreds of thousands from which one could select an illustration.

Children Who Are Not Headliners

The family consists of Mona Stay, twenty-three, and her common-law husband Frank Brown, aged twenty-six. There are three children: Frank Stay, three and a half, Sylvia Stay, eighteen months, and Wilma, seven months. The Stay-Browns have been together over five years. Although they quarrel and separate periodically, they seem very mutually dependent and likely to remain a couple.

Their original referral was from a nurse who had become aware of the eldest child's, Frank's, condition. He was difficult to discipline, was eating dirt and paint chips, and seemed hyperactive. Although over two, he was not speaking. His father reacted to him with impatience. He was often slapped, and hardly ever spoken to with fondness. The case worker got Mona to cooperate in taking young Frank in for a test for lead poisoning, and for a full developmental evaluation. This child had had several bouts with impetigo, had been bitten through the eyelid by a stray dog, and had a series of ear infections resulting in a slight hearing loss. Although physically normal, developmentally he appeared already nearly a year retarded.

Often this child was found outside the house alone when the caseworker came to see the family. On one occasion he was seen hanging from a broken fire escape on the second floor. The worker was unable to rouse his mother, or to enter the house until she got help from the nearby landlord, after which she ran upstairs and rescued the child. Only then did the sleeping Mona awaken!

With much effort having been expended on his behalf, this child had been attending a therapeutic nursery. His speech is already improved after four or five months, and his hyperactivity has calmed. He comes through as a lovable little boy.

Sylvia is surprisingly pale for an interracial child and, indeed, suffers from severe anemia. This child has had recurrent eye infections, and had a bout with spinal meningitis at age three months which, fortunately, seems to have left no residua. Much effort has gone into working with Mona concerning Sylvia's need for proper diet and iron supplement. After a year of contact this is still a problem.

The baby was born after the family had become known to the agency. Despite the agency's urging, Mona refused to go for prenatal care until she was in her second trimester, but she did maintain a fairly good diet, helped by small "loans" from the agency when her money for food ran out. When Wilma was born, she had to remain for a time at the hospital for treatment of jaundice. After she went home, she was left to lie most of the time in her bassinet, receiving very little attention from either parent. At four months of age, Wilma weighed only five pounds and was tentatively diagnosed as exhibiting "failure to thrive" by the hospital. Thereafter the mother avoided going to the clinic, and the caseworker spent much effort concerning the feeding and sheer survival of Wilma. The baby is now slowly gaining weight but is still limp and inactive.

In addition to an active caseworker, a homemaker was assigned to this family for months. Much more was involved than trying to help Mona learn to organize her day: she had almost no motivation to get started. Rather than learning how to manage, she tried to manipulate the homemaker into doing her housework for her. However, with time and patience, Mona has been persuaded to go with the caseworker on shopping trips, is learning how to buy groceries to best advantage, and from time to time manages to get the laundry into and out of the laundromat. So far as her plans for herself, Mona has talked of seeking training as a beauty operator, but has never followed through on this or on other positive plans.

The family's sole support is public assistance. Frank Brown, the father, was on drugs earlier in their relationship, but managed to get off them. Now, however, he drinks heavily, and although he manages to work, he never contributes to the household. The fact that theirs is an interracial liaison (Mona is white and Frank black), does not seem important against the background of their other problems.

Mona, apparently, was herself a neglected child, and was removed from her parents in infancy. Placed with an adoptive family, there was constant friction during her growing up, and she ran away from home several times. During her teens, she was placed in an institution for incorrigible girls. Later she spent a period in a mental hospital during which she was withdrawn from heroin addiction. It is a commentary on her life that she regards this period in the adolescent ward as one of her happiest ever. Her adoptive mother is now dead, and her father wants nothing more to do with her, so she was more or less living on the streets when she met with Frank and set up their present establishment.

Frank and Mona, despite his obvious exploitativeness, seem to love each other and their children, and to want to keep the family together. They are able to relate to those who try to help them, so at least one is not operating constantly against hostile resistance. Mona is an intelligent woman and now shows adequate ability to handle the children. She can be an excellent cook—when there is food. Yet this remains a disorganized household. Bills are never paid, clothes are thrown around, the children never sleep on clean sheets, trash is piled around the house so that flies and maggots abound. Mona still leaves the youngsters quite alone for brief periods. There is no heat in the house, and the family will soon have to move, with neither any idea where to go nor funds for rent deposits and the like. Mona, at least, is currently wearing an IUD.

The Stay-Brown ménage was not invented, although of course we have altered names and some facts to protect all concerned. These are real people, and they are clearly involved in child neglect. The failures center on poor feeding, uncleanliness, extremely bad housing, filthy circumstances which make the children prone to infections, lack of medical care, inadequate supervision and protections from danger, lack of intellectual stimulation, inattentiveness to the children bordering on rejection—one could go on. What chance does a Wilma, malnourished to the point of near death in infancy, have of resolving her first life crisis on the side of Erikson's (1959) Basic Trust? By what models is young Frank to acquire control over his impulses, and joy in productive work?

These are obvious questions, but it is hard to ask them without seeming to sneer. There are those in the legal profession who believe we have to right to intervene in families like this one because our ability to predict the future harm to the youngsters is yet so poor. And what would they predict? Three Nobel Prize winners? Three factory workers? Three happy adults of whatever sort? Yet, these are people about to miss on their only chances for happy lives, unless something is done to save them. Indeed, it is hard simply to condemn their parents, given what we have learned about Mona's history. Frank, who is not an admirable man, does not talk. But something about his background might be gleaned from the fact that his own parents have recently asked to move in with him!

What we see, in other words, is that these are very real people, that there must be many, many Mona-Frank households, and "something should be done." We also see, immediately, that the problem is not easy, and that our knowledge concerning what to do is inadequate. The fine staff trying to help Mona improve her child care finally gave up and closed her case after about fifteen months of effort. The care was improving slowly, if at all, and there were recurrent instances of regression. Frank proved superficially amenable to suggestions when he could be seen, but in fact evaded any real responsibility for the household. The time, money, and—more importantly—motivation for hard work with such families are chronically in short supply. So the decision was made to try to help someone else who might be more treatable.

Meanwhile these children are with their parents. Since they have not literally been abandoned, it is uncertain whether a local judge would decide the home is so bad that the children must be removed. If a catastrophe were to occur, if one were to read that these three children had burned to death in a fire, one would be saddened but not greatly surprised. If one of the three were to die of an infectious disease, or an undiagnosed appendicitis, one would not be surprised either. For the present, however, they are among the group child-protection workers know well, but that the public does not, because they do not make headlines—or at least not yet.

Later Careers of Neglected Children

Does the neglected child resent his fate? It is rare that the resentment is conscious, and is certainly not present at the ages of the children in this household. We have had many dealings with parents who were themselves neglected as children, a fact we could gather from obvious clues or from others who had known their families. Rarely do they cite this fact themselves.

Generally, for the children this is the only life they have known. They are not participants in our century of rising expectations. The agony of an ear infection, the sore nose and upper lip that go with a winter-long respiratory infection, the shivering and discomfort of an unheated bedroom and too few blankets are the way the world is. Not for this child planned meals with a mother urging him or her to eat. When there is bread and sliced bologna, you make yourself a sandwich. You do not wake your parents simply because you are hungry. Does someone run to comfort you when you bruise your knees? Does anyone care how long you sit, passively mesmerized, watching cartoons and casual violence on TV? Does Grandpa come to visit bringing toys and his pockets stuffed with nuts and candy? Do you believe in trolls and elves? What are trolls and elves?

The adult's remembrance of childhood deprivation and pains is masked by the merciful process of repression, which is part of the adaptability of the human ego. And the child's current awareness of his lot is obscured by the lack of anything with which to compare it. Besides, who could bear to know he was being neglected? If your parents, on whom you are dependent for life itself, are unwilling or unable to care for you, you are in terrible danger. So there is denial of the present reality.

Yet in their later careers these children often act as if, at some level, they were encumbered with reservoirs of aching resentment. We still have very few follow-up studies of maltreated children. However, one research project in New York State (see chapter 9) yielded evidence that such youngsters are more likely to become delinquent than are average children, and are more likely to be involved in violence against people than are other delinquents.

Fontana (1973) has detailed the histories of a number of famous assassins of our time. It appears that Lee Harvey Oswald, the killer of John F. Kennedy, James Earl Ray, who shot Martin Luther King, and Sirhan Sirhan, the killer of Robert Kennedy, were all maltreated as children. It is easy to understand violence in an abused child as an instance of identification with the aggressor, but a substantial proportion of assailants were not abused so much as neglected. Dollard and his associates (1939) would have understood these observations in terms of their "frustration-aggression hypothesis." Our own thoughts incline toward a process we have called the "deprivation-detachment" sequence (Polansky, Borgman, and DeSaix 1972). The massive inhibition of feeling that derives from indifferent and unempathetic mothering amounts, we think, to a kind of splitting in the ego. Since the person is unable to be aware of his own hurts and suffering, he is certainly unable to empathize with those of others. Such a person can inflict suffering on other people, then, with a coldness and calculation of which more normal persons would be quite incapable.

The Monetary Costs

The expense to the nation stemming from the ultimate effects of child neglect has to be enormous. We believe a large proportion of the inmates of prisons and, certainly, of juvenile correctional institutions were neglected. So were at least a large minority of those who spend their lives checking in and out of state mental hospitals. In this country little attention is paid to the unemployed and the underemployed rich, some of whom were emotionally neglected. But among the poor whose unproductivity concerns us more, it seems likely that a majority of the able-bodied unemployable are victims of developmental failures related to inadequate nurture. To the current financial costs of maintaining all these people must also be added the more distal expenditures: damages to victims of crimes, participation, in turn (like Mona), in offering inadequate care to the next generation of youngsters.

If the more distal costs of neglect are undoubtedly enormous, so are the more proximate, such as rearing children outside their biological families. Anyone who has worked in a children's institution, in which twenty-four-hour-a-day coverage must be arranged with staffs working forty-hour weeks, on hourly pay and with time off for vacations and holidays, must become aware of how costly it is to provide substitutes for parental care. Indeed, the natural family offering its youngsters at least acceptable care is, if nothing more, an enormous convenience to the remainder of society.

Shyne and Schroeder (1978) studied a representative sample of 9,597 cases of children under care in public auspices as of March, 1977. At that time there were an estimated 1.8 million children being served by the public social services. Of these, 395,000 were in foster care, a figure triple the 132,000 of 1961, although children under eighteen had increased by only 3%. They tabulated the "most important reason" for the children being under care cited by the worker carrying the case. Child neglect accounted for 268,000, abandonment was cited for 51,000, and unwillingness to care for the child another 51,000 (p. 82). A quarter of all children regarded as neglected by their parents were in foster families, and over 60% of those who were abandoned, or whose parents were unwilling to keep them. The potential financial costs to a reasonably humane society become enormous. Some figures cited by Fanshel and Shinn (1972) for New York City may, by now, be applicable in less expensive living areas as well. They estimated the cost to the public of keeping an infant in foster care until age eighteen would be $122,500, allowing for cost of living increments of 5%, a figure which, alas, has proven all too conservative. Among 161 families they studied with children then in foster care, "at least four families seem destined ultimately to cost the community over $500,000 in fees from the Charitable Institutions Budget" (p. 25).

But these figures on the numbers of neglected and unwanted children ought not astonish us, if we have been attending to related research. Podell (1973), for instance, reported a study of a representative sample of mothers on welfare in New York City. Their fertility was relatively high. Among those over thirty, the majority had five or more children; among those in their teens and twenties, a quarter had already borne five children or more. But when they were asked, "If you were starting all over again, how many children would you want altogether?" almost six in ten wanted no more than two, and a quarter would have wanted none! Nevertheless, only 40% of those for whom birth control was applicable (e.g., under 45, and not surgically sterilized) were presently using contraception. The ambivalence about parenthood in the middle and upper-middle classes, which is reflected in a magazine like *Esquire* devoting a whole issue (March, 1974) to the topic, "Do Americans Suddenly Hate Kids?" is not confined to the affluent.

We end this chapter, then, on the note on which we began. Numerous children are being born to a mixed reception, or to parents unable to give them what they need. The costs to them, and to the rest of us, are becoming nearly unbearable. We need to learn all we can about the parents involved in such families in order to find means for preventing or repairing the chaos they are in. We have come to think of the majority of these as damaged parents. Why we have come to think this way, what the nature of the damage seems to be, and what to do in the face of it form the subject-matter of the rest of this book.

Two

How Much Is Enough?

At what point do we decide that a child's care has become so poor it is "neglectful"? Extreme circumstances, like outright abandonment or failure to provide food, are clear enough. But most of the time the situation is not that obvious. Child-rearing practices that are regarded as unacceptable vary with the society's general standard of living, its cultural mores, its social prejudices, the degree to which people are in communication and able to observe each other, and so forth. The definition of neglect has changed, over the years, in our own country.

For those who came earliest, immigration to America meant a life filled with hardships. Child mortality was high, and then as now parents tried to foster their children's abilities to survive. Some of their methods would seem strange today. For example, one sage advised his fellow Puritans "that boys should go without hats to harden them and children's feet should be wet in cold water and also they should wear thin-soled shoes in order to toughen their feet" (Chrisman 1920, p. 381). Parents must have leavened such prescriptions with a modicum of common sense, for many Puritans lived to adulthood. Still, even if they had added the inculcation of hardiness to the hardships children already underwent, parents would not have been thought harsh. Assessing failure to provide medical care depends very much on the state of medical knowledge, and if parents' intentions seem "good," specific practices are less likely to be scrutinized. Moreover, when children living in squalor are sharing their parents' mode of life, should one consider them neglected or merely unfortunate?

But even care generally agreed to be substandard might not have led to community intervention. Frontier Americans have shown a tolerance for suffering of other people's children that often bordered on indifference. Those who recall *Huckleberry Finn* are aware that Huck was portrayed as a neglected and abused child. In one memorable scene, Huck's father raged in drunken self-righteousness against the busybodies who threatened to interfere with his doing as he pleased with his own child. The scene was, of course, a satire on how respect for parental rights may impose a terrible fate on the child. In an earlier study of local variations in child-placement practices in America, Maas and Engler (1959) repeatedly encountered reluctance to interfere between parents and child, sometimes as a rationalization to avoid hard decisions.

Fortunately for our children, indifference to the sufferings of others has never been total or universal in our country. When we read studies which bring to light the cynical manipulations at the top that hamper efforts to improve the lives of children (Schorr 1974; Steiner 1976), we feel a need to protest. If there were not also a substantial body of citizens which feels compassion and translates it into philanthropy and law, there would be no child welfare apparatus at all. Careerists may contaminate the apparatus, but they have, traditionally, been unable to control it. The majority of the social workers involved really does care about children, and those who mean well are not without skills in maneuvering.

Nor are those who exploit the public's compassion the only problem. Charles Loring Brace, who founded and led the Children's Aid Society of New York City for forty years, is one of the heros of the field (Becker 1971). Under the slogan of ridding the city of its "dangerous classes," he actually rescued hundreds of homeless boys and girls wandering the streets of New York, and sent them off to foster homes in upstate New York and the Middle West. Yet stories began to filter back of farmers taking youngsters in simply to use them as work animals, of the bodies of underfed children found floating in upstate creeks, and so on. While Brace could protest that the rumors were false, we do have copies of some of his sermons to youngsters in his home for newsboys. His disparaging and bitter remarks about their drunken and uncaring parents may have been all too accurate, but he seems to have been obtuse to the damage the children's own self-images would suffer from such descriptions of their parents by a person in authority. Brace came from a prominent New England family and self-doubt was not his problem. So the field of child welfare has always been riddled with imperfections, and it still is. Perfection, on the other hand, can be found in this world only in the life of the mind.

That definitions of neglect are always culturally relative hardly requires belaboring by examples of infanticide in classical Sparta and nineteenth-century India. Evidence of differences in frames of reference is easily demonstrated in the present-day United States. Thus, in a strange twist of ethnic discrimination, one worker found miserable living conditions in a family of eight black children unremarkable because "that's how those people live." But what would one expect? Nearly all social judgments of any complexity and ambiguity are culturally relative, and the attempt to find a universal definition of neglect, equally applicable for Ghana or Scranton, strikes us as footless. To a considerable extent, the definition of neglect is a matter of our agreeing about what standard is minimal.

Most significant social action in a democracy takes places in a setting in which the many are indifferent but a few are zealous; opinions differ but a core of common judgment may be found; eventually "something is done about it," but the effort is less than wholehearted. The movement to identify and treat the child victims of poor care, for better or worse, is very typical.

Legal and Social Work Definitions of Neglect

The two professions most concerned with neglect have traditionally been social workers and legal authorities: judges, lawyers, and other court officials. Meier (1964) has contributed a remarkably perceptive and foresighted paper which deals, in part, with similarities and differences in the two points of view. Legally, she notes,

> the conditions that constitute neglect are variously defined, but rather characteristically the laws cite these circumstances: (1) inadequate physical care; (2) absence of or inadequate medical care; (3) cruel or abusive treatment; (4) improper supervision; (5) exploitation of the child's earning capacity; (6) unlawfully keeping the child out of school; (7) exposing the child to criminal or immoral influence that endangers his morals. [p. 157]

A more recent and exhaustive analysis is that contributed by Katz, Howe, and McGrath (1975). They found that, after much legislative activity in this area during the 1970s, the grounds for adjudicating neglect found most frequently in the various states and other territorial jurisdictions were "in 56 jurisdictions: 'lack of proper parental control or guardianship'... in 46 jurisdictions:

'parental refusal or inability to provide necessary medical, surgical or other special care made necessary by the child's particular condition'... and 'abandonment' in 44 jurisdictions" (p. 56). Neglect was commonly dealt with under the civil code, which has relevance to parental custody of the child or its termination; however eight jurisdictions also mention it in the criminal code. The authors found that whether the child was termed neglected, dependent, or deprived was not of critical significance, since the most common grounds were found in conjunction with all these terms. The major distinction among states, rather, was "between language which stresses parental fault or which focuses upon the condition of the child without any mention of parental fault" (p. 57).

Meier correctly noted that, since both legislators and social workers are heavily influenced by community norms, and look to such norms for their legitimation, it is not surprising to find that their definitions of neglect have always had much in common. Over the years we have had definitions of neglect, or of conditions warranting protective action by social agencies, by social workers and committees of professional organizations. These social work statements, however, tend to be more inclusive than the legal definitions. This is evident, for example, in a statement of the Child Welfare League of America's Committee on Standards of Child Protective Service:

> In our society, both parents and children have natural and legal rights which are accompanied by corresponding responsibilities enforceable by law. Parents are responsible for giving their children the love, care and protection which they need; and for providing, within their ability and the resources available to them, all of the following, until their children can care for themselves:
> · adequate food, shelter, clothing
> · medical care
> · education
> · supervision and protection
> · moral and social guidance
> ... The rights of parents may be limited or abrogated by reason of parental failure or incompetence. [Committee on Standards for Child Protective Services 1960, pp. 5–6]

One reason that the social work definition is more inclusive is the legal reluctance to rely on inference in adjudicating neglect, an attitude that is embedded in our democratic tradition. None of us, for example, would accept being put under surveillance on the grounds that, given what is known of his or her background, one is likely to try to overthrow the government in ten years. "Law cannot be concerned with causative factors or with predictions of future behavior" (Meier 1964, p. 161).

More recently a legal scholar, Wald (1976), has published an influential analysis in which he urged that state intervention on behalf of neglected children be limited to those who are demonstrably suffering a present "harm," especially if the child's removal from his home is the issue. Wald is at pains to remind us that our ability to predict future disability from present life circumstances is still very limited, and that there is very little relevant research. But some of his strictures appear legalistic, if not laughable, to a social worker. For example, he expresses concern about the harm that might be done by social workers, and others, intervening in homes to offer their services. When one observes, first hand, the physical violence, criminality, dilapidation, and miserable poverty with which many potentially neglectful urban families are bombarded all the time, the notion that a well-meaning young caseworker might add a significant threat is ludicrous. The social work definition of neglect does include concern about what a child's future will be if nothing is done in the present. And since we are dealing with people rather than principles, we cannot await the final outcome of research (which is not being financed, anyhow), but must act now on the basis of our clinical experiences.

But social work can afford to be more inclusive in its definition because our judgment results in an offer of help. More drastic action down the line, like removal of children or termination of parental rights, is a matter for courts to decide. Meier noted that social workers are sensitized to seeing "emotional neglect," but doubts that legislators would want to enter that legal thicket because of its ambiguities, which leave so much to the discretion of the particular judge.

Finally, there is the fact that the law needs a decision that a child's circumstances are, or are not, neglectful in order for a court to assume jurisdiction or decline it. In effect, child care is measured by a simple dichotomy. To the child welfare worker, however, it is obvious that the quality of child care has to be seen as a *continuum,* ranging from excellent on the one hand to severely neglectful on the other. Dividing the continuum into a dichotomy is necessarily somewhat arbitrary. Moreover, as we shall see in the measurement of the caliber of care used in our own studies, the dimension is not simple and univocal, but multifarious, involving a number of subscales for physical and psychological nurture. In short, if social workers are concerned to protect individual children in trouble, and lawyers are geared to safeguarding the rights of "all families and children" against capricious intrusion by the state, they will often disagree in their assessments of families, and in the way they would write the laws. Indeed, they should disagree, for a tension between the two differing societal functions is healthy in a democracy, and one would worry if it did not exist.

With all this in mind, we advanced the following definition of neglect to guide our work:

> Child neglect may be defined as a condition in which a care-taker responsible for the child either deliberately or by extra-ordinary inattentiveness permits the child to experience avoidable present suffering and/or fails to provide one or more of the ingredients generally deemed essential for developing a person's physical, intellectual, and emotional capacities. [Polansky, Hally, and Polansky 1975]

There are a number of implications of this definition, some of which represent stands taken on issues discussed above. Neglect, for example, is not thought of as limited to consciously motivated behavior by a parent; indeed, the approach emphasizes the circumstances of the child's life, rather than characteristics of his parents. "Avoidable present suffering" is in the definition. For a child to go to school in bitter cold weather with no more protection than a cotton jacket may not result in dramatic long-term damage to his health, but it cannot be good for him emotionally. Children may, and do, lie in pain from ear infections that remain untreated and escape permanent auditory damage, but this, too, seems unconscionable. But to speak of *avoidable* suffering is to rely on the current state of medical knowledge, so that any definition of neglect must be relative to what is known, in a given era, especially about pediatrics and child development. And with respect to the latter, our definition is in line with the thinking of a number of experts that the key issue in adjudicating neglect or considering removal of children must be the probable impact on the child of any action taken (cf. Goldstein, Freud, and Solnit 1973; Fraiberg 1977). The child's need for mothering, then, is paramount, but one ought not presume that only emotional well-being is at stake. Neglect, like abuse, occasionally proves lethal. Nor is all neglect the fault of natural mothers and fathers; children may also be neglected by others who stand *parens patriae:* by institutions, foster homes, placement agencies, day care centers, and nurseries.

This, then, was our working definition of neglect, verbally or conceptually. Bringing it to operational terms has been challenging and arduous. We have operationalized the thinking involved in a Childhood Level of Living Scale whose development and content are described in chapter 6.

The Prevalence of Child Neglect

Most statistics descriptive of social pathology are collected in terms of incidence, that is, the number of new cases of a given condition identified during a given year. A measure of this sort seems proper when we are dealing with a condition that is specific and short-lived. Neglect, however, tends to be chronic and long-term. So the identification of a family typically does not mean that it has just "committed an act of neglect," but rather, that a continuously neglecting family has come to official attention. It is more appropriate, therefore, to think of statistics on neglect as reflecting *prevalence,* the level of neglect that exists as an ongoing, chronic phenomenon.

The main impression one gains about the statistics we have had on child maltreatment during the past decade or so is that there is more of it "out there" than we had initially anticipated. Events in Florida have been a striking case in point. In 1971, their legislature passed new laws requiring that suspected cases coming to the attention of health, welfare, and other personnel in touch with children must be reported to the responsible local department. The liability to suit for damages was correspondingly reduced. Florida also set up a twenty-four-hour telephone monitoring service to take referrals, and initiated a modest advertising campaign to alert citizens and to encourage their taking action. In 1970, the year preceding, there had been seventeen reports of abuse. However, during the first year under the new system, there were 19,120 reports of maltreatment of children under age seventeen, and in the second year there were 29,013. According to Nagi (1977, pp. 36ff.) this was a reporting rate of 14.2 per thousand children. Projected nationally, this rate implied slightly over a million cases of abuse and neglect in 1972.

Nearly all who are professionally concerned with child maltreatment are dubious about figures that have become available. Because most people hesitate to interfere in others' family lives, much abuse and neglect that is suspected goes unreported. The sharp rises in numbers of reports that follow public awareness campaigns or stories in the news media, demonstrate that the general level of public consciousness of the problem markedly affects its being reported. When reporting is not only said to be mandatory, but the law is also enforced, more cases also become "official." An interesting new facet of this process, by the way, may have been introduced by a ruling of the California Supreme Court in 1976. The court ruled that failure to report child abuse was grounds for a suit for damages against a professional, when brought on behalf of the child (Martin 1976). A socioeconomic bias is alleged, in which affluent families' maltreatment is not referred for action by their private physicians, although similar circumstances in families known to clinics lead to referrals. Some agency workers have told us that unavailability of resources in their counties designed to help such families makes teachers and others hesitate to report them. When one's experience is that nothing good comes of a referral, it seems pointless to make one except in the most severe instances. These are some of the main factors influencing our statistics.

The increase in estimates of the extent of the problem of child maltreatment has been dramatic, to say the least.

> One of the first attempts to estimate the incidence of abuse was by De Francis (1963) who used as his source cases of abuse reported in newspapers of 48 states and the District of Columbia in 1962. He found 662 cases. In the same year, Kempe, et al. (1962) surveyed 71 hospitals, finding 302 cases, and surveyed 77 district attorneys, who knew of 447 cases in that year. [Martin 1978, p. 7]

Recognizing the difficulties of getting an exact measure of the size of our burden, nationally, an effort was subsequently made to get counties to send reports of cases to a central register in each state. The Children's Division of the American Humane Association then undertook to assemble these figures into national totals. Cooperation varied at every level. Many front-line workers found the forms involved irksome additions to their paper work; whole states simply ignored the effort. However, for the year 1975, the Children's Division totaled 289,837 reports of abuse and/or neglect, involving 304,329 children. Of these, 228,899 had been investigated by responsible local agencies, and about 60% were found valid—that is, there was good reason for the report. Of these cases, the ratio of neglect to abuse was 63:37. But neglect was clearly understated. Seven states included did not even carry statistics on neglect, and a number did not require it to be registerd centrally unless it was very severe (i.e., life-threatening) (Reports 1977). Still, even these incomplete figures are enormously greater than those that were recorded twelve or thirteen years earlier.

The most authoritative review we have of all the available compilations and estimates is that by Martin and Klaus (1978). They cite an estimate from Nagi of a probable 666,000 cases of *neglect* nationally in 1972–73, of which he anticipated about two-thirds would have actually been reported. It is also commonly believed among students of the problem that identified neglect predominates over abuse, in the average jurisdiction, in a ratio of about five to one. It is obvious that there is an enormous number of families known to be neglectful in these United States.

Are Things Getting Worse?

One has to be impressed by the remarkable increase in the estimates of child maltreatment in our country. Drawing on newspaper accounts, De Francis found 662 cases of abuse in 1962. By 1975, a compilation of states' central registrations, which were very probably substantially incomplete, came to several hundred thousand, The estimate of 666,000 cases of neglect drawn from the work of Nagi (1977) is particularly impressive because of the caliber of his methods. Area sampling of households was used to identify and weight a representative national sample of political entities (usually counties) having jurisdiction over child maltreatment. The researchers could then deal more thoroughly with a limited number of reporting agencies to try to secure more reliable and valid reports from which to project the national estimates. Nevertheless, Nagi found enormous variations in rates of reported maltreatment among the 129 jurisdictions sampled, from a low of one child in every 4,000 under age eighteen, to a high of 59.6 per thousand. It is far more credible that most of the variation was due to factors of the sort mentioned above which appear to affect the rate of reporting than to assume we have counties in this country which differ by a factor of 238 in the real extent of the problem.

Thus, as we remarked earlier, the available figures are all suspect, but there clearly has proven to be a great deal more child maltreatment going on than was originally thought. Gil's (1970) estimate of two and a half million cases of abuse per year, as of 1965, seems less preposterous now than it did when his results were first published. When he compared estimates from his sampling survey with a subsequent attempt to compile reports of known cases of abuse from the various states, he himself came to question how large a problem, numerically, abuse was.

Meanwhile, the number of reports submitted and compiled continues to increase. A very recent report from the American Humane Association is based on data from forty-eight states, the District of Columbia, Guam, Puerto Rico, and the Virgin Islands. The total number of cases of both neglect and abuse in 1976 was 412,972; in 1977 it was 512,494, a 24% gain among the states and territories participating in the study (Reports 1979).

What about trends? Is there now, in fact, more neglect of children than there was? Or are these families simply now more likely to come to official attention? We have been at pains to describe the state of the art as one in which we probably do not have valid statistics from any recent year. It is patently impossible to make inferences, scientifically, by comparing unreliable data in the present with unbelievable data from the past.

Social workers, of course, are under no illusion that this problem is new. Caring for the neglected children of alcoholic or otherwise damaged parents was a major concern to the amateurs who helped found our field in Hamburg in the eighteenth century, and to those in the Charity Organization Society movement in London, in the middle of the nineteenth. Twenty years ago, the term for families very like those now thought of as maltreating was "multi-problem" (Schlesinger 1970). No, neglect may have been newly brought to public awareness, but it is certainly not new.

Under such circumstances, one can only offer one's impressions. Ours is that the proportion of children being "neglected," in our conception of it, probably waxes and wanes in any society, in line with other major social occurrences and trends in the culture. As compared with, say, the period shortly after World War II when so many young couples were, if not greatly optimistic, at least free from the threat of Hitler and eager to start living, Americans of late have been less in love with the idea of rearing children. In the urban poverty areas, particularly, as life becomes ever more dangerous and difficult in nearly every aspect, we believe the rate of child neglect has been steadily rising. Many front-line workers have come to us at meetings to express concern about the deterioration of child-rearing standards, however, in affluent areas of their counties. In these areas, the neglect is thought of more in terms of failing to instill emotional security, or to work at developing children's superegos to a level compatible with living maturely, than it is in terms of sheer physical care. For what it is worth, therefore, it does seem that the increase in rates of cases identified reflect more than improved case-finding; rather, protective service workers do seem to be trying to cope with an evermounting human flood.

Three

What about the Parents?

Those working to help neglected children have usually been motivated by concerns far more humane than mere intellectual curiosity. Their approach to the task has been eclectic and, above all, pragmatic, in William James's meaning: following those principles that appear to work best. But they have not been totally lacking in theoretical commitment, for it is nearly impossible to make a serious try at doing something about a social problem without making assumptions about its probable causes.

If these assumptions cannot be dignified as "scientific theories," they do provide part of an ideology—a system of beliefs and values—that lends intellectual coherence to the work. Followers of such a treatment ideology think of it as their rationale; skeptical onlookers, as their rationalization. Working in the 1850s, Charles Loring Brace certainly had an explicit hypothesis about the eventual fate of neglected, lower-class children:

> the class of a large city most dangerous to its property, its morals and its political life, are the ignorant, destitute, untrained and abandoned youth: the outcast street children grown up to be voters, to be the implements of demagogues, the "feeders" of the criminals, and the sources of domestic outbreaks and violations of the law. [Brace 1872, p. i]

A century later, we cannot totally discount his hypothesis, however archaic or objectionable we find its phrasing.

Although a staunch Darwinist, Brace had the happy thought that evil traits in man tend to be eliminated by the process of natural selection. Hence, he shared with modern social workers a preoccupation with environmental influences as prime determiner of individual character. Among these influences social class played the greatest role. Brace admired the middle class as the repository of puritan virtues; as the head of a great charity he was unimpressed with the social consciences of the very rich and recommended their numbers be limited on the boards of agencies. The lower class he divided into three, in a manner somewhat reminiscent of Karl Marx: the industrious poor, the paupers, and the dangerous classes, whose children needed rescue. His feeling about their parenting is captured in a sermon he delivered to newsboys staying in a lodging house which Brace's Children's Aid Society had set up for them:

> Providence has granted you very little of the world's greatest blessing—the affection of the home. Your father, if you ever knew him, probably beat you when he was drunk, and worked you like a beast of burden when he was sober. Your mother, very likely, half-starved you and whipped you, and finally, in her intoxication, drove you out of house and home. Your faces are worn and your bodies scarred often with the abuse of those who ought to have loved you. [Brace 1886, p. 140]

Let us try, for a moment, not to be too judgmental of Brace's judgmentalism. What, objectively, seems so wrong about what he was saying to the boys? He does seem a man who has spent time in direct work, and who has made some accurate observations. His words contain evidence of passion and compassion. But they are so insensitive! To Brace, a boy's continuing attachment to his mother must have been mystifying, the denial of a mother's weaknesses beyond belief. Scientifically, by the unfair standard of a century later, one would tax him with oversimplicity, with lack of empathy, with superficiality. In short, he too soon gave up asking the question: Why?

How far have we come since then in our understanding? Several lines of theory have been pursued in the search for the causes of neglect: the *economic*, emphasizing the role of material deprivation and poverty; the *ecological*, in which a family's behavior is seen as responsive to the larger social context in which it is embedded; and the *personalistic*, which attributes poor child care to individual differences among parental personalities, particularly their character structures. Although our own work adopts the personalistic approach, we do not believe a family's poverty or its social environment may be discounted in understanding the caliber of its child caring.

Poverty

Several investigators have noted a general association between poverty and child maltreatment; they believe it plays the greater role in neglect than in abuse. Kadushin has ably phrased the prevailing opinion:

> Neglect appears to be a response to social stress. More often than not the neglectful mother has no husband, is living on a marginal income in substandard housing, and is responsible for the care of an atypically large family of children.
>
> Abuse appears to be a response to psychological stress. The parent in reacting to internal conflicts, selects one child in the family as a victim and responds to his misbehavior in a disproportionate manner. [Kadushin 1974, p. 283]

Sheer iteration of the poverty-neglect association by various writers extends credibility to the observation. But some study designs, when carefully scrutinized, do not permit drawing conclusions about the relationship.

Young (1964) studied records of 300 families known to public and private child welfare agencies in selected urban and suburban areas of the United States. Both abusive and neglectful families were studied, and an effort was made to identify factors that distinguish the two forms of maltreatment. Although her major conclusion about the cause of neglect stresses the childlike characters of the parents (see p. 101), Young also noted that nearly all were multiproblem families, and poverty was widespread among them. Since her data were from cases under care of agencies, with no control sample, Young's observations are to be considered suggestive rather than definitive. Meier (1964) also mentioned being overwhelmed by the external pressures, such as poverty, which are a potential cause of neglect.

The study by Giovannoni and Billingsley (1970) did not rely solely on agency records and, moreover, they did include a control group. In their work in the Los Angeles area, 186 mothers were interviewed once about their current lives and their pasts. Drawn from several ethnic backgrounds (Black, Caucasian, Spanish-speaking), the women were sorted into three groups in terms of the level of child caring indicated in their case records: neglectful, potentially neglectful, and adequate. As compared with the adequate mother, the neglectful mother was found more likely to have had more children; to be without a husband; to have had recent marital problems; and to have less money than the controls for material resources useful in child care (e.g., no telephone, no watch).

The authors determined that the severity of current life conditions brought on by poverty was the main causative factor. They did not find differences related to earlier life circumstances, and this negative finding reinforced their conclusion that current life pressures were primarily to blame. Hence, the treatment proposed would consist of giving these families more money to live on and improved facilities, like better housing, an idea that hardly seem arguable. Yet the failure to find differences in life backgrounds, which they report, is negative evidence. It could be due to measurement error, or to not having examined the right variables. For, in our own research, we have had no difficulty establishing differences between neglectful and nonneglectful low-income mothers in terms of the kinds of families they come from and their earlier life adjustments, nor have Wolock and Horowitz (1979). These differences, however, are not at the level of social class or ethnicity (see chapter 11). An overall conclusion of theirs with which one can agree, however, is "that poverty exposes parents to the increased likelihood of additional stresses that may have deleterious effects upon their capacities to care adequately for their children" (Giovannoni and Billingsley 1970, p. 204).

Wolock and Horowitz (1979) have recently reported a large and fruitful study which bears on the same issue. The aim of the study was to identify factors associated with child maltreatment among impoverished families. Cases were drawn from the rolls of families receiving Aid to Families of Dependent Children (AFDC) in Northern New Jersey. Five hundred fifty-two mothers were screened into the study as having been known to public child welfare personnel for child maltreatment, that is, neglect, abuse, or both, and they were able to interview 380 of these. Interviews with these mothers were compared with those obtained from a representative sample of 191 other mothers on AFDC, of whom they were able to reach 141. The authors noted that many of the most serious forms of maltreatment are not included, since frequently all children would have been removed from the home, but that their sample did include the sorts of maltreating families commonly known to public agencies.

Of the sample of 380 maltreating families, neglect only was reported for 246, and both neglect and abuse for another 106. There were only 28 families interviewed whose problem was child abuse alone. One might, then, interpret most of their findings with respect to child maltreatment as germane to child neglect. However, the combination with child abuse, in their study, proved larger than we had anticipated.

Wolock and Horowitz's results might be interpreted as supporting any of the three theoretical approaches to explaining neglect. While severe material deprivation characterized all the families present in this AFDC sample, the authors describe the maltreating group as the "poorest of the poor" (p. 186). Statistically, they were shown less likely than the nonmaltreating to possess a telephone, an air conditioner, or a color TV, items taken as representative of their generally lower standard of living. Now, one might argue that to define neglect, in part, as material deprivation in the household, and then to find that maltreating families were indeed living at a lower level, was simply a validation of one's grouping of cases. Moreover, as the authors acknowledge, taking all cases from the rolls of AFDC hardly provides the best opportunity to examine the role of poverty in causing neglect since, if anything, family incomes should be essentially matched. Hence, differences in living standards could reasonably be attributed to how well the same income was being used by the parents involved. The latter would then reflect personal adequacy.

There were other differences found by these authors worth bearing in mind in relation to the studies to be mentioned below. Respondents in the maltreating group were significantly more negative than the nonmaltreating about two aspects of their neighborhoods: the state of the housing and neighborliness. They were more socially isolated, having fewer contacts with friends, relatives, and formal organizations; they reported high levels of alienation on a scale for measuring this, but these levels were no greater than those of the comparison group; they reported they had been themselves beaten and neglected as children more frequently than did nonmaltreating mothers; and they had larger numbers of children per household, averaging 3.9 versus 2.7 in the control families ($P < .0001$). Their children were also born closer together.

To provide an overview, the authors list the main factors that emerged from a discriminate function analysis. These factors were: number of children in the family; family background of the mother; present material level of living; and social isolation. However, much of the variance remained unexplained, for the Canonical correlation in the multivariate analysis was .319. These findings will be recalled when we report our results.

Despite the relative parsimony by which an interpretation in terms of maternal character structures would integrate their various findings, the authors focus their conclusions around the issue of inadequate income. What can one say? That we admire their values, but wish their inferences were better supported by their own reported results? For if one wanted to design a study that would highlight factors *other* than poverty as causes of child neglect, selecting all cases from a common eligibility for AFDC would be a reasonable design.

We are left with a puzzling state of affairs. One would have to be recently arrived from Mars not to think that family income affects the likelihood of child neglect. Yet neither of these studies, conducted by sociologically oriented researchers, actually supports so highly credible a hypothesis. They do, nonetheless, help reinforce an impression we had formed. Their descriptions of life among the very poor remind us that those mothers living in extreme poverty whose children are *not* neglected are little short of heroic.

What sort of design, then, would be required to test the proposition that economics has a greater influence in causing neglect than does parental personality? A truly exquisite design would be required. On the side of personality, one would select those traits that have most to do with influencing parenting; but, to prevent circularity, they must be measurable independently from actual child-caring behavior. One would then have to achieve measurement definition of these traits at a high level of validity, and use the measurement in a sampling design that provides maximal variability on each dimension so that each trait-factor has its best chance of becoming statistically visible. A similar operation would have to be performed simultaneously on the side of the economic variables.

Such a design is clearly beyond the present state of the art, not to mention the available financial support. We introduce it, at this point, as an ideal type, along with a caution as to what can be expected in this field. At a time when we are just beginning to get confirmations from independent investigators as to which variables have any significant association at all with neglect, it is premature to assign weights. Analogous logic, of course, applies to the interpretation of discriminant-function analyses, factor analyses, and the like, even within a single study.

Regardless of the causes, when it comes to actual level of living, these studies do suggest strongly that neglectful families may be described as the "poorest of the poor." It would be heartless to react self-righteously to an inferred "misuse" of income when the amounts involved are so trivial by middle-class standards, as our own study will also demonstrate. But if parental personality plays a major role in determining how much income is available, as well as how it is handled, then programs aimed simply at increasing income will not solve the problem of neglect. For increased income may prove a necessary by *not sufficient* condition for solving the problem in most households. We are concerned, then, not with a theory but with potentiallly dangerous realities in the lives of children.

Ecology

Implicit in the work on human ecology, as in other field theoretical approaches, is a synthetic mode of theorizing. Rather than analyzing the whole into its constituent, fundamental components, we ask: "Of what larger whole is this present unit a part?" For it is assumed that the part partakes of qualities of the whole to which it belongs, and that this principle, of itself, may be explanatory. Moreover, as Kurt Lewin (1951) has often emphasized, since the parts of a whole are interdependent, it is more efficient to undertake to change the whole, rather than its constituents, one by one. Lewin's dictum is usually understood as applying to mezzosystems, such as families and face-to-face groups, but it is equally germane to the individual ego.

Garbarino and his colleagues have been pursuing the idea that an analogous idea might also apply to larger aggregates, such as neighborhoods, and prove relevant to reducing child maltreatment. "Socially impoverished families may be particularly vulnerable to socially impoverished environments and susceptible to amelioration only in socially rich environments" (Garbarino and Sherman 1978a, p. 3). In view of this, they believed that the study of families with the potential for child abuse must be accompanied by the study of high-risk neighborhoods.

Working with data from one county in Nebraska, their first studies sought to correlate the rate of child maltreatment with other variables descriptive of the same neighborhoods. Incidence of child maltreatment was calculated in terms of numbers of cases reported; the authors believe this to be a more valid index than number substantiated, since the latter is more susceptible to political and other extraneous pressure. Using 1970 census data, an index of economic status of the neighborhood was developed that consisted of combining percentage of households with incomes over $15,000 per year with the obversely weighted percentage of those under $8,000. The 93 census tracts in the county were combined into 20 "subareas," or natural neighborhoods, since most correlations were somewhat higher, this way, than when the census tract was the unit of analysis. The multiple correlation of neighborhood income with the rate of child neglect reported per thousand families was $R = .78$. The multiple correlation with child abuse was nearly as high, $R = .65$, so there is reason to doubt whether, as Kadushin proposed (see p. 22), the causes of abuse are more internal, and those of neglect more a matter of external stresses.

In the New Jersey study by Wolock and Horowitz (1979), it will be recalled that maltreating mothers were more negative about their neighborhoods than were the comparisons, reporting their housing more dilapidated and their neighbors less friendly. Their negative attitudes, of course, could have derived from their own low morale or bitterness rather than from their surroundings. Data from another study by Garbarino and Crouter (1979) are therefore of especial interest because they are drawn more or less at random from neighborhood residents, not just from those implicated in neglect or abuse. An index of the percentage rating their neighborhood "very desirable" was compared with rates of maltreatment reported. The overall correlation with child maltreatment was $-.22$, which was not significant; neither was the correlation with the rate of reported neglect, $-.13$. However, the correlation with rate of reported abuse was $R = -.49$ ($P < .05$, $N = 20$). Low *neighborhood* morale, as well as individual morale, may have something to do, then, with child abuse; its status with respect to child neglect remains uncertain. The authors also found that the percentage of those who think having good neighbors is important, which may be another sort of indicator of relatedness in a neighborhood, correlates fairly well with the rate of reported child neglect: $R = -.47$ ($P < .05$), but this finding did not hold up when the analysis was repeated at the level of comparisons among the 93 census tracts, so we do not know how seriously to regard it.

The same group has also undertaken other research that appears potentially fruitful. For example, two census tracts were identified, each of which would have been expected to have a rather high rate of cases reported based on a regression formula from the larger study, but which contrasted markedly in the numbers actually reported. Thus, one "should" have had 69 cases per thousand, but actually had 130; the other should have had 66 cases, but reported only 16. In an exploratory way, relatively small samples of respondents were interviewed from each neighborhood (Garbarino and Sherman 1978b). More from the nonmaltreating neighborhood said the neighbors were friendly and that they were familiar with them. About the same amount of help among neighbors was being exchanged in both neighborhoods, but since the need was greater in the high-incidence area, more need remained unmet. Fewer in the high-incidence area seemed able to use resources of the larger community. These findings will bear comparison with our own work on the relative isolation of neglectful parents (see chapter 7).

Based on the psychology of reference groups, one might wonder whether community attitudes regarding child caring differ among neighborhoods, and therefore influence the reported rates of child neglect. However, in a pilot study in southern Appalachia in which mothers identified as being severely neglectful were interviewed with a standard schedule concerning child-caring practices, they gave knowledgeable and highly acceptable answers (Polansky, Borgman, and DeSaix 1972). Similarly, Wolock and Horowitz (1979) found no differences between maltreating and nonmaltreating mothers in their professed child-rearing attitudes. Either we are dealing with what used to be termed the difference between "public," or professed, and "private," or seriously believed attitudes, or values among societal groups do not really differ with respect to minimal standards of child care. If this were so, we would have to conclude that the neglectful parent is unable, or unmotivated, to conform to the standards of his or her own reference group.

The social supports, or lack of them, for reinforcing values that dictate good child care are also part of a family's ecology. Obviously there is less social support if one lives in a neighborhood characterized by absence of consensus about values (*anomie*); obviously, too, the pressure to conform is lessened if the parent is generally out of touch with his neighbors. The fundamental processes involved were laid bare by social psychologists three decades ago (Festinger, Schachter, and Back 1950). We will return to these issues in our own studies of whether there are class differences in values relevant to basic child care (chapter 6), and of the isolation of neglectful parents (chapter 7).

A conception well known among social workers, and one related to the ecological approach, is that of "community neglect."

> I consider *parental neglect* as existing in families where there is evidence of persistent, inadequate, insufficient provision of child care by the adult, or adults, responsible for the child or children and where the adult's behavior and attitude offer little or no likelihood of improved care without some outside intervention. I consider *community neglect* as existing where there is evidence of persistent, inadequate, insufficient provision of resources for child care by community authorities and where the behavior and attitudes of such authorities offer little or no likelihood of improved provision of resources without some outside intervention. . . . The child protection program must be concerned with both types of neglect. [Lewis 1969]

Those working in protective services often feel they are encountering a lack of support from the communities where they work. Their own agencies are usually understaffed and lack resources such as emergency foster care, emergency financial assistance, and the like. They also keep discovering gaps in services that "ought to be available" for all disadvantaged children in the larger community, e.g., free dental care. So there is considerable appeal in labeling such instances community neglect. In order for it to be effective, however, it is important that Lewis's conception serve needs that go beyond the perjorative and rhetorical, the assigning of blame to power elites who are incapable of guilt or shame, and therefore unresponsive to name-calling.

More scientifically, we might say that since the family unit is part of a larger whole, which is the community, provisions for care of *all* children in the community are likely, for better or worse, to affect care given in a particular family. Thus free lunch programs help nourish the neglected along with other low-income children in a school. But even within larger wholes, there may be degrees of interdependence of the parts. To the extent that neglectful families are out of touch with the majority, their children are less likely to benefit from programs geared to "average expectable families" (Hally, Polansky, and Polansky 1980). We will return to these conceptual formulations below (p. 171).

Let us close our reference to the ecological approach by appending another of Lewin's field-theoretical notions, the *quasi-stationary* equilibrium (Lewin 1951). The care in a given family resembles an equilibrium in the sense that it attains a level that seems typical of the given family. Some days things are better, some days worse, but there is a tendency to return to a familiar level. When protective services recognize the equilibrium effects in neglect, they usually are impressed with forces that act to resist efforts to raise the level of child care. But have we not been overlooking dynamics at work in other households whose effects are beneficial? In more fortunate families, a life mishap such as hospitalization or even imprisonment triggers spontaneous help from grandparents, neighbors, and workmates who are able and willing to step in. To borrow a term from sailing, families at risk have equilibriums that are "tender," that is, easily upset. Moreover, the forces maintaining the equilibrium are asymmetrical in their effects: improvement occurs with difficulty, but child-care standards are not very resistant to deterioration.

Developmental Failures in Parents

In pursuing the personalistic approach, we have followed the scientific method of "successive approximation." Questions raised in studies become progressively more pointed: Are there any enduring personality features, or factors of personal background, that distinguish between neglectful parents and others whose care of their children is adequate? If there are characteristic differences, how may we specify the traits, capacities, and attitudes marking off neglectful parents? Are there characteristic diagnostic syndromes? Typical sets of underlying dynamics?

From her study of agency cases, Young (1964) attempted some generalizations about the personalities of parents implicated in neglect. She noted the prevalence of poverty, poor housing alcoholism, mental illness, and of large numbers of children per family. With regard to personality, the parents appeared childlike, exhibiting dependence, impulsivity, inability to carry responsibility, poor judgment, narcissistic orientation, and other evidences of failure to mature. Meier (1964), too, remarked that many of these parents evidently have severe defects in ego development. Indeed, she commented that many skills and attitudes inculcated into social workers, such as permissiveness, acceptance, exploration of the parent's own deprivations, would be inappropriate to working with a client with severe ego defects. The setting of limits and the use of authority might be more to the point.

At the same time our own work was under way, a fascinating experiment in the use of the ego psychological approach (Wasserman 1974) was under way in Chicago. Thirty-five severely neglectful families were taken under intensive care in a program integrating a range of services through one agency. From their sustained, intimate contacts, Sullivan, Spasser, and Penner (1977) were able to synthesize some common characteristics of the parents:

> An almost universal personality aspect . . . was a basic feeling of "badness" and self-reproach. . . . They were . . . bad people to whom nothing good would happen. This attitude was related to their negative early experiences and was held to tenaciously. . . . Another phenomenon that was almost universal was the prevalence of rather severe depersonalization experiences and anxiety. . . . Perhaps the most serious underlying problem common to these mothers was depression. . . . Closely related to the foregoing problem . . . was a serious arrest in development. [pp. 104–5]

The aspect of developmental failure most crucial to this group of investigators was the subjects' sense of incompleteness because of not having achieved an internalized separate identity. "This was manifested in many ways; e.g., by clinging to their children, by the presence of abusive and unfulfilling relationships, and by the inability to tolerate being alone" (p. 105). The parents also feared taking responsibility and making decisions and had severe difficulties in verbal communication—a nexus of defensive traits Polansky (1971) had earlier related to Kaiser's concept of the "delusion of fusion." Feelings of sadness and need were especially hard to put into words. Because of the pervasive incapacity to tolerate conscious anxiety, feelings were split off from events and anxiety was customarily discharged directly into activity. Whether or not one follows the developmental map proposed by Mahler, Pine, and Bergman (1975), the observations by Sullivan, Spasser, and Penner certainly imply seriously depriving early relationships and massive "splitting in the ego" (Kernberg 1966).

Many of those studying child abuse have also isolated parental traits bespeaking gross immaturity. Steele (1975) cited dependency, poor self-esteem, difficulty in seeking or obtaining pleasure, impaired ability to empathize with the child's needs, and distorted perceptions of the child. The familiar observation that abusive parents try to practice role-reversal with their children (Morris and Gould 1963) would be expected of parents who are themselves needful and immature. Not enough attention has been given to the possibility that such parents' murderous rage toward their own mothers, often split off and repressed, actually derives ultimately from neglect in their own childhoods. A series of intrapsychic transactions may result in a view of the mother as hostile when she was, in fact, indifferent (Klein et al. 1952; Guntrip 1969). Thus it becomes tempting to speculate that "at a deeper level" neglectful and abusive parents are much the same—which would account for the overlap of problems identified by Wolock and Horowitz (p. 23). But the problem with analyses "at the deeper level" is their lack of problem-specificity (Steele and Pollock 1974). It is not enough to recognize the commonality of developmental failure; immaturity is also present among parents who neither neglect nor batter their children. Why the choice of symptom? Symptom choice, as we are well aware from more general work, is a perennial theoretical problem of psychopathology (Shapiro 1965).

Child Placement and Neglect in Southern Appalachia

Empirical work directed by the senior author on the causes of substandard child caring began in the spring of 1964. Through Charles Gershenson of the Children's Bureau, he was given a programmatic grant to study how to prevent the institutionalization of children living in southern Appalachia. The work began with scouting the problem by talking with local social workers, visiting homes, reading records of children who had been placed. Even after a lifetime of social work in prisons, mental hospitals, and social agencies, the case histories of many youngsters confined in a local delinquency institution made sickening reading. Hungry, dirty, clothed in rags, there were boys who were essentially on their own as early as seven or eight and living on the occasional largesse of strangers. These were not the tough and hostile "punks" one had known in urban settings; these youngsters were simply pitiful, and to them confinement in an "evaluation center" (what a euphemism!) first of all meant shelter and regular meals.

Many rural counties had no budgets at all for the foster care of children. Therefore numerous youngsters were being sent to "schools" conducted by charitable groups with strong religious ties. These schools seemed to vary wildly in the caliber of child care offered, as well as in the degree of fanaticism to which young children were being exposed. At best they seemed to offer a benign environment in which a child could grow up to take his place in the community and in the religious tradition espoused. Placement in such schools was likely to last until maturity, because they often saw no reason, and had no program, for moving their charges into foster homes. They were operating in the manner of the congregate institutions for dependent and neglected children we thought had been given up in this country. Few of these children were full orphans. Most seemed to come from backgrounds of family troubles and collapse, so that institutionalization was undertaken to provide essential child protection.

In short, it seemed that there were a number of services badly needed in these rural mountain counties in which workers, some of whom were heartening in their dedication and perceptiveness, had so little to work with in trying to rescue children. One such resource, the availability of AFDC payments for children in foster care, is an example of something missing at that time which has since been instituted. Research, however, is not the same as providing services. Services are, or ought to be provided when their need is obvious. Only matters that are truly not understood, that are nonobvious, warrant research.

The question repeatedly asked by thoughtful county directors of public welfare and their staffs was, How can we help these families improve their child care? What can be done other than removing children from their homes? Doing something about these families presupposed that one had reasonably clear formulations about what was wrong with them. But insight into causes was also missing. It turned out that the questions being raised in our professionally isolated corner of the country were very similar to those that were, or would be, raised nationally within a few years. We had no idea of that at the time, having had some expertise about the treatment of children in institutions and very little about where they came from.

So we approached the Children's Bureau with a request to recast the focus of our inquiry. The institutionalization of dependent children did not represent a puzzle, intellectually; it represented an unmet need for alternative facilities. However, the majority of children being placed, at least in this area, seemed first to have been deprived, neglected children. The prevention of institutionalization would require improving the level of care in their own homes. But no one seemed at all clear about what was typically going wrong in such families, what the "causes" were of the child neglect. Lacking such knowledge, how could one start a rational program for treating them?

We seemed, then, to have come upon a major gap in our knowledge, affecting the fates of hundreds of pathetic children. One could not hope to close the gap with a single study, but there was no doubt the effort should be made. Accordingly, we proposed to the Children's Bureau a program of studies into the causes of child neglect in southern Appalachia. Charles Gershenson, who seemed more like a fellow researcher than a grant manager, saw immediately the logical progression, and managed the bureaucratic rationale so that support could be continued. Some years later, when then-senator Mondale became exercised about child abuse, and, *sotto voce,* neglect, our little group in a field office in Asheville, North Carolina proved at times the only one in the country actively studying neglect. But it was not depth of experience, perspicacity, or knowledge, then, of the statistics recorded in chapter 2 that brought us to the problem. Rather, it was a combination of events, of ordinary logic, and of a willingness to tackle questions that are unwieldy but clinically meaningful. For in all such areas of "dirty" research, where the multiplicity of variables and lack of controls make definitive findings impossible, a scientist can keep going only by reiterating the slogan, "Some information is better than no information."

The Significance of Character

One approaches the study of a complex and relatively unmapped phenomenon with an open mind but, preferably, not an empty one. The latter should disqualify one from an area of inquiry, for the risk of wasting one's own research years and others' money becomes too great. Moreover, it is axiomatic that if the research aims to cast a rather wide net, it becomes doubly important to mark the boundary of the fishing grounds.

From preliminary scouting of the problem, our impression was that identified neglect in southern Appalachia, at least, was usually accompanied by family poverty. We did not assume that only the poor neglect their children. Previous work experience as therapists and researchers in private psychiatric facilities had offered too many instances of emotional and even physical neglect of children from upper-income families. We, of all social workers, were *less* likely to "blame the poor." Neither did the direction of causation, if there was such an association, seem at all clear. For example, the same personality inadequacies that led to neglect of children might also hinder the parent's efforts to earn and keep a decent income level. The decision to concentrate on low-income families, therefore, only implied an interest in making the results of the research as useful as possible to those doing the front-line work with neglectful families. But the decision to concentrate only on low-income families meant that the effects of income, as such, could not be brought under systematic scrutiny, for there was to be no comparison made with higher-income families. (The logic is identical with that in our critique, above, of the studies of the effects of poverty.)

We were also of the impression that there would be other researchers more committed to economic determinism than we were, who would be very likely to raise the poverty hypothesis. Our interest and, to an extent, expertise were in personality theory and clinical work, so it seemed reasonable we would be better able to make a contribution in these areas. Hence the study question became: What factors, other than low income, affect the level of care parents are providing their children?

A second major limitation of our initial research effort was the focus on the mother in each family. It was not presumed that fathers are irrelevant, or make no difference to the level of care. But given the reticence of most families we meant to study—especially to outsiders but even within the home—coupled with the nonverbal stance of most low-income mountain men, we simply did not believe it would be possible to engage very many fathers in our research. In fact, the very request that they participate themselves might well provoke some into forbidding their wives to enter the study. So the decision was to limit the study to the women only as informants and as the persons we might hope to interview and observe directly. It hardly seems necessary to state that to accept a limitation on one's research is *not* the same as to draw a conclusion or to presume what one might have found. We regretted the wisdom of this limitation the more since, in the majority of families being served in our area, there were two parents present. A further limitation, therefore, was to confine the study to two-parent homes.

The results of these studies have been previously reported in a monograph (Polansky, Borgman, and DeSaix 1972), so we will not detail them here. From an initial, descriptive pilot study of ten or eleven families identified as severely neglectful, a couple of leads emerged. One was the fact that when the mothers were interviewed regarding their child-rearing attitudes and practices, they gave answers that were often knowledgeable and socially acceptable. In other words, if one were to limit his data on child caring to what the mothers *said,* one would have a picture of the actual care that was at variance not only with that of the agency workers who had known the family over a period of months, but also with observations being made by our own research social workers. This finding has left a residual doubt about the probable validity of data from "one-shot interviews" that has never left our group. Instead, we rely on the greater openness about how a mother's life really is that seems to come with four or five contacts with her, supplemented by making use of what the worker observes while visiting the home, although these data are not without problems. The second lead to emerge was that, in studying the character structures of neglectful mothers, we would find ourselves preoccupied with two major themes: detachment and impulsivity. But we did not take the latter lead seriously at first.

Instead, our initial presumption was that we would find many instances of child neglect based in dynamics that were delimitable and that could be precisely phrased. For example, a woman who otherwise functioned reasonably well, but who had been resentful at being made to care for younger siblings when she was herself a child, might be too conflict-ridden to carry out the mothering role. Another, who had markedly unresolved Oedipal strivings would find her own motherhood too symbolic of a bitter competition with her own mother. The expectation was that one might find in child neglect instances of one or more genotypes analogous, let us say, to the "role-reversal" discovered among abusive parents. Once the forms of neurotic invasion of the child-caring function had been identified, the hope was to devise treatment approaches that were reasonably specific and could be taught to front-line workers. An example would be the mother whose poor child care was due to a reactive depression, so that the child neglect was secondary to self-neglect. There is a lot known about the interview treatment of mild depression in otherwise fairly intact people, and we would draw on this to help those working with the woman.

There was, of course, another possibility. The poor child care might prove but one expression of a pattern of traits pervading the maternal personality. But we were less interested in this and, in our naïveté, it appeared far less likely. In retrospect, it is clear that we preferred to see the women involved as neurotic, rather than character-disordered. Entranced by the clinical experience from which we recognized emotional dynamics the workers were unable to see, we underestimated the character pathology. But after several years of systematic work, that was not how things worked out. Comparing women whose children were receiving adequate care with a group whose care was poor to marginal, the evidence of systematic differences in enduring personality was unmistakable. As compared with identifying the character traits involved, the locating of encapsulated dynamic genotypes shrank in significance.

It is not that one never finds interesting dynamic constellations: rather, it synthesizes one's ideas better to see them within the context of the total character structure. For instance, we observed the need of many neglectful parents always to have a helpless infant; we remarked their lessening interest as the child achieved mobility. Thus we concluded that the baby was being used in large measure as an "adult pacifier," a bulwark against loneliness. Hence the threat "to make more" if the child is removed is not an idle one. But all these phenomena really stem from intense, unresolved separation anxiety, which is endemic in clients who are immature. In short, there are some fairly common dynamic constellations found in neglect; they are intriguing; they may prove important to case management. But from a scientific standpoint, it is parsimonious to recognize their roots in the structured aspect of personality we term "character."

The fact that one responds to the conjoint occurrence of traits by thinking, "But, of course . . ." ought not mislead us. One can seldom derive the constellation of traits by sheer logic, even though once they are discovered, their psychological symmetry is recognizable. Expressions of emotional immaturity, after all, are multifarious; it requires empirical work to identify the modes it will take in damaged parenting.

We also now see, as we did not then, that the meaning to be ascribed to a behavior also depends very much on its context in character. In a fairly intact neurotic, anxious clinging to one's infant might well represent the reaction-formation against destructive wishes that David Levy (1943) presumed. But in infantile persons elaborate defenses are rather rare; it is more efficient to infer simple separation anxiety as the basis for the clinging. Similarly, when our psychiatric consultant suggested concerning a depressed woman that "her child neglect is secondary to her self-neglect," he might have been assuming more ability to groom oneself than is typical of disorganized people, whether or not they are depressed at the moment (Polansky et al. 1968).

It was research, then rather than preference that pushed us from viewing neglectful behavior as an encapsulated symptom, and toward seeing it as more an expression of a pervasive style of life.

Four

The Apathy-futility Syndrome and Infantilism

Charles Loring Brace referred to the maltreating parents he knew as members of the "dangerous classes." Our studies led us reluctantly to conclude that chronically neglectful mothers are very likely to be character-disordered. Was this an advance for our profession, or had we merely fallen into a twentieth century version of labeling?

True, to diagnose someone as character-disordered does not mean that person is not worthy of respect. Neither should it convey that she is without many of the same feelings and strivings that are also present, at some level, in the rest of us. We have been at pains to point out that these mothers were understandable human beings, people with whom one could empathize and sympathize. They employed defense mechanisms familiar among clients and patients encountered in family counseling and mental health practice. So impressive was this that, at first, we overlooked how ominous many of their patterns really are. But character diagnosis that is not demonstrably relevant to guiding treatment may, in fact, amount to invidious labeling (Polansky 1979). What are the useful implications of this conception?

From a clinical standpoint, there are several. Most importantly, it suggests that the disability resides in large part inside the mother. Students of neglect who emphasize economic causes assume the parents involved are "average-expectable people," victims of external accidents of fate, such as poverty. But to describe someone as character-disordered is to acknowledge she is also life-accident-prone. Many of the external pressures she experiences are self-induced. Of course, poverty makes it all the more difficult for such a mother to cope; in fact, she is less able to cope than other mothers in the same miserable circumstances. For, unfortunately, it is nowhere written that one will have but a single disadvantage in this life.

A second implication is that the adjustment problems are pervasive, and not limited to poor child care. A third is that the evidences of inadequacy will prove to have been long-standing: it will be hard to trace them to either one or several events in the recent past which destroyed an otherwise promising course of living. And if there is anything most practitioners have learned well, it is that problems which are long-standing usually do not yield easily and readily to treatment. Hence one must be prepared for a process which will require considerable effort and money if it is to succeed; and the treatment may well not succeed, so that a variety of backup arrangements must also be readied. These implications associated with the term character-disorder may be treated as hypotheses for the research which will be described in chapters 8 and 11. The reader will then be in position to decide to what extent these hypotheses seem valid for a sample of neglectful parents.

The term character-disorder is a rather vague one. What are these parents like, more specifically? If there is a "modal personality" (Kardiner 1945) in parents whose children are being cared for poorly, our Appalachian studies strongly suggested that personality is markedly childlike. We found ourselves adopting an expression first used by Ruesch (1948) to describe patients most prone to psychosomatic illness: his term was "infantile personality." Although the word infantile sounds condescending, it does denote massive fixation better than does a word like "immature." The later is often used euphemistically, as in "I guess I'm a little immature."

To summarize our clinical and research findings for training purposes, we developed a list of types of women likely to be encountered in treating neglect situations (Polansky, DeSaix, and Sharlin 1971). Of course, we had nothing systematic to contribute about the fathers. Included, then, were five types: the apathetic-futile; the impulse-ridden; the mentally retarded; the woman in a reactive depression; and the woman who is borderline or even psychotic, which is rare. The listing was highly impressionistic, and so we have tried here to go beyond it (see chapter 8). All but one of these "types" could be expected chronically to show infantile features, and a mother in a reactive depression might show them in her temporary regression.

If its acceptance by protective service workers elsewhere is an indication, the listing was not without general validity. There has also been a related study that is intriguing because of its setting. Most work on neglect has occurred in areas where malnutrition is not a widespread problem. However Kerr, Bogues, and Kerr (1978) worked with families living in desperate poverty in the West Indies. Eleven mothers, whose children were pediatrically judged to be severely malnourished, were compared with others whose children had medical problems, but were not malnourished. The authors noted marked differences in the general psychosocial functioning of the two groups of women, all natives of the islands. They described the malnourishing mothers as fitting either the apathetic-futile or the impulse-ridden diagnoses that we had developed in southern Appalachia. One does not know whether to be pleased or appalled by the implied generality of our categories.

The Syndrome

Of the kinds of mothers indicated, the ones who interested us most were those fitting the "apathy-futility syndrome." They interested us because they included most of the women called to our attention by agencies offering protective services in the mountain counties. These were women who appeared passive, withdrawn, lacking in expression. Upon being interviewed, they showed many schizoid features, resembling in this way a number of patients from more fortunate economic backgrounds with whom we were familiar in private psychiatric hospitals. Their workers found them disorganized in their life-styles and child caring; they were also frustrating because, although they did not oppose the suggestions offered, neither did their care improve. The agency personnel did not know what to make of them or how to treat them and neither did we. After a time we were able to identify the following features, or character traits, as making up the pattern involved in the syndrome:

1. A pervasive conviction that nothing is worth doing. The feeling of futility predominates, as in the schizoid personality. As one patient used to say, "What's the use of eating supper; you'll only be hungry before breakfast."
2. Emotional numbness sometimes mistaken for depression. It is beyond depression; it represents massive affect-inhibition from early splitting in the ego.
3. Interpersonal relationships typified by desperate clinging; they are superficial, essentially lacking in pleasure, and accompanied by intense loneliness.
4. Lack of competence in many areas of living, partially caused by the unwillingness to risk failure in acquiring skills.

5. Expression of anger passive-aggressively and through hostile compliance.
6. Noncommitment to positive stands; even the stubborn negativism is a last-ditch assertion that one exists.
7. Verbal inaccessibility to others, and a related crippling in problem solving because of the absence of internal dialogue.
8. An uncanny skill in bringing to consciousness the same feelings of futility in others; this is used as a major interpersonal defense against efforts to bring about change. [Polansky 1979]

As with other ideal types, whether proposed for analytical purposes in sociology or for analogous reasons in clinical social work, we do not mean to imply all the parents who call this syndrome to mind embody it exactly. Rather, there are a number who typify it in every essential aspect; there are even more who resemble the syndrome closely, who have many apathy-futility features, but not all. In the latter cases, one suspects that much of the same underlying pathology has been at work, but perhaps not with the same severity that afflicted those most typical of the syndrome.

The reaction of front-line protective service workers in numerous workshops at which the syndrome has been discussed has been an encouraging sign of the syndrome's face validity. They find the constellation described recognizable in their caseloads, and have often expressed pleasure that it has been identified and organized. The last feature mentioned—that these client's feelings of futility are highly contagious to those charged with helping them—seems to be particularly apt. For this generation of nonpsychoanalytically trained workers, the notion that the contagion was unconsciously intentional (in the service of resistance) seems a new idea, albeit a believable one. They are more troubled by a related observation, namely, that no one outside the individual can stir such feelings *ex nihilo*, that they must be present in a repressed state in nearly all of us in order to be brought out.

There are other characteristics one might add: the tendency toward concreteness in thinking, all-or-none stereotyping, conversion reactions, and, more dangerously to the parent, psychosomatic illnesses due to an inability to resolve life's problems or express feelings verbally. A quality worth emphasizing is a serious deficiency in the capacity for self-observation. It is not only that these people have distorted self-images; it is that they are unable to take distance and observe themselves at all, as if such a separable organization within the ego—a splitting in the service of the ego—were impossible for them. But all these additions are traits common to all infantile personalities, including, for example, the impulse-ridden character.

These mothers almost never abandon their children outright.

Nor, indeed, do they break up their marriages, for they are too desperately attached to their husbands. But they are likely to be involved in the most chronic, severe child neglect that falls just short of the point at which children are simply removed. Our impression from talking to workers was that this was the most ominous parental diagnosis and, when we devised a way of rating the mothers studied along a scale measuring the *degree* of apathy-futility, it correlated negatively and substantially with the quality of care the children were receiving. The syndrome, in other words, seemed highly significant to child neglect.

Accordingly, we made efforts to trace the etiology involved, asking two quite different questions. First, to what extent did the apathy-futility appear to derive from very early deprivations in these mother's own lives? Second, was the apathy-futility related to other major forces at work in the mountain culture? These questions lie at different levels of theorizing, to be sure, but they are not mutually exclusive.

Cultural Influences

As compared with most of the rest of America, the population of southern Appalachia is geographically stable and homogeneous with regard to variables like race, religion, even income. This is WASP country, but a place in which average income is well below the national norm. Many families are Scotch-Irish in origin, others, English and German, with a few from other northern European countries. However, those of us who had lived in other rural areas found the characteristics of neighbor-watching and reserve toward outsiders typical of small communities everywhere. The culture, however, is no more monolithic than is any other, viewed from close up. The middle- and upper-middle income classes are nearly indistinguishable from country club sets throughout American small towns. What, then, were some distinctive themes? Our interest, of course, was not in the positive values, of which there were many, but in those we labeled "regressive" (Polansky, Borgman, and DeSaix 1972, p. 75), which seemed to contribute to lowering standards of child caring. These themes were:
1. Penis worship and infantilizing the males.
2. Separation anxiety, conformity, and trying to maintain the fusion-fantasy.
3. Inexpressiveness and verbal inaccessibility.
4. Fatalism and powerlessness as defenses against blame and guilt.

The participant observation through which these themes were identified and formulated was supplemented by a couple of small quantitative studies. From these, it appeared that the reported feelings of powerlessness were greater among lower-class children than among those higher in socioeconomic status. Verbal accessibility also appeared class-linked in the mountains—the lower the class, the less accessibility. These results were fragmentary, but they suggested that the traits we might consider regressive were more visible among teenagers of lower-class background than those who were more advantaged. Cultural support for attitudes of conformity, powerlessness, inexpressiveness, and the like might well contribute to the personality structure we termed apathetic-futile, or to immaturity in general.

Generalizing beyond Appalachia, one might argue that the themes identified are widely prevalent among the poor. Those preferring economic explanations may insist that these attitudes were both inaccurate reflections of the actual powerlessness of the very poor in our society, or adaptations to the hardships of poverty. We, however, found this formulation hard to accept. For one thing, there were such wide variations among women's responses to being poor. Some were energetic and humorous in struggling against it; others were resigned; still others immobilized. Only a small minority are truly apathetic-futile. Hardly any strike us as "fully mature," rich or poor. But certainly most of the poor are not infantile.

Character Traits of Neglectful Mothers

A sample of mothers at or below the poverty level was recruited. Using our Childhood Level of Living Scale (see chapter 6), the level of child care was quantified. The women were then judged to be high or low on child care. Many of the latter provided care that was poor or marginal, and the thinking was that differences detected among these women would, by extension, help to explicate outright neglect.

All mothers in the study were interviewed and social histories obtained using an outline standard in psychiatric settings. The women also participated in psychological testing that included shortened versions of the usual clinical battery: Wechsler, Rorschach, TAT. Based on the research caseworkers' observations and impressions, mothers' personalities were also scaled on a variety of personality dimensions, using our Maternal Characteristics Scale. Since this was an exploratory study, attempting personality exploration under difficult field conditions, our methods of measurement often had to be developed *ad hoc*. Moreover, as in all such exploratory-diagnostic studies, we were not very clear about what we were looking for. But we emerged with the following sketch of the typical mother-at-risk:

She is of limited intelligence (IQ below 70), has failed to achieve more than an eighth-grade education, and has never held public employment. She married the first or second man who showed an interest in her, and he proved to be ill equipped in education and in vocational skills. She has at best a vague, or extremely limited, idea of what her children need emotionally and physically. She seldom is able to see things from the point of view of others and cannot take their needs into consideration when responding to a conflict they experience. She herself has grown up in a family in which her parents were retarded or showed deviant or criminal behavior. [Polansky, Borgman, and DeSaix 1972, p. 120]

This is obviously a portrait of a generally poorly functioning, adaptively limited person who might be expected to fit the conception of the infantile personality. Why were these women infantile? The main etiological lead we had was that they had been deprived in early life, quite probably in their first year, by their own parents. But we were not able to demonstrate this so much as to remark the congruence of their characters with patterns predictable from the clinical theories of Spitz (1945), Bowlby (1961), Guntrip (1969), and others. From the evidence of inadequacies in their families of orientation, we also identified what we termed "an intergenerational cycle of neglect." We hypothesized that this came, ultimately, from the passing on of infantilism, mother to daughter, through processes of deprivation leading to detachment (the "deprivation-detachment hypothesis"), failure to provide stimulation, and the child's identification with an inadequate role model. Hence the cycle of neglect might be said to derive from a cycle of infantilism.

This, then, was about where we had arrived in our more structured empirical work. Because the work was exploratory, there were deficiencies in design and methodology of which we were all too conscious. Even more serious, in the opinion of many colleagues, was the fact that the study had been done in an area that was not only rural, but that was widely thought to have a culture rather different from most of America. Our own feelings about the latter issue were mixed. Appalachia is somewhat "special," but do American mothers differ very much in their values about basic child care? Moreover, our observations were being read, and presumably used, by workers in distant, urban areas. Still, the real test would be to repeat the study, in improved form, in an urban setting. To this we turn next.

Five

The Design of
the Philadelphia Study

Six years after completing the diagnostic study of the causes of neglect in the mountains of southern Appalachia, the senior author set out to replicate it in Philadelphia. A grant was obtained from the National Center on Child Abuse and Neglect, and the investigator moved the study to the School of Social Work of the University of Pennsylvania. The aims of the replication were several. First, there was a need to cross-validate the associations originally found, that is, to see whether similar results would obtain when the study was repeated. For in a study with many variables, some associations that appear statistically reliable could be chance occurrences. Cross-validating, of course, requires that the repetition be done with instruments identical with, or at least very similar to, those used in the first study. A second aim of the replication was to make certain improvements in the design of the study. Based on what one learned from the first effort, and what one regretted about it, several elaborations could be introduced.

But the biggest reason for repeating the study stemmed from a question frequently asked when its results were presented: "This is very interesting about rural Appalachians, but do you think it applies to a big city like the one I work in?" The only way to test the generality of the results of studies like our is to repeat them in other places. Ideally, one would repeat the study in a sample of localities elsewhere, but such a procedure is seldom feasible. We chose the alternative, namely, to redo the study in a setting which was obviously widely different from the first. Moving from a rural mountainous area, thinly settled, to a metropolis of the North provided an enormous contrast—in characteristics of the underlying populations, in housing, in style of life.

So great was the alteration in the investigator's daily round that it was hard to believe he was the same person, conducting this related study, and in the same lifetime. Except for having an eerie familiarity with details of the study's conception and execution, it could have been done by someone else. Maintaining objectivity was hardly a problem, since there was not all that marked a sense of owning the previous work. We wonder whether colleagues who have done the same sorts of replications have experienced similar sensations.

In the opening pages of the earlier work, *Roots of Futility,* the scene was set by describing the breathtaking beauty of the Great Smoky Mountains in which the research took place. How anomalous the bitter neglect of children seemed against the backdrop of God's creativity. And how ironic the contrast between the Smokies and the neighborhood in which we set up our field office so as to be more accessible to the families among whom we worked.

Urban Pathways to Neglect

Pathways lead to a city. A city of row houses, boat houses, townhouses, apartments, soft pretzels, Philadelphia cheese steaks, and the Liberty Bell. A city of neighborhoods—Fishtown, Kensington, South Philadelphia, Manayunk, Germantown—each with its own history and flavor; each adding to the historical patchwork quilt called Philadelphia. This is the city where we worked for two years. Into its colorful ethnic neighborhoods we were welcomed as learners and observers.

It was the summer of America's two hundredth birthday, and in Philadelphia's blue collar neighborhoods the celebration went on for weeks. The early, tentative decorations were sparse: a lone manhole cover painted blue with a white "'76" in the middle. By the weekend of the Fourth, restraint had given way to a frenzy of red, white, and blue. The narrow streets, lined with two-story row houses on both sides, turned into striped roadways. Every fire hydrant sported stars and stripes, every street sign was outlined in red and blue. The American eagle, executed with varying degrees of skill, adorned sidewalks and streets, but most ubiquitous were the stars, the '76's, and the stripes. Plastic triangular flags were strung across the streets, from second story to second story. Their loud flapping in the summer breezes was a reminder, for weeks afterwards, of the great American birthday party.

Even in a time of high unemployment, not contributing extra money to the kitty for block decorations would have been an unpatriotic act. Pride in the neighborhood, in the block, in the good life in America was unashamed. It was toasted with beer, by the case. Here was a party to which everyone in the neighborhood was invited.

Philadelphia, "the city of neighborhoods," was settled by immigrants from many European countries. The inhabitants recognize vast differences among themselves, but to the researcher the similarities in their ways of life, and in the look and feel of the various neighborhoods, are more striking. Always there is "the Avenue," that center of the community where the Army recruiter in a trailer in front of the largest bank is joined in March by representatives from the Internal Revenue Service. Stores, large and small, abound, offering easy credit. In the spring, mothers promenading along the avenue display for general admiration the winter crop of babies in their carriages, and maternity tops over their jeans announce things to come. Parades in a more formal sense also add to the sociability, a favorite being the Baby Parade at Halloween with prizes for costumes in many categories. Pictures announcing the winners are always published in the local weekly, and when there are no prizes to announce, photographs of children celebrating birthdays, sent by proud mothers, often appear.

The smallest unit in the neighborhood is the block, and a cluster of a relatively few blocks encompasses a named section. In many sections, factories intrude into the residential area; only the best sections do not share their living space with industry. Housed in the second floor of a renovated storefront row house was our office, graciously rented to us by the local community center. Some of our neighbors became participants in the study. Across the street, facing our row of houses, stood a meat-packing plant. In the course of a year we watched the men on their cigarette breaks, then we saw them picketing, and finally, when they left, auction signs went up. Critical to the life of our block was the corner store, whose owner, knowing that we were social workers, tried each lunchtime to find out a bit more local gossip. A drugstore and two bars, one of which stayed closed because its owners had been caught selling liquor to minors, completed the block.

The trees which survived beyond the sapling stage were rare, although most blocks showed space dug out of the sidewalks where attempts at growing them had been made. Newly broken saplings along one block evoked some mourning from the women, who complained about teenagers becoming drunk and destructive. Rationalizing the loss, they also acknowledged that the trees got in the way of the cars, which also used the sidewalk for navigation or for parking.

When the weather is warm, the street is welcomed as an extension of the house. A place to socialize, not only for the children, it is the meeting place for mothers, for teenagers (who get off the blocks and onto the corners—a little out of sight, if possible), and at night, for couples. Lawn chairs are brought out, along with beer and pretzels, to while away the hot summer nights and hope for a drop in the humidity. In spite of the lure of television, summer still calls forth the tradition of sitting on the stoop.

There is a quality of togetherness to this life, of neighborhoods where life has its own rhythm and stability. Comings and goings are known to everyone. For the families who were raised in the neighborhood, whose parents, brothers, sisters, and cousins still live here, living anywhere else or in any other way is unthinkable. Friends are friends from high school, and the security of having known one another for many years adds to the feeling of being connected—and also to that of being detached from the rest of the city. Visits to downtown are reserved for special occasions: to take the kids to see Santa Claus and the "Enchanted Village" at the recently defunct Lit Brothers department store or to see the Liberty Bell. But the real celebrations, the real evenings out—to the movies or to dinner—take place right in the neighborhood, in its movie theater, in its bars and small restaurants. Physically and psychologically, the local territory provides enough, and most people are satisfied with it.

All families, however, do not share in the comfortable stability which is the hallmark of the area. Many blocks now have renters instead of home owners. Money and skills to keep the houses in good repair through painting, replacing rotted window frames and old roofs, and thus preserving these fifty- to eighty-year-old homes for comfortable habitation, are too often in short supply. Time and again we visited home which were in the process of renovation. There is a mystique in the neighborhood that its men have all sorts of skills—for carpentry, plumbing, and electrical work—which in fact they possess only minimally. Thus panelling would be installed which was not plumb; the popular dropped ceiling would be left unfinished because "it didn't come out even"; the toilet wouldn't flush quite right because "something is wrong with it." Frequently skills are traded, but even more often one's house is left in a state of incompletion. Sometimes this is because of a lack of knowledge about how to fix what goes wrong, or because of a decline of interest in the project, or because money is needed for more essential things. Often the men who work at physically demanding jobs do not want to do more hard work when they come home, and those who are unemployed lack the spirit to face the added frustration of working at something they do not do very well. So piles of panelling sit in living rooms, sometimes for years at a time.

For these politically powerless areas, municipal services are frequently sporadic or nonexistent. When the sanitation workers had a "slow-down," weeks with no garbage collection whatsoever went by, making the summer-baked streets reek while rats and flies feasted. Gas company repairmen left a half-finished job which led to a gathering of rats, a situation corrected only when outraged residents, unable to force a response from appropriate authorities, finally called in television's "Action News." Although there are some well-equipped playgrounds, the small city parks are mostly dusty, bottle-strewn wastelands, both unsafe and unappealing. Promises to build a community swimming pool in one area progressed to the hole-in-the-ground phase and stayed that way for two years. Some community mobilization has occurred through the efforts of a small number of social workers based in the few remaining settlement houses, or through neighborhood action groups. However, to get an equal share for these low-priority sections of the city demands a real struggle—one for which most residents have no heart.

For in spite of the positive qualities of these neighborhoods, there is also a "dead end" feeling about them. A high dropout rate in the schools, young marriages frequently forced by unexpected pregnancy, low job expectations, and personal problems of alcoholism, marital difficulties, and depression all feed into the same sense that "no one cares about us." Services to help solve the problems of living are scarce and overburdened. Outreach to those in need is not generally accomplished. For those families not well-woven into the tightly knit fabric of community life—those less successful, more struggling families—life is a strain, stretching the capacity of people to survive. The built-in insularity of the neighborhoods, of which they are a part, but not an accepted part, often permits them to go unnoticed and neglected.

Among the urban poor, as among the rural, life was hard for everyone. But their children were nearly universally loved and most of them were being well cared for. Some, alas, were not. As in the mountains, the overall question for study was: in families, all of whom are low-income, what distinguishes parents whose children are being neglected from the parents of those who are not?

The Sampling Design

To answer this question required locating a sample of low-income households identified by a social agency as neglectful, in order to make an intensive study of the personalities of the parents involved.

However, in order to ensure that our findings had to do with low standards of child caring, rather that with poverty, we would need a comparison sample made up of parents whose incomes were also low, but who were not regarded as neglecting their children. Other factors could be controlled for or varied systematically by the way cases were incorporated into the study. Some variables were controlled by the imposition of "sampling conditions," that is, criteria setting boundaries for the sorts of families to be included in the study, whether in the neglect or nonneglect group. The Appalachian study had been done in an area so homogeneous that the matching of subsamples on factors like race and birthplace was more or less automatic. For example, well over 90% of current residents of several mountain counties we encountered had been born in the same county. Few American cities approach such homogeneity, of course, so we will now list the factors that were taken into account in the sampling.

Income

The parents studied in the Appalachians were low-income, but self-supporting for the most part. It required considerable thought to try to set standards to recruit a group that would be comparable in Philadelphia. One idea was to take a local figure said to represent the poverty level, multiply it by 1.25, and use the result as our ceiling. Unfortunately, this standard would have yielded a sample made up entirely of households on public assistance. So we shifted to the Bureau of Labor Statistics Low Budget figure for Philadelphia. When we began recruiting cases in the fall of 1975, the most recent figure available was for fall 1974. Based on this, the ceiling was set at about $9400 for a family of four. By the fall of 1976 there had been an upward shift in the cost of living revising the Low Budget upwards, and so our ceiling was moved to around $10,000 for a family of four. The ceilings guaranteed that all families included were low-income in that place and time. But there could be variation beneath the ceiling. The degree of match between the samples obtained will be discussed later in this chapter, where we will report our method for making incomes comparable among families varying in composition and size.

Race

Substantial numbers of Philadelphians are black, and the neglect of black children is as significant as it is in any group. It would have been appropriate and desirable to have included black families in our study. However, one could not simply pool cases, regardless of ethnicity, unless it were safe to presume that race has no impact on life-style on the one hand, or personality on the other. To be conservative, one ought not make such an assumption, but instead conduct identical studies in both groups and determine empirically whether the associations obtained are similar. This extension would have required our running, in effect, two parallel studies.

Our grant provided neither the financial resources nor the authorization to attempt such a major elaboration of our original work, which was involved almost wholly with whites. Given the difficulty of the study of whites only, we cannot argue with the wisdom of the review committee in so limiting us. At the time of our research, there was considerable racial animosity in the City of Brotherly Love. During a period of declining research support, we also encountered much guarding of professional turf. In short, the politics of behavioral science suggested that extensions into other racial groups would have better chances of success when conducted by scientists from those groups. Later in the work, we shared all our instruments and preliminary results with several black researchers, but there was no follow through. Perhaps this report will encourage others to undertake the extensions, for we strongly suspect that the parental character traits associated with child neglect in this country are about the same in all cultural groups.

The Focal Child

Studying a family's level of child caring presupposes there is a child in the picture whose care can be observed and scaled for measurements. However, the care that is necessary to sustain life in a six-month-old would have a grossly retarding effect if given a child of eight. A way to reduce the complexity of measuring care is to confine the age-range under study. In this research, therefore, all families included had at least one child living in the home who was between four and seven years old at the time of the study. If there were two children between these ages, the one to be studied was picked at random, and was termed the "focal child" in our research.

The measurement of the level of care each focal child was receiving was taken as representative of the care being generally given by those parents. The scaling involved is described in chapter 6. Several investigators have reported that abuse is often practiced on one child in a family with the other children exempted. Picking a child at random to represent the abuse in the family, then, would be dubious procedure. But neglect, we had already learned, is rarely so selective.

Requiring the presence of a focal child as a sampling condition of course influenced the types of parents our study might include. Automatically ruled out were households of such squalor and debilitation that protective service workers had already succeeded in having all the children removed. Remaining, then, were families whose care might be seriously deficient, and others for whom removal of the children was at least a possibility. The most severely neglectful were excluded.

Presence or Absence of the Father

All households in the mountain study included both parents. The couples were married and the father figure, in nearly every instance, was the biological father as well. In Philadelphia, inclusion of a group identified as neglectful brought this sampling condition into question, for a very large proportion of neglect cases were said to be fatherless households. Eliminating such cases would make the group sampled very atypical; moreover, it would hamper efforts to obtain a reasonably sized group of neglect cases. With the advice of our late colleague Leonard Kogan, therefore, we decided to make a virtue of necessity and study the ways in which presence or absence of the father seemed to affect nurture in both neglect and nonneglect households.

The decision required that the sampling recruit substantial numbers with both types of family structure in both comparison groups. Our original intention was to obtain fifty families containing both parents for the control group, since this pattern was, of course, normative in the subculture under study. Twenty-five families with the father absent were to have been included as well to provide contrast with this variable, but we found ourselves in negotiations with more than that number about the time we meant to close intake, and rather than disappoint any, we ended up with twenty-nine. Among families identified as neglectful, a far smaller group from which to draw recruits, no effort was made to select on this dimension. However, of those who cooperated with the study, the sample was divided nearly equally between families with the father present and those with the father absent.

Recruiting Cases

Having developed a sampling design, we were ready to invite families to participate in the study. How to proceed with the list for invitations? A purist would argue that the control sample ought to consist of families drawn at random from metropolitan Philadelphia. The principles for generating a reasonable degree of representation through stratified area sampling are pretty well understood. Unfortunately, the operations required simply to identify households in locations to be approached would have used up much of our budget. And having identified such households, their members would then have to agree to a minimal screening interview for ethnicity, income level (a sore topic for some), and presence of a focal child, enormously reducing the sample in this urban area. One would emerge from this phase with only a residuum of families to invite into the study. Some of them could be expected to decline, so that the sample obtained, despite the pains taken, would still not be a random one.

All this would have to take place before any serious data collection could get under way, in a study with a two-year limit on funds granted. The thought occurred that there must be issues in studies like this that are more significant than the precise degree of representativeness of the comparison sample. The main purpose of the sampling design, after all, was to provide groups with contrasting levels of child care, the variable of interest. So we turned to the task of purposive sampling.

Philadelphia is, indeed, a city of neighborhoods. Several are made up of people who are predominately white and low-income, and they also have community newspapers. A major means for recruiting families into the study was the placement of small advertisements which read, "Help others and earn good money for your family by participating in our study of urban childhood," followed by a telephone number. Persons who responded were told about the study in general terms, and an appointment was made to visit and secure signed agreement to participate after detailed explanation, if that was the decision. The offer of fifty dollars for each family who cooperated in the study was an important inducement, of course, especially since there was a mild recession in the city about the time we began our work.

Another important channel for contacts with potential nonneglect families was referral from agencies (e.g., community centers) of families who seemed to fit our criteria and needed the money; we also had an interesting number of parents who had already entered the study referring their friends. Some effort was made to reach out to various parts of Philadelphia for control families to make the samples more comparable to the neglect sample. For example, there were hardly any low-income Jewish families with young children still in our neighborhood, but there were several in the neglect sample, so we recruited a number known to workers at the Jewish Community Center some miles away.

Recruiting control cases and sustaining their collaboration with our study required both casework skills and patience. It also required, in part, a scrupulous adherence to absolute confidentiality, as in any good social agency. No person is a "case" until one begins analyzing the data statistically, and the personal and social history shared often involves painful facts and feelings necessarily kept secret. Thus no case was identified by name, only by a number. And not only were all case records kept constantly under lock, but the master list matching names to cases was hidden securely. No information was shared except with the parents' express permission, even with the agency which may have referred the family to the study in the first place. Such measures to maintain confidentiality are not only part of our ethics, they are a necessary part of the research social workers' assurance in dealing with families. And our workers needed all the assurance that could be mustered, particularly in working with many in the neglect sample.

If accumulating control cases went fairly routinely, recruiting parents for the neglect sample was something else again. Of course one anticipated that there would be difficulty in making and keeping contact with a study population of parents of whom nearly all were beleaguered and most were suspicious. A great many led disorganized lives and were vastly indifferent to matters like appointment times, worker's job pressures, and the like. It was also expected that there would be families who fit the study criteria and were known to be agencies, but who could not be referred. In some instances the client might be too fragile to bear an additional intrusion; in more, the relationship to the protective services worker might be too fragile to bear the load of any suggestion extraneous to the worker's immediate job with the family. So we were under no illusion that this aspect of the study would be at all easy. Indeed, it was knowledge of the complexity, as well as the need to have personnel sensitive to clients' needs and anxieties, which led the senior author to employ only well-trained, experienced caseworkers to undertake the work of interviewing.

It was also expected, however, that most agency personnel would lend support to serious efforts to research the causes of neglect. None could claim that the problems of these parents were yet well understood, nor that their treatment showed many successes. While research cannot promise results, there is always the possibility that from more knowledge will come better designed methods of treatment. Regarding possible effects arising from our research interventions, it really did not seem likely that asking some questions of a person who was always in the position of being able to evade or avoid answering—and who was, moreover, being interviewed by a person trained to "back off" sensitive areas if necessary—could be damaging. Compared to the barrage of physical violence they experienced outside the doors of their apartments, and sometimes within them, our assaults on clients' "defenses" were trivial. There was also the legitimate question of clients' rights to be, or not be, studied. But it must be obvious that no one can be included in an interview study except willingly.

Nevertheless, we encountered massive resistance to the proposed research in the local agency we had counted on to refer the bulk of the identified cases, the Philadelphia Department of Public Welfare's protective services units. The resistance did not come from the administrators involved, so far as we could tell. The feeling came to a head in a tense meeting of the staff workers at which we explained the study and asked for their help in referring families. No family, by the way, was to be "referred" directly to the study; agency referral simply meant the client would have been approached about his willingness to have the study explained to him. Only after receiving signed permission to be approached by us would we contact the family. Then, as with the control sample, the client could decide to enter the study or decline, taking into account what was expected and what they would be paid for the six to ten hours of time involved. A minimum, actually, was being asked of any protective services worker, since we had been repeatedly warned of their large caseloads and work pressure.

The reasons for the workers' resistance to the research were several, at least as expressed by some. First, they felt money was being wasted on research that would be better spent on clients. This opinion was most strongly held among those who regarded the parents as "victims of the system," people whose troubles stemmed primarily from dire poverty. Second, some felt the research was a violation of "clients' rights," a term that of course is definable *ad libidem* by whomever is using it. Third, there was some concern about damage to relationships with clients. This latter concern seemed inconsistent when combined with statements to the effect that they seldom saw most of their cases, but were completely occupied handling emergencies that arose in their very large caseloads. In the background was the fact that worker-administrator relationships were very strained, in part because of a strike by the workers that had occupied most of the previous summer. Also in the background was a contempt for the seeking of knowledge which was generally characteristic of their generation at that time. The social workers' contempt was exacerbated by the profitable studies which academic entrepreneurs and "hustlers" from Philadelphia's many universities had been conducting among the community's poor for two decades to no useful effect. But much of this we learned too late. Meanwhile, only a few cases were referred from the agency, which should have been our main source. It was liking hosting a party to which no one came.

One group of protective service workers nearly destroyed the study; another group of social workers saved it. Our rescuers were the administrators and staffs of private social agencies dealing with children and their families, and the leaders and staff of the Delaware County Care Service, which served areas coterminous with the city of Philadelphia. Our gratitude to these thoughtful people is very great, for without their assistance there would have been no study. The Delaware County Child Care Service was the public protective services agency for its county. Private agencies were of course involved in cases of neglect either through referral for service from the responsible public agency, the Department of Public Welfare, or because families who had come to them, or had been referred to them, had proven to be neglectful. They screened their caseloads for families that appeared to fit our criteria and, unless it were professionally inadvisable, mentioned our study to them. Through these channels and others, we eventually recruited a total of forty-six families into the neglect sample.

What criteria did the agency workers use in identifying cases as "neglectful"? Naturally they asked us for our definition of neglect, since we were doing the research. Yet it was important to the design that this judgment be made independently. Therefore the definition offered them was deliberately rather general, encouraging them to use the definitions "common in our field." As a result, we are able to study in chapter 6 the question of whether our measurement of the child's level of care proved valid against judgments by colleagues that were made independently.

Despite the worrisome fashion in which it had to be accumulated, the neglect sample as finally obtained appeared representative. (Later we shall compare the neglect and nonneglect cases on a number of demographic characteristics. Several factors distinguishing the neglect are in line with previous reports in the literature.)

Before describing the methods of data collection, we should state the rationale of the study as it was given to prospective participants. The research was interpreted as an effort to learn more about things that affect how children are reared in cities, with the hope that such knowledge would help in planning services really needed by them and by their families. We were particularly interested in including families whose incomes were limited, or who might otherwise have been dealing with difficulties. Parents referred by an agency were told, in addition, that we understood from their workers that things had not been easy for them, and therefore we were the more eager to know how things seemed to them. The name given our operation was Urban Childhood; it appeared on our stationery, cards, and so forth, and is preserved on T-shirts which were presented us by the clerical staff at the end of the project. The advantages of this rationale were that it was relatively uncomplicated, that it was short, and that it was tactful but accurate. The offer of money played a major role in most people's motivation to enter the study, but once in it, the majority were also interested in helping us find out "how it is," in their situations.

The Method of Collecting Data

Although the present study aimed, in part, to replicate that in the mountains, it would have been foolish to have collected its data in an identical manner. The original work was heavily exploratory, asking "Are there any discernible differences?" It culminated, really, with the generation of hypotheses. A subsequent study, therefore, could be far more pointed; it could ask, "Is this characteristic of parents who offer substandard care confirmable and general?"

How Close the Replication?

That we could be more specific about questions and hypotheses under study permitted extension and improvement in a couple of ways. Some directions of exploraiton had proved unpromising; they could be dropped from the replication, making room for new avenues not originally considered. Examples of such elaboration were the studies of paternal personality and role in neglect (chapters 8, 10) and of helping networks (chapter 7). Previous experience, of course, facilitated the design of instruments that were more complete and more clearly focused, as well. Thus the initial study collected maternal social history following a standard, rather loose guide devised by the investigator from his clinical and hospital experience. For the replication, much history could be collected with a semistructured interview outline, since the elements of greater interest were already identified. The advantages of the latter were, of course, in ensuring similar matters were being covered by all three interviewers in about the same way, and in greatly easing the later task of ordering a mass of material for statistical analysis. (The interview outlines for the study, including those for women living with a man in the home, for mothers living single, and for fathers constitute altogether some fifty pages of typescript. In the interest of economy, it was decided not to reproduce them in the appendixes. Researchers who have need for the instruments can obtain them by writing the senior author at the School of Social Work, University of Georgia, Athens, Georgia, 30602.)

We even discovered that to adhere too closely to the original may invalidate a replication study. For example, a Childhood Level of Living Scale (or CLL) had been devised to facilitate rating the caliber of care of the focal child. Perhaps because there was nothing quite like it, the scale had proved interesting to other students of neglect, most of whom were working in cities. But the original CLL was fitted to discriminating differences among rural, low-income families, most of whom lived in small, single homes, often isolated and lacking such amenities as telephone service. It certainly did not seem to us that slavish use of the same instrument would be a valid indicator of the quality of nuture in one of Philadelphia's older row houses. With an instrument of such doubtful validity, how could one test for an association between a parental characteristic and resultant child care? The pursuit of *content* hypotheses, then, argued in favor of modifying certain instruments to fit the changed environment of the study (see chapter 6). While this was not the senior author's first experience of replicating a complicated field study, the issues of scientific method raised by this one were unique in his experience. Throughout, the decision was to opt for validity over constancy of measurement, although the latter is also highly desirable in replications.

An Overview of the Measurements

Details of measurement operations are seldom memorable except when presented in reasonably close conjunction with the hypotheses and questions involved, as well as the results. Therefore, specifics of questions asked, scale items utilized, and the like, will be reserved for later chapters as they become relevant. It can be said, generally, that the methodology represented a marriage of behavioral science with the clinical practice of social work. Thus in talking with a parent, the research caseworker followed an interview outline which included probes, and recorded the parent's answers verbatim on the form. When the worker returned to the office, the record of the interview was supplemented with narrative dictation of interactions with the client that had seemed meaningful and revealing, observations of the home, additional information about his or her experiences, and attitudes the parent might have volunteered. The narrative records proved extremely useful in a number of ways. For example, we were able to retrieve enough information from these to test several hypotheses not thought of in advance. They were, naturally, absolutely essential to the worker's efforts, later in the process, to write sketches of parents who might serve as exemplars of personalities or situations encountered.

Narrative records have been used traditionally as bases for coding or scaling clients and their life-situations. Ours were later used in just that way, in obtaining assessments from outside judges or case readers (chapter 8). However, as in the original study, it seemed to us that the person best equipped to quantify the data by rating what was observed was the person who was in the home, the research caseworker. Consequently, we repeated the device of asking that the worker himself or herself fill out several scales that served to summarize observations made. Examples of these scales were the Childhood Level of Living Scale (chapter 6) and the Maternal Characteristics Scale (chapter 8).

The impressions informing the workers's ratings came from

interviewing, from interacting and observing in the home, and, at times, from others who knew the family and told us about it. For while we were wary of sharing what we knew, we did not hesitate to listen. There were many instances in which, as it turned out, we ended knowing more about a household than the referring worker, if only because our role became less threatening; but there were probably as many others in which the validity of our ratings was helped considerably by additional information.

Data collection also included psychological testing by a person on our staff, using abbreviated versions of the Wechsler Adult Intelligence Scale, the Rorschach, the Thematic Apperception Test and the Draw-a-Person with mother and father. Children were tested with the Wechsler Scale that was age-appropriate, with the Draw-a-Person, and with the Bender Gestalt. Parents also verbally completed a short scale having to do with alienation, which proved revealing, and a tedious scale concerning values about child rearing which, to the dismay of the senior author, came to naught and will not be much mentioned.

The process of interviewing began with a conference in the mother's home during which she was given questions about the developmental history of the focal child. One or, more often, two more visits were needed to complete getting her own social history. In families where the father was in the home, an effort was made to see him for a single, fairly lengthy interview, which also yielded social history, but not in the detail elicited from the mother. Next, mother and focal child came to the field office or, more typically, were brought by the research social worker for psychological testing. The psychologist was not told whether the case was neglect or control. It was usual for the father to be tested at another time, outside working hours. Some mother-child pairs also accompanied the worker to a local public hospital, where the mother was given a physical by a nurse-practitioner and the child was examined by a pediatrician. At this point the family would have fulfilled its contract, and the parents were paid the fee promised. However we offered in all instances to provide an interpretation of the results of psychological testing. A very high proportion of the parents were interested in getting those concerning the focal children, especially, and also those about themselves.

This, let us say, was the process: when cooperation was good, parents were organized and considerate and did not suffer mishaps like illness or hospitalizations or jailings, and there were no slip-ups on our side. No experienced protective services worker would have expected this process to be routine with very many of the neglect families.

The Comparability of the Samples

In recruiting parents into the study, the sampling conditions described above were followed. Because all cases met these criteria there was automatically a certain amount of matching between neglectful and nonneglectful samples. Variables held constant in this way included ethnicity, locus of residence, and having a young child in the household. There was also a ceiling on family income, although this was a rough figure during the recruitment, permitting variability within the groups. Thus one question to be addressed is the degree of matching that occurred between our two main samples. A second question emerges from the fact that the difficulties in assembling neglect cases for study raise questions about the representativeness of that sample. Was it like some others described in related studies in the literature?

Income

Family incomes could be expressed simply as dollars per month, but this figure would be misleading as a sign of standard of living. For a household of three, an income of $600 per month meant one thing; to a family of seven, it meant something else. How, then, to weight the actual figures given us by families in order to make incomes comparable, taking family size and composition into account? With the help of Dr. June Axinn of the University of Pennsylvania, we discovered the "Revised equivalence scale for urban families" published by the Bureau of Labor Statistics (1960–61). When this scale was combined with the Bureau's Lower Budget for Autumn, 1976, it was possible to calculate a figure required for each family to achieve that budget. The actual income of each family could then be divided by the standard computed to fit it, and family income could then be expressed as a decimal, that is, the proportion of the standard which its own income met. If the Bureau of Labor Statistics figures indicated a family needed $750 per month to achieve the lower budget but the family income was $600, the family's ratio would be .800; if their income was $900, the ratio would be 1.200.

The mean income ratios for the various subsamples were then calculated (these are reserved for chapter 10, where they become relevant to understanding the plight of families living without a father in the home). For present purposes, we may note that the mean ratios of the neglect and nonneglect samples did not differ significantly ($P < .19$ by ANOVA). However, if we simply classify cases in terms of whether or not they were below the low budget standard, we find that 84% of the neglect families were below as were 65% of the controls. This difference was significant at beyond

.05 by Chi-square test. In their study, Giovannoni and Billingsley (1970) reported that 63% of the adequate mothers, 84% of the potentially neglectful, and 88% of the neglectful families were living in extreme poverty: "Thus, even within a group of families all of whom can be considered 'poor,' there was higher incidence of extreme poverty among neglectful parents" (p. 199). So, even though the statistical evidence about lower income among the neglect families proved mixed, as a precaution we tested a number of relationships reported below with partial correlations and analyses of covariance to hold income constant.

That public assistance was the main source of income in neglectful households was reported earlier by Young (1964). Public assistance was very unusual in our group of fifty control families with a father in the home, involving only 6%; among the neglect father-present families, however, the figure was 54.5% ($P < .001$ by Chi-square test). Among female-headed families, over half (58.6%) of the nonneglect mothers were on public assistance; for the neglect, the figure was 87.5% ($P < .05$ by Chi-square test). Thus public assistance was common in all father-absent households, but it was most characteristic of those implicated in substandard child care. In this respect, the neglect sample is analogous to others in the literature. The reliance on financial assistance, by the way, was not a new phenomenon for most of these families. Of those receiving public assistance when studied, over 60% had been on it for over three years.

Socioeconomic Status

How did the groups compare in social class? After reviewing some other measures available, we concluded that Hollingshead's Two-factor Index of Social Position (ISP) dating from 1957 was as valid for our purposes as those developed later, and eminently suited for use. The ISP bases its score on a weighted sum of credits for education and the status of one's occupation. In father-present households, the family's score was the father's; in father-absent, the mother, of course, was head of the household. Distributions of scores are tabulated in table 5.1.

Most families fell into classes 4 and 5, which one often thinks of as the "working class." As we shall show in chapter 11, they also derive nearly entirely from these strata. Somewhat more of the neglect cases fell into class 5, the lowest, than did the control (50.0% vs. 30.4%, $P < .05$ by Chi-square test). So once again the samples proved substantially similar, but with some disadvantage to the neglects. Perhaps because of the mothers' marginal employment, we also found that families headed by a woman were also

Table 5.1: Social Class of Study Families

Social Class	Neglect Families		Control Families	
	Father Present	Father Absent	Father Present	Father Absent
2	0	0	4	1
3	2	0	7	2
4	12	9	26	15
5	8	15	13	11
Total	22	24	50	29

more likely to fall into class 5 (49.1% vs. 29.2%, $P < .05$ by Chi-square test).

Focal Children

No attempt was made to select cases with sex of the child in mind, and our hope was that this factor would balance out. There proved to be more boys that girls among study families (72 vs. 53), but this was true in both major samples. Boys made up 55.7% of the controls, and 60.9% of the neglects (i.e., 44 and 28 boys, respectively).

The difficulties in finding cases led us to be a bit flexible about the age ranges studied, especially among the families involving substandard care. We were also misled in a couple of cases, and did not get the child's true age until well into the study. The discrepancies, however, were slight: two neglect children were over 7 but under 8; two were slightly younger than age 4; one nonneglect child proved slightly older than 7. The mean ages, however, were very close: 5.15 for the neglect; 4.94 for the nonneglect. It appears that age and sex of the focal child may be regarded as having been well matched by the sampling. In any event, only one difference related to sex of the child was found in the study (see chapter 9).

Family Structure

Most mothers in the homes labeled father-present were legally married to the father, the majority for the first time. Households in which the mother was living with a person quaintly termed, in Philadelphia social work circles, a "paramour" were treated as father-present only if the relationship was of some duration and the man played a regular role in family life—even if that included the child neglect. Seventy-two men were regarded as the father in the families studied. In the nonneglect families, 94% were married to the mother; in the neglect, 81%, which is not a significant difference. Only three of these men had never been married, only three of the mothers had never been married. The varieties of structures are depicted in table 5.2. Overall, the formal and in-

Table 5.2: Mother's Current Marital Status

	Neglect Families		Control Families	
Mother's Status	Father Present	Father Absent	Father Present	Father Absent
Married				
first time	15		44	
second time	2		3	
Separated				
alone		10		12
with paramour	3	1	1	
Divorced				
alone		8		14
with paramour	2	2	2	2
Widowed				1
Unmarried		3		
Total	22	24	50	29

formal arrangements by which people were living together or apart were not markedly different in the families offering poorer care.

Parents' Ages

The age of parents in all subsamples averaged in the late twenties or early thirties. Hall (1979) working in a clinic in Texas reported the mothers involved in neglect were often young, although they could be found in all age brackets. But in our study the neglect mothers were, if anything, slightly older than the controls. The mean age for neglect women was 31.2, with father-absent about two years older, on the average, than father-present (32.4 vs. 30.3). Control mothers averaged 29, and both father-present and -absent had means nearly the same. Control fathers averaged slightly older than neglect: 33.6 vs. 30.5 years of age. So the samples turned out quite well-matched in this respect, too.

Family Size

It has been observed by a number of investigators that families implicated in neglect are likely to have more children than those in comparison groups (Young 1964; Giovannoni and Billingsley 1970; Wolock and Horowitz 1979). Was this also true of the families we have recruited? Our study proved typical in this respect, too. In the neglect sample, 33 families, or 71.7% had three children or more, with a median of 3.5; in the comparison group, 36 or 45.6% had three children or more, and the median number was 2.0. Difference between the samples with respect to having two children or less or three or more was significant beyond .005 by Chi-square test. Four of the families identified as neglectful contained nine children or more, while the largest family in the control group was eight. On this basic aspect of family composition, then, the two samples differed, but in a way that resembles findings in other studies. From a questionnaire administered to 75 low-income families in New Haven, Geismar and LaSorte (1963, p. 480) said of those rated disorganized that "a relatively high value was placed on the sexual experience, but this was not matched by a general satisfaction in marriage or an interest in children living and yet to be born."

The basic demographic information has been given in order to provide a beginning impression of the people in our study. It also appears that despite the scrambling that entered into our recruitment process, the parents who entered the study are not atypical of those encountered in other researches on neglect. Might this imply that there are features found so universally among such parents that they outweigh the circumstances of the sampling?

Six

Assessing the Quality of Child Care

The study design was meant to expose factors associated with child neglect. Its logic involved comparing a group of families identified as neglectful with another group that was socioeconomically comparable, drawn from the community at large. The methods of sampling could be presumed to have generated a difference between the groups as to their caliber of child care, but one could not be sure it had done so. As is often true of so-called control groups, making a choice on the basis that a case was not known to possess a trait did not prove the trait was absent. Although such an outcome was most unlikely, it was at least conceivable that a large proportion of the families who volunteered for the study from the community were actually neglectful. It was desirable, therefore, to have an additional measure of the caliber of nurture in each family, as a validity check. Was the logic of the *ex post facto* experimental design really followed? An obvious way to have the check was to make our own assessment of the quality of child care in each home studied.

Another reason for undertaking such a measurement was the vague way in which the term "neglect" has been in use. From the writings summarized in chapter 2, one could not argue that this has been a term with a clear meaning, conceptually or operationally. So, having asked the agencies to refer families whom *they* considered neglectful, one might still wonder: What did these people have in common? How did their child care differ from that of other

64

low-income families? What criteria were the agencies using? To end the study without being able to answer such questions would have been most unsatisfying. There was a need for a way of describing each family's child care that would yield specifics about the care given. One would also like to be able to integrate the specifics into an overall score, or a set of scores, so that groups of families could be compared with each other on their general level of nurture.

In this chapter, we shall describe the rationale, development, content, and validity of the Childhood Level of Living Scale, or CLL. The scale, devised to discriminate among households on gut-level issues of child caring, was first developed in the Appalachian study. It was revised to permit analogous measurement in an urban setting.

Considerations in Scaling Adequacy of Scaling

Legally, we have observed, neglect is based on a dichotomy: the child is or is not neglected. But to social workers, child care is graded on a continuous dimension. Some families fall at so low a point on the scale they are clearly neglectful. However, since the scale is continuous, it is inevitable there will be marginal cases, and that the specific point we deem the boundary of "neglectful" parenting might be hard to specify.

Operational definition is not made easier by the fact that the dimension involved is evidently multiplex, resembling a telephone cable, rather than univocal, like a single wire. A quick review of relevant statutes and position papers of professionals brings the complexity to attention:

> Physical, emotional and intellectual growth and welfare are
> being jeopardized when, for example, the child is:
> —malnourished, without proper shelter or sleeping arrange-
> ments —without supervision or unattended —ill and lacking
> essential medical care . . . —denied normal experiences that pro-
> duce feelings of being loved, wanted, secure and worthy . . .
> —exploited, overworked, exposed to unwholesome and de-
> moralizing circumstances. [Child Welfare League of America
> 1973, p. 12]

How many dimensions of nuture are implied by such a statement? Without reflection one can list: financial support, feeding, housing, protection, moral guidance, empathy, loving, constancy of presence. And one could go on. None of these matters is irrelevant to child care, nor can one readily set priorities among the congeries to make measurement more convenient, the scale more univocal. Is it more important to be well fed than to be kept from freezing in the winter? Is it worse that a child die from appendicitis or mirasmus?

It was conceivable, of course, that there were elements of child care which could be taken as representative of the whole. An analogue, for example, would be that the score on vocabulary correlates very highly with the score arrived at when one administers the other nine subtests of the Wechsler Adult Intelligence Scale. Are there certain parental actions that are especially indicative? For this to be true would require that the caliber of rearing be "all of a piece." A reanalysis of the data from the earlier mountain study had strongly implied that it is (Polansky and Pollane 1975). Having household possessions and amenities for living proved to be substantially correlated with what parents did in physically caring for the child. Moreover, the physical care the child received, overall, correlated substantially with his psychological care ($r = .67$).

We know of no other study confirming this observation, namely, that quality of parenting tends to be pervasive. Of course hardly any of the child development literature deals with comparable problems. That the child-subject will survive is taken for granted. Thus the finding about parenting had to be retested, and this argued further for measuring child care extensively. Once a wide range of measures had been employed, factor analytic methods would tell us which variables could be taken as most representative of the whole. Such knowledge would be helpful for subsequent studies.

In trying to characterize family life by extensive measurement, one plan employed has been to identify the general dimensions that seem salient. Each dimension is then structured into a ratio scale, and the family is assigned a score on it by some knowledgeable observer. The raw data of specific impressions and facts are synthesized by the rater or judge into these scale scores. Geismar (1973), for instance, has made extensive use of this pattern in his studies of "family functioning." An advantage of this method lies in exploiting the human professional as a recording instrument who is also capable of synthesizing. But for present purposes, there were two distinct disadvantages of such an approach. Once the judgments had been made on the various scales, the scale scores became the data of the study: it is not possible to work one's way back to the facts and incidents on which each was based. If one were to search for "what social workers mean by neglect" in this fashion, he would end with a high-level abstraction defined in terms of other abstractions, at a level only slightly less removed from reality.

The second disadvantage of the use of global ratings was the likelihood of contamination among them, of "halo effect." Because of the difficulties of entering these families and gaining their trust, there could be no thought of introducing second and third observers to make independent judgments of the parents. Therefore most of the data would have to come through the research social worker. If one could design instruments made up of specific, concrete items, the hope would be that the worker's halo effect, positive or negative toward a family, would play less of a role in the scores obtained. So in this study, as in the previous one, the decision was to develop scales for measuring child care which consisted of reports on limited, concrete issues, items as specific and unsusceptible to distortion as possible.

Ought one employ the same pool of items developed for the CLL in the mountains in Philadelphia? Some protective service workers in cities had, we knew, made use of the earlier CLL and told us it was useful. But that could have been an instance, as the French say, of *faute de mieux,* lacking better. Arguing in favor was familiarity with characteristics of the scales already constructed and the fact that this study was, after all, a replication. Arguing against were the matters of validity and precision. Is it really a replication to use, say, an item about warning children against poisonous snakes where none exist? Obviously not. But which items to keep, which to delete? Rather than relying solely on our own judgment, a panel of mothers from the area near our field office was gathered and the items reviewed with them. They suggested some additions and counseled some deletions; they also gave us a few surprises. For example, the senior author had assumed an item about teaching children about poisonous berries would be irrelevant, but it turned out there were bushes with such berries "down at the tracks." So the decision was to include as much of the previous CLL as seemed appropriate, but to add new items to fit the urban setting.

The final selection of items, however, emerged from a process that was, of course, more organized, and made use of experiences with the instruments and statistical procedures. Let us turn, then, to the process of constructing the CLL out of the original pool of items we collected.

Development of the Childhood Level of Living Scale

The CLL consisted of a series of declarative sentences, each of which was possibly descriptive of the parent's child-rearing practices, or the household in which the child lived. Examples from the rural version were: "The roof leaks" or "Mother threatens punishment by imagined or fright objects." In its original format, part A of the scale dealt with physical care and consisted of eighty-seven items grouped under nine subheadings. Part B dealt with emotional/cognitive care, or psychological nurture, and contained forty-eight items under seven subheadings. The scale was constructed rationally, but cluster analysis was also used to locate assignments of questionable items or to delete others that did not seem to fit the scale. Factor analysis was not undertaken at that time. The statistical work was done in our field office, 170 miles from our university, using desk calculators. In Pennsylvania, of course, we had ready access to excellent computer facilities.

It seems worthwhile to point out here a departure from standard research practice involved in developing both versions of the CLL. Ordinarily, construction of a scale as critical to the research as was this one is organized as a research undertaking in its own right, a preliminary investigation. But such a study would have required getting a sample of families identified as neglectful, recruiting a contrasting sample, securing cooperation, and so forth. To know each family well, one would have to end with a preliminary study nearly as costly as the main content study one had in mind. So, as we had done in other studies, we telescoped the process of instrument construction and made it part of the conduct of the main study. When such a shortcut succeeds there are several gains. There is a saving in time, money, and investigator-years. And the fact that a number of other measurements is also being made facilitates using construct validity as a check on the instrument being constructed. This kind of telescopic gambling on one's experience and intuition in setting up operational definitions *a priori* was characteristic of the work of the late Kurt Lewin and his students. There are also risks in doing this, the worst being the use of measurements for major variables which prove highly unreliable and/or invalid. However, many social work researchers have great clinical familiarity with the area being researched, and can minimize such risks. Pilot interviews, of course, must still be used.

Development of the urban revision of the CLL began with a pool of 220 items. Each was borrowed from the rural version or invented for this one; each seemed relevant to quality of nurture, probably observable, and probably usable for discriminating among families. The first screening of the items began after about fifty families had been studied, and consisted of deleting items that were not working out. Some were removed because the three research social workers, in comparing notes, decided they were very unclear about the concept the item was supposedly measuring. Others had proven very hard to observe, or to acquire credible information about, and the worker felt no confidence in his or her rating. A few turned out to be age-linked: that an item was true or false meant something quite different for a four-year-old than a seven-year-old, and the study spanned these ages. The sampling included numerous fatherless households but, it turned out, there were items that were meaningful only in the context of there being a male figure present. Many items proved nondiscriminating. For example, in the mountain study, whether or not the family had a telephone correlated with the general level of child care. However, all but two of the first fifty families in the present study had telephones. All these families had hot water piped into the house; none used kerosene to start fires if, indeed, they had stoves at all; leaking roofs were not common occurrences even in Philadelphia's poorer housing. Pilot interviews with about ten families had, of course, been done before the main study began in order to familiarize the research caseworkers with their tasks and to permit polishing of instruments. Nevertheless a substantial set of items remained whose faults could not be established until a larger group of cases had been seen.

How was the CLL actually administered and scored? It was a kind of true/false questionnaire, but it was not given to the client. Rather, it was self-administered by the research social worker after he or she had nearly completed contacts with the family, on the basis of what had been directly observed, what had been learned from others, and by direct questions of the parents concerning matters the worker still did not know. While parents' responses cannot be taken at face value as descriptive of their child care, neither ought one automatically assume all parents distort their reports. Once reasonable rapport had been established, most experienced no great need to conceal what they were doing, if only because they, themselves, do not question their practices. But, to repeat, the CLL was a scale completed by a knowledgeable professional.

Each item was scored yes or no. There are items for which a yes notation appeared desirable and earned the family a point on the scale; others yielded a point for no. Each item can be scored one or zero. Thus, item 1, "Mother plans at least one meal consisting of two courses" yields a point if answered yes, zero if scored no; item 26, "There are food scraps on the floor and furniture." yields a point if scored no, a zero when scored yes.

At the end of the data collection, our statistical consultant, Dr. Sam Snyder, assisted by John Norcini, did a factor analysis of all the CLL protocols, including all items which had survived the original screening step. The effect of the factor analysis was to determine empirically which items clustered, that is, which had been scored across all families, neglect and nonneglect, in such a way that they seemed to be part of separable dimensions. Because a matrix of the large number of items involved would have exceeded the capacity of the available computer, the two halves of the CLL, physical care and cognitive/emotional care, were factor analyzed separately.

The full Childhood Level of Living Scale, directions for scoring and tentative standards for interpretation, are given in appendix 1. However we will abstract the scale here for the reader's convenience in following further discussion.

Physical Care

I. *General positive child care.* Contains 15 items, for example: "Mother uses good judgment about leaving child alone in the house." "Bedtime for the child is set by the parent(s) for about the same time each night." Eigen value 19.54, accounting for 53.2% of the variance of physical care items.

II. *State of repair of house.* Includes 10 items, e.g., "Storm sashes or equivalent are present." Eigen value 3.83; 10.4% of variance.

III. *Negligence* (reciprocal meaning, since scoring is of desired practices). Seven items, e.g., "There are food scraps on the floor and furniture." Eigen value 3.36; 9.2% of variance.

IV. *Quality of household maintenance.* Eight items, e.g., "There are leaky faucets." Eigen value 2.81; 7.7% of variance.

V. *Quality of health care and grooming.* Seven items, e.g., "Mother has encouraged child to wash hands before meals." Eigen value 2.02; 5.5% of variance.

Emotional/Cognitive Care

VI. *Encouraging competence.* Includes 20 items, e.g., "Planned overnight vacation trip has been taken by family." "There are magazines available." Eigen value 17.94, accounting for 49.4% of variance of the items in the cognitive/emotional segment.

VII. *Inconsistency of discipline and coldness* (reciprocal meaning). Fourteen items, e.g., "Mother seems not to follow through on rewards." "The child is often pushed aside when he shows need for love." Eigen value 7.36; 20.3% of variance.

VIII. *Encouraging superego development.* Fourteen items, e.g., "Parents guard language in front of children." Eigen value 2.62; 7.2% of variance.

XI. *Material giving.* Four items, e.g., "Crayons are made available to the child." Eigen value 2.24; 6.2% of variance.

We have had numerous requests for copies of the scale since it was first published (Polansky, Chalmers, Buttenwieser, and Williams 1978), mostly from colleagues in social work and public health. It is, of course, a rather long scale, and some have wondered how to shorten it to make it more palatable for practitioners to use.

The Eigen values and information on variances may be interpreted to mean that subscale I, general positive child care, adequately samples the physical care aspect with only fifteen items; and subscale VI, encouraging competence, does the same for the psychological aspect with twenty items.

A family's score on the CLL can be taken as simply the number of points scored, from a minimum of zero (which we never encountered), to a maximum of 99, which six control families did in fact achieve. The factor analysis was done after 120 families had been seen and, at that point, there were of course many more than ninety-nine items still in the pool. Besides providing us with the factor structure of the CLL, the analysis also identified items which did not "belong" to any cluster, or which were in a couple of clusters with Eigen values so low they were dropped. Our ending with ninety-nine items was unplanned, but it was a considerable convenience in scoring, for if all items are scored, the number of points achieved is nearly the same as a score for *percentage* of items passed out of all attempted. This means that if an occasional item cannot be scored, because of lack of knowledge about it or the like, one can resort to a score of "percentage of all possible" and have a figure that is numerically equivalent to one yielded by the full scale.

Based on our families, we considered that scores from zero to 62 (the fortieth percentile) represented care that should be termed neglectful. Acceptable child care began with a score of 77, which was the fiftieth percentile of our sample, and good child care, characterizing the top quintile of the study families, began with a score of 88 (the latter figure was in error in the original publication). These norms are, of course, advanced tentatively, as befits so small a standardizing sample. Indeed, we should be grateful if agencies who have utilized the scale already would provide us information regarding their results with it, and the demography of those with whom it has been used.

A further note about utilizing the scale has to do with the possibility of halo-effect, mentioned above. The items were clustered empirically, that is, according to how items actually intercorrelated when the scale was applied. If the scale were to be given on a form structured like the one we have published, the worker would find herself or himself scoring a series of items all of which are obviously related in content. The danger is that the decision about one item would have a carry-over effect on the next one, if it were similar in content, and that this would partly dissipate the gain from using discrete, reasonably concrete items. Therefore we recommend that the items be placed on scoring forms more or less at random, thereby breaking up the clusters for the person assessing the family. This is how the scale was composed, at least, in the present study.

Reliability of the Childhood Level of Living Scale

One meaning of reliability in appraising research instruments is especially noteworthy for those instruments made up of large numbers of discrete items, or subscores, as is the CLL. Sometimes called internal reliability, the issue concerns whether all the items in the scale are measuring phenomena in the same area of discourse. Do all these items have to do with quality of child nuture? Does the statement, "Window are caulked sealed against drafts" belong in the same realm with "A prayer is said before some meals"? One could argue *a priori,* without collecting any data, that such diverse observations do indeed have to do with child care; but one could argue equally persuasively that they do not. The best test is to collect the data, run the required statistical analyses, and find out. If answers to these two questions are systematically associated, if they belong, at least, to subscales that prove to be correlated significantly, then we may conclude they are, in fact, part of the same universe of measurement.

The internal consistency of the CLL was guaranteed by its method of construction. Items that did not correlate with each other, or with total score, were discarded after the factor analysis. But the *degree* of internal consistency that was found was surprising; it has a meaning that goes beyond the methodological to the substance of the study. For in this replication, as in the first study, parenting again appeared "all of a piece." Among the fifty-two families in the mountain study, few of whom we regarded as outright neglectful, the correlation between physical care and psychological care was, it will be recalled, .67. The correlation between the analogous segments in the present research was even higher, .81.

Now, one could attribute this correlation simply to halo effect, but that would discount the discreteness and substantial diversity among the actual items in the scale. The correlation was also found among this sample of families of which all were low-income, a fact which must have limited the spread of scores to some extent. The fact is that there were exceptions, but "in general and on the average" one could fairly well estimate a family's psychological care of the focal child from a knowledge of the physical care being given. This is an important observation, theoretically, for it accounts for the difficulty encountered when we tried to identify isolated dynamic constellations associated with child neglect. Quality of parenting, rather, seems related to the whole caliber of functioning, the warp and woof of parental personality termed character.

All parts of the CLL intercorrelate, at least moderately. The correlations of subscales, with total score, ranged from .64 to .88. Hence this is a "sturdy" scale in the sense that the loss of some items from the scoring would probably not greatly affect comparability between scores, after they are numerically adjusted as was suggested above.

The other form of reliability of interest was interobserver reliability. "Interobserver reliability, of course, has to do with the agreement that exists among observers in their independent observations of the same phenomenon by means of the same instrument" (Rosen and Polansky 1975, p. 170). The sensitive nature of the contacts made it impossible to run an experimental test of interobserver reliability among our workers using the scale with the neglect families, in particular. As a substitute, we conducted analyses of variance of the scores on the various subscales given by the three research caseworkers. If their cases were drawn at random from the same population, then there should have been no significant differences among their mean scores. However, from other evidence, this was not thought to be precisely true. The results of the analysis of variance, in any event, showed only a scattering of significant differences among the workers, and in each instance these were in the same direction as were apparent differences among their cases. We believe the scale is capable of good interobserver reliability because such unreliability would have added to the error factor and, as will be shown, the CLL did show substantial associations with other variables, independently measured, which were theoretically expectable. Nevertheless the direct test of this form of reliability remains a project for the future.

Validity of the Childhood Level of Living Scale

Thus the CLL was univocal, internally consistent, which is a desirable attribute in most scales. But the fact that a group of items measures the same thing does not tell us whether it is measuring what we want it to measure. Child neglect was conceived to represent one extreme on a general scale of child caring, and the CLL was proposed as an operational definition of quality of child care. If validity is the degree to which the operational definition fits the concept, was the CLL valid?

A scanning of the items included is persuasive that the CLL does have *content* validity, that the "measurement procedure samples the universe of situations or subject matter about which conclusions are to be drawn" (Kogan 1975, p. 88). In an older phrasing, one might have said that the CLL is "valid on the face of it."

We were able to use two other forms of validation of the CLL in this investigation. Both are preferred by most researchers over content validity because they are less susceptible to benign distortion of judgment and because they more closely resemble the ultimate uses to which a research instrument is likely to be put. The first of these types of validity is *concurrent,* by which it is shown that "measures correspond to concurrent criterion performance or status" (Kogan 1975, p. 88). The second type is *construct* validity, in which the scale is inferred to be a reasonable operational definition because its associations with measures of other concepts are found to accord with predictions from theory. The construct validity of the CLL, whether or not we mention it explicitly, will be one of the matters at stake in subsequent chapters dealing with the fate of several of our hypotheses. The focus here will be on concurrent validity, the extent to which the family's CLL score proved to be associated with an external criterion.

The sampling design ensured the availability of the external criterion, for the group of cases of greater interest were all identified as neglectful by a referring agency. It will be recalled that we did not choose which case should be referred, and that we avoided explicitly defining neglect for the agencies. Thus the agency's judgment may be treated as having been independent of our conception. Were we, however, influenced by their judgments? We can only say that we did not take their assessments for granted, which is one reason the CLL was in use, after all.

There is a tendency in instrument construction to treat the external criterion as if its validity were beyond scrutiny, and the instrument being developed has to measure up to it. Some researchers show a bias toward behavior over verbal statements, for example, in inferring attitudes. If an individual working in an office dislikes his superior, which observation is more valid: that he treats the employer politely, or that he remarks to the interviewer, in confidence, "My boss is impossible"? There are times when statements are, in fact, better indicators than behavior. So we thought of the agency identification as a judgment external to us and to the CLL, but not necessarily more valid simply because we did not make it.

This was really a situation in which there were at hand alternative operational definitions of the same concept (Polansky 1975, p. 23f). One operation yielded a dichotomy, agency identification versus absence of identification; the other, the CLL, yielded continuous scaling, and could be thought of as a ratio scale. If both were reasonable operational definitions of the same concept, the quality of child care, they should correlate with each other. An analogy may be made to developing a test of children's intelligence. Should the test correlate with grades in school? It is well known that factors other than intelligence enter into school grades, factors like motivation and teachers' attitudes toward grading, but we do expect intelligence to become visible in grades, to some extent, and over a group of students. Similarly, one anticipates that trying to sample an aspect of personality that affects competence as pervasively as does intelligence through a series of tasks to be completed in forty minutes is a procedure prone to error, too. Hence a perfect correlation between two patently imperfect alternative operational definitions is not to be expected. But if the correlation were zero, this would be unnerving news to the constructor of the test.

How high, then, should we expect the correlation between agency identification and the CLL score to be? We hoped for a moderately strong correlation, but had no clear way of anticipating how strong. Meanwhile, comparing the CLL against the identifications by agency workers was a way of validating both assessments. The detail provided by the CLL might, indeed, help to reveal the bases used by agency workers in labeling child neglect.

It will be recalled that the score on the total CLL represents, really, the percentage of items "passed" out of all those attempted. The same would apply to scoring individual families on subscales, even clusters with as few as seven, or even four, items. Therefore each family had a score on every subscale, as well as a score on each major segment of the CLL and on the total. So one way to test whether the CLL and the source of the case were associated was to compare the mean scores from each group. Results for this analysis are given in table 6.1. They demonstrate that, on every cluster of the CLL, the control families scored higher than did the neglect. All these differences were significant beyond .001 by ANOVA.

Table 6.1: Relation of Childhood Level of Living Scale Score to the Control/Neglect Dimension

CLL Factor	Mean Score*		Point Biserial Correlation
	Control	Neglect	
I. Positive general child care	.912	.566	.63
II. State of repair of house	.842	.534	.47
III. Negligence	.928	.682	.46
IV. Household maintenance	.829	.514	.49
V. Health care	.631	.294	.60
Total physical care	.839	.522	.68
VI. Encouraging competence	.729	.354	.67
VII. Inconsistent discipline and coldness	.797	.453	.64
VIII. Encouraging superego development	.794	.416	.66
IX. Material giving	.910	.678	.43
Total emotional/cognitive care	.777	.420	.72
Total CLL scale	.806	.468	.74

*P of each difference less than .001 by ANOVA.

(Analyses of variance were used, rather than t-tests, to facilitate analogous study of mean differences associated with father presence/absence. See chapter 10.)

It was tempting, by the way, also to compare mean scores of clusters with one another while scanning the table, so we might remind the reader that this would not be meaningful. The items used in measuring positive child care, for example, might be somehow easier to pass than those for health care, on which neglect families scored very poorly. In other words, we do not know that they are particularly lacking in health care because there is no way of determining that the scaling for this was as demanding as that for positive general child care—and no more. Comparison among groups, on the other hand, is based on the same contents.

The usual way to reveal strength of association is by a correlation coefficient. Treating one variable as continuous and the other as a discontinuous dichotomy, the coefficient of choice was point-biserial correlation. Results with this statistic are listed as the right-hand column of the table 6.1. From the pattern of associations it is evident that all elements measured played a role in agency identification. The correlation of the total CLL score with agency identification was .74, a rather strong association in research of this sort. The correlations for physical and psychological nurture were of the same order, .68 and .72. So one can conclude that all these aspects were playing a part in the reactions of the agency workers to their families; one can also conclude that the concurrent validity of the Childhood Level of Living Scale was strongly supported.

We have lately received corroboration of the probably precision of the CLL. Magura and De Rubeis (1980) have been evaluating the effectiveness of a program for treating families of abused, neglected, and/or emotionally disturbed children in Hudson County, New Jersey. Among their measures were the CLL and Geismar's (1971) Family Functioning Scale. The latter involves rating each family on ten seven-point ordinal scales. Ratings were done by the workers on each case three months after they began working with the family and again after nine months on cases that continued in treatment. Ratings were available for twenty-two families. Magura and De Rubeis correlated *changes* on each of the Geismar subscales with the change on the total CLL score (p. 73). All correlations were positive, and three were significant: family relationships and unity ($r = .70; p < .01$); social activities ($r = .53, p < .02$); and adjustment of the female caretaker ($r = .53, p < .02$). (The levels of significance given by the authors in the original report were in error; see Glass and Stanley 1970, p. 539.)

Lest there be confusion on this matter, by the way, let us add that the external criterion played no part in the selection of which items were included and which deleted from the scale. The criterion was not whether an item discriminated between neglect and nonneglect families, but whether there was enough yes/no distribution among all families on the item so that it *might* discriminate. The major considerations in retaining items were their feasibility for use in the field and their compatibility with the remainder of the instrument, that is, their contribution to internal consistency.

Marginal and Nonfitting Cases

In evaluating diagnostic procedures used by physicians, medical researchers speak of the *sensitivity* and of the *specificity* of the tests invented. A score of .75 on the CLL included all neglect cases in this study, all the "pathology," so at that score the test had a sensitivity of 100% in medical parlance. However, setting the cut-off that high also included 16 control cases. The specificity of measurement, then, was 63/79, or about 80%. If one were case-finding a kind of cancer that is highly curable when detected early, one would be very willing to cause concern to one out of five healthy patients, the false-positives, to save the others. Whether there should be the same readiness to trade specificity for sensitivity, that is, to reduce false-negatives to zero in identifying neglect, is a good question. What this would mean in practice would be the judge's taking the agency worker's evaluation of the family as gospel, since he or she would be so unlikely to miss an instance of neglect, and the children of parents falsely accused probably could use protection in any case.

The medical indices, of course, are but another way of looking at the degree of correlation found between the CLL and whether or not families were referred by an agency. A correlation of .74 meant 55% of the variance was accounted for; it also mean 45% was not. So we took a closer look at the cases that did not quite fit the pattern of association. There were five families who were referred, but who scored above the median score of all 125 families in the study, that is, 69.5 on the CLL. None, as it happened, scored more than five points above the median. Three of the mothers involved were living with their own parents, the maternal grandparents, at the time we studied them. Such an arrangement can operate well to protect the children.

Judy P. is separated from her husband, whom she left because of frequent beatings. She has two sons, aged six and five, and is currently pregnant by her boyfriend, who is in jail for armed robbery. Judy is shy, and giggles when she admits that much of the boys' early child care fell on her mother, with whom she lived much of the time. Actually, because of the efforts of the maternal grandmother, the mother's two sisters, and the community center,

Judy's boys are presently fairly well cared for. She, herself, has benefitted from talks with her social worker, and recently has settled down, no longer absconding for weeks at a time to stay with friends. She thinks of herself as now more grown up than when she became intentionally pregnant to get away from her mother and school. "That was dumb, but I didn't know any better," she says. The family hardly needs another infant to nurture, but hopes for the best.

Another woman is married to a drug addict who exploits her, and she seems to function much better when he is not around. Still another is an arrested alcoholic who appears to be benefitting from her sessions with a psychiatrist. The research social worker felt that this referral for neglect might have been more appropriate earlier in the agency's work with the mother.

Fifteen families of the seventy-nine in the control group scored below the overall median, which is not far out of line with their proportion of the sample of 125. However, we found that in about half these families, the score for psychological care was dramatically lower than that for physical care, ranging from 13 to 43 points lower. If the physical care was at least marginal, there was much less likelihood that the family would be referred to a child welfare agency as neglectful, either by the school counselor or by the caseworker with the Department of Public Assistance, the local agency responsible for income maintenance, to which many of these families were also known.

Mary F., a mousy-looking, frightened young woman of twenty-nine has children aged seven, six, four, and three. She and her husband have had repeated separations over the past six years; each reunion resulted in another baby. During these separations, Mrs. F. usually moved in with her own parents, but five months ago she took her own apartment, where she has been living on a combination of Social Security, since she is legally blind, and public assistance.

Mrs. F.'s school-age boys have brought her to the attention of the school counselor. The boys have been doing badly in school, in large part because they are so frequently absent. This came out, in our contact, when she talked of being tempted to stay in bed that day, but getting up to get the children off to school because, "I promised the counselor." On the third day of school, she added with a sigh, "It's going to be a long year."

Mrs. F. makes efforts to keep her apartment clean, but has a hard time. "Notice how the bathroom stinks," she says, "I can't help it if the boys pee on the floor." "If they want candy, I use what money I have to buy it," and, again, "If they don't like to go to the doctor to get their shots, I can't make them." It is startling to have Mrs. F. get all excited that her three- and four-year-olds have left their toys across the street, when she does not seem to notice they are crossing a busy avenue without supervision. "I can't help it if they want to play over there all the time."

These children appear as neglected as any in our study. But the school counselor cannot know the family well, and the Department of Public Assistance seemed content with having transferred the burden of support to the federal level. Attempts by the research social worker to get Mrs. F. involved with the other social services were sabotaged by her, as she has done before. Speaking of her plan to reunite with Mr. F., she says, "It will solve all my problems."

In short, there were a few cases recruited to the study as part of the control sample who might easily have qualified for the neglect. However, we did not delete these cases from the research because to do so would have represented an intrusion of our assessment into the neglect/nonneglect dichotomy. To reiterate an earlier statement, selection of cases for a control group on the basis that they are not *known* to have a particular characteristic when sampled leaves open the possibility that this characteristic is, in fact, present.

Nevertheless, we felt it better to leave the neglect/nonneglect division independent of our judgment. Even though this meant some imprecision of measurement in the external criterion, later chapters will show that a large number of significant differences between the groups was found. One incident did help matters, and seems worth mentioning. The level of care in one nonneglect family was such that the research caseworker found it painful to leave the case in that sample and, moreover, ethically disturbing to take no action. Fortunately, through a series of events unconnected with the research, another agency reported the family for neglect and we changed its status accordingly.

Poverty in the Measurement of Quality of Care

We did not intend in this study either to prove or to disprove the hypothesis that the main cause of child neglect is inadequate income. Indeed, by imposing the sampling condition that all families be low-income, we may have so truncated the range of family incomes that effects of this variable could not be studied. Yet even among families recruited at or below the income used, variations remained. Several authors have referred to neglectful families as the poorest of the poor (Giovannoni and Billingsley 1970; Wolock and Horowitz 1979). Might it be that the agency workers, and we too, were simply grading people's relative poverty and terming the poorest neglectful? Did this practice account for our agreement?

Income level, in our study, was expressed as the proportion of the Bureau of Labor Statistics low-income living standard which a family in our study had, after correcting for family size. When this index of income adequacy was compared with scores on the CLL, correlations emerged that were low, but were statistically significant. Product-moment r for income with the physical care segment of the CLL was .28 ($P < .001$); with emotional/cognitive care, .21 ($P < .01$); and with the total CLL score, .25 ($P < .002$). So even within the constricted range in the present study, family income had something to do with level of child care.

Did relative poverty, then, explain the correspondence between our assessments and those of the agencies? To test this proposition, the ANOVAs of the CLL scores according to whether or not the families were referred by an agency or controls were repeated. This time, however, analyses of covariance were done holding family income constant. If our agreement had been based on income, the covariance analyses should have been statistically insignificant. In fact, the results were practically identical with those given in table 6.1; no level of significance was altered, and the estimated differences between means, with family income held constant, were each within a percentage point of those in the original table. Obviously we were not jointly grading poverty; our agreement was uninfluenced by it.

There is another way of viewing poverty, of course. One might speak of "a poverty life-style," a way of living that is partly affected by sheer income, but also affected by the values about what is important among families of low social class status. Our measure for socioeconomic status (SES) was Hollingshead's Two-Factor Index (see chapter 5). Correlations between the CLL and SES ran somewhat higher that those with family income. For physical care, $r = .37$ ($P < .001$); for emotional/cognitive care, $r = .24$ ($P < .004$); and for the CLL total score, $r = .31$ ($P < .001$). Yet if we were to reprint the point-biserial correlation coefficients given in table 6.1 with socioeconomic status *partialled out,* they would be identical with those already given.

So there is no reason to believe that we and our agency colleagues were simply grading poverty or the culture of poverty. Instead the evidence heavily favors the supposition that what was agreed upon was the phenomenon intended. Quality of child care is related adversely to poverty, but is separable from it.

Class-related Values and Neglect

Although it was found that the degree of agreement between the agency workers and us did not rest primarily on the clients' incomes or on their socioeconomic statuses, it does not follow that class played no role in the measurements involved. There is the matter of the class orientation of those doing the research. Most social workers are of middle-class status and origin. Yet, as was shown in chapter 5, parents in the neglectful families were predominately from classes 4 and 5, so there was a class difference between us. If the parent implicated in neglect so often feels relatively guiltless, is it because his standards are different from ours? When we score an item in the CLL as desirable or undesirable are we applying middle-class values?

Several investigators have reported that variations in how children are reared, and values about how they should be reared, are associated with the parents' social class. Early on, Davis and Havighurst (1946), working in Chicago, noted that middle-class parents there appeared more demanding of self-control and conformity in their children than did working-class parents. The opposite was found by Sears, Maccoby, and Levin (1957) in greater Boston in 1951–52. Bronfenbrenner (1958) tried to reconcile these conflicting trends with the thesis that child-rearing practices slowly change in all classes, but change more rapidly in the middle class because those parents are more educated, more aware of newer teachings propounded by those thought to be experts. In line with Marxist theory, Kohn (1968) postulated that class attitudes reflect families' objective positions in the class structure. Working-class families are less in control of their fates than are middle-class families; therefore they rear their children toward conformity and toward gearing behavior in terms of external consequences. Middle-class parents are more likely, he reported, to emphasize self-directedness and knowing why one should accept controls.

Although the evidence is mixed, and theories differ somewhat, there is very good reason to believe that each of us makes judgments that are influenced, to greater or lesser degree, by the reference groups to which we belong. The more ambiguous the judgment, the more influence. Whether or not one accepts Marxist theory in all its details, it also seems highly likely that our values will resemble those in similar positions in life and with whom we associate the most—those in our own social class. Have social workers fallen victim to this obvious process in judging neglect?

Previous studies do not really deal with this issue because, as we remarked earlier, child development studies seldom deal with the critical issues we address in child protection. Housing, clothing, medicine, protection against assault—things that keep social workers up nights—are not studied. It occurred to us, however, that these were issues worked on in developing the CLL, and that the content in it could be readily converted from a scale for measuring

quality of child care actually practiced to an instrument for studying values about child-caring practices. All that was necessary was
to take the same set of described conditions and ask the respondent
her attitude about each.

The respondent, then, was presented with a questionnare. This
could be in written form or the subject could be interviewed. The
statement introducing the questionnaire read:

> This is about a child between the ages of four and seven and the
> situation in which he lives. Some of these things will strike you
> as good and you will be glad about them. Some will strike you
> as awful and you'll feel they should be reported. Some might
> not seem that important, or kind of good or kind of bad, but
> you don't have any strong feelings about it. After each state-
> ment, just place a check mark in one of the six columns to mark
> your answer. Put down your first reaction. We want to know
> what mothers like you think about those situations in which
> many children live. Remember, every item is true of at least
> some children.

There then followed 214 of the items originally collected in developing the CLL. Each item, however, was followed by a Likert-type
scale on which it was to be evaluated. Thus:

199. The child is often pushed aside when he shows the need for
     love.
     ____Report
     ____Very bad
     ____Bad
     ____Doesn't matter
     ____Good
     ____Excellent

The reader may share our amusement about an occurrence during
the pretesting. A number of seemingly rather minor things were
being graded "Report," that it, "should be reported," for example,
that there were leaking faucets in the household. Women who were
apartment-dwellers in the Northeast interpreted this as meaning
"should be reported to the super," the building superintendent or
janitor. Thereafter, it was explained that on the scale "Report"
meant to the legal authorities.

The sample was given to a sample of white working-class
mothers residing across the Delaware River from Philadelphia, in
and near Camden, New Jersey, because we did not want this side
study to contaminate the major effort. Fifty-seven of those interviewed were found to fit the desired demographic conditions. That
is, 51% were in Hollinghead's class 4, 43% were in class 5. Half
were high school graduates, but none had completed college, and
their median income was about $10,000 per annum.

We calculated the mean score of the respondents on the Likert-type scale, which was scored from 1 to 6. Each mean could then be related to the verbal label on the scale it most closely approximated, numerically. Thus a mean of 1.2 would signify "Report"; a mean of 1.9 indicated a group judgment of "Very bad," and so forth. The items which were included in the final version of the CLL were, of course, of greatest concern. Would these working-class mothers, on the average, have scored the CLL differently from us middle-class social workers? Comparing their positive and negative evaluations of items with our own showed agreement on ninety-six of the ninety-nine items! In other words, with the exception of three items on which they averaged responses in the range "doesn't matter," the working-class mothers evaluated the circumstances in a child's life the same as we and, by implication, the same as the agency workers had been doing.

This raised the interesting question of what a sample of middle- and upper-middle-class women might think of the same matters. To provide information about this, a sample of fifty-eight white mothers was recruited, this time, however, from the Philadelphia suburbs, chiefly in Bucks County. Of these women, 96.6% were college graduates and, indeed, over half had attended graduate school. Family incomes were nearly entirely beyond $11,500 per annum and some were very far beyond. Clearly, the sample's class status contrasted with that of the women from New Jersey and with most of those in our study. Again, however, there was agreement of their average evaluations with those used in scoring the CLL on ninety-six of ninety-nine items.

There were two items on which we placed an evaluation, but both mothers' groups scored them "Doesn't matter": "Clothing usually appears to be hand-me-downs" and "Mother mentions use of TV to teach child." We scored "Mother uses good judgment about leaving child alone in the house" a positive, and the middle-class women agreed, but the working class said, "Doesn't matter." On the item, "There are leaky faucets," working-class women agreed with scoring it negatively, but the middle class felt it didn't matter. These were the only items that would have affected scoring.

Indeed, the similarity of responses of the two samples was very striking. A product-moment correlation was done between the mean evaluations of the groups. Agreement among means on the forty-seven CLL items having to do with physical care yielded an $r = .9832$. This was almost embarrassingly high, so we looked at the correlation among means for the fifty-two items concerning psychological care, and the $r = .9824$. Many of the means of the two groups were so nearly identical that researchers inventing their data would have been more conservative. In short, the mothers were almost surprisingly homogeneous in their evaluations of these basic issues of child care. Differences between them, or with us, were always matters of degree, never of direction of evaluation.

Were there, then, no differences among the mothers? Did social class play no role in the judgments? Such a finding would be contrary to previous work in the field; one would feel more comfortable about results of this small auxiliary study if it were, in fact, in accord with what was already known. So those items on which there were significant differences between the means of the two groups were examined. These differences, to reiterate, were matters of emphasis, not of direction of evaluation. Analysis of these items indicates that the middle-class women placed the greater emphasis on psychological care; working-class mothers on physical care. Details are given elsewhere (Polansky and Williams 1978). The pattern of psychological versus physical concerns accords with the findings of others, and therefore is reassuring concerning the validity of the other findings from our study.

A study which was published as this manuscript neared completion offered strong support to our conclusions. Giovannoni and Becerra (1979) studied how various professional and community groups reacted to concrete instances of child abuse and neglect. The method used was to present the respondent with a series of vignettes, and ask him or her to rate each on a nine-point scale of "seriousness of the act" involved. They found that the lay community did not make fine distinctions among different acts that various professional groups had utilized, because they rated 85% of all vignettes with average scores of 6.0 or higher. Persons of low socioeconomic status in the community generally viewed mistreatment as *more* serious than did those with higher status. And "the more highly educated the respondents, the lower their seriousness ratings" (Giovannoni and Becerra 1979, p. 189). Were black and Hispanic respondents more tolerant than whites? Quite the contrary, say the authors. "In 94% of the vignettes the white sample rated the incidents as *less* serious than did either the Black or Hispanic groups" (p. 184). They report disagreement among the groups, statistically, because of the relatively lower mean ratings in the white sample. But if one looks at the group means obtained, the disagreement is always over how extreme the ratings were of seriousness of the actions, not the white group's differing in the direction of its ratings.

The results, then, strongly suggest that on gut-level issues of child caring, opinions of white mothers are uniform. The same is probably true for mothers from other ethnic groups, as well, but time and money did not permit our extending the study to pursue this. So far as the matter of the validity of the CLL, the implication is that within the general American culture studied, assessments from it are not just a matter of imposing middle-class values on the families being studied. Another implication, too, is that the poor child care witnessed is not being supported by attitudes prevalent in any very large segment of the population. Either those involved are members of small, unusual reference groups or, as seems more likely, the care given is not a matter of following permissive values so much as a matter of incapacity to provide better.

Seven

Isolation from Helping
Networks

We begin the discussion of what was learned about damaged parents with an issue that came to attention in the Appalachian study. In the mountains great value is placed on neighborliness and on mutual helping. It was troubling to find, therefore, how isolated were many of the families who concerned us. Little, if any, neighborliness was being shown them, and this was sad. For if anyone's children needed neighborly help and protection, theirs did.

Kurt Lewin once remarked in a long ago seminar that "friendly power fields are additive." He meant by this that the span of things over which you "have power," which you can control and use, may be greatly extended by the readiness of those who love you to grant access to their possessions as well. But if there are few or none who care about you, you do not have friends, you have cronies. To lack the resources caring people offer one another is to be that much more at the mercy of chance. Social workers have traditionally assumed most people have such friends and relatives. Indeed, when discussing a client's resources, it was common practice to review not only what the client could call upon or liquidate, but whether there was not someone else willing to help out informally. Were we wrong in this assumption?

That neglectful parents were isolated from helping networks was not, however, an established fact from the first study. The issue had not been foreseen, and there was no arrangement to collect relevant data systematically on all families. Rather, we had an impression, a hypothesis for future study. So in designing the replication, provision was made to study the degree of informal support being received by all families, neglect and nonneglect.

Subsequently, we have learned from our colleague David Guttman of Catholic University that what we call "helping networks" were also under study in the field of aging. A problem for the elderly is the gradual disappearance of relatives and friends from their lives because of deaths and disabilities. They lose their helping networks, that is, their "informal support systems" (Cantor 1975). But with neglectful parents, averaging in their early thirties, the question is not one of loss but of whether they have ever had a network.

The Family Support Index

The guide for maternal interviews contained questions about mothers' relationships with their families of origin, that is, their siblings and parents, who were termed maternal grandparents in this study. Questions dealt with frequency of communication. They were also asked if they ever received help from their families and if there were others they felt able to call upon for help. The interviewing of fathers on these issues was not as detailed, since they were usually seen only once as compared with the three or more conferences held with mothers. They were, however, asked about relationships with coworkers and neighbors, and if they ever helped each other. From collating answers to these various questions, parents were classified in terms of the following ordinal scale, which we call the Family Support Index.

1. *Completely isolated.* No one helps or client stated only person to be counted on was a social worker or other professional helper.
2. *Family dyad.* One parent or one sibling can be counted on to help.
3. *Friend dependent.* Only one friend can be called on; no family member can be.
4. *Family bound.* Two or more members of the immediate family—parent(s) or sibling(s)—can be called on.
5. *Family and friend related.* At least one member of immediate family and one friend or more distant relative can be called on.
6. *Supported.* At least one member of immediate family and at least two friends can be called on to help.

Each parent's responses were classified according to the Family Support Index. The family unit was also assigned a score, based on the higher of the two in two-parent households, or on the mother in

Table 7.1: Distribution of Parents on the Family Support Index (Frequencies)

Family Support Index	Mothers Only		Fathers Only		Family	
	Neglect	Control	Neglect	Control	Neglect	Control
1. Completely isolated	13	3	6	7	10	3
2. Family dyad	2	2	5	4	3	2
3. Friend dependent	6	2	2	4	6	1
4. Family bound	11	6	4	5	12	5
5. Family and friend related	7	8	1	3	7	6
6. Supported	6	58	3	24	7	62
Insufficient data	1	0	1	3	1	0
Total	46	79	22	50	46	79

one-parent households. The outcome of the scoring is given in table 7.1.

It may seem to the reader that this was not a very demanding scale. It did not prove so for parents in the control group, for 62 of these 79 families were classified supported, the highest point. Only 7 of the neglect, or 15% of those classified, reached this position. So the familiar social work assumption that "everybody has friends" did prove justified among these low-income, urban, white families, but not for those implicated in neglect. Differences between groups were tested by comparing proportions low on the index (ratings 1, 2, and 3) with those high (ratings 4, 5, and 6). Nonneglect mothers scored higher than neglect ($P < .001$ by Chi-square test); nonneglect fathers higher than neglect ($P < .01$); and nonneglect families higher than neglect ($P < .001$). So far as the ready access to informal sources of help is concerned, our neglectful parents were not in an average-expectable position of others of similar social backgrounds. The impression from the mountain study was confirmed. Wolock and Horowitz (1979) were conducting their research at the same time as we and, it will be recalled, found that maltreating mothers saw their neighbors as less friendly than did the controls (chapter 3).

Other researchers have also commented on the relative isolation of parents involved in maltreatment. The characteristic is especially mentioned in connection with abusive parents, but also has been cited in instances of failure to thrive (Evans, Reinhart, and Succop 1972; Martin 1976; Elmer 1967; Smith, Hanson, and Noble 1974). Although the great majority of the control parents scored at the highest point on the Family Support Index, neglect families were distributed throughout and a fifth of them were rated completely isolated.

What are the explanations for these differences? Were more of the neglect parents geographically mobile newcomers to the area?

Some Relevant Demography

In the course of collecting histories from the parents a number of matters were touched on which are germane to the question. As is shown in table 7.2, the parents in both groups were, predominantly, born in Philadelphia, and the majority were, in fact, second generation native-born.

In the neglect father-present households, half the mothers still resided in the neighborhoods of their childhood; among the father absent, the figure was lower, 33%. Among the nonneglect, the comparable figures were 62% and 48%. Just about half the fathers in each sample still resided in their home neighborhoods. Thus

Table 7.2: Backgrounds of Study Parents*

| | Percentage of | |
Factor	Neglect	Control
Mother born in Philadelphia or suburbs	78.3	92.4
Father born in Philadelphia or suburbs	85.7	85.1
Maternal grandmother born in Philadelphia	56.8	83.5
Maternal grandfather born in Philadelphia	57.8	66.2
Paternal grandmother born in Philadelphia	75.0	73.9
Paternal grandfather born in Philadelphia	80.0	57.4
Maternal grandmother still lives in Philadelphia	70.5	74.7
Paternal grandmother still lives in Philadelphia	47.6	78.7
Mother from family of 4 or more	63.0	63.3
Father from family of 4 or more	61.9	68.1
Maternal grandmother deceased	11.4	12.7
Maternal grandfather deceased	45.5	32.0
Paternal grandmother deceased	28.6	6.4
Paternal grandfather deceased	52.4	21.7
Mother never married	6.5	0.0

*Percentages refer to cases on which data were known.

there were some discrepancies between the groups favoring the control parents, but these were not at all of the order of the differences found regarding placement in helping networks.

Over three-fifths of each group had three or more siblings, most of whom were geographically reasonably accessible. However, they reported quite different relationships with them. Forty-two percent of the neglect mothers rarely or never visited with their brothers and sisters; this was true of only 3% of the control mothers. Forty percent of the neglect fathers rarely or never visited with siblings as compared with 18% of the nonneglect. In chapter 11, we will give more detail on the distant and/or ambivalent relationship that many parents involved in neglect have toward their own families of origin.

There was one index of mobility on which the two samples showed a sharp difference. The nonneglect parents reported a median of 1.2 changes of residence during or since the present marriage; the neglectful, a median of 3.4. Proximity does have much to do with the formation of attachments in urban settings, and even a move of several blocks could, one supposes, rupture some of these. But one must still wonder whether their moving made these parents more isolated, or whether their lack of ties made it easier for them to move. In any event, it is clear that we were rarely dealing with mobility problems of the sort that have afflicted rural black families coming north from Mississippi, or Appalachian whites working in Toledo and Detroit. The opportunities to become members of helping networks were not really that different between the groups.

Alienation

Are neglectful parents likely to be rejected by their neighbors? Are they perceived as unlikely to return favors, or as objects of scorn? In the mountains, we became aware that these attitudes were often present. However, one would have to interview the neighbors, as well as the families in the study, to establish their sociometric positions, and this, of course, was not done. There are, however, data regarding the parents' own attitudes which proved revealing.

Most parents offering the poorer child care showed little or no interest in events in the larger society; the same was often as true about happenings in their local communities. Several sociologists have theorized that those in the lower socioeconomic statuses tend to be alienated. Since so much is beyond them they feel futile, and withdraw from participating in social movements. One of our own studies suggested that among adolescents from mountain communities a feeling of powerlessness was greater among those more socioeconomically disadvantaged (Polansky 1969). The impression, nevertheless, was that alienation among these parents was noticeably greater than for most other poor people. There are others living in poverty who retain humor and bounce, who challenge the fates and city hall—but not these parents.

Each parent interviewed was administered Srole's scale for anomia (1956). The scale consists of only five statements. The respondent is asked to agree or disagree with each. They are:
1. These days a person doesn't really know whom he can count on.
2. In spite of what people say, the lot of the average man is getting worse, not better.
3. Most public officials are not really interested in the problems of the average man.
4. Nowadays, a person has to live pretty much for today and let tomorrow take care of itself.
5. It's hardly fair to bring children into the world the way things look for the future.

Scores range from zero to five, depending on how many of these statements are agreed with. While Srole, as a sociologist, sees his scale as measuring the individual response to societal *anomie*, the scale has seemed to us also to reflect what we regard clinically as feelings of futility (Polansky 1973). Average scores for the various groups of respondents are in table 7.3.

In both father absent and father present circumstances, the mothers identified as neglectful showed more alienation than those recruited from the community ($P < .001$ by analysts of variance). The difference between the fathers was also significant ($P < .05$ by

Table 7.3: Mean Scores on Srole's Anomia Scale

	Fathers	Mothers	
		Father Present	Father Absent
Neglect	3.10	3.64	3.74
Control	2.19	2.42	3.17

t-test). So our impression that these people tend to be more alienated than are other poor people was confirmed by the parents themselves.

Women living with a father figure in the home reported less alienation ($P < .05$ by ANOVA), a fact to which we will return in chapter 10. And the mothers in each group scored higher than the fathers (overall female mean 3.06 vs. 2.47 for males), a difference that was also statistically significant ($P < .01$ by t-test), a result that some might interpret, again, as reflecting their relative power positions in social classes 4 and 5. But the key difference, for present purposes, was that between the neglect and nonneglect samples. This suggests that, whether or not the less adequate parents are being rejected, they are less likely to seek others out.

A Pattern of Nonparticipation

Does this relative isolation extend in other areas as well, such as participation in formal organizations? This has been a matter much studied over the years, and it has been found repeatedly that lower-class respondents have fewer such memberships.

To summarize the interviewing on formal social organizations, respondents were grouped into three categories. A low rating meant either no memberships, or only *pro forma* membership (e.g., residing in a Catholic parish, belonging to a compulsory union). Those active in one formal organization, and belonging to at least another were adjudged medium. An example would be a mother active in P.T.A. and a member of her church. Those active in two or more groups were rated high. The results are given in table 7.4.

The overall difference between neglect and nonneglect mothers rated low was significant at beyond .001 (by Chi-square test); that between the fathers was also significant at .001. Parents implicated in neglect, then, are much less likely than are those of similar socio-economic background to participate in formal organizational activities. Among the mothers there was an interesting interaction, to which we shall again refer in chapter 10. The married controls were more likely to participate than those living fatherless ($P < .001$); but among the neglectful, those living father absent were more participatory ($P = .025$, Fisher's Exact Test).

Table 7.4: Parents' Formal Organizational Activity (Frequency)

| | Mothers | | | | Fathers | |
| | Neglect | | Control | | | |
Level of Activity	Father Present	Father Absent	Father Present	Father Absent	Neglect	Control
High	0	5	28	5	3	19
Medium	3	4	16	14	0	13
Low	19	14	6	10	18	15
Insufficient data	0	1	0	0	1	3
Total	22	24	50	29	22	50

Table 7.5: Informal Socializing by Parents (Numbers)

"Going-out" Score	Mothers		Fathers	
	Neglect	Control	Neglect	Control
High	16	54	9	22
Medium	9	17	7	19
Low	20	8	5	6
Insufficient data	1	0	1	3
Total	46	79	22	50

The results with regard to formal organizational involvement were, of course, hardly surprising. But what about informal socializing? Were our neglectful parents gadabouts, thus contributing to their children's problems, or did they seem relatively withdrawn? To study this, we developed a scale which, in local parlance, we termed the "Going-out" score. Parents were rated, again, high, medium, or low on their socializing, whether in bars, restaurants, or neighbors' homes. Assessments of our groups are given in table 7.5.

Among the neglectful mothers, 44% reported themselves low on going-out, as compared with only 10% of the controls. Differences between the fathers were not nearly as great, although they tended toward the same direction. One might have thought that the neglect woman living without a man would be the more active socially, but actually 93.7% of the control single mothers reported at least a medium level of such socializing, versus 54.2% of the neglect. The difference was of just about the same order among those living father present (88% vs. 54.5%). Both members of the control couples socialized to the same degree, but among the neglect couples fathers more often left the women at home.

The lack of social participation was not a new phenomenon in the lives of parents in the neglect sample. We constructed a scale to measure level of ego functioning in adolescence which also included the person's socialization at that stage of his or her life. Called the Education-Dating-Occupation (E-D-O) scale, it had correlated, in the Appalachian study, with the level of care parents were giving their children as adults. Shuford (1978) also compared rural mothers identified as abusive with women on Aid to Families of Dependent Children and with mothers of emotionally disturbed children, using the original version of the E-D-O. The mean score for the abusive women was 1.3; for the other two samples the means were 3.2 and 2.9 ($P < .01$ by t-test). Criteria for the E-D-O were changed in Philadelphia to fit the urban environment. For example, graduation from high school appeared to be the norm there, whereas graduation from eighth grade had been more typical of the low-income rural sample. The current scoring awarded one point for each of the following:

· graduation from high school;

· having dated at least one person other than the one married;

· having participated in extracurricular activities in high school;

· having worked outside the home for a year or more prior to marriage.

Hence there was a five-point scale, from zero to four, with the higher score reflecting more participation during adolescence. Mean scores of the various subsamples are listed in table 7.6.

For most average-expectable youngsters, the E-D-O would not be a very demanding scale. Thus the low scores attained by women in the neglect sample were the more striking, averaging half that of the control women. Difference between fathers, on the other hand, was not so noteworthy. Speaking especially of the mothers, then, it appears that they were starting to fall outside the mainstream already in adolescence. Lack of participation, in other words, was not a new thing in their lives.

Indeed, it appeared that their being outside the ordinary informal network of mutual support reflected something relatively enduring about their personalities. If this were the case, one might expect that how they responded to the Srole at the time of our study might have some association with their level of adolescent adjustment as compiled in the E-D-O. This possibility was tested and, indeed, there was a low but significant inverse relationship between the amount of futility expressed on the Srole and index of adolescent adaptation ($r = -.26$, $P < .001$) among all parents in the study.

Helplessness and Futility

The review of results commenced with an observation about the social ecology of the neglectful parents. As compared with the pattern usual among families who were similar in background, they were isolated from helping networks. It turned out, however, that the isolation was more general than at first appeared, extending to both formal and informal participation with others, and it was

Table 7.6: Mean Scores on the E-D-O Scale

Parent	Sample	
	Neglect	Control
Father-present mothers	1.09	2.76
Father-absent mothers	1.70	2.62
All mothers	1.40	2.71
Fathers	2.43	2.91

accompanied by feelings of alienation to a degree that was unusual, again, even among families on limited incomes. Moreover, the lack of social involvement was visible already in adolescence, prior to their becoming parents. The data led, in other words, from a fact about their ecology to observations on character structure.

This is not to discount the ecological approach. Life, as we shall reiterate, is not fair. If anxieties and hostilities limit contacts with others, if personality limitations leave one with little to give to others, then there is, in fact, an additional disadvantage: one lacks the supports other people can take for granted. One is left with a "spiral of causation," as they say in general systems theory, leading downward. So the ecological and personalistic approaches must be seen as complementary rather than mutually exclusive.

The interplay of situation with personality reactions can be seen in a related connection. Most depressed people are more or less immobilized; they also experience a feeling of helplessness to do anything about their state. Thus it has been usual to regard feelings of helplessness as an affective state symptomatic of, or brought on by, the underlying dynamics of depression (Rapaport 1967). Edward Bibring, however, saw the relationship differently. He wrote: "Depression can be defined . . . as the emotional expression of a state of helplessness in the ego" (1953, p. 760). It seems that the experience of helplessness reactivates an infantile state that is both perilous for life and accompanied by depression.

But helplessness is not just a subjective state. How one experiences the world does not precisely mirror it, of course. Yet reality also strongly affects our perceptions and reactions. To be unable to manage for oneself *and* to have no one else to turn to must magnify the feeling of helplessness to which Bibring alluded. The results of this unhappy combination of subjective and objective isolation were visible in the lonely women we encountered.

Moreover, there is mounting evidence that isolation is dangerous to one's physical survival as well. A recent study by Berkman and Syme (1979) reported on a nine-year mortality follow-up of a random sample of residents in Alameda County, California. "The age-adjusted relative risks for those most isolated when compared with those with the most social contacts were 2.3 for men and 2.8 for women" (p. 186). This was true even when such factors as previous state of health, smoking, drinking, and so forth were controlled for. Whether the neglectful mother had her isolation imposed on her or brought it on herself, its effects were serious for her and for her children.

Eight

Character Problems of
the Parents

Among parents who are neglectful or in danger of becoming
neglectful of their children there are those who are simply overwhelmed by external pressures, those who are unknowing of
standards expected from them in a community whose ways are
strange to them, those whose physical stamina is unequal to the
task of child rearing, those reacting to their children in terms of
their own unresolved conflicts and unmet needs within their
own past or present circumstances, and those who are mentally
ill. There are also likely to be a considerable number of parents
with defects in ego development who are diagnosed clinically as
character disorders. [Meier 1964, p. 186]

When Meier made her informed list of conditions leading to
neglect she had little research on which to draw. Her statements
were really hypotheses drawn from her own and her colleagues'
practice. Each of these possible causes seems plausible; one ought to
be able to cite one or more cases demonstrating each causal chain.
But if one is planning a program for treating neglect or for training
protective service workers in ways of dealing with it, information is
needed that goes beyond the listing. How frequently is a given cause
at work? Which forms of character disorder are most often in evidence? Are there other low-income parents who show the same ego
defects, but whose children are well cared for? As an example, we
might note that not knowing the standards expected of them in a
new community was not much at issue among the parents in our

Philadelphia study, since the majority had been there all their lives.

In this chapter, we shall set down our main findings regarding the personalities of the parents. It has already been shown that quality of child care tends to be "all of a piece"; it was then shown that failure of neglectful parents to participate in helping networks is part of a more general pattern of unrelatedness. The suggestion has been strong that whatever is wrong with the parents is pervasive. Theoretically, failure to provide adequate nurture could derive from what Meier termed "unresolved conflicts" in an otherwise intact personality; practically, the damage found has not seemed so delimitable. The findings thus far imply deficits with the warp and woof of functioning, involving both character traits and character disorders. On which traits, then, on which ego functions do neglectful parents differ from others?

The Maternal Characteristics Scale

The person on our staff who knew the mothers best was the research caseworker. Although information collected by the worker can be (and was) later submitted to assessment by a reader, it seemed essential to take advantage of the worker's own impressions. Therefore a way had to be devised by which such clinical learning could be summarized and quantified for statistical analysis.

It was also important that the process of rating parents be made as objective and discrete as possible, to counter the danger of contamination among judgments. The caseworker knew which family had been referred as neglectful; the worker was also responsible for the Childhood Level of Living Scale. In the worst case of circularity, correlations obtained would not reflect the realities of the parents so much as the workers' expectations of them.

As with the CLL, the way in which we tried to combat halo effects was by reducing the scope and ambiguity of each judgment the worker had to make. The Maternal Characteristics Scale (or MCS) was made up of a large number of declarative statements. Each described a way of acting that the worker could affirm as true (yes) about the mother or false (no). The items included in the original Maternal Characteristics Scale in the Appalachian study were in part borrowed from a scale used in evaluating psychiatric patients. Since that scale, however, was too oriented toward severe pathology to fit our clientele, a number of items were replaced by forms of behavior we thought indicative, diagnostically, of various character neuroses or character disorders. Many of the latter came, of course, from the senior author's clinical background.

The rural study was more exploratory than the replication, of course, and at the time of the latter there was much more clarity about the traits, or dimensions of character, of interest. Specifically, the traits about which we had hypotheses were: degree of *apathy-futility*, by which was meant the relative prevalence of elements typical of the apathy-futility syndrome; degree of *impulsivity*, that is, presence of elements associated with the impulse-ridden character; and *verbal accessibility*, or the willingness to talk about one's most important attitudes and feelings. Based on intercorrelations in the earlier study, sixty items were chosen from the rural version of the MCS, selecting the twenty that seemed to load most heavily into each of the traits we wished to measure. As with the Childhood Level of Living Scale, the items were placed randomly on the forms used by the research caseworkers. Indeed, they were not told the dimensions to which each judgment was expected to contribute.

Of the 125 women in the study, only one was regarded by her worker as having been too elusive to permit ratings. Using the 124 forms available, Dr. Snyder then subjected the sixty items to factor analysis. The results were only partially supportive of the grouping of the items we had had in mind. Some fitted together as we had expected on rational grounds, but others fell empirically into factors that were different from those projected. Four factors were found which, together, accounted for 79.5% of the variance of the item pool. The thirty-five items involved are given in appendix 2. It is important to bear in mind that the scales were developed, of course, without reference to an external criterion, such as whether or not the mother being scored was deemed neglectful.

We should mention here something that also applies to the CLL. It would have been easy to set up a Beta weight for each item, but this did not seem appropriate. In our experience, such intricate loadings are very likely to require recasting when new studies with new samples are done, so there seems little to gain by complicating the scoring. Hence, each item is scored as a plus or a zero, unweighted. Thus with respect to factor I, relatedness, item 10, "It is hard for her to consider a new way of looking at the same thing" is scored plus if no, zero if yes, and 26, "Can laugh at herself" is scored plus for a yes, zero for a no.

As with the CLL, the score on each factor was simply the percentage of pluses scored out of all items rated. The use of percentages made scores comparable from parent to parent even though one or two items had not been scored. Sometimes failure to score an item represented an oversight, but there were occasions when the worker felt absolutely unable to make the rating, despite the injunction always to attempt one if at all possible.

The four factors on the Maternal Characteristics Scale, to which we shall refer in this chapter, were as follows:

I.   *Relatedness* (absence of apathy and detachment)

Consists of 13 items, e.g., "Says she enjoys living"; see above p. 99. Eigen value 17.62, accounting for 55.5% of variance of the measurement universe sampled by the MCS.

II. *Impulse-control*

Includes 10 items, e.g., "Has engaged in behavior not acceptable in her own community"; "Apparently married to escape an unpleasant home situation." Eigen value 3.13; accounts for 9.9% of the variance.

III. *Confidence* (Absence of Futility)

Has 7 items, e.g., "Has a sad expression or holds her body in a dejected or despondent manner"; "Mentions she is aimless, or getting nowhere." Eigen value 2.43; 7.7% of variance.

IV. *Verbal Accessibility*

Contains only 5 items, e.g., "Answers questions with a single word or phrase only"; "Shows warmth in tone in discussing her children." Eigen value 2.03; 6.4% of variance.

Since each of these factors, as scored, reflected something positive about ego strength, it was not surprising that they were intercorrelated. The intercorrelations proved substantial, ranging from .44 to .66. That degree of association naturally raised question about the independence of the factors and of the traits scaled. However, differential relationships to other measures emerged that seemed meaningful, so for some analyses, the scores were handled separately. The intercorrelation made it legitimate to combine factors as well. Relatedness and confidence, factors I and III, were combined into a measure termed "reciprocal of apathy-futility"; it was termed reciprocal because the higher the score, the fewer the elements of the syndrome. It also seemed that these two factors could also be combined with impulse-control to yield an overall score termed "reciprocal of infantilism."

Is the Maternal Characteristics Scale susceptible to worker biases? Might one research caseworker depict less pathology in applying the scale than would another? The best answer would come from independent assessments of the same sample of mothers, who were known equally well to all workers. Such an experimental test of interrater reliability was not possible in this study. But if one could assume that case assignment, which was done pretty much by rotation, meant the sample of mothers known to one worker was probably the same as that known to another, then the failure to find systematic differences among the workers would be reassurance that their scaling was being done evenly. Analyses of variance were done, comparing distributions of scores of the three workers. For relatedness and impulse-control the probabilities were .157 and .100 respectively, implying no significant differences among average ratings made. On confidence, the scores of one worker (EB) were more generous than were those of the other two, but we felt this could by accounted for by the nature of the cases she had. But the small scale for verbal accessibility proved to have been applied in such fashion that each worker's mean score was significantly different from that of the other two, with EB most generous, and MAC the least. This small scale, therefore, proved highly susceptible to worker bias. The findings from this analysis resulted in our not including the verbal accessibility items in the overall reciprocal of infantilism score. Fortunately, other ratings of verbal accessibility were being made.

How did the mothers identified as neglectful compare with the nonneglect women on these scales? Table 8.1 gives the outcome of the relevant data analyses in a manner analogous with that employed with respect to the Childhood Level of Living Scale. Differences between means were tested by ANOVA and all were highly significant. The strength of each association between MCS factor and the neglect/control dichotomy was calculated as a point-biserial correlation, as before. The strongest association was with impulse-control. Absence of apathy-futility elements also proved substantially correlated in this study.

The same ANOVAs also related MCS factors to whether the mother was living father present or father absent. Only impulse-control showed a significant relationship. The mean for father present mothers was .77; that for father absent .54 ($P < .001$ by ANOVA). The relationship, nevertheless, was not nearly as strong as with neglect/control ($r_{pt.-bis.} = .37$).

Subsequent to our Appalachian studies, Shuford (1978) completed a small extension of the work with the help of our colleague, Robert D. Borgman. Shuford compared ten mothers identified as abusive with two other samples: mothers of disturbed or "problem" children and mothers simply on Aid to Families of Dependent Children. Both the investigator and the caseworker completed

Table 8.1: Comparison of Neglect with Control Mothers on the Maternal Characteristics Scale

MCS Factor	Mean Score*		Point-Biserial Correlation
	Neglect	Control	
I. Relatedness	.27	.65	.54
II. Impulse-control	.40	.83	.70
III. Confidence	.29	.70	.53
IV. Verbal accessibility	.47	.78	.49
I. + III. Apathy-futility (reciprocal)	.28	.67	.58
I., II., III. Infantilism (reciprocal)	.34	.73	.69

*All mean differences significant at $P < .001$ by ANOVA: N = 124.

Childhood Level of Living Scales on the families; the original rural version of the Maternal Characteristics Scale was also filled out. Interrater reliability of $r = .81$ was achieved overall. The abusive mothers scored significantly higher than the other two samples on apathy-futility and on childish impulsivity ratings. They were also found to be offering a substantially poorer level of child care, far poorer than that of the women on welfare.

Our Appalachian research had turned our attention to the apathy-futility syndrome. The research in Philadelphia impressed us with the significance of impulsivity in the character structures of neglectful mothers. We also concluded from these analyses that the reciprocal of infantilism measure was a good summary rating of the mother's overall level of functioning, and this combined index played a major role in later discriminant function analyses (see p. 112).

Aspects of Ego Strength Assessed by Cases Judges

Much of the data for our study were recorded directly on the interview outline. However, following each contact, the worker also dictated a narrative record in the style usual in social work. The dictation included the circumstances involved in obtaining cooperation, incidents encountered while visiting, worker-client exchanges that seemed meaningful, and the like. Many of the vignettes our workers were able to write, which are so useful in bringing the participants to life, were drawn from such narrative material. The narrative was also used to provide a partial reliability check of the workers' judgments about parental personalities.

Each case record was gone over carefully by a case reader or judge. All three case judges were trained and experienced psychiatric social workers. Two were employed specifically for this task. Gertrude Persky's many years of experience were in Chicago; Myra Singer's largely in Cincinnati. The other judges was David Williams, who for a period was assigned to coordinate this phase of our work. Of course, he did not participate in the rating of records of cases on which he himself had been the research social worker. It is important to note that in reviewing the record for the ratings he or she was to make, the judge had access to all of the narrative, and to client's responses to questions on the interview outline, but the judge did not have the worker's ratings of the Maternal Characteristics Scale, nor—at first—the psychologist's report. The latter was made available only for the final judgment, which was to classify the parent according to a standard diagnosis.

The research caseworkers, it will be recalled, had not attempted to rate the fathers in the study with the specificity demanded from an instrument such as the Maternal Characteristics Scale. For one thing, there was much more contact with the mothers, while many fathers were seen only for one long interview. The judges' ratings, however, were more global, and so they tried to assess the fathers as well as the mothers. How valid these ratings of fathers proved to be can be assessed from results given below.

As all experienced researchers know, in devising a scheme for coding written documents one strikes a compromise between all things one would like to scale and the limitations imposed by the available data. We began our code with a list of character traits that interested us, and on which we suspected there were differences between the parents implicated in neglect and the others. Only those that survived the process of screening for feasibility and re-liability of judgments (i.e., intercoder reliability) will be reported. Each of these traits is a facet of "ego strength," by which we mean the *adaptive capacity* of the personality.

Reliability of coding was tested by having each of a pair of the judges rate a sample of cases independently, and by then comparing their scores on each variable rated. Coefficients of reliability were then calculated using the statistic appropriate to the type of scale on which the judgment was being made (Rosen and Polansky 1975). Judgments on dimensions that could be assumed to be interval scales were expressed by the product-moment correlation r; several scales did not seem to have interval properties, so for these we applied Cohen's Kappa (Cohen 1960; Rosen and Polansky 1975). In the instance of a multiply coded nominal scale, we were reduced to the percent-agreement score.

Two reliability checks were run with independent samples in the course of coding the cases. Since there were three possible pairs among the three judges, we had a total of six comparisons of the coding on each scale. Some of the reliabilities achieved were not as high as one would wish. However, the measures retained for later analyses in the study were kept because of their theoretical interest, and also because there were evidences of construct validity in later phases of the study. In a further effort to ensure valid ratings, each case was coded by two judges. Discrepancies were resolved by con-ference, so that the final score represents a pooled judgment in each instance. Out of the processes of checking reliability and agreeing on final coding, the concepts were refined and clarified and, in several instances, reformulated. We are grateful to the judges not only for their enduring so tedious a task, but also for their sub-stantive contributions to the study.

The character traits associated with the scales retained in the study included the following:

Apathy-futility. The definition employed by the judges was taken verbatim from previous publications (see chapter 4). Converting the syndrome into a scale meant assessing the degree to which elements of the diagnosis were present in the personality. The scale had such anchoring points as "Typifies the a-f syndrome"; "Several elements of the a-f syndrome are observable"; "No evidence of apathy-futility."

Let us take this scale to illustrate concretely how reliability was tested. Three judges permitted three possible pairings, that is, Persky-Singer; Persky-Williams; Singer-Williams. Each pair read a common group of cases and rated them. Assuming the ratings were being made on interval scales, we calculated three product-moment correlations. On a later occasion, the procedure was repeated, so we now had six product-moment correlations (r) representing the interjudge reliability of the apathy-futility scale. To average a group of r's, one transforms each into its equivalent z-score, gets the mean of the z-scores and then transforms back into an equivalent which is the average r. On apathy-futility, the mean r was .72. We should have preferred this to be higher, but it did suggest that the scaling would be usable in comparisons between groups. Certainly there was substantial agreement among the judges.

Impulsivity. This was defined as failure to have developed normal control systems for binding drive-discharge and/or acting out in the service of defense. It was typified by such attitudes as "I want what I want when I want it"; low tolerance for frustration or delay; frequent absence of planning; shortened time perspective; and poor judgment about consequences of action. Judgments were based primarily on recorded behavior, rather than inference from life-circumstances. The scale included: "Typifies impulse-ridden character"; "Impulsivity present but there are no significant consequences"; "No real evidence of impulsivity." Average r among judgments was .70.

Verbal Accessibility. This is the readiness of a client to express in words, and to permit others to talk with him about, his most important attitudes and feelings (cf. Polansky, Borgman, DeSaix, and Sharlin 1971). To achieve a high score there must, of course, be willingness to talk. However, verbal accessibility is not to be confused with verbosity or circumlocution. The scale used by the judge was the same as that used by the psychologist, and also by the research caseworker (i.e., the global rating of VA, not the index derived from the Maternal Characteristics Scale). The six-point scale ranges from "Spontaneous verbalization" to "Responsive, equal give and take with caseworker" to "Avoids or evades verbal expression." Average r was .65, for the judges, which we found disappointing, and was probably due to the nature of the narrative data they had to work with.

Workmanship. This was defined as the ability, and desire, to become engrossed in tasks even if the steps involved are neither intrinsically nor immediately rewarding. In a reasonably mature level of workmanship, work is invested with pleasure and there is capacity to value accomplishment or the work-product in relatively nonnarcissistic ways. An extreme example of investment of work might be termed "a passion" (Lowenstein 1976). Child caring, housekeeping, and home chores entered into the ratings of mothers. If the father had a job, his rating related primarily to his paid employment. Scale points included, "Works relatively happily and steadily much of the day"; "Experiences work as a necessary evil"; "Work is resented and avoided whenever possible." The average intercoder *r* was .74, which seemed to us rather promising for this attempt to bring to measureable terms one of Erikson's (1959) significant concepts.

Capacity for Object Relations involved an overall clinical judgment of the parent's ability to relate warmly and to give to a younger person. Evidence was taken from various questions on the interview outline concerning attitudes, along with other data. The nine-point scale included "Able to offer supportive, nurturing, individuating relationship with reasonable consistency"; "Capacity good although occasionally breaks down because of internal stress, i.e., intrapsychic problems"; "Often unable to nurture appropriately because of external stress"; "Unable to separate child's needs from own and/or relate to them; unable to provide minimal emotional support." In the final data analyses, we decided this could be treated as an interval scale. However, at first we treated it conservatively as nominal, and its reliability was tested by Cohen's Kappa. The six obtained Kappas ranged by .35 to .54; all were significantly better than chance.

Noteworthy Symptoms were recorded by a judge using a prepared check-list. Most frequently listed were complaints regarded as psychosomatic, e.g., headaches, gastrointestinal distress, dizziness. A few were defined psychological symptoms, e.g., irritability, early waking. Symptoms reported present in the past were also listed, but general traits of character were not. The resulting variety was very large and, since the average parent reported more than one symptom, Kappa could not be used. The percent-agreement score (see Rosen and Polansky 1975, p. 175) averaged 74%.

Of specific symptoms, only three were more prevalent in one group than the other. Neglect mothers more frequently reported palpitations ($P < .01$ by Chi-square); weight gain ($P < .02$ by Chi-square with Yates's correction); and alcoholism ($P < .02$, Chi-square, corrected). In subsequent analyses of data, a parent's symptoms score represented simply a count of all the different

Table 8.2: Numbers of Symptoms Reported by Parents

	Mean Number	
Parent	Neglect	Control
Mother: father absent	4.52	3.41
Mother: father present	4.05	2.96
Father	1.57	1.36

symptoms agreed to be present by two readers of that case.

Because we hypothesized more character disorder among them, it occurred to us that the neglect parents might bind anxiety by acting out, and so show fewer delineable symptoms. The other possibility, however, was that if anxiety tolerance were less, they would be more likely to form symptoms. As things worked out, more symptomatology was noted in this group than among the control (see table 8.2).

No significance was attached to the fact that means for fathers ran so much lower than the mothers', since the interviewing was briefer with them. However, in both neglect and control groups. women living father absent reported more symptoms than those in intact households. We were also struck by the amount of symptomatology found in women in the control group. Of course, ours is by no means the first study to find evidence of fairly wide-spread emotional problems in working-class populations (Brown and Harris 1978).

Parental Ego Strength Related to Child Caring

Which traits rated by the judges have most to do with the quality of child care? The measure of caliber of care was the family's score on the Childhood Level of Living Scale. These ratings were not reviewed by the judge and, indeed, the final scoring had not yet been

Table 8.3: Relation of Indices of Maternal Ego-Strength to Score on Childhood Level of Living Scale

	Correlation (r) with CLL:	
Judges' Rating of Mother's:	Physical Care Total	Emotional/Cognitive Total
Absence of apathy-futility	.69	.77
Absence of impulsivity	.54	.55
Verbal accessibility	.51	.62
Workmanship	.77	.73
Capacity for object relations	.64	.72
Number of reported symptoms	−.24*	−.30

*$P < .01$; all others $< .001$ by t-test $N = 124$.

done when the cases were being read. On the other hand, whether the case was neglect or nonneglect could not be concealed from the judge. Relevant correlations of judges' assessments with CLL indices are summarized in table 8.3.

All correlations proved significant beyond the .001 level of ANOVA, and most were strong. The data strongly implied that there was a substantial relationship between maternal character and the caliber of care focal children were receiving. As for the fathers, similar correlations for them are presented in table 8.4.

With the exception of the zero-order association to the symptoms score, correlations between judges' ratings of paternal traits having to do with ego strength and the CLL indices were also significantly different from zero. Although these associations were weaker than the mothers', it appears that such parental traits as a capacity for object relations, workmanship, and the absence of apathy-futility all have at least moderate correlations with the Childhood Level of Living Scale. It is evident that, in those families in which fathers are present, paternal character was also associated with the quality of care.

Interobserver Reliabilities of Personality Ratings

Ratings by the research social workers, naturally, were not independent of the narratives they dictated. Still, the ratings by a judge at least represent impressions gained from the evidence by another experienced professional. To the extent that the formation of these impressions was independent, rating by the judge served as a partial check of the interobserver reliability of the trait scale under consideration.

In the case of one trait, the study design provided an instance of true independence of ratings. The verbal accessibility of the subject

Table 8.4: Relation of Indices of Paternal Ego-Strength to Score on Childhood Level of Living Scale

	Correlation (r) with CLL·	
Judges' Rating of Father's:	Physical Care Total	Emotional/Cognitive Total
Absence of apathy-futility	.45	.47
Absence of impulsivity	.32*	.35*
Verbal accessibility	.26**	.32*
Workmanship	.45	.47
Capacity for object relations	.56	.63
Number of reported symptoms	.07†	.02†

*$P < .01$; **$P < .02$; †P not significant by test.
All others, $P < .001$. N = 68.

being tested was also rated by the psychologist, on the "global scale" for this judgment. The psychologist, it will be recalled, conducted his or her testing "blind," i.e., not knowing whether the parent or child being seen was from the neglect or the control sample. The relevant correlations are given in table 8.5.

None of the obtained correlations attained the level of agreement we demand, for example, in instruments for observations of groups by observers who watch the group simultaneously. But the psychologist's appraisal was limited by the structure of the situation. Moreover, the worker typically dealt with the parents in their home rather than in our office. It is not at all clear that most people become less open about important feelings in strange situations; some become more open. But the home/office difference was at least an additional factor which conceivably lowered reliability. Nevertheless, we noted that both worker and judge had significant agreement with the psychologist in rating verbal accessibility. In the assessments of mothers, the agreement was substantial. We may conclude that verbal accessibility was rated with agreement that went far beyond chance; we may also conclude that terming verbal accessibility a "trait," an aspect of character (Polansky 1971) was further supported in the present study. Its expression was sufficiently stable across situations to have led to agreement between caseworker and psychologist. Finally, the social worker's ratings of verbal accessibility on the global scale showed higher correlations with those of others than did their ratings on the composite index derived from the Maternal Characteristics Scale (factor IV).

Table 8.5 Interobserver Reliabilities of Various Ratings of Verbal Accessibility

Ratings Compared	Correlation* r
A. On mother	
research social worker (global) X judge (global)	.66
research social worker (MCS IV) X judge (global)	.53
research social worker (global) X psychologist (global)	.54
judge X psychologist	.52
B. On father	
research social worker (global) X judge	.58
research social worker X psychologist	.33
judge X psychologist	.30

*All r's significant at $P < .001$ by t-test.

Two other trait ratings were directly comparable between the judges and workers. A reciprocal of apathy-futility had been composed by combining factors I and III from the Maternal Characteristics Scale. Similarly, the judge's global rating of the prevalence of apathy-futility elements was so scored that a higher score reflected less of the syndrome. Judgments were available on 124 mothers, and the correlation was again substantial, $r = +.78$ $(P < .001)$. The reciprocal of impulsivity as rated by the research caseworker was also correlated with the judge's global rating of the trait, and yielded $r = +.73$ $(P < .001)$. Using the recordings available to them, the judges corroborated the social workers on both these indices. We found the reliability encouraging as to the probable validity of the judgments being made by each.

Diagnoses

What have we learned about the neglectful parents thus far? These parents were certainly functioning on a level far better, say, than that of regressed psychotics or severely retarded adults. But their standard for comparison was other adults of similar cultural background who were also caring for young children. The assessment by the research caseworkers, which was corroborated by the case judges, depicted a group of people with a modal personality: less able to love, less capable of working productively, less open about feelings, more prone to living planlessly and impulsively, but also susceptible to psychological symptoms and to phases of passive inactivity and numb fatalism. The image is one of men and women who do not cope well with life. Based on what has now been learned about residua of chronic deprivation and life accidents on the personality, one assumes their histories have left them with developmental failures and fixations. Perhaps the term infantile will now appear to the reader less bizarre or extreme than when it was first introduced.

There is another language for summarizing personality which is, of course, more familiar to our readers than the concepts we have been using. These are the standard diagnoses. The final task of the case reader was to arrive at a diagnostic "impression" (we are not psychiatrists) of each parent. For this judgment, all phases of the record, including the psychologist's report, were made available. The nosology used was from the American Psychiatric Association's *Diagnostic Manual of Mental Disorders* 2 (1968), with a few additions of our own character types. Intercoder reliability of assignment to diagnostic category was tested by Cohen's Kappa. The six obtained ranged from .365 to .726; all were statistically significant.

Table 8.6: Parental Diagnosis (Frequencies)

	Mother		Father	
Diagnostic Impression	Neglect	Control	Neglect	Control
Essentially normal	0	15	0	9
Neurosis	2	29	0	12
Mental retardation	0	0	1	0
Psychosis	2	0	0	0
Character disorder:				
Apathy-futility syndrome	17	10	4	1
Impulse-ridden character	10	3	0	1
Addictive personality	0	0	2	2
Antisocial personality	3	0	3	1
Narcissistic character	5	7	1	0
Passive-aggressive personality	0	3	3	8
Inadequate personality	1	1	1	5
Paranoid character	0	0	1	2
Borderline personality state	4	3	3	6
Other character disorder	1	8	2	0
Insufficient data for diagnosis	1	0	1	3
Total	46	79	22	50

Distributions of the diagnoses are given in table 8.6. The mothers were not separated in terms of father presence/absence because there was only one noteworthy difference related to this. In the nonneglect group, when a male figure was present in the home, 67.3% of the mothers were classified normal or neurotic; in the nonneglect father absent, fewer, 37.9%, had these healthier diagnoses ($P < .02$ by Chi-square test).

Outstanding among the diagnostic impressions is the greater pathology attributed to the neglect parents. Only two mothers and none of the fathers were classified as simply neurotic, by which we mean a definable set of symptoms in an otherwise reasonably intact personality. Many of the control parents were seen as having character neuroses and disorders, but character disorder was nearly universal among the neglect sample. In these samples, if a woman was diagnosed simply normal or neurotic, she had a 96% chance of being in the nonneglect group.

The apathy-futility syndrome accounted for 17, or 38.6%, of neglectful mothers classiffied, which reinforced the concern about this characterformation that had grown during our mountain studies. Mothers labeled impulse-ridden accounted for 22.7% of the neglects. The two character types were not unknown among low-income women from the community, but the proportions were far smaller (12.7% and 3.8% respectively). Thus they were not simply common responses to being poor.

Apathy-futility and Child Care

How ominous, then, is the diagnosis "apathy-futility syndrome"? What does it imply about child care? To throw some light on this question, we grouped all cases together: those referred as neglectful and the controls. There were 46 mothers diagnosed as normal or neurotic. The mean score on the Childhood Level of Living Scale of this group was .85. Of all possible positive ratings, they received an average of 85%. On the other hand, the mean CLL score for the 27 women diagnosed as exhibiting the apathy-futility syndrome was .48, which was in the lowest quintile of our distribution, and which we considered severely neglectful. The remainder included the 51 mothers with all other character diagnoses, and their mean score was .64, which we thought of as marginal child care, but not neglectful. Differences among these means were significant, of course, by ANOVA ($P < .001$).

There is, of course, possible circularity involved in these associations. Although the case reader did not have the CLL, the narratives also contained comments about the state of the house, parent-child interactions, and so forth, which might have led the child care to be influential in the diagnosis. Yet there were other diagnoses which are, clinically, also very ominous (e.g., borderline personality state) but evidently were not associated with as poor a level of child caring. From our impression, we believe the apathy-futility pattern is the most ominous of those commonly encountered with regard to the level of child caring in these families.

Identifying Risk-prone Mothers

As the reader is by now well aware, a substantial number of measures of parental personality was employed in this study. Some obviously overlapped. A major reason for the overlap was that many instruments had not previously been used, and we were unsure of their validity and reliability. The design permitted us to examine the instruments with respect to these two important issues. The dimensions measured were certainly not picked at random, nor were they pulled out of the grab bag of someone else's personality inventory. Each was an attribute believed to set off the parents identified as neglectful from average low-income people. In that sense, each relationship tested on the neglect/nonneglect dimension was a hypothesis, or at least a corollary of the general hypothesis that such parents are characterized by "weak egos," to use an imprecise expression.

The particular ego functions measured by the various scales

helped to specify the particular ego deficits involved, and in that sense the process followed the scientific method of successive approximation. But so far as specificity is concerned, the positive results also represented a true embarrassment of riches, for to clinicians, the deficits were rather pervasive. True, we did not encounter outright psychosis, neither did we find severe mental retardation. But reality testing left much to be desired, problem solving and conceptual abilities were also typically limited. One could continue. Overall, the findings describe a modal personality functioning at an immature level of ego integration.

If one were screening a group of parents to identify those most at risk of becoming implicated in neglect, how would one select them? To what facts about them ought one assign the most weight in making the judgment? The question of relative weights of factors has obvious significance in designing programs of case-finding, and in early intervention. The weight attributable to an area of deficit is also significant in training protective service workers. What can one anticipate finding that will be common among such parents? What do we know about how best to help, or change, people with these sorts of damage?

Selecting and weighting the factors most useful for prediction is the task to which a statistical procedure, in this case discriminant function analysis (Kerlinger and Pedhazer 1973; Tatsuoka 1971) addresses itself. We will next report the outcome of applying the procedure among the parents in our study.

Before undertaking the main discriminant function analysis, it occurred to us that some one index might be useful to represent a cluster of all having to do with character maturity. For reasons given above, it seemed that the Reciprocal of Infantilism Scale, combining factors I, II, and III of the Maternal Characteristics Scale, might serve that function. The first step, then, was to see to what extent other assessments about the women in the study contributed to the measure of infantilism. The reciprocal of infantilism dimension, broken into high versus low scores, was treated as the criterion to be predicted in a preliminary discriminant function analysis, using the Statistical Program for the Social Sciences package. Results of this analysis are presented in table 8.7.

Five variables correlated against the infantilism measure were ratings by the case judges: intelligence came from the psychological testing, and the other was our own E-D-O scale (chapter 7). The coefficients may be read as if they were on a ratio scale, that is, the judges' ratings of impulsivity had about half the weight in predicting the research caseworkers' scoring on infantilism as did their ratings of the presence of apathy-futility elements. Intelligence and evidences of involvement in adolescence were also associated. The

Table 8.7: Contribution of Various Attributes to Mother's Absence of Infantilism

Maternal Attributes	Discriminant Function Coefficient
Absence of apathy-futility*	.32727
Capacity for object relations*	.29057
Intelligence (IQ on WAIS)	.19147
Absence of impulsivity*	.15079
Verbal accessibility*	.14594
Role fulfillment*	.11754
Education-dating-occupation score	.09937

*As rated by case judges.

canonical correlation was .805; 89.3% of the women were correctly classified as to degree of infantilism. To simplify subsequent analyses, therefore, the reciprocal of infantilism score was taken to stand for the mother's general maturity of psychological functioning. The Eigen-values on the MCS indicated that the score for infantilism was itself heavily weighted by the factor of relatedness.

Which maternal attributes proved most predictive of membership in the neglect sample? For this analysis we had necessary data on all 79 control mothers and 44 neglect. Results of this discriminant function analysis are given in table 8.8.

In this study, by far the strongest predictor of maternal involvement in neglect was an evaluation of her general maturity. Following this were two indices derived from social history, her participation in formal organizations, and embeddedness in informal helping networks. The MCS rating of verbal accessibility came next, followed by still another indicator of relatedness, the going-out score (see chapter 7).

Maternal intelligence was weighted opposite to the other scales. This did not imply that neglect mothers averaged higher in IQ; the control mothers' mean was significantly higher. Rather, the negative correlation revealed something about the way factors combined

Table 8.8: Mother's Attributes Predictive of Identified Neglect

Maternal Attribute	Discriminant Function Coefficient
Absence of infantilism (MCS I, II, III)	.57966
Social participation score	.23388
Family support index	.22374
Verbal accessibility (MCS IV)	.18971
Going-out Score	.16019
Intelligence	−.11315

in predicting neglect. Since all the other variables were similar in sign, their effects were simply additive. But the negative correlation means that when good intellectual capacity is, nevertheless, coupled with an infantile adaptation, the results are ominous for child caring. On the other hand, when personality is seen as mature, but intelligence is relatively low, child care is likely to be adequate. The canonical correlation of these factors was .735; the six correctly classified 84.5% of the mothers. It was noteworthy that one of the variables which did not add significantly to the discrimination, and was thus deleted, was family income.

Does one's definition of neglect affect the variables that will prove predictive? In other words, was the constellation of predictors different for physical care than for psychological? Parallel discriminant function analyses were run with the mothers dichotomized, this time, into those high versus low on the physical care segment of the CLL, and those high versus low on the emotional cognitive care segment. Results are recorded in table 8.9.

Table 8.9: Mother's Attributes Predictive of Physical vs. Psychological Level of Care

Maternal Attribute Predicting:	Discriminant Function Coefficient
A. Physical care score on the CLL*	
Absence of infantilism (MCS I, II, III)	.85031
Family support index	.18403
Family income	.11449
B. Emotional/cognitive care score on the CLL**	
Absence of infantilism	.66985
Verbal accessibility (MCS IV)	.25985
Going-out Score	.17667
Social participation score	.16059

*Canonical correlation .641.
**Canonical correlation .722.

Once again the mother's degree of infantilism played the predominant role in discrimination, somewhat more with regard to physical care than psychological. The differential among determinants emerged among the auxiliary variables. In addition to the mother's character structure, elements of her situation entered into predicting physical care, that is, having a helping network and family income. The other determinants of psychological care, on the other hand, all had to do with interpersonal ease and relatedness—to the caseworker (verbal accessibility), to "playmates" (going-out score), and in formal organizations.

The Father's Character Structure

What was learned about the elements in the father that were associated with whether or not his children were being adequately cared for? For this analysis, our data were sufficient on 39 of the control and 17 of the neglect fathers to conduct a discriminant function analysis. Since there was no scale as representative of paternal personality as was infantilism for the mothers, each rating by the case judges was included in the analysis. Three variables correctly classified 89.3% of the fathers, with a canonical correlation of .705. Most influential was capacity for object relations, which yielded a coefficient of .5228; next was the score on social participation, with a coefficient of .35490. The measure for workmanship was the other variable, and its coefficient was .31205. One could say, then, that the ability to love and to invest onself in work are the facets of parental personality to be kept in mind in estimating fathers-at-risk. Such other factors as the father's apathy-futility, impulsivity, and his score on the family support index were all significantly associated with neglect/control, but these did not add to the predictive power of the three listed above.

When there are two parents present, whose personality makes the greater difference in determining the level of child caring? Up until now, we have been pursuing this line of questions with control/ neglect taken as the predictive criterion. To answer the present question, however, we decided to test prediction of status on the Childhood Level of Living Scale. While ratings on this scale are somewhat less independent than agency identifications, we believe our own CLL scaling to be more valid. Accordingly, scores on the CLL were dichotomized at 69.5, which was the median for all the 125 families. The 56 two-parent families who had all the necessary ratings, however, averaged above the median of the whole group. Thirty-seven scored above 69.5 and 19 below.

When measures on both mother and father were utilized, the discriminant function analysis selected five variables which contributed incrementally to predicting CLL status. The cluster correctly classified 92.9% of the cases, with a canonical correlation of 0.825 or 68% of the criterion variance accounted for. The five variables are given in table 8.10.

In this subsample of cases, as in others, we see the predominant role played by the mother's degree of maturity. Her linkages with formal organizations and with informal helping networks also improved prediction. For the father, the key issues appeared to be freedom from apathy-futility and having *more* neurotic symptoms.

A simple count by the judges of the number of different

Table 8.10: Parental Attributes Predictive of Score on Childhood Level of Living Scale in Two-parent Families

Parental Attribute	Discriminant Function Coefficient
Mother's absence of infantilism (MCS)	.68124
Father's absence of apathy-futility (judge)	.35999
Mother's social participation score	.34201
Mother's family support index	.31980
Father's reported symptoms	.27915

NOTE: Canonical correlation .825.

symptoms noted for the father also had important predictive value when father variables were tested for ability to discriminate the CLL score, without including the mother's as well. Indeed, in the father-only analysis, it bore the strongest predictive weight. Ordinarily, one interprets numerous symptoms as evidence of pathology. But in this study there was a problem with that idea. A large proportion of neglectful parents appeared character-disordered. Such persons do not handle anxiety by forming symptoms or by experiencing it consciously; they try to rid themselves of it through action. Hence it occurred to us that in the present sampling the presence of specifiable symptoms might be a sign of more impulse control. Sullivan, Spasser, and Penner (1977), for example had found that a couple of their neglectful mothers, having been helped to try to organize their households better, developed psychotic reactions! Among the present cases, the 19 fathers low on the CLL had a mean number of symptoms of 1.2105; the 37 high, 1.5135. Although the difference between the means was not statistically significant, the discriminant function analysis showed, in the context of other predictor variables, a higher number of symptoms was associated with a better CLL rating.

But what about the question we posed for the last analysis? To whose attributes ought one attend more in estimating probable level of care of young children in such two-parent households, the father's or the mother's? The results strongly imply that the weight should be on the maternal personality. Related issues will be discussed in chapter 10.

Evidence from Psychological Testing

Projective testing is notorious for the difficulty it presents researchers. Promising and rich as its content appears, it has an unfortunate tendency to yield zero-order correlations with other variables. Still, for evidence of the maturity or promitivity of thought processes and perceptual style, psychological testing does seem the most appropriate method of measurement. Armond Aserinsky, who headed our psychological testing during the latter half of our project, undertook to explore the Rorschach recorded by himself and other psychologists for the project.

Following a model of mental development formulated by Heinz Werner (1948), Rorschach specialists have developed a method of scoring responses which should be indicative of psychological maturity. Responses which appear primitive, diffuse, and un-organized are contrasted with perceptions indicating thought and perceptions which are more differentiated and articulated. Thus "mud" would be a primitive response; "two Russians in capes balancing on a pole" (no pun intended!) would be highly articulated.

Protocols were scored for development level according to a method developed by Friedman (1953), Becker (1956), and Wilensky (1959). Since the scoring was laborious and our time was running short, only 29 neglect and 28 control parents, chosen at random, could be rescored with this method. The developmental level mean for the neglect sample was 3.296 (S.D. = .6487); for the control, 3.463 (S.D. = .4053). Although the obtained mean difference, then, was small, it was significant at beyond the 5% level by t-test (t = 2.2302). Upon inspection, the difference was due primarily to the mothers' lower scores in the neglect sample. The greater neglect/control difference between mothers than between fathers recurs elsewhere in our data, for example in intelligence. The similarity, however, is not surprising, since the Wechsler measures ego functions comparable to those in question here. Indeed, the score for developmental level from the Rorschach has been found to correlate +.44 with IQ (Goldfried 1962).

Results of projective testing regarding primitivity versus organization of thought and perception were in accord with the other data regarding parental ego functioning.

To sum up, it may be concluded that the major findings of the Appalachian study were substantially supported in the Philadelphia replication. The mother's maturity or degree of infantilism was again underscored, as was its expression in the forms of apathy-futility or impulsivity. The assumption that, among white low-income families the mother's personality plays the major role in how well the children are protected, proved justified. It will be recalled that conclusions about families involved in outright neglect were drawn by extension of trends in marginal families in the Appalachian study. The confirmations found were reassuring regarding the accuracy of those projections and the theory on which they were based.

The improved instrumentation in the present study also permitted us better to specify the character traits at stake. Much more was learned, of course, about the significant aspects of the father's character. And the larger samples permitted us to use more elaborate statistics, such as discriminant function analysis, so that we were better able to select those factors to emphasize in identifying families at risk.

Nine

Sequelae in Neglected Children

The chief concern of most who work in child protection is, of course, not the parent but the child. Their concern is understandable. It is not at all certain the child will escape an early death although, fortunately, nearly all live. But there is a fair chance the child will have been damaged physically in ways that will show up later. And there is a probability he will have suffered emotional damage, sequelae of which will be unpleasant for him and for those around him. Mature humans who are capable of empathy—it does not require exquisite sensitivity—find it painful to witness others whose emotions alternate between an anger-laden anxiety and numbness, and whose limited lives are plagued by loneliness.

Most people do not have to be intimately connected with neglect and its sequelae and they avoid them. But social workers undertake to help all comers and cannot turn their faces away. We are pained by youngsters who have futures but no prospects, who have survived physically but are socially and emotionally dead.

As yet there has been no major study of consequences in people's lives of having been reared in neglectful families. However, much can be inferred from other studies. Child neglect is multifarious. Thus any study linking a definable lack in earlier caring to a later developmental deficit or crippling symptom is relevant. Much of this literature was summarized by Polansky, Hally, and Polansky (1975) in the monograph *Profile of Neglect*.

Despite their morbid nature, we were fascinated by the sheer diversity of scientific findings which illuminate the concerns of child protection worker. The pediatric services of hospitals, for example, are concerned about the infants exhibiting "failure to thrive." (Powell, Brazel, and Blizzard 1967; Bullard et al. 1967). These infants sometimes perish, thus fulfilling wishes of which their mothers are more or less unconscious. There is an opinion that these death wishes are the same as other women express by battering their babies (Smith and Hanson 1972).

The cells of an infant's brain may turn out far smaller than is normal if the pregnant mother experiences protein deficiency (Vore 1973; Scrimshaw 1969). There is other evidence that neglect may start before birth. The newborn of a woman addicted to narcotics may die of withdrawal seizures if the obstetric team is not alerted to institute preventative measures (Densen-Gerber, Hochstedler, and Weiner 1973; Glass 1974). What is the fate of children born to mothers who requested an abortion which did not take place? Follow-up studies of such children were done in Sweden by Forssman and Thuwe (1971) and in Czechoslovakia by Dytrych et al. (1974). In both studies these children showed more social pathology and were, in general, living less successful lives than were their age-mates. It seems that neglect often begins in the act of conception.

Maltreatment and Delinquency

There has recently become available a study supporting a connection many have suspected, but have not been able to prove—that child maltreatment probably has a causal connection with delinquency. This investigation was sponsored by a select committee of ,the New York State Assembly (Alfaro 1978). This group had access to records of public agencies to an extent that is not ordinarily possible for outside researchers.

The research involved two separate *ex post facto* studies. The first proceeded from a known cause to a hypothesized effect. Five reasonably representative counties in New York State were involved. A total of 5,136 children were identified as members of the 1,423 families who had been reported for suspected abuse or neglect in 1952–53, of which 78% were considered "founded" or verified. The subsequent juvenile court records were traced to see if these children appeared later among children brought to court for delinquency or ungovernability. A number of factors could have interfered with finding later references to these children: destruction of records, removal of the family from that county, the children's passing an age at which they were no longer answerable within the juvenile justice system, and so forth. Yet of families with at least one "founded" referral for maltreatment, 42% had one or more children later taken to court as delinquent or ungovernable, and this ratio (which must have been a conservative figure) was five times that expectable in the general population of the counties studied. Indeed, the association appeared stronger in those counties having the more complete records, affecting 64% of the maltreating families in one county.

In the companion study, the reasoning proceeded from a known effect to a hypothesized cause. A total of 1963 children were identified as having been reported for delinquency and/or ungovernability in 1971–72. Of all the boys in this total, 21% had earlier been reported as abused and/or neglected as were 29% of the girls (In New York County the figures were 31% for the boys, 45% for the girls!) It no longer seems appropriate to say, "We just don't know where these delinquents are coming from." Moreover, when the children's delinquencies were compared with those of others, they were found to be more violent in nature. This tendency toward violence, by the way, did not depend on whether the parents were guilty of neglect or of abuse. Violence is often explained as the expression of accumulated frustration or as identification with an abusive parent. But we have also noticed among neglected children the "deprivation-detachment" sequence (Polansky, Borgman, and DeSaix 1972) and the massive repression of feelings that accompany it. This kind of affect-inhibition makes it far less likely such children will empathize with others' pain, so they may prove peculiarly capable of cold-blooded torture or businesslike brutality.

Finally, we might add that more of the children identified as neglected were removed than were the abused (20.3% vs. 16.0%). "This figure indicates that neglect may be more difficult to treat than abuse, that protective agencies find abuse more amenable to treatment." (Alfaro 1978, p. 22).

In a working paper submitted to the Joint Commission on the Mental Health of Children over a decade ago, Polansky and Polansky (1968) proposed that a "watch" be placed on any family with an adjudicated delinquent, just as one might do with a precancerous lesion in dermatology. Our guess was that such an event could be a warning of possible child neglect in the household which would also affect the siblings of the youngster already apprehended. Alfaro's study supports this suggestion.

Jenkins and Boyer (1967) reanalyzed data on 300 delinquents committed to the New York State Training School for Boys at Warwick. Three delinquent types of behavior were identified through cluster analyses: the socialized cooperative delinquent; the unsocialized aggressive delinquent; and the unsocialized runaway delinquent. Of the three, the latter two were thought to have the most disorganized personalities and to have suffered the greatest early parental rejections. The socialized cooperative type, on the other hand, was thought capable of relating, but to have become acculturated to an amoral group code in the living environment. In a personal communication, Jenkins told the senior author he also believed the socialized type most treatable, as one would expect. This study, too, has implications regarding the role of neglect in producing a certain type of delinquent.

These, then, are the kinds of evidence we have from others' efforts that may be indicative of effects of neglect. However, the main focus of our Philadelphia study was, of course, on the personalities of parents and how they affected their caring for their children. Sequelae of neglect in their children were studied mostly with respect to the child's intelligence. We focused on this because intelligence may be taken as a fair indicator of many aspect of competence. Intelligence is also a developmental characteristic that has been much studied, and for which there are measuring instruments generally regarded as valid. A secondary concern was the child's verbal accessibility, and a study was made of this as well.

The Focal Children

Before describing our findings about the apparent effects of neglect on intellectual functioning, we shall pause to review the nature of our obtained samples of focal children. One of our sampling conditions was that each family contain a child between the ages of four and seven. Two children proved to be a bit older, that is, aged 8, but the rest were within the limits required. The mean age of those in the neglect group was 5.15; in the controls, 4.94. Seventy percent of all the children were four or five.

The neglect sample contained 28 boys and 18 girls (i.e. 61% vs. 39%), and the nonneglect sample was very similar, with 44 boys and 35 girls (56% vs. 44%). Thus the two samples, as obtained, did not differ significantly on age or sex of the focal children. There was a difference, however, in the numbers of siblings each had. The mean number of children in the families identified neglectful was 4.09, as compared with a mean of 2.52 in the nonneglectful. Put another way, 50% of the neglectful contained four or more children while a quarter (24%) of the nonneglectful were that large ($P < .01$ by Chi-square test). Thus our study proved representative of others in that problematic families also contained more children.

Early Development

In the course of our gathering developmental histories, each mother was asked when she first saw a doctor for the pregnancy of the focal child. Of the nonneglectful women, 57 of 79, or 72%, reported seeing a physician during the first trimester, a figure which was noticeably higher than that reported by the neglectful, of whom 19, or 41.3%, checked with a doctor during the first trimester ($P < .01$ by Chi-square test). A higher proportion of the mothers from whom we had relevant information in the neglect group reported gaining over 35 pounds in this pregnancy—16, or 40%, versus 15, or 19%—but since they were a minority in both groups, the difference was not significant. As far as we could tell, there were also no differences in birth weight, prolonged or complicated delivery, and the length of the babies' stay in the hospital. So, with the exception of the mothers' report regarding how early in the pregnancy a doctor was sought, our samples resembled each other regarding perinatal events.

Of course, all the above information was based on retrospection, and retrospective data are always to be taken with a grain of salt. Nevertheless, a couple of findings may be indicative. In the course of asking about development, we asked for the timing of three developmental milestones: the age of the child (1) when he or she sat up; (2) was able to stand without support; and (3) could walk unassisted. Of the 79 women in the control group, 76 gave answers to all three of the questions. If they did not know the answer off-hand, they referred to "baby books" on the child or other records. Of the 46 mothers deemed neglectful, however, 23 simply answered "don't know" or "can't remember" to at least one of the three questions ($P < .001$ by Chi-square test). The mother was also asked whether she thought her child's "learning ability" was fast, average, or slow, as compared with other children's. A majority of the control mothers, 53%, described the focal child as fast, whereas only around a third (35%) of the neglect chose this adjective ($P < .05$ by Chi-square test). We believe the difference to be more an expression of the mother's pride—or lack of it—in her child than of an objective appraisal, although as we shall see below there could have been some factual basis for the discrepancy.

Measuring Intelligence

Intelligence of the children was measured, in all but one case, with either the Wechsler Intelligence Scale for Children (WISC) or the Wechsler Preschool and Primary Scale of Intelligence (WPPSI); the other child received a Stanford-Binet. For mothers and fathers, the Wechsler Adult Intelligence Scale (WAIS) was used. In order to reduce the burden of the testing session on the subjects "short forms" of the test were used. These included three verbal subscales, Comprehension, Similarities, and Vocabulary, and two performance subscales, Picture Completion and Block Design. The advantage of shortening the session is that results are more likely to be valid when subjects are feeling cooperative. The disadvantage, of course, is that more refined breakdowns of the data may become impossible. Silverstein (1970) has reported correlations of .9 between five-subscale short forms and full scale testing, which was reassuring. On the other hand, shortening the scale may affect the precision of measurement (Kramer and Francis 1965). Loss in precision would be of particular concern were we to correlate other variables with, say, the verbal IQ and the performance IQ separately, but this was not at issue in our study.

Those doing comparable research will be interested in our experience with eliciting cooperation from the families studied to participate in psychological testing. We have been warned not even to mention the word "psychological," but the resistance encountered was fortunately not so great that the social workers could not work it through. Of the fifty control families with father present, all mothers were tested as were forty-nine children. The omitted child clung so fearfully to her mother that after two attempts to test, we gave up. Eleven out of the fifty fathers in these families refused to undergo the tests, although eight of these did participate in an interview. All mothers and children in the nonneglect fatherless families were tested. All the mothers in the neglect families with father present were tested, but five of the fathers were not tested. Of these, four refused the psychological tests, although they did grant interviews; the other man was jailed while the study was under way. Two of the women in the neglect fatherless group refused testing, but one of these participated fully in interviews. Six children out of the neglect sample were not tested. Of these, two were not seen at all by the psychologist, but the other four were regarded as untestable (e.g., two appeared to be autistic).

It appeared, then, that at least some resistance to testing was specific to that phase of the study, since most of the same parents participated reasonably willingly in other aspects. Incidentally, the necessity of coming to the office for testing was not the decisive issue in failures to elicit testing. The office setting was preferred for obvious reasons of convenience and quietness, but our psychologists were good about going out to the homes when necessary.

How valid was the psychological testing? The status of the various Wechsler indices was not at issue; they were assumed to be valid. But one might wonder how their use worked out with these populations, and under the circumstances of the study. The important issue, in the present instance, relates to construct validity: the reasonableness of associations found between the IQ and other unrelated measures on theoretical grounds. However, we did have an opportunity, also, for a direct comparison with another scale that also had to do with cognitive functioning. This scale was the Human Figure Drawings, or the Draw-a-Person test.

In order to ensure the independence of these data, the psychologist was never told whether the family being tested was neglect or nonneglect. Great care was exercised among the staff to sustain this independence. Although the psychologist sometimes thought he or she could guess from what was observed about child or parents, it was better not to. For if the tester leaned over backward to be independent about a neglect case, the result would be invalid; wrong guesses would simply add to error, and so forth.

Participants' drawings were scored "blind," i.e., without knowledge of who made the drawing, or from which sample the person came. The scoring was done by David Williams and two members of our clerical staff, Denise Graham and Karen Corcoran, after training in the method by Dr. Aserinsky. Scoring consists of comparing the obtained drawing with standardized drawings (Harris 1963) and assigning the appropriate mental age. The median mental age estimated by the technique was 7.5 for the mothers involved in neglect and 10 for those from the nonneglect group, a difference significant at .05 by Chi-square test. No other differences were significant.

From the estimated mental ages, one can also derive an IQ for each subject. The intelligence scores obtained in this fashion were correlated with those from the Wechsler. Correlations between these sets of scores among the mothers, fathers, and children in the study are summarized in table 9.1.

The correlation (*r*) was highest among mothers and lowest among the children. And despite their smaller numbers, the correlations were higher among neglect parents and children than among the control. Since we had anticipated that, if anything, persons from the control sample would test more consistently, we have no explanation for the finding. For present purposes, we note that all but one of the correlations were positive and significant, and some were substantial. The validity of the Wechsler testing, therefore, was supported by results from drawings of the human figure. In subsequent analyses of data, the subject's intelligence was operationally defined by the Wechsler.

Table 9.1: Correlations Between IQs Estimated from Human
Figure Drawings Test and from Wechslers

Sample	No. of cases (n)	Product-moment Correlation (r)	Significance of r* (p)
Mothers			
Neglect	38	.80	.005
Control	69	.59	.005
All available	107	.71	.005
Fathers			
Neglect	16	.59	.01
Control	35	.36	.02
All available	51	.45	.005
Children			
Neglect	33	.42	.01
Control	67	.17	n.s.
All available	100	.29	.01

*By t-test.

Intellectual Deficit

Have the neglected children suffered a stunting of their intellectual
growth? If they began with the same potential as other children, but
then averaged significantly lower in intelligence at the time of our
study, the difference might be due to the deprivation they experienced. There were, at the same time, a number of matters making it
less likely that a difference would be found. The testing of children
is acknowledged to be unreliable in the younger ages. There were
also conditions in our study which removed some of the children's
scores which might have proven lowest. Six out of forty-six in the
neglect sample had no test scores, in four instances because the
psychologist found them untestable. The reader will also recall that
children in the most severe neglect situations would probably have
already been removed, so such families would not be in our study.
The mean scores are given in table 9.2,

The average IQs of both the neglect and nonneglect children for
whom we had scores were within normal limits. The neglected,
however, had a mean eight points lower, a difference significant at
the 1% level of confidence by ANOVA. Differences between means
related to father presence/absence were trivial and not significant;
the interaction of this variable with neglect/control was also not significant. There was then, intellectual deficit found among neglected
children.

Sandgrund, Gaines, and Green (1974), working in Brooklyn,
New York, compared the mean IQs of a sample of abused children
with others identified as neglected and a sample of controls. Their

Table 9.2: Mean IQs of Children in Control/Neglect and Father
Present/Absent Samples

| Father | Sample | | Total |
	Neglect	Control	
Present	95.45	104.82	102.10
	(20)*	(49)	(69)
Absent	97.75	103.97	101.43
	(20)	(29)	(49)
Total	96.60	104.50	101.82
	(40)	(78)	(118)

*Number in parentheses is *n*.

testing also used the Wechsler Intelligence Scale for Children and
the Wechsler Preschool and Primary Scale for Intelligence.
Significant differences emerged among the group means on both
verbal and performance IQs. For total scores, the relative means
were: control, 91.57; abused, 81.83; neglected, 79.97. Abused and
neglected children did not differ from each other, on the average,
but both averaged lower in intelligence than the nonmaltreated.
The average difference between those neglected and the controls
was of the same order as ours, although their mean scores averaged
lower.

How shall we account for the difference found? One is reminded,
naturally, of the classic issue of heredity versus environmental determinants. In the Appalachian study, a correlation was found between the mother's IQ and her score on the Childhood Level of
Living Scale. The median score of those mothers was an IQ of 78.
Mothers in the Philadelphia study tested higher overall, but those
identified neglectful had a mean IQ lower than the comparisons
(91.25 vs. 100.87 respectively). Among those fathers who cooperated with the testing, the neglect fathers' mean was also lower than
the nonneglects' (101.6 vs. 106.08). And, of course, the children's
environments were also very different.

One way to test the possible contribution of other factors to the
child's measured intelligence is to calculate their correlations. Those
that seemed of greatest interest are listed in table 9.3. There we see
that the quality of childcare, as measured with the Childhood Level
of Living Scale, is correlated significantly with the child's IQ. As
might be expected, the correlation is somewhat higher with psychological than with physical care. The child's IQ also correlated
significantly with the income level of the household, but had no
relationship to Hollingshead's Index of Social Position, the measure
of socioeconomic status employed. An overall assessment of the
mother's maturity level was also correlated.

Table 9.3: Correlation of Other Variables with the Focal
Child's IQ

Variable	Correlation with IQ (r)	Significance of r* (p)
Childhood Level of Living Scale score		
physical care	.33	.001
emotional/cognitive care	.45	.001
total CLL	.41	.001
Mother's IQ	.40	.001
Father's IQ	.15	.135
Household income	.23	.006
Mother's infantilism score (MCS)	.39	.001
Family's socioeconomic status	−.10	.151

*By t-test.

The correlation of the child's with the mother's IQ was of the same order as that with the CLL, and it also was highly significant. However, among two-parent families where it could be tested, there was no correlation with paternal IQ—and this despite the fact that the mother's intelligence correlated with the father's at .53 ($P <$ .001), which was greater than between mother and child!

So, we were left with our question. Did the child's mode of life affect his intelligence? For it was also possible that the mother's IQ was transmitted to her child and *also* determined the CLL score of the household. In fact, analysis showed that the association between maternal IQ and total score on the CLL was .44, while that between maternal IQ and the psychological care score was .48 ($P < .001$). Fortunately, light may be cast on the issues involved through the use of partial correlations. Through these, we may estimate how much correlation between one factor and another might remain with a third factor partialed out or held constant.

The results of the necessary computations are presented in table 9.4. It appears that with mother's intelligence held constant, there was still a significant association between the child's IQ and the quality of care, in general, and the psychological care in particular. On the other hand, when effects of the child care were partialled

Table 9.4: Partial Correlation with Child's IQ

Variable Correlated	Variable "Held Constant"	Partial Correlation (r)*
Mother's IQ	CLL total score	.27
CLL total score	Mother's IQ	.29
Mother's IQ	CLL emotional/cognitive score	.25
CLL emotional/cognitive score	Mother's IQ	.33

*All significant beyond .001.

out, there was still a significant association with the mother's intelligence. Perhaps because of the constricted ranges involved, the correlations were all low, but they were significant. The evidence indicates that both heredity *and* environment influenced the children's intelligence, additively. Since such a finding is familiar in the related literature, the substantive finding also supports the construct validity of our measures.

Similarity to Appalachian Research

The work in Philadelphia was designed to replicate previous research in Appalachia. However, there were few instances in which actual *numerical* indices were so directly comparable as in the present set of analyses, and we decided to compile a number of correlations reported from our Appalachian work and compare them with those from Philadelphia. The comparisons are given in table 9.5.

With the exception of the principal investigator, the staffs of both studies were totally different. The Childhood Level of Living Scale used in Philadelphia was a revised, urbanized version of that used in Appalachia. Robert Borgman did all our psychological testing in the mountains, while the larger volume in Philadelphia was distributed among a number of psychometricians. Nevertheless, the correlations with maternal intelligence were strikingly similar, while those with the child's intelligence were also much the same. In the mountains, the level of care seemed to have a greater influence on the child's intelligence, as evidenced in the partial correlations, but otherwise both studies demonstrated a joint contribution from both what the mother was and what the mother did.

Such replicability of important hypotheses is substantively of interest, of course. Methodologically, it is a tribute to the

Table 9.5: Comparison of Correlations from the Philadelphia Study with the Same from the Appalachian

Variables Correlated	Philadelphia Correlation (r)	Appalachian Correlation (r)
Mother's IQ with:		
CLL physical care	.35	.40
CLL cognitive/emotional care	.48	.49
CLL total	.44	.45
Child's IQ	.40	.45
Child's IQ X mother's IQ		
with CLL total partialed out	.27	.17
Child's IQ X CLL total		
with mother's IQ partialed out	.29	.36

craftsmanship of the research social workers and psychologists employed on the work. Without scrupulous efforts such results do not appear, even if the constancy is present in nature.

There were other determinants of the strengths of associations which seem worth preserving here. The correlation of mother's IQ with her child's was higher in two-parent families ($r = .52$) than in the whole sample studied ($r = .40$); the correlation of mother's with child's intelligence was also greater among the control families ($r = .42$) than among the neglect ($r = .29$).

In our Appalachian study, there was some suggestion that boys were more vulnerable to the nature of the care they were receiving, which was reflected in the fact that some correlations between life-situation and personality were stronger among boys than girls. However, in the Philadelphia study, other factors consistently correlated higher with girls' IQ than with boys'. For example, the correlation of the emotional/cognitive score on the CLL with IQ among girls was .62; among boys, .34. Although the latter r was significant at .002, it was clearly lower than that for the girls. The correlation of maternal reciprocal of infantilism (factors I, II, and III on the MCS) with girls' IQs was .52; with boys', .31. Yet there were more boys tested than girls (68 vs. 50) and IQ averaged about the same for both sexes. Perhaps the Wechsler results were more valid for the girls; we know no other way to account for the difference.

Results with the Bender Gestalt

The Bender Gestalt as used with children requires only that the youngster copy a set of nine printed designs presented one at a time. There is no time limit. Verbal interaction plays a limited role, so the test can be used with deaf children or with those who speak a language other than the examiner's. The test has been found related to visual-motor capability, intelligence, and general developmental maturity.

The scoring system most commonly used was developed by Koppitz (1964) for subjects between ages five and ten. Koppitz's method yields an overall "error" score and a set of possible indicators of brain injury, but we were interested only in the former. For present purposes, the child's error score was compared with the norms for his age. Scores within one standard deviation of the mean were called "average"; those more distant were termed, fittingly, "above average" or "below average." Our psychologist, Armond Aserinsky, had little confidence in scores for children aged four and five in this study, and, indeed, he found no significant differences on them. A somewhat greater number of the neglected children proved unscoreable. However, for those children in the study aged six years and over who were able to be tested, and whose protocols were scoreable, there were some interesting differences. Of ten children with scoreable records in the neglect group, seven scored below average; of thirteen in the control, four scored below average, and nine average or above ($P = .012$ by Fisher's Exact Test). Thus in our sample of children, all of low-income background, developmental deficit was found in those identified as neglected, according to the Bender Gestalt. The results confirmed those with the Wechslers.

Deprivation-detachment and the Child's Verbal Accessibility

The Appalachian research drew its sample from children currently enrolled in a year-round Headstart program. A consequent advantage was that each child's teacher was able to help us by providing knowledgeable, independent ratings of aspects of his personality. Two traits in the children were found significantly correlated with traits in their mothers. Aggressive defiance was associated with impulsivity in the mother, but showed no relationship to the Childhood Level of Living Scale as an index of quality of care. Withdrawal in the children, on the other hand, was associated with prevalence of apathy-futility elements in the mother; it was also connected with lower scores on the CLL (Polansky, Borgman, DeSaix, and Smith 1970).

While a number of processes may be adduced to explain the transmission of patterns from one generation to the next, the correlations found were clearly consistent with the hypothesis that children identified with their mother's patterns. However, the association between withdrawal and poor child care appeared the product of a different mechanism. Delinquency is often explained as an instance of the frustration-aggression hypothesis, namely, that deprivation leads to frustration, which results in anger and generalized hostility. More commonly associated with neglect, however, was what we termed the deprivation-detachment sequence. Rather than responding with anger, severely deprived youngsters turn to fantasy, or to other self-assuaging operations that turn attention aside from the environment. Of course, we are not implying that any momentary failure of mothering leads to such results. Citing Mahler (1963) and others, Miller (1977, p. 20) has written

> Optimally, in the initial separation/individuation stage, the toddler who has idealized a caring parent figure encounters gradual non-traumatic disappointments due to the parent's transient unavailability, failures in empathic appreciation of the child's needs, and other human frailities. . . . Normal progression through this phase is impeded by either a precipitous withdrawal of support,

creating massive disappointment, or a too perfect and too sustained need-meeting relationship experience.

A "too sustained need-meeting experience" was not exactly at issue in neglectful homes.

In the Philadelphia study we were unable to devise a method for getting independent ratings of the children which would be consistently available on all, use the same rating instrument, and be feasible under the geographic conditions of our work. Indeed, the only convenient data source on the children's condition was the psychological testing. So in addition to the formal tests in use, we also asked our psychologists to rate each child on his or her verbal accessibility, using the global scale that was also used for the parents (see chapter 8).

After completing the testing session, the psychologist scored each child's verbal accessibility. It will be recalled he had not been told whether the child was from the neglect sample. The mean rating of youngsters from the nonneglect families was 4.18, corresponding to scale point "Responsive; with equal give and take." The mean for youngsters from neglectful families was 2.78, that is, "Receptive; little give, lots of take." Difference between means was significant at .001 by ANOVA; difference between sexes was not significant. So neglected children were visibly less open, less relaxed, on first meeting with a strange adult.

Previous research had suggested that there are family patterns affecting verbal accessibility (Haring 1965). The present design afforded us a chance to see whether the psychologist's observations on the child correlated with what had been found out about his parents and about his general level of child care. The relevant correlations are given in table 9.6.

None of the measures of the father's verbal accessibility correlated with the child's. However, ratings of maternal openness by the psychologist, caseworker, and case judge were all significantly associated with the child's albeit weakly. Thus there is more evidence for identification with the mother than with familial norms about accessibility. It will also be noted that the child's relatedness, as thus measured, is also correlated with a general index of maternal maturity (the reciprocal of infantilism), and with the level of child care being received. Negatively stated, the poorer the level of care, the less open the child. The latter finding, like the association with withdrawal in our mountain study, is consistent with the deprivation-detachment hypothesis.

The senior author had argued elsewhere that verbal accessibility is an almost surprisingly representative index of overall personality function, and, moreover, one that is readily observable in relatively

Table 9.6: Correlates of Focal Child's Verbal Accessibility as Rated by the Psychologist

Variable Correlated	Correlation r	Significance of r* p
Psychologist's rating (global) of:		
mother's verbal accessibility (VA)	.25	.003
father's VA	.20	.074
Judges' ratings (global) of:		
mother's VA	.42	.001
father's VA	−.05	.360
Research caseworker's ratings of:		
mother's VA (global)	.26	.002
mother's VA (MCS IV)	.27	.002
father's VA	.04	.368
Childhood Level of Living Scale		
physical care total	.37	.001
emotional/cognitive care total	.45	.001
total CLL score	.43	.001
Mother's (absence of) apathy-futility (MCS I, III)	.41	.001

*By t-test.

short order by most experienced clinicians in the ordinary course of their work (Polansky 1971). No emphasis was placed on this concept in the present study and the conception was, of course, unfamiliar to the psychologists who shared the psychometric work. Once again the trait has shown significant relationships to a variety of others which may be taken as indicative of its observability and construct validity. Evidences of its interobserver reliability, despite minimal training concerning it, will be recalled from chapter 8.

Let us now synthesize the results of these various explorations of the impact of neglect on the focal children.

Conclusions

This chapter has dealt with deficiencies in the focal children associated with their receiving a poorer quality of child care. The main source of relevant data was the psychological testing program.

Our testing program gained confidence by finding that estimates of intellectual functioning from human figure drawings correlated for parents and children in both the neglect and the nonneglect groups. Of the two, the consistency of test scores was higher in the neglect group. Although we had not anticipated this, it was encouraging with regard to the validity of their testing.

Intelligence of children from neglectful families averaged significantly lower than among those from the nonneglectful. However, at least at the ages tested (leaving out the greater number untested among the neglects) the averages were within normal limits. Was the lowered intelligence in the neglected children a product of their level of living or of their heredity? Children's intelligence, in our samples, did not correlate with their fathers', or the father-figures' in the families, although the parents' scores were correlated. But they did correlate significantly with mothers' scores. They were also correlated with the CLL, especially with the psychological care received. By partial correlation, it was shown that "what the mother does" makes a difference to the child's level, along with "what the mother is." These findings confirmed those from Appalachia and, in fact, were strikingly similar to them.

Results from the Bender Gestalt were fragmentary, but in the same direction. The latter essentially nonverbal test, tapping visual-motor facility, also indicated developmental deficit among those whose tests were scoreable.

We may say then that within the limitations of this study, performance on the measures of cognitive development was significantly associated with the caliber of child care; we may also conclude that this association was in addition to that demonstrably related to the capability of the chief child-caring agent, the mother. One cannot, of course, conclude from an association that there is a cause-and-effect relationship present, but the findings are certainly consistent with this hypothesis, which has been validated in many other studies. Some of these have shown a progressive decrement in the intellectual development of children in poverty vis à vis children from families comfortably off. Our results suggest that the decrement is probably even more marked among neglected children. And, of course, these were still young children.

Also studied was the child's relatedness to an adult in a strange situation, as indicated by the psychologist on the global scale for verbal accessibility. This facet of the child's personality was found to differ, also, between neglected children and others of very similar social backgrounds. Exploration of the data suggests that with respect to this trait, too, the general caliber of child care ("what the mother does") and the mother's own verbal accessibility ("what the mother is") each contributed.

Once again, however, among those cases in which father-figures were present in the home, there was little correlation with the measures of paternal personality. Because of the question as to whether data from fathers were as complete as those from mothers, we have been conservative about concluding that maternal personality had much the greater impact on the child's personality among these families. But we are certainly not the first to encounter such a suggestion. An older study by Jenkins and Boyer (1970) dealt with a very large number of children seen in clinics of the Illinois Institute of Juvenile Research. In their study, too, both hostile rebelliousness and inhibitory symptoms in children were correlated with "inadequate maternal response"; deficient fathering showed much weaker correlations.

Two theoretical formulations were supported by these data. The first is that lack of adequate cognitive stimulation leads to a decrement in general intellectual ability. The second is that emotional deprivation in early childhood leads to detachment and withdrawal in the personality. The latter were already visible in the focal children from neglectful households. However, the age-level of the focal children studied did not permit testing of another hypothesis we have come to hold. We believe that around eleven or twelve, a fairly high proportion of these withdrawn and pitiable youngsters undergo a reorganization of defenses. Their anxious emptiness becomes hidden behind a shield of brittle, hostile defiance; in other words, they "turn mean." It was in relation to these processes that we speculated that massive affect-inhibition prevents normal empathizing with others, and makes it easier for massively deprived children to commit violence and even to murder.

Ten

Observations of Marital Patterns

The replication of our Appalachian study went even further in that households were included in which no father was present. Reliable national data are lacking, of course, but most practitioners believe that neglectful households are more often fatherless than are the general run of other low-income families. Giovannoni and Billingsley (1970) also reported such women were more often living without husbands than were their controls. Because homes with both father present and father absent were included in the sampling, it became possible to raise such questions as: Does the absence of a male parent contribute to child neglect? Does it affect the form the neglect takes? In this chapter we shall also consider other observations on the marriages studied, including some striking similarities of personality in the marital pairs.

The question of the effects of absence of a father in the home is a general one, and is raised about situations in which neglect is not at all at issue. Students of delinquency, for example, have long been aware of its association with broken homes. There has been professional concern about the impact of father absence on male children in particular, a problem that has become more widespread with rising rates of divorce in America. A substantial review of this literature by Herzog and Sudia appeared in 1970. Being without a father is probably disadvantageous to a boy. While studies showing more pathology among such children have often not been confirmed by others, there are none which show more pathology among those with the father present. Herzog and Sudia made the point that if there were truly "no relationship" one would expect results of studies to vary evenly with regard to the presence or absence of a father.

If fatherlessness is disadvantageous for children, both theory and research remain unclear as to why. Jacob (1975, p. 64) concluded from his review: "Family interaction studies . . . have not isolated family patterns that differentiated disturbed from nondisturbed groups." Doubting that father absence is automatically deleterious for the child, Herzog and Sudia (p. 85) also cited "the individual characteristics of the mother, including her ability to cope with her current situation." Other investigators have looked at the interaction between father absence and other features of the home atmosphere, such as familial warmth and expressiveness, which may serve to counteract it (Kagel, White, and Coyne 1978). Because of our unusually detailed measurements of child rearing practices and our efforts to appraise parental personality, it seemed we might be able to contribute to the more general understanding of corollaries of father absence, as well as its role in child neglect.

If we consider the possible impact of father absence on the child's way of life, how shall we understand it? For heuristic purposes, two hypotheses were set forth differing strongly in the significance attributed to the father. These may be labeled the *contributory father* and the *maternal character* hypotheses.

According to the contributory father proposition, the father who is in the home makes a direct and useful contribution to child care. He has a beneficent indirect effect on it, as well, by providing emotional support to the mother. The father is seen as a resource for household income, keeping up the home physically, ministering to the children physically and psychologically, and giving comfort, advice, and protection from loneliness to the mother. The culture studied is one in which "having a man" is valued in women's intrasexual competition; presence of a husband, then, could itself help a woman's morale.

The maternal character hypothesis emphasizes the role of the mother, and of her enduring traits, on the child's lifestyle. In blue-collar groups such as those under study, she is the source of nearly all direct child care; her values and energy are also the main determinants of how well the home is maintained. Moreover, her personality can be seen as having an indirect effect as well, for her attitudes and traits determine whether, in fact, there will be a father-figure present, and, if so, what sort of person he will be. Each of these two hypotheses has considerable plausibility; in fact, both may be true. They have been phrased to differ sharply in order to explicate and dramatize dynamics which could be operative in our families.

Before describing the results, a couple of definitional clarifications must be repeated from chapter 5. In our study, "father absent" is not equivalent to unmarried parenthood. Even among the father absent homes, fifty of the fifty-three mothers had been married. There was only one widow, so the other forty-nine were divided about evenly between being divorced and separated. In instances of separation, father absent meant permanent removal of the man from his family; brief or recurrent absence was not counted. There were a few homes treated as father present although the man was a paramour, since the arrangement was long-term, and definitely meant presence of a male figure in the family, but most were first marriages.

Household Income

We had not been fully aware, when our research began, of the extent to which female-headed households are also low-income in the United States. As of 1974, husband-wife households reportedly had a median income of around $13,000; female-headed of $6,000 (America's Children 1976). Was the discrepancy also visible in our samples? Despite the ceiling on income imposed by the sampling conditions there was, as we remarked earlier, margin for variation among the families recruited. In the nonneglect or control group, the mean monthly income of father present households was $730.50, and of father absent households $415.48, a difference of over $300 per month. In the neglect group, the mean among father present families was $662.86, for fatherless households $408.95, a difference of over $250 per month.

But these were raw income figures, not corrected for elements in family composition which affect living costs, for example, the number and ages of persons in the household. As was described in chapter 5, we converted monthly income into a percentage of the Bureau of Labor Statistics' Low Budget Equivalence Scale. One could then compute means of these percentages for each of the samples on which we wished to make comparisons. The fifty control father present families had a mean of 99% of the low budget; the father present families identified as neglectful had a mean nearly as high, 96%. The female-headed households were disadvantaged by comparison, with the control fatherless families averaging 86% of low budget, and the neglect only 70%. Using these corrected figures, difference between means was *not* related to the neglect/control dichotomy, but there was a significant difference on the father present/absent (*P* < .008 by ANOVA). Among fatherless households in the study, 100% of the neglect and 72.4% of the nonneglect fell below the BLS figure, whereas with a man present, the figures were 63.7% and 60%.

The discrepancy in family incomes, then, extended into our study families, even though they were sampled purposively. In this regard the sampling proved representative. To be fatherless was to be low-income. Moreover, as the Bureau of Labor Statistics' figures imply, the income deficit was such that having one less adult to feed and clothe did not make up the difference. The deficiency was both absolute and relative.

Level of Child Care

Given the measurements already reviewed, we were in the fortunate position to explore other possible concomitants of fatherlessness in these households. How, for example, did absence of a father relate to the caliber of care the children were experiencing? To explore this, the mean subscale scores on the Childhood Level of Living Scale were calculated for father present and father absent families. Three-way analyses of variance were also done, with the other independent variable being neglect/control, which also permitted isolating significant interactions. Results of this analysis are given in table 10.1.

The mean differences were not of the same order as those be-

Table 10.1: Relation of Childhood Level of Living Scale Score to Father's Presence/Absence (Mean Scores)

| | Father | | |
CLL Factor	Present	Absent	*p**
I. Positive general child care	.844	.706	.013
II. State of repair of house	.804	.627	.008
III. Negligence	.905	.747	.003
IV. Household maintenance	.795	.603	.002
V. Health care	.526	.485	.999
Total Physical Care	.783	.642	.001
VI. Encouraging competence	.634	.535	.999
VII. Inconsistent discipline and coldness	.690	.636	.999
VIII. Encouraging super-ego development	.636	.617	.999
IX. Material giving	.843	.803	.999
Total Emotional/Cognitive Care	.680	.602	.999
Total CLL Scale	.729	.621	.020

*By ANOVA.

tween neglect and nonneglect, shown in chapter 6. Nevertheless, on four of the five subscales having to do with physical care, the fatherless focal children were deemed disadvantaged. Significant interactions appeared on two of these variables. For IV, household maintenance, the interaction was significant at .026; inspection revealed the difference favoring father present was found only in the control families. On health care, subscale V, interaction was significant at .007, and was due to reversal of trends. Control children were better cared for with a father-figure present, but neglects were actually better *without* one. The latter two variables, however, accounted for only 13% of the variance for physical care, so the general result was that lack of a father was associated with poorer physical care.

On the other hand, and despite the intercorrelations among CLL subscales, there were no significant effects of fatherlessness on the focal child's psychological care. The differential result was consistent throughout the latter subscales. It is a striking fact to have encountered, and of course could not have occurred without measurements that were specific.

It will be recalled that there was a low but significant correlation between the CLL and the adjusted score for household income. Could his contribution of money explain the better physical care in families having a father? The relationship of physical care to father presence/absence was calculated as a point-biserial correlation, and $r_{pt.-bis.} = .31$, $(P < .001)$. However, with income held constant by partial correlation, the correlation was still $r = .26$ $(P < .001)$. The results strongly suggest that the father's contribution to the children's physical care could not be accounted for solely by the additional income he brought in.

Thus the data indicated that the absent father may be missed as "the other pair of hands" in physical care of the children and the house, but the absence of a father was not associated with lower psychological care of focal children. There was partial support, then, for the contributory father hypothesis.

The significant interactions drew attention to a further issue. How much the missing father is missed depends on the sort of father he is. All the mothers living single were in financial distress. However, one reason the controls were a bit better off was that more of their ex-husbands were paying child support (37.9% vs. 10.8%). Only one neglect father absent mother was making payments on her home; the rest were renters but a fifth of the nonneglect single women were in homes purchased while the marriage was still intact. All but three of the neglect father absent households were receiving public assistance at time of the study, most of whom were long-term recipients.

Noncontributing Fathers

It seems inevitable that a country which lost men in World War II, Korea, and Vietnam during one person's lifetime would have a surplus of marriageable women, but this fact is rarely emphasized. Instead, in the blue-collar group in which we were working, there is, as we remarked, a stigma attached to being without a man. Does such a male presence provide indirectly to the care of the children by boosting the mother's morale, as we postulated?

Let us review, here, some of the data reported in chapter 7. The Anomia scale may be regarded as a fair index of mood or morale. From table 7.3 we note that women living father absent average more anomia, a difference significant at .05 by ANOVA. But this difference really exists primarily in the control group; in the neglect, the maternal anomia scores are nearly identical. Presence of the fathers did not improve the scores for these women. Since the neglectful fathers themselves scored worse than the nonneglectful men, one wonders whether they are able to help their wives' morale. Similarly, the addition of father's contacts to the mother's on the Family Support Index did little to improve the status of their families' memberships in helping networks (see table 7.1).

As compared with the controls, neglectful women had very little participation in formal organizations. But in that group the women living single were somewhat more active than those with a father in the home. This was opposite to the pattern among the nonneglectful mothers, where those who were married were much more active. In informal socializing, the neglectful fathers more often left their wives at home than was the case in the control marriages. If the presence of a man in the home contributed to the mother's morale, it was happening in the control families, not in the neglectful.

Burgess and Conger (1978) collected observational data on behavioral interactions in the homes of seventeen abusive, seventeen neglectful, and nineteen control families in rural areas of Pennsylvania. They found that the neglectful mothers "stand out for their extremely negative behavior and their low rates of positive interaction" (p. 1169). While children in the neglectful households treated their mothers no differently than did the controls, they spoke to their fathers less often, interacted less positively with them, and initiated fewer physical contacts with them. The fathers were characterized by their low rates of positive response and failure to comply with children's requests of them.

We may conclude, then, that living single was disadvantageous for all the mothers of that status in our study, but living as a couple did not help very much for the neglectful women. Was this because of the severity of the mothers' own pathology? Or was it because the men with whom they became involved had so little to give? In our research, it appeared the answer to both questions was yes.

Parental Similarities

In reporting the Appalachian research, we proposed that people of the same psychosexual stage of development find each other and get married. The proposal was half in jest, because the data on which it was based were so fragmentary at the time. However, in this study, too, the impression grew that if one parent proved competent, the other was also likely to be a strong parent. Earlier we postulated that the mother's character may, in fact, determine the father's, in the sense that it influences her choice of a mate. In the opinions of the researchers in this study, there were substantial similarities in marital pairs.

In table 10.2 are tabulated the results of the judges' ratings of the fathers as correlated with ratings given the mother in the same family. Data were available for this analysis on a total of sixty-eight pairs. There was a substantial similarity on the capacity for object relations, a trait that proved weighted for fathers' contributions to the level of child care (see chapter 8). More generally, then, we wondered whether the more mature women were paired with men who were judged more competent. For this analysis, correlations were with the reciprocal of infantilism score on the Maternal Characteristics Scale. Again, the evidence indicates that the more mature the mother, the more capable of loving, the better a workman, and the less prone to apathy-futility and impulsivity her husband.

These ratings, however, were susceptible to halo effect, so other available associations were also examined, with a particular regard for those that were more objective. The mother's score on the Family Support Index correlated with the father's $r = .47$ $(P < .001)$; the Social Participation index correlated .55 $(P < .001)$; and the

Table 10.2: Correlation of Father's Traits with Mother's and with Mother's Infantilism Score

Parental Trait	Mother's Same Trait	MCS I, II, III
Apathy-futility	.49	.52
Impulsivity	.42	.44
Verbal accessibility	.31*	.34**
Workmanship	.58	.57
Role fulfillment	.39	.14†
Capacity for object relations	.68	.61
Symptom formation	.28*	−.06†

*$P < .01$ by t-test; **$p < .002$; † not significant; all others $p < .001$.

going-out scores correlated .57 (*P* < .001). Most striking were the results of the intelligence testing. The correlation of father's IQ with mother's was *r* = .53 (*P* < .001). This association was stronger than that between mother and focal child, in this study. The correlation between their anomia scores was also significant, although not strong.

These results were in accord with the clinical impression. More mature women had chosen husbands whose character was better suited for fatherhood. There was thus support for the maternal character hypothesis. But if our findings were good for the hypothesis, they were often disastrous for the children. While some children were doubly blessed, others were being doubly cheated. That is, when a household needed a strong parent to compensate for the other who was not functioning well, the odds were that such compensation was atypical. Rather, the mother's lacks were typically matched by similar problems in her husband.

Finally, we may ask what was learned about those patterns in the mother which determined whether there was a man in the home at all, and whether she and the father were still living together. One is very leery of attaching value to the sheer intactness of marriages, of course, given some of the earlier findings about the father's roles. However, the results were perhaps indicative.

It will be recalled that there were significant differences on all four factors of the Maternal Characteristics Scale that distinguished women giving better child care from those giving poorer. The same analyses of variance also tested for differences related to father presence/absence. The only maternal trait correlating significantly with this variable was impulse-control (*r* = .37, *P* < .001). The more impulse-ridden the mother, the more likely she was to be living fatherless.

Values taken over from the family of origin were the other force identified in whether families remained intact. Of the control mothers, 62.1% of those living fatherless came from homes which had experienced divorce or separation at some point; this was true of 20% of those living father present. The figures were in the same direction in the neglect sample, 41.7% versus 22.7%. Of the fathers still in the homes, three-quarters of those in the control sample and six-sevenths of those in the neglect were also from families whose parents had remained together. We did not, unfortunately, collect comparable data on the families of the fathers who were out of the homes. But it did appear that a major determinant of whether the woman remained with her husband, in the neglectful as in the control households, was her attitude about whether one should give up one's marriage.

Despite the father's minimal contributions to the family and, frequently, his unpleasant habits such as drunkenness and unfaithfulness, many of the neglectful pairings are extremely stable. Earlier in our social work the concept of a sadomasochistic pair formation would have come to mind, but this is very rarely the basis for such an attachment. More often the mother is so terrified of loneliness, so ridden with unresolved separation anxiety that it is nearly impossible for her to break a relationship.

One also observes instances of another dynamic at work in certain families. No matter which room you enter, if one member of the family is there, then the whole group is likely to be. Especially among the mother and her preteenage children, there seems to be a unity, as if they were joined within a common boundary. Fathers, too, may be part of the huddle. One family therapist (Bowen 1975) has used the term "undifferentiated ego mass," and it seemed very apt for several families we had known. One is also reminded of the theories of Mahler and her colleagues (1975) regarding the development of identity which, in the young child, means "I exist; I am an independent entity." At least some of the interpersonal clinging observable seems to represent, in mother or in child, a psychological symbiosis: "Without you, I am incomplete; I will cease to be."

Child-rearing Attitudes

It was earlier noted that, during the Appalachian research, an attempt to measure the attitudes about various child-rearing practices among neglectful mothers indicated they were aware of the responses that were, at least, socially acceptable, and were very likely to give them on interview. As a further test of the hypothesis that parents implicated in neglect would not differ in their professed values about child-rearing practices, we included in the research interview thirty-two items taken from the Parental Attitude Research Instrument (PARI) (Schaefer and Bell 1958). In selecting items, we drew on the work of Radin and Glasser (1963), who identified items most likely to differentiate attitudes among culturally deprived mothers. A factor analysis was run, and we then tested for mean differences in expressed attitudes on factors we labeled closeness and communication; strictness; suppression of aggression; and maternal martyrdom. In this much more systematic test of the hypothesis—which we had hoped, this time, to disprove with better measurement—no differences emerged between the neglect and control samples.

Disappointed to have got no yield out of so much laborious interviewing, we advanced another hypothesis. It was theorized that intrafamilial communication about child rearing would occur less often in the neglect households, and therefore that these marital pairs would show greater differences in expressed attitudes, as measured by our PARI factors. Discrepancies between parental scores for all two-parent households were then calculated (Cronbach and Gleser 1953). The mean discrepancies were nearly identical in the neglect and control pairs, and t-test yielded a value less than 1. So, again, there was no difference found concerning parental attitudes as measured.

These data reinforce the conviction we have had that interviewing must be supplemented by observation in this kind of research. They also suggest that neglectful parents are well aware of values about child rearing common among parents of similar socioeconomic status.

Eleven

The Stunting of Parenting Instincts

To label as instinctual the complicated activities of adult humans engaged in caring for children has an archaic ring. The instinctivist approach to explaining behavior has not been popular in this country for many years. Early in the twentieth century, however, it had powerful adherents among American psychologists—Dewey, Woodworth, and Thorndike among others. The most vigorous proponent of the position was William McDougall, a transplanted Scot. McDougall wrote of "native propensities," one of which was the "protective or parental propensity" (1932).

There were good reasons for the decline of instinctivism in personality theory. Trying to account for all motivated behavior by referring to instincts or propensities led to unwieldy lists. McDougall's eighteen propensities, for example, included the acquisitive propensity, the migratory propensity, and the propensity to laughter. The resulting hodge-podge hardly led toward parsimonious theory. As Gordon Allport (1954) also pointed out, the view of human motivation as fixed in the nature of man has been distasteful to most American behavioral scientists. They have preferred a more optimistic view, one that sees motivation as modifiable through learning and habit formation. The process of operant conditioning is also highly observable and verifiable by experiment (Skinner 1969). Instincts, on the other hand, are constructs; they have to be inferred. But the notion that there are at least some innate drives or instincts cannot totally be discounted. Even in the process of operant conditioning one starts with assumptions about experiences that make for pleasure or discomfort.

We think of a motivation as perhaps instinctual when it is nearly universally present among humans despite wide variations in cultural and economic background. The idea that it might be instinctual is reinforced when the drive has obvious survival value for the species in terms of human evolution. The impulse to care for the young appears to meet these criteria. Beliefs and practices about how one ought to rear children differ widely around the world. But the impulses to protect them, to nurture them, even to fondle and entertain them are almost surprisingly ubiquitous, and are visible in both sexes. If the parenting drive is not in our genes, it was evidently laid down so early that it might as well be treated as innate. People who do not show these urges, especially toward their own children, arouse shock and dismay in others. Such parents are regarded as unnatural.

How then shall we think of the parents involved in child neglect? Is their behavior counterinstinctual? Martin (1979) has brought one aspect of the problem out sharply: "Neglect must be understood as a situation wherein the child is not getting an adequate quantity of parenting. . . . In most clinical situations, there is a lack of investment or cathexis from the parent onto the child" (p. 5). The array of actions and attitudes that is predictable for average-expectable adults seems absent; the impulse to nurture seems weak and indiscernible. We believe that in most such parents the psychic energy ordinarily available for investment in child caring has been dissipated. The instinct to parent has become distorted in its aim or overwhelmed by problems of personal survival as a result of massive early deprivations.

Man is not the only species of which it has been observed that early deprivation may stunt parenting behavior. Harlow and Harlow (1962) reported that great difficulties appeared among female rhesus monkeys who were deprived of mothering and social interaction during the first six months of life. For one thing, isolated monkeys were hard to breed. Of a series of fifty-one such females, only twenty were able to be impregnated by experienced males, even under optimum conditions. Of these twenty, only five were thought to be adequate mothers. Eight abused their first-born offspring physically, four of them fatally; seven were indifferent mothers (Harlow et al. 1966). The abusive mothers were, however, much less violent toward their second-born. From this, Harlow and his group concluded that females who had developed no affectional ties had no restraints to use when their aggression matured. They theorized that monkeys with more social experience are likely to have developed such restraints.

In child neglect, however, although naked aggression is sometimes also present (Wolock and Horowitz 1979), the major problem is failure to invest care in the child. One is reminded of Freud's dictum that "so long as a man suffers, he ceases to love." Suffering that occurred in the past leaves its marks in the present. In this chapter, we shall bring together what we have been able to learn about the lives our parents lead, how—in a manner of speaking— their "parenting instincts" have been stunted.

These data are, of course, retrospective and self-reported. There are methodological concerns about such information. If a person is depressed on a given day, his mood will color how he recalls his past. While attitudes and feelings are probably most subject to retrospective distortion, even facts may be recalled selectively. Thus the methodological limitations of the next group of findings have to be borne in mind.

Class Origins

One stereotype we have encountered about families that function poorly is that they are usually victims of geographic mobility and cultural conflict. Social workers recall the Appalachian people who migrated to Detroit to work in the auto plants. More recent were the many black families displaced from the tenant farms of Mississippi by the machinery of agribusiness. But this kind of mobility was not at issue in our study. As was recounted in chapter 7, both samples of parents were reared predominantly in Philadelphia and its environs. A majority of the grandparents were from the same area, and the grandparents, if alive, still resided there.

What about social mobility, changes in socioeconomic status which are also often stressful? Information on occupation and education of most grandparents was able to be obtained. Converted into Hollingshead scores on his Index of Social Position (1957), they were then grouped into the classes he specified. The results are in table 11.1.

The great majority of all parents in these low-income families were from families in Hollingshead's classes 4 and 5. Among the mothers, a higher proportion of the neglectful originated in class 5, but the difference from the control (50% vs. 34%) was not significant. The father presence/absence dimension was unrelated to class origin.

The tendency among blue-collar families to show upward mobility on indices like these from the last generation to this one is well

Table 11.1: Social Class of Family of Origin (Frequencies)

Social Class	Neglect		Control	
	Mothers	Fathers	Mothers	Fathers
1–3	3	3	11	4
4	17	9	39	23
5	20	6	26	18
Insufficient data	6	4	3	5
Total	46	22	79	50

known. Of the control fathers, fourteen were ranked a class higher than their own fathers and five lower. The ratio for the neglect fathers was not as favorable, three higher and five lower. As compared with their origins, thirty nonneglect mothers had moved upward in class and eleven downward, whereas the ratio for the neglect women was seven to six. This difference, again, was not statistically significant, and if it had been, would have been attributable largely to the greater proportion of women in the control sample in intact marriages. In our samples, at least, socioeconomic mobility did not appear to be an important explanatory factor. Neither, in fact, did class origin.

Composition of Families of Origin

The families our parents came from were large by modern standards. As we commented earlier, having at least three brothers and sisters was common, and a few had eleven or twelve. Size of family of origin, however, did not distinguish the neglect sample.

In the last chapter, it was noted that both neglect and control women living single were more frequently from broken homes than were those in intact relationships. However, the percentages from marriages broken eventually by divorce or separation were nearly identical in the neglect and nonneglect groups: 31.6% versus 35.4% for mothers, 22.7% versus 23.4% for fathers. Somewhat more of the neglectful mothers had their homes broken while they were still fairly young, that is, below age twelve (30.4% vs. 15.4%). There are some interesting newer statistics indicating that the younger a person was when his parents divorced, the more prone he is to feelings of loneliness (Rubinstein, Shaver, and Peplau 1979). But this difference between the samples was not significant, either.

Thus if one looks at parental case histories at the demographic level indicated here, one might conclude with Giovannoni and Billingsley (1970) that variations in personal background do not account for the occurrence of neglect. The relevant data are of another order. Consider the life of Mrs. Damper.

Recollections of Placement

Mrs. Damper is a thirty-four-year-old separated mother of six children. Her eldest daughter is Pat, now eighteen. Pat has lived since birth in the home of the maternal grandmother. Mrs. Damper's long, frizzy blond hair accentuates her 250 pounds. She seldom alters her position on a sagging green sofa. From this dubious throne, she chain smokes, talks on the telephone, screams obscenities at her children and conducts business with a stream of bill collectors.

Born to a seventeen-year-old mother and a father she never knew, Mrs. Damper describes herself as "the unfortunate accident." After five years in an institution in a southern state, she passed into the life-style sometimes known as foster care. Mrs. Damper recalled vividly each of the five foster homes from which "I was always removed because they couldn't stand the stink." She had both diurnal and nocturnal enuresis. Eventually, the foster mother called the social worker who "finally got me out because he or she couldn't take the complaints any more. . . . All of this was blamed on my nerves but I never got any help." At age fourteen she was placed in her last foster home. "They kept me and a few more to pay for their house," sobbed Mrs. Damper, "and put me out before I was sixteen." At this point, she returned to her mother who was then living in New York. "No one else wanted me, not even the social workers, so I got dumped back on her." She stayed with her mother for a year, until she became pregnant and had her first child, Pat.

Over the years, the maternal grandmother had had three other children. She placed each in turn, keeping the baby. "She was only able to love one person at a time," says Mrs. Damper. The youngest, Jane, has fared better than the other two, "the only sane one in the bunch." Now the loved one is the eldest granddaughter, Pat.

Mrs. Damper has been cut off from her family. Her mother, she says, "calls me a whore" and rejects any effort at reunion. She has lost contact with the other two sisters who were placed in foster homes. Only Jane, the luckiest, "sends a card at Christmas," and lends a listening ear—from a distance.

Mrs. Damper left home at eighteen and found employment in a Philadelphia baking plant cutting cookies. "When you only got to the eighth grade, you can't find a better job." After several months, she met Bill, with whom she lived for twelve years. "We never married; he had a woman somewhere else." Eighteen months ago they separated for the sixth and "final time" after a stormy relationship. Although she was articulate about her life, her manner remained consistently flat during her tale of rebuff and loss. The children bear the scars of a mother unable to communicate joy, warmth, excitement, or even love. Meanwhile she clings to them all the more because "they are my whole life." The children are referred to as "the little bastards," and Mrs. Damper feels that Sue, the eleven-year-old, should "take care of these kids for me." Sue has other ideas and will often leave the home in the morning to go wandering in downtown Philadelphia. Mrs. Damper blames the father for this. "She feels rejected. She used to be his 'little gipsy.' " The focal child for the study is Bob, aged six, who is restless and often stays home from school. In one and the same breath, his mother speaks of him as her "little man" and about how happy she is when he wants to sleep with her, and then says how concerned she is that he has no friends and is failing in school. Four-year-old Andy spends his days watching TV. When Mrs. Damper is alone with two-year-old Mary Jane, she uses the washing machine to entertain her. "I sit her on top, and she sings while it vibrates. It keeps her out of my hair."

Once Mrs. Damper went to a mental health clinic to get help for Sue, but never found anything to say during her formal sessions. Yet she felt abandoned because the worker "was never there when I wanted to talk." Such an attitude presents a formidable problem for outpatient treatment.

Experiences of Childhood Losses

We present the story of Mrs. Damper because in our research there were many poignant moments which were masked by tables of statistics. The research caseworkers found especially memorable some of the women's responses to such questions as "Did your parents ever say they wished they had not had children?" and "Did you ever feel that they sometimes wished they had not had children?" Those reared in long-term foster care responded in terms of their foster parents, since they regarded them as the only families they had known. These questions were not included in the father interviews, so there are data only on the mothers.

Some answers were quite straightforward, especially those of women who simply said no to both questions. Others answered uncertainly, saying "Only my mother wanted me" or "I'm not sure how they felt." But the strength of other answers was unnerving: "I always felt like excess baggage"; "My mother used to say, 'I cursed the day you were born!' " The responses were categorized, and are given in table 11.2. Of the neglectful women, 56.5% felt unwanted as children; less than a quarter were sure they were wanted. Similar insecurities were found among control mothers in the father absent sample, but not with the same prevalence.

Occurrence of such feelings was not surprising when our samples were compared with respect to the subjects' having been reared

Table 11.2: Mother's Feelings of Being Wanted as a Child
(Frequencies)

Reported Feeling	Neglect		Control	
	Father-Present	Father-Absent	Father-Present	Father-Absent
Wanted	5	6	36	12
Uncertain	4	5	8	5
Unwanted	13	13	6	12
Total	22	24	50	29

away from the parents during childhood. Only placements of six years or more duration were counted for this analysis. Eleven of the neglect mothers had been placed at birth or before the age of two in placements that continued until they were eighteen. Altogether, 41.3% of the neglect mothers had experienced long-term removal from their natural parents—most in formal or agency placements, a few in arrangements such as being reared by relatives. Lest one consider such placements typical of children from low-income families of their generation, we noted that only four of the control women had been in formal placement, and two more in informal, a total of 7.2% of that sample. Placements were also uncommon among the fathers interviewed, affecting four of the neglect but only two of the controls. The term "throw-away children" did not exist when these parents were children, but the condition may exist without the name.

It was definitely known in a few cases, and strongly suspected in others, that the neglectful women were removed from their families of origin to protect them from neglect. In our Appalachian studies, we were sufficiently impressed with the similarities between mother and grandmother to have written of a possible "intergenerational cycle of neglect." Was it found here? It was, but not with the frequency we had hypothesized. About seven or eight women, we believe, really represented such a sequence, between a sixth and a seventh of the group.

But when we found a woman like Mrs. Damper, who was the product of years of foster care under the supervision of a public social agency, and saw that other neglectful mothers from Philadelphia were known to private agencies, two responses were inescapable. First, we were impressed by the extent of damage to the personality that had usually already occurred prior to placement, so that routine foster care left in its wake a severely crippled adult. And second, we were chagrined as fellow professionals at each agency's failure to do more to repair the specific damage to the child's personality.

Ours was not the first research group to become concerned about intergenerational cycles of neglect. Lewis, Jahn, and Bishop (1967) cited a study by the National Study Service in the 1960s:

> Perhaps most serious of all is the fact that children who have experienced poor parental care, deprivation and lack of opportunity, are likely themselves to spawn another generation of deprived, neglected or mistreated children. . . . This cycle was illustrated in an NSS study of foster care in the Massachusetts public welfare system. . . . In nearly one-fourth of the families encountered in the study . . . at least one of the parents and in three instances both of the parents had themselves been neglected children. Three families out of the sample have a history of unresolved child neglect and unsatisfying foster care experience covering three generations. [p. 45]

Similar impressions were recorded by Young (1964), Gunn (1970), and Oliver and Taylor (1971). The histories of neglected parents are ominous regarding treatment of their children. We shall return to these themes later in chapter 15.

Experiences of Violence

There is a device we use in workshops when we need to make something about the parent-child relationship vivid. The class is formed into pairs. Then one partner climbs on a chair, after which the two look each other in the eye. Most participants immediately associate the position, and the discrepancy in height, with a mother and her preschool child. Looked at from far below, the adult is enormous, formidable. To be attacked physically by a person so huge and on whom, moreover, one is totally dependent for security, is psychologically devastating.

A number of authors have noted that it is common among abusive parents to have been abused themselves as children (Spinetta and Rigler 1972). Behaviorists formulate the sequence as an instance of parents modeling their behavior after their parents'; psychoanalytically oriented workers refer to identification with the aggressor. However, since this etiological factor is far from universal, these formulations have limited power to explain abuse. Moreover, somewhat to our surprise, we found that many of the parents in our study, who were neglectful but not abusive of their children, reported experiencing violence in their own childhoods from their parents.

Each parent was asked, "What did your parents do to get you to mind?" followed by probes about the disciplinary policies each experienced. A further question was, "Do you think either parent used too much physical punishment?" Their responses were coded as follows:

·*Within normal limits* referred to discipline administered in a planned and consistent way;

·*Both parents abusive* referred to reports of physical abuse by both parents or parent surrogates;

·*One parent abusive* included the pattern in which one parent beats or tortures the child while the other silently acquiesces;

·*Inconsistent* meant grandparents were sometimes strict, sometimes lenient, according to whim;

·*Excessively strict* was reported by a number of fathers; and

·*Permissive* was applied to homes that appeared to set no limits.

The numbers of parents reporting each kind of treatment predominating in their homes are given in table 11.3.

Abuse was reported by over three-fifths of the neglect mothers, but by less than a fifth of the nonneglect ($P < .001$ by Chi-square test). Many more of the control mothers, on the other hand, reported discipline that was within normal limits, as far as we could tell. Differences between the fathers interviewed were not as striking, although here, too, fewer of the men involved in neglect reported treatment rated normal. Given the lack of organization in the way they lived, we had hypothesized that neglectful parents would come from homes characterized by permissiveness, absence of limits, and inconsistency of disciplining. But this problem did not especially characterize that group. Evidently, then, the results of abuse are not always as specific as one would presume from the defense mechanism of identification. Perhaps because it so often occurs in a general atmosphere of emotional coldness, the damage to the personality may be more diffuse; we get people who are angry, but we also get people who are just inadequate.

What about the parents' own disciplinary styles? Among the forty-five neglect families for whom data were sufficient to permit ratings, four were thought to be abusive of their own children, as compared with only one in the seventy-nine controls. Of the remainder, twenty were thought permissive, and another nineteen inconsistent or (in six cases) conflictual, meaning parents disagreed about practices. Only one marital pair was rated within normal limits in discipline in the neglect sample, but forty-two of the seventy-nine controls were so rated. As in other areas, the distinguishing marks of the concerned parents were sins of omission: permissiveness that stemmed from their own inattentiveness or withdrawal as often as not; and inconsistency that reflected either disorganization or, again, an alternation of withdrawal with becoming provoked. As Martin pointed out above, we seem to witness recurrent failures "to cathect," or to invest the children. Few, of course, show an awareness of long-range effects of disciplinary practices on children's personalities.

Table 11.3: Discipline Experienced by Parents in Youth
(Frequencies)

Discipline Reported	Neglect		Control	
	Mothers	Fathers	Mothers	Fathers
Both parents abusive	15	0	5	0
One parent abusive	13	3	9	9
Excessive strictness	0	4	0	5
Inconsistent	1	3	4	4
Permissive	6	7	13	9
Within normal limits	10	2	48	20
Insufficient data	1	3	0	3
Total	46	22	79	50

The study by Wolock and Horowitz (1970) which was done contemporaneously with ours has been cited several times earlier. Theirs was a study of maltreating mothers on AFDC. Only a few, however, were judged only abusive; about a third were involved in both abuse and neglect; and about 65% were considered simply neglectful. Of these mothers, 29% reported having been severely beaten as children, a proportion significantly greater than that among their control sample. As we had expected, Wolock and Horowitz found the effects of experiencing violence in childhood were not limited to abusive behavior in adulthood, but could show up more diffusely.

Pathology in Families of Origin

Data about parents' early lives have indicated, thus far, that such factors as geographic mobility, social mobility, social class, family size, and broken homes did not distinguish the neglectful. Yet the mothers experienced more placements and had been disciplined more violently than was true of others of similar backgrounds. Thus there were many signs of varying degrees of emotional disturbance in their own parents.

When the women spoke of their parents, it was often possible to take their descriptions as representing signs of pathology in their own parents. On the other hand, we were also interested in evidences of strength among others.

Of course, if a woman spoke of her mother as cold or of her father as distant, one did not automatically assume that these traits were so extreme as to have grossly interfered with her development. Remarks about frequent quarreling, or poverty, or overly large families, or even obviously limited intellect in parents did not always seem noteworthy. But even discounting such comments, the mothers now offering poorer care did seem to come from homes containing serious personal pathology in their parents. One might have suspected this from the fact that they had more frequently been placed outside their natural families.

Pathology seemed most prevalent among neglectful mothers living father absent. Of these twenty-four women, sixteen reported severe problems in both parents. Nine had fathers who severely beat the mothers; thirteen had fathers who abused alcohol. Only one woman spoke of parents with many strengths and, interestingly, this was one of the women referred as neglectful whom we did not consider to be.

Six of the twenty-two father present neglect mothers also described serious pathology in both parents. Again, the most prevalent problem was alcoholism. Desertion, promiscuity, mental illness, and child molestation were among the matters brought up. In general, locating strengths among the parents of neglectful women was difficult.

The nonneglect father present mothers appeared to have come from the most competent families. Out of fifty cases, there were evidences of strength in at least thirty-six; four others appeared to show no serious pathology. Support to their own families of origin from the grandparents was specifically cited by seven.

While living without a man can hardly be taken as diagnostic or as indicative that the woman has problems in sustaining relationships, we were interested to find somewhat more pathology among control women in father absent status. Ten of these twenty-nine mothers reported serious pathology in both parents, with alcoholism again most widespread. A few cited wife abuse, and six had a mother or father who was recurrently mentally ill.

The fathers were asked similar questions about their own earlier lives, but, in view of our briefer contacts with them, their responses were less rich and detailed. We were impressed, nevertheless, with the amount of pathology reported by them. Of the forty-seven fathers in the control sample interviewed, twenty-seven had at least one parent with noteworthy pathology, with alcoholism leading the list. Six had both parents incapacitated. On the other hand, a number of these control fathers mentioned strengths in one parent which compensated for the other who was less able to function. As a consequence, few of the control fathers seemed to have come from disorganized homes. Among the fathers implicated in neglect from whom we had enough data to attempt a judgment, we did not find one who came from parents without serious problems.

These notations were, of course, highly impressionistic, and we have couched them that way. They fall short of all one would like to know in order to understand how each of these adult human beings became the person he or she is. Still, these data were consistent with the other findings that indicated neglectful behavior toward one's offspring stemmed from deficiencies in one's own upbringing. As any social worker would anticipate, the caliber of current parenting is, in part, predictable from social history. We certainly did not find neglect usually, or even very often, to be an emergent response to current stress. Quite the contrary.

Unexpected Strengths

The prevalence of pathology in the families of origin of people doing a poor job of parenting, then, was expectable. But what about the people who, despite similar early disadvantages, were now doing a reasonably good job of parenting? Ours is a book mainly about parental pathology and the stunting of parental expression, but among these parents, who have never known and probably never will know real financial security, there were also many instances of grace under adversity which restored one's continuing wonder at what man can be.

In the control group, especially, we encountered adults who have survived life insults and emerged remarkably intact. Sometimes this was because of the presence of one strong parent who held things together and who provided an ego ideal. A few came from families in which they were the eldest, or among the elder, and in which they must have had good, basic emotional nourishment before the parents' neuroses caught up with them. Several represented the successful outcome of efforts by social workers and teachers who helped them overcome potentially crippling homes. There were a number of instances in which a couple's mutual love made the difference. One of the men from the father present nonneglect group who was *not* seen comes to mind. His wife told us that his own background was so full of loss and pain that whenever he was forcibly reminded of it, he became anxious and depressed, and that she did not want him interviewed. Still, he works hard, is a considerate father, and evidently finds in his sensitive and loving wife belated substitution for the mothering he never had. It was good to encounter people healing each other in their marriages.

Parenting ability may be, and often is, damaged along with the stunting of the rest of the personality. But the control parents also demonstrated how many neurotics manage to keep these ego functions exempted, relatively autonomous (Rapaport 1951) from the rest of their conflicts and weaknesses. In a fair proportion of such neurotic parents, the level of child caring was strengthened by values and strongly held convictions were maintained in the face of anxiety and phobic reactions. Several parents were able to be quite verbal about their determination that their children would have better lives than they had led, including the need to hold the family intact at all costs. With the case of George Bernard Shaw, Erikson (1956) taught us that a *negative identity* need not always be destructive in its effect. To interview two people, each reared in a succession of foster homes, and learn that they had come together in order to "have somebody" was touching even when their parenting was not. How much more moving, therefore, it was to encounter a pair with similar needs who were also bent on offering their children, too, something they themselves had never had. Who would want to bring up the substratum of defiance beneath the good intent?

A close look at the life histories of our nonneglectful parents reveals us, once again, as a generation short on miracles but not lacking altogether in happy accidents. And a close look at the histories of the neglectful mothers and fathers helps to restore them to full humanity. Although for good and scientific reasons we have been at pains to expose the degree to which neglect rests in parental character pathology, this does not mean that they are "poor protoplasm," somehow less than people. They act and change; they feel and they hunger; they are often enormously lonely and bereft. And their life stories remind us of something which indignant concern for their children may lead us to forget: neglectful parents did not mean to be this way.

Twelve

A Rationale for
Intervention

Two series of studies, each containing a major study of the personalities of neglectful parents, have been recounted in this book, as well as several ancillary studies. The first major study was done in southern Appalachia; its replication in metropolitan Philadelphia. The mountain families lived in small, rural homes, some of which were over a mile from the nearest neighbors. The urban families resided in apartment houses or row houses, usually in densely populated areas with grass and trees scarcely to be seen. In their means of livelihood, their national origins, their tastes in entertainment, and the like, the two populations seemed poles apart. Yet in each setting, the parents offering their children marginal or neglectful care had character traits differing from the norms of their communities in ways that were surprisingly similar. It has been said that all happy families are much alike. The same, alas, might be said of these unhappy households. Parental personalities were found distorted to a degree that, in ordinary clinical work, presupposes damage early in their own lives, a supposition which was largely supported by the facts that were available.

The similarities of the two sets of findings indicated success for the replication, but they had ominous implications for treatment. Whether in a rural or an urban setting, the planning of programs of treatment of character-disordered persons is very difficult. It is hard for social workers to find treatment approaches that show high 159 rates of success, if by success one means bringing about alterations in parental life-style so that the children may remain in the family secure from further damage to their own personalities and with a good chance of happiness when they mature. The difficulty of finding methods of treatment that are effective, cheap, and reasonably rapid must foster an unfortunate and inaccurate impression of the state of knowledge in our field.

When social workers speculate about what might be done with the Mrs. Dampers on their caseloads they do with constraints in the background of their thinking which are largely unspoken, for each family they meet participates in the larger American culture; the parents and children are members of a democracy, the same democracy shared by all of us. It is not really all that hard to conceive of modes of treatment that might have high rates of success. Based on our experiences, there is much to be said, for example, in favor of treating people who are character-disordered in settings in which their social environments can be substantially controlled. Such a setting might be a residential treatment institution or a psychiatric hospital. In a monitored environment, one need be far less cautious about high levels of anxiety that might result from confrontations used in uncovering brittle defenses; group influences can be more effectively and consistently marshaled; opportunities for acting out and exacerbating life crises to distract oneself from conflicts can be better restricted. These were the sorts of elements Maxwell Jones (1953), for example, had in mind when he helped to pioneer milieu therapy for substantially similar people in England shortly after World War II. But will such parents commit themselves to inpatient treatment and subject themselves to its disciplines? The experience of Fontana (1973), a New York administrative pediatrician with means and influence greater than most, was that few severely neglectful women availed themselves of the offer of inpatient care, and even fewer stayed with the treatment course.

One might also imagine an outpatient community setting combining group support and pressure to bring about change in parents' modes of adaptation. Suppose each parent were a member of a face-to-face group with his or her neighbors, a group chaired by a leader from the controlling political party. The neglectful parent, accused by his neighbors, might be repeatedly required to stand in meeting and confess his aberrations and try to correct them under threats of ostracism and legal punishment. Severe moral pressure could be applied, because none could leave the group. On the other hand, if a job or improved housing were needed, the group leader could arrange these through ties with the hierarchy that dominated the community's political and economic systems. A setting like that described might have a fair chance of imposing order in a household in which the parents' own lack of internalized structure was such that they could not manage to establish order on their own. But such a plan does not sound feasible. It does not, because we are not practicing in China—or our image of what China must be like—but in the United States.

No, the difficulty does not come from our lack of creativity or perspicacity; it comes from the nature of the greater society in which we live and from the fact that, in common with others in that society, we believe in democracy. To deprive any of freedom arbitrarily is to endanger it for us all. So we search for modes of treatment that are largely voluntary and still have a fair probability of success.

There are social workers who take it as an article of faith that treatment to bring about personality change cannot be imposed. We know, after all, that numerous clients with problems less severe than are those of the majority of neglectful parents have difficulty changing even when they seek out the treatment and commit themselves to it. Indeed, all social influence relies in the last analysis on offering the person choices among alternatives of which one proves the more persuasive. This is true even when the alternative to the "offer he can't refuse" as the saying goes, is death, for in Hitler's concentration camps, numerous inmates chose death over dishonor. Nevertheless, there are too many instances in which authoritarian regimes of our own time have succeeded in inducing marked attitude changes by the use of force or threats of force for us to conclude that "treatment" has to be purely voluntary. The matter is complex, and the evidence is not yet all in—even though we want no part of collecting it. For all practical purposes, however, the social treatment offered the parents we work with is entered into essentially voluntarily.

Even the threat by a judge to remove children from a home deemed neglectful, painful as it is to most parents, does not routinely result in efforts to change. For there are further characteristics of infantile personalities which need to be emphasized here, since they affect treatment so heavily. Few infantile persons have much capacity for self-observation. They are quite unable to take distance, as we say, and observe their own roles in bringing on their troubles. Most of the time, in fact, social workers deal with people whose initial approach to their own unhappiness is alloplastic: they want others to change, or their situations to change. Rarely are they motivated from the beginning autoplastically, toward altering their own ways of operating. Neglectful parents almost never seek autoplastic solutions. Thus the protective service worker too often finds himself or herself involved with a client who is unmotivated to change, or even to look hard at what she is doing. And the worker is dealing with neglect within a system that presumes the average-expectable American adult is mature, decent, and able to conduct his or her life to the family's best advantage. The average-expectable neglectful parent does not fit this image, but this does not mean she or he is a subhuman monster with whom one cannot sympathize.

If all this seems complicated, the reason may be that, in fact, it is. Nor will its complexity be reduced simply by being impatient with it. A rationale for doing something definitive about child neglect has to take into account the social context in which the neglect is identified and in which the treatment will take place. The positional relationships can be expressed as follows:

The neglected
·*child* is a part of a
·*family* residing in a
·*neighborhood*. The latter, in turn, helps make up a
·*community* which is part of a larger
·*society* whose natural *economic* and *political* variations it shares and whose *cultural values,* including those about child rearing, largely determine its own. [Hally, Polansky, and Polansky 1980, p. 1]

We have shown that there was substantial agreement among mothers in evaluating what constitutes good or poor care and in judging circumstances of children's lives. But this does not indicate what action the mothers would want taken in families where their standards were being violated. In a democracy, for protective services to intervene in families presumes they are acting with substantial moral support from the rest of the community. What does "public opinion" say ought to be done about neglect?

Public Opinion and Interventions in Neglect

That social values predominant in a community affect child welfare services was underscored by the study done by Maas and Engler (1959). These authors found that whether a child was removed from his home and placed in foster care depended very much on beliefs about parental rights in that community. Collecting the opinions of community leaders in Minneapolis, Minnesota, Boehm (1964) found that they supported intervening into the family in the event of physical neglect, but not for emotional neglect. A small study by Varon (1964) in Boston brought into focus the double bind in which the public often places protectives services personnel. Her working-class respondents professed great concern about the problems of children dealt with by the local private protective service agency, but regarded removal of children from their homes as wrong and punitive.

Nagi (1977) adduced that how one deals with the parent in a case of child maltreatment may vary in accordance with whether he is seen as criminal or "sick." A scale was devised to study attitudes among personnel from the variety of agencies that have a role in handling abuse and neglect. Nagi reported that the majority response, overall, was to regard maltreating parents as sick, but the espousal of such a therapeutic orientation varied markedly. In child protection agencies, 91.8% had a therapeutic orientation toward such clients; among the police the figure was 44.7%

From the few previous studies that were relevant to the issue, we learned that the public's wish that something be done about neglect does not, of course, extend equally to all methods of helping. So another ancillary study was undertaken, this time to explore the values that are widely held in this country as to what actions should be taken in handling neglect, and *why* people make the choices they do (Polansky, Doroff, et al. 1978). In carrying out this study, the authors were very interested in finding a research technology suitable for the study of values about interventions in general, as well as those having to do with child neglect. For the question of whether we have widespread support for what we do extends into other areas of protective intervention, as in work with the mentally ill or with people physically incapacitated by age or illness. It is clear we cannot simply take the preferences of elected officials as representative, since they are very often at least as uncertain about what "the public" wants as we are.

Method of Measuring Values

Most studies of values have the respondents place the matter to be evaluated on a simple scale representing positive/negative, approach/avoidance or like/dislike. But this type of univocal scaling may mask the full process of evaluation. Thus removing the child from a neglectful home might be thought to be in the interest of his safety, but not a kind thing to do; one might also feel the action was harsh on the parents. It seemed desirable, therefore, to find a convenient method of scaling which would, in getting an evaluation of a social work intervention, lay bare at least some of the mixture of reactions entering into it. It occurred to the senior author that Osgood's semantic differential technique might be modified to fit the need for multidimensional scaling (Osgood, Suci, and Tannenbaum 1957).

The semantic differential has customarily been employed by presenting the respondent with an abstraction, usually a noun (e.g., rape, friendship), and then asking him to place the noun on a series of seven-point scales. Each scale has a pair of antonyms as its poles. Naturally, many such scales tend to associate with each other. After a series of trials, Osgood, Suci, and Tannenbaum succeeded in isolating three general dimensions which appear essentially independent of each other: the evaluative, the activity, and the potency dimensions.

Rather than ask the respondent to rate an abstract noun, the present researchers presented him with an intervention, that is, something which might be done to ameliorate child neglect. The intervention being considered was then rated by the respondent on five scales. For the evaluative dimension, the antonymic scales were "kind/cruel" and "sufficient/insufficient"; for the activity dimension, the scale was simply "active/passive"; for the potency dimension, the antonyms used were "hard/soft." To these we also added a dimension, "risky/safe," because this is an issue much thought about by those of us who have to choose among courses of action in trying to help others.

Procedure

Respondents were told they were being asked to help us learn more about a serious social problem by completing a questionnaire that would require only five to eight minutes of their time. The questionnaire would ask their opinion about how a case of child neglect ought to be handled. The version of the form used by one set of respondents read as follows:

> Recently there was a court case in which the judge had to decide what to do about a child who some witnesses testified was being neglected by his parents. Although these witnesses were probably correct, it is always hard to decide what to do in cases like this. There were a number of actions the judge could have taken. Each is listed on one of the following pages. We are interested in knowing how each of the actions would seem to you if you were the child. Beneath each action are five scales. Please read the action, and then rapidly circle the number on the scale that corresponds to *your* first reaction. Your spontaneous reaction is the best. Remember, you are taking the point of view of the child.

The nature of the neglect was deliberately left vague for two reasons. First, the researchers wanted the rating to be about neglect in general, and did not want to get lost in the complications of some particularity. Second, the average person's knowledge of a neglect case, in real life, is also usually vague, so the stimulus was realistic.

It will be noted that in the statement read by the respondent, he or she was asked to identify with the child, to have the child's interest in mind in making the scalings. There are other interests one might bear in mind in thinking about an action with respect to neglect, for example, how one's action might affect the parent. Or one might be thinking of the impact of the action taken, in this case, on the larger community, of which the rater is a part. It seemed inappropriate to ask the same subject to respond to all the interventions three times on five scales, each time from the viewpoint of a different interest group. So, what we did was to compose three cover sheets, varying the directions on each to induce identification with one of the three interest groups, and we distributed these three versions at random among each group sampled.

After reading the directions on the cover sheet, the respondent turned to the next eleven pages of the booklet. Each was headed by a possible action the judge might take; beneath were the five scales on which the action was to be rated. To control for effects of order of presentation, the sequences among these eleven pages were arranged at random.

The Interventions

What were the interventions to be rated? We tried to come up with a listing of decisions the judge might well take, based on knowledge of cases or on those of which we had heard. Thus these were all actions that are taken by judges. Unfortunately, our resources did not permit investigating which are most in use, and whether there are others we might have wanted to include. Here is the set given each respondent:

- Jail parent(s) for criminal neglect.
- Remove the child from his parents' home temporarily and place him in a foster home.
- Remove the child from his parents' home permanently and find another place for him to live.
- Assign a social worker to visit the family regularly and try to help them to improve their care of the child.
- Require the parents to see a qualified mental health practitioner (social worker, psychiatrist, psychologist) regularly.
- Request more information—trial to resume in thirty days.
- Persuade parents to give the child up for adoption.
- Dismiss the case.
- Assign a social worker to check up on the family regularly and report to the judge whether the care of the child has improved.
- Refer the family for welfare help to improve the child's standard of living.
- Urge the family to leave town.

Samples

The first sample obtained was, for convenience, a group of students from the University of Georgia. While the results even from this sample might have been of interest as a test of the methodology employed, the students could not, of course, be thought of as representative of the general population. Lacking resources for area-probability sampling, we did succeed in getting two other samples purposively, which contrasted markedly with the student group.

The blue-collar sample included forty-nine people working in a grain elevator, a planing mill, and a furniture factory in Hagerstown, Maryland. Less than half in this sample were high school graduates, and only one had finished college. Twenty-three of the forty-nine were female; twenty-eight were between twenty and forty years of age. This sample made us aware that our technique assumed a certain level of literacy, for sixteen other questionnaires given out to the Hagerstown blue-collar workers were spoiled and unusable. A third sample consisted of waitresses employed in downtown Philadelphia restaurants, who were approached during their coffee breaks in groups of two or more. Although the researcher offered them money to participate, only six out of forty-five accepted it. Thirty-eight were between twenty and forty years of age; thirty had finished high school, of whom four had graduated from college.

Data Analysis

The method of analyzing the data is set down with some care because it was initially preplexing as to which computer program to use and which statistical analysis was appropriate. Each scale was scored from 1 to 7. For example, on the kind/cruel dimension, 1 represented kind and 7 represented cruel, with the midpoint rating being 4. In analyzing the data, a factorial repeated-measures analysis of variance for unequal n's was used; the ratings for the eleven interventions were treated as repeated measurements, and the interest and sample were treated as the two other grouping variables (Winer 1971). The complexity of the design was found to exceed the capacity of most of the familiar computer packages. The BMD-P2V program was used, as being convenient and economical and reliable in its accuracy.

Humaneness

Which of those interventions the judge might order seemed to our groups the most humane, which the most cruel? The mean ratings of each of the interventions, along with the verbal equivalent on the scale to which the rating corresponded, are given in table 12.1 The

Table 12.1: Possible Interventions Ranked from Kindest to Cruelest

Intervention	Respondents' Mean Rating*
Assign social worker to improve child care	2.49
Assign social worker for surveillance	2.76
Parents to mental health practitioner	3.07
Refer for welfare	3.23
Delay for more information	3.80
Remove child temporarily	4.19
Remove child permanently	5.03
Obtain's child's release for adoption	5.11
Dismiss case	5.21
Jail the parent(s)	5.36
Urge family to leave town	5.84

*Ratings from 3.50–4.49 meant neutral; 4.50 and above cruel.

results of the analysis of variance are given in table 12.2.

Protective service workers will be interested to see that rated most kind was referral to them: assigning a social worker to try to help the parents improve care of their child, or assigning a social worker to check on the family regularly. Also favored was assigning parents to see a mental health practitioner. A number of actions were adjudged cruel, such as urging the parents to leave town or jailing them out of hand. Temporary removal of the youngster averaged a neutral rating overall, but permanent removal was adjudged cruel.

From the results of the repeated-measures analysis of variance it appeared that by far the greatest determinant of the kind/cruel rating, across all three samples, was the intervention being judged. This was what we hoped for, and it indicates that the possible interventions were differentially regarded on this dimension. The

Table 12.2: Repeated-measures Analysis of Variance of Ratings as Kind/Cruel

Source of Variance	Degrees of Freedom	Mean Square	F	P
Intervention	10	218.43*	72.82*	.0001
Intervention X sample	20	10.88	3.62	.0001
Intervention X interest	20	16.83	5.61	.0001
Intervention X sample X interest	40	4.78	1.59	.011
Error	2060	3.00		
Sample	2	117.38	19.27	.0001
Interest	2	5.83	0.96	.3860
Sample X interest	4	7.02	1.15	.333
Error	206	6.09		

*Rounded to two decimals.

significant main effect for sample was not anticipated. It derived from the fact that the blue-collar respondents rated all interventions more kind than did the others. Did this reflect a greater tolerance in this sample toward intervening in families, in line with the "law and order" stance blue-collar workers have shown in a number of surveys? Or were they just choosing agreeable ratings?

The interest variable did not show significant main effects, but it did enter into signficant interactions with interventions. Thus in all three samples, jailing the parents was rated crueler from the parents' standpoint than from that of the child; to dismiss the case was judged cruel according to the community's and child's interests, but neutral for the parents.

Effectiveness

The other evaluative dimension was sufficient/insufficient, according to Osgood, Suci, and Tannenbaum. Sufficient was given a score of 1 and insufficient, the negatively evaluated end of the scale, a score of 7. Table 12.3 gives the means of the eleven interventions, rank-ordered on this dimension. As one would expect from the fact that sufficient/insufficient was assumed to correlate with kind/cruel, the two rank-orderings of the interventions which we obtained did resemble each other. The rank-difference correlation of the two orders (rho) was +.97. (When $n = 10$ and rho $= .733$, $P < .01$, as tabled by Edwards 1954, p. 512).

Once again, the differences among interventions yielded main effects on analysis of variance which were highly significant; and once again the main effect for sample was significant because of the more positive ratings by the blue-collar group (see table 12.4).

Table 12.3: Possible Interventions Ranked from Sufficient to Insufficient

Intervention	Respondents' Mean Rating*
Assign social worker to improve child care	2.94
Parents to mental health practitioner	3.28
Assign social worker for surveillance	3.49
Delay for more information	4.18
Refer for welfare	4.38
Remove child temporarily	4.42
Remove child permanently	4.55
Obtain child's release for adoption	4.64
Jail the parent(s)	5.08
Dismiss case	5.63
Urge family to leave town	5.97

*Ratings from 3.50–4.49 meant neutral; 4.50 and above, insufficient. Only two were in the zone of sufficient.

Table 12.4: Repeated-measures Analysis of Variance of Ratings as Sufficient/Insufficient

Source of Variance	Degrees of Freedom	Mean Square	F	P
Intervention	10	128.64	40.24	.0001
Intervention X sample	20	13.35	4.18	.0001
Intervention X interest	20	15.98	4.99	.0001
Intervention X sample X interest	40	5.29	1.66	.0060
Error	2020	3.20		
Sample	2	176.75	19.03	.0001
Interest	2	27.65	2.98	.0530
Sample X interest	4	11.20	1.21	.309
Error	202	9.29		

Nevertheless, only assigning a social worker to try to help the family and requiring the parents to see a mental health practitioner were deemed likely to be effective. The blue-collar group, in particular, took a dim view of referral for welfare help. Rated least useful were urging the family to leave town—which has been done—or simply dismissing the case.

The adaptation of the semantic differential technique, we believe, is an economical and promising way by which social workers may explore societal values affecting what we do, and we have also employed it in a pilot study of values about the handling of persons deemed psychotic. But for present purposes the suggestion is clear. On average these respondents favored assigning a social worker to try to help the family improve its child care as the kindest thing to do and as the action most likely to be effective. These data offer reassurance to those doing the work, for they indicate that much of the public agrees that to disregard the occurrence of neglect, on the one hand, is wrong, but to take sudden and drastic action is also wrong. On the whole, the respondents' reactions seem reasonable to those of us who have far more occasion to be well acquainted with the problem.

What do these results add to our knowledge of the neglected child? They imply that there is, indeed, community sanction for intervening in families in which the caliber of care is neglectful. These sanctions, too, are part of the ecology of neglect.

Social Strategy and the Medical Model

Thus far, in discussing treatment, we have recognized public reluctance to intervene forcibly in families on two counts. One stems from respect for the Bill of Rights in our Constitution; the other from humane concern for the feelings of the mothers, fathers, and children whom the intervention affects. Yet these values conflict with the desire to rescue the child.

A way to resolve the conflict, of course, is to treat the state of functioning in the family as an aberration, a kind of sickness. Ill people are not expected to be handled in the same way as everyone else. Hence the proper approach, and one which resolves the conflict, is to follow the "medical model." According to this pattern, the physician is sympathetic to the patient, but he has no doubt the illness lies within the patient. In his special role, the physician reaches into the patient's life to cure him. To cure means to help the patient get over the illness and become like everyone else. Supposedly, it never enters the physician's mind that, in fact, the patient already *is* like everybody else, perhaps more so, and that what is wrong with him is wrong with everyone, including the physician. It would be outside the physician's imaginings to think that, as a member of the larger society, he was also a participant in the etiology of the patient's illness. Practitioners in the various helping occupations who follow the medical model are typically unaware of doing so; they do not question their assumptions or their ingrained patterns of understanding causation. They feel responsible if the family fails to improve or deteriorates further because treatment was in error or poorly applied. But they take little responsibility for its initial condition.

For those who question the model, however, matters are different and questions of responsibility may be more intricate. Now, there is one group questioning the model who strike us as engrossed in playing games with the morality and blame involved according to rules of their own devising. We have little patience with professional oratory when its intent seems to be to evade responsibility for not doing well with those on one's caseload because "in the last analysis, society is to blame." As unabashed caseworkers, we are not interested in justifying failures but in trying to get ourselves to face them when they occur, in the hope of finding ways to provide better treatment. Meanwhile, we are under no illusion that the power elite of our society, our clients—or we—operate by ideal moral principles.

There is a different reason for questioning the medical model, nonetheless, which commands attention. The thought pattern for understanding causality which most of us were taught was analytic. The program for theorizing aimed at understanding by reduction, that is, by analyzing phenomena into their most basic elements. From these fundamental units, one might try parsimoniously to construct an image of causality based on the way the elements fit together. But there is another way of understanding causality which is synthetic and expansive. Rather than asking what parts make up the whole, one asks, "Of what larger whole is this particular event a part?" For if one can assume that all parts participate in characteristics of their wholes, then identifying the larger wholes may be the key to parsimonious theorizing. Such an approach to understanding neglect, for example, would see its rising rate as but one aspect of more general deterioration in the community or neighborhood in which that family is contained. We certainly do not discount such a manner of thinking and chapter 3 summarized the evidence that Garbarino and his colleagues have begun to bring together in support of it.

From this standpoint, it would be desirable to try to treat not only the neglectful family but the neighborhood of which it is a part. Indeed, it would be logical to go on and treat the whole community or even the whole society. At the latter levels, however, the worker is involved either with politics or megalomania, so there is a continuing discussion whether both do not transcend expectations reasonable for social workers. We believe that what one sees in protective services is certainly an incentive to political involvement, both as citizen and as professional.

It does not seem that, as a group, the social workers involved with neglect must or should choose between the highly individualized activity of casework and efforts to improve the clients' social environment. We say "as a group," because realistically some who are talented at direct family service are made uncomfortable trying to do community organization. On the other hand, there are social workers who do well at marshaling and administering services but who lack the perceptiveness or the patience for intensive casework. Together we may undertake the whole.

Treating the Social Context

Garbarino and his colleagues postulated that vulnerable families would be more likely to deteriorate in "socially impoverished" neighborhoods than in those in which the neighbors were more friendly and supportive (Garbarino and Sherman 1978a). Their hypothesis seems reasonable, on the face of it. But how would one decide which families were most at risk, which parents were the most likely to succumb in a hostile or indifferent environment? One realizes, then, that their statistics, like other social indices (Kogan and Jenkins 1974) serve to identify neighborhoods at risk, or whole counties at risk, but not the specific families. To identify parents at risk, one needs the studies we have been doing on parental personality. Vulnerable families, then, would be those in which the parents were impulse-ridden, or showed many elements of the apathy-futility syndrome. In short, the two lines of theory do not conflict; rather, they complement each other.

That the family's social context makes a difference can be further illustrated by concrete examples. In rural Appalachian counties, medical care for children was a problem, especially for poor children. In Philadelphia, with its five medical schools and many hospitals, medical care did not seem so lacking, even among neglected children. Dental care was another matter, in Philadelphia, and we understand free dental treatment is harder to obtain throughout the country, in part because dentists volunteer less time.

In Sweden, as in Canada, children's allowances are universal regardless of income level. In Sweden, good day care is very widely accessible, with a sliding fee scale. We have been in a rural home in which the only balanced meal of the day that the eldest child had was the free lunch he was given in school. It was poignant to witness this boy's return home, each day, bearing in his pockets pieces of bread and cake he had saved from his lunch for his younger brother and sister. The school lunch program, aimed at improving the nutrition of all poor children, was particularly helpful to this neglected child, as it must have been to many others like him. Thus the social amenities that exist for all children are also likely—but not certain—to benefit neglected children. Sometimes they do not.

Consider Aid to Families of Dependent Children, AFDC. Historically, AFDC derived from the Mothers' Pensions provided by New York State in the 1920s under a law sponsored by Alfred E. Smith. Smith was once governor of New York, it will be recalled, and the first Catholic to be nominated for the presidency. He was sympathetic to the plight of widows with young children because his own father died when he was a child, and his mother had to find work the day after the funeral. Later, Franklin Roosevelt, who had also been governor of New York, and a member of his cabinet, Frances Perkins, brought AFDC to the whole country with the New Deal.

The original purpose of AFDC, and a continuing one, was to make it possible for families to remain together despite the death or disablement of the breadwinner. It picks up where our Social Security leaves off, aiding families without Social Security coverage. AFDC is presently under attack from a number of quarters. Some of the complaints against it are justified. It is true that we have successive generations, in some families, living on AFDC; it is true that we have the spectacle of adolescents defiantly becoming pregnant and "going into business for themselves" on AFDC. But if one doubts that AFDC also does the job it was created for, namely, to provide basic support for mothers with children when none other is available, one need only visit a country without AFDC, which includes much of the world. A fair number of the families in our study were on AFDC, including a very large proportion of the father absent neglect households, and the children in fact were fed and housed by this basic program.

Yet we are also aware that among families on AFDC, there are wide variations in children's level of care, a finding of the study of Wolock and Horowitz (1979). Programs set up with an image of an average-expectable parent in mind may fail to benefit neglected children because their parents are not average-expectable. AFDC is hardly a munificent program anywhere, and in some states it is niggardly, but the notion is that with the money provided, the parent will be able to manage the care of her children. This does not always happen. We regard the current separation within AFDC work, with one set of people determining eligibility and another poised to offer services when requested, as most unfortunate. When caseworkers made frequent visits to the families, they were able, in the course of offering financial aid, to monitor the level of child care to some extent; they also had an ongoing relationship with the parents. Now we have counties in which casework service to the family is offered only when requested, an unlikely event in many families we have come to know.

Efforts at treating neglect, or preventing it, by enriching the neighborhood in which the family resides are attractive, but they must be looked at critically as well as sympathetically. An example comes from one of the Family Service Units in England. The Family Service Units are an esteemed organization which was originally made up of conscientious objectors who volunteered to help families bombed out of their homes in English cities during World War II. Their movement survived after the war and, since they were accustomed to going into homes to offer very concrete manual help with cleaning and cooking, as well as psychological support, Family Service Units have since tried their hands at assisting multiproblem families. Wardle (1970), a member of the movement, has recounted an experiment designed to aid "family development." Eight social work and education students were brought into an urban neighborhood to work for a month during the school holidays. They provided sports and other activities for children, and a place for them to go, thus relieving pressure on parents during the long vacation weeks. The hope was also to reach at least some of the parents through their children's involvement.

Programs of this type are, of course, familiar to us from American urban social settlements and, indeed, it will be recalled that Jane Addams had neighborhood improvement very much on her mind when she took the job of sanitation inspector for the area in which Hull House is located. The settlement workers undertook to reside in their areas and to work in them for years at a time. Moreover, given what we have learned about the neglectful parents' role in their own social isolation, one is always dubious that they will be found among the small numbers of neighborhood residents who involve themselves in neighborhood improvement. There is always the chance that they will benefit from positive changes in their neighborhoods along with everyone else—and also the chance they will not, for they are among life's losers. Opportunity has a way of passing them by and vice versa. If this is true of AFDC, it may well be true of neighborhood development programs. Experienced settlement and neighborhood workers have always supplemented their group work and educational activities with much individual contact and reaching out to families. The latter activities take time each week; they also take time as measured in years of the worker's professional life. Hence, one feels better about the probable impact of efforts to treat neglectful families' neighborhoods when they include in their design continued contact with their communities over a period of years and arrangements for individualized reaching-out.

These comments concern neighborhood organization and development from the standpoint of the protective services only. We pretend to no expertise regarding that whole field of practice, but we have formed opinions about the manner in which such programs affect child neglect. We resent the squandering of scarce resources on organizations trading in trivia under the guise that they are preventing child maltreatment; but we welcome the help of serious and effective neighborhood workers. In the first place, improved neighborhood morale, mutual supportiveness, buying cooperatives, child care centers, and the like, make substantial contributions toward helping marginal families pull themselves up. For those involved in severe and chronic neglect, the social treatment is difficult and each worker needs all the help she or he can get. Some specific helps, which one would hope to find within the neighborhood, will be described as we go along.

Summing up, we have encountered few arenas of social effort which make one more conscious of society's ailments and unfairness than work among the children in these families, which are so justifiably regarded as "the poorest of the poor." Caseworkers in protective services are very unlikely to lose sight of the "big picture." They repeatedly encounter exploitation of the helpless, gaps in services, indifference to suffering which cannot help but turn their attention to the way the whole society functions. Work, which is hard at best, begins to seem impossible.

Yet the children are there, their needs are there, and they cannot wait for long-range processes of change. Viewing the "big picture" can be used as a rationale for withdrawal and flight. One hopes, instead, that it will provide a blueprint for cooperative work among all agencies which might contribute to the effort.

Thirteen

Toward Intentional
Change

Many of those who read this book, like those who wrote it, have
received pamphlets and brochures describing one or another new
service that may be used in child protection. Two of the more
recent, in our collection, concern the use of volunteers and
twenty-four-hour hotlines. No one has issued a pamphlet about the
use of social casework. One implication, not very thinly veiled, is
that casework with neglectful families is passé. There is even a
growing literature to the effect that casework has no value in any
setting.

Each of these fine innovations, nevertheless, carries with it an
unspoken assumption.

> Somewhere in the picture there is a woman or a man pounding
> a district in a car, or on foot, who makes the investigations,
> who makes contact with the parents and the children, who has
> to decide what service is needed, who seeks out the service or
> the facility or the money, and who offers, threatens, cajoles, rea-
> sons, entices, argues, or seduces some of the clients into using it.
> Every design for services, however advanced and fancy, some-
> where assumes a *liaison* between a client and facility, and that
> liaison proves to be a human being. As we dwell on what that
> person is supposed to do, and the kinds of equipment he had
> better have in order to do it, he or she may not be called a social
> caseworker, but sounds suspiciously like one. [Polansky 1979]   176

The person who acts as a liaison ought to have a practical knowledge of the world, especially the world of families implicated in neglect. This practical knowledge, however, needs to be combined with an awareness of clients' emotional needs and sensitivities. For in truth there is no "objective reality," only the world as the client is experiencing it. Without such sensitivity to the feelings and motivations of clients involved and skill in working in terms of them, parents and children seldom profit from the resources intended to assist them. It does not matter very much what title is borne by the person who carries the multiple role of comforter-threatener-adviser-courier-benefactor, but we have known that person as a social caseworker.

Those who question the value of casework have in mind a person who remains fixed in his or her office, and who relies entirely on interviewing and on processes of interpersonal influence to effect change. What is changed is almost never the client's circumstances. Rather, according to this model, the caseworker focuses on changing the client's attitudes and some of his ways of operating so that, primarily, he tolerates his circumstances with less discomfort and, secondarily, he manages to improve them a little. Prominent among the various objections raised against this image is the conviction that trying to help people tolerate the intolerable is a waste of effort. The image, in other words, is couched in a way that emphasizes the overlap which exists between casework and psychotherapy.

This is not our image of casework. In the first place, it has not been our experience that responsible psychotherapy really consists in making the "intolerable" tolerable or in "blaming the victim." Even Heinz Hartman, the theoretician, who probably had only a dim idea of the lives of families like those that concern us, said that psychoanalysis assumes "an average expectable environment" (1958). One would have to be an idiot to suppose that the world of Mona and her boyfriend, Frank, described in chapter 1, resembles the average American mode. In order to simplify theorizing about the operations of the human personality, in order to highlight, for example, the ways in which women like Mona participate in exacerbating their hardships, it may be convenient to *assume* that their world is very like everyone else's world, an "average expectable environment." But, of course, it is not, and no perspicacious therapist would treat it as if it were.

Now, it is true that many experts on personality are very inexpert about conditions of families living on low incomes in embattled neighborhoods. Since they are inexpert, they may try to fill in the void by assuming that these conditions are similar to those with which they are familiar. Or they may rely on "common sense" in estimating Mona's environment. Common sense is a dubious resource. In the first place, it is never abundantly available; in the second, "common sense knowledge" consists in taking as factual conscious impressions of the world without asking whether or not we might be distorting or repressing information to fit our own unconscious predilections. A psychoanalyst would be aghast at basing his or her assessment of a client's personality on common sense. Thus if a psychotherapist operates out of ignorance in responding to someone like Mona, it is because of a human limitation in the therapist and not because of something inevitable about personality theory.

It is useful for understanding the nature of social casework, in general, to review its place in child protective services. It is immediately apparent that what is meant by casework may, at times, involve the worker in trying to bring about attitude changes in the client. But casework is far more than this, if only because the worker we have been describing, who is in and out of the homes of neglectful families, is quite unable to sustain the theoretical fiction that such a family's housing, food, clothing, and place in the community are the same as those of everyone else. It is certainly not irrelevant to helping Mona and her children to understand how her own impulses and limitations make it inevitable that they will all be, again and again, out of money, cold, and hungry; neither is it irrelevant that, whether her fate is imposed on her, invited by her, or both, once the utility company shuts off the gas, the family is cold. An acute awareness of both person and situation is intrinsic to social casework in what has been termed "the psychosocial approach" (Hollis 1964). Because neither the person nor her situation can be discounted, one would like to be expert concerning both. However, we encounter our own human limitations, and so become as expert as we can about as much as we can. Our field tries to make it possible for large social organizations to become focused, humanized, and individualized in order to meet the needs of the individual person or family, the "case."

In evaluating casework, then, it is important to differentiate between the conditions that are *necessary* and those that are *sufficient* for treatment success. Most protective services agencies assume, and we agree, that to bring about an improvement in the level of care of the children involved requires that the worker represent financial resources and concrete services, the possibility of child placement, the authority of the state. The worker cannot carry out the work equipped, like Willie Loman in *Death of a Salesman*, with no more than "a shoeshine and a smile." Even the full panoply of resources and psychological treatment may not prove sufficient to eliminate the neglect. But without someone prepared to undertake the liaison role, no treatment takes place at all. Even if the casework proves not to be a sufficient condition for treatment, how can the process which is a necessary condition for treatment have no value?

In this chapter on intentional change as a goal in treating neglectful families, then, we shall be speaking from the standpoint of casework. Of course, we will not review basic theory of casework practice, for that is a task beyond the scope of this book. Rather, we shall try to set down some conceptions of the work that stem, in large part, from our research and which seem fundamental to treating child neglect.

The Significance of Character

The gist of the diagnostic approach to social work is that one's treatment fit the case. Consider Martha M.

Martha is a ten-year-old referred to her school social worker around Thanksgiving. Now in the fifth grade of a school she entered in the first, she is well known to several teachers. She has always been a lively, cheerful youngster, eager to learn and standing near the top of her class. However, for the past two months she has been arriving at school listless and unresponsive. She spends much time staring out the window; she has become aloof from her playmates; her school work is at a standstill.

Martha's attendance is now so irregular it is cause for concern. Often she arrives at school without having had breakfast. Moreover, for a child who was usually well groomed, the change in her appearance is striking. Buttons are missing, her hair needs washing and brushing, her personal hygiene in general is not good.

Mrs. M., the mother, is a hard-working divorcee who has been rearing Martha single-handed since she entered school. Despite her job, she has been accessible to the teachers for conferences, in the past, and has always seemed a loving, competent, and cheerful woman. However, Mrs. M. has not responded to notes sent home with Martha, nor has she seemed willing to come to the school to discuss the child when the teacher has reached her by phone.

After several attempts, the school social worker did succeed in arranging to see Mrs. M. at her home. She found the four room apartment well furnished but untidy. Mrs. M. was morose, but fairly willing to talk. The mother is aware of the difficulties for Martha, but at the moment cannot seem to do anything about them, for she has been feeling badly herself. In June, her mother was found to have cancer, which metastasized rapidly, and she died in great pain over the summer. Mrs. M. was terribly saddened at her mother's fate and, because of her understanding that her mother's illness means she and Martha are also at greater risk, she has become concerned about them, too. She is now a woman of thirty-five and, in the midst of all this, a man with whom she has had a relationship for five or six years broke off with her. Now she is worried about her job, for she has been absent a number of times when neither she nor Martha could seem to "get organized" in the morning. She works as a legal secretary, and is highly paid, but dependability and accuracy are essential to her work. In Mrs. M's state of mind, the school social worker felt her home visit seemed just an additional burden. Everything seems harder to do. She feels constantly tired, irritable, and has lost fifteen pounds since June.

So, what have we here? We have a set of facts, of course, not all the facts one might wish, but enough to form an impression of the dynamics at work. Martha has been reacting to a marked change in her mother and, since she lives in a situation in which her mother is her sole source of security, this is not surprising. At the moment, the key to Martha's protection, then, is her mother's state of competence. What is wrong with Mrs. M.? Obviously, she is experiencing a reactive depression. It is reactive in the sense that we are able to relate it, in time, rather clearly to a series of realistic events beginning with loss of her mother, receiving very unwelcome news about risks to her own life, and then loss of her lover. So, this depression is not the form called endogenous, which comes upon people like the unfolding of an inner process, without clear external events we can relate it to.

As a consequence of her state, Mrs. M. is more anxious, withdrawn, generally slowed, self-preoccupied. She is hardly in a position to handle her demanding daily routine as she had been; she is also hardly in position to give Martha the emotional support, or even the physical care, she had been giving her. We take the latter seriously, because most women with values and competences as substantial as the ones Martha's mother has shown maintain their child's basic care despite physical illness or emotional upset. She must be under severe stress for there to have been a letdown in Martha's grooming. Note, then, that the "kind of person" Mrs. M. is influences our impression of how depressed she must be.

The kind of person she is also influences our thoughts about what actions to take. We think of her as undergoing reactive depression because, among other things, there has been significant change in her behavior and mood, the onset of which can be pinpointed. We think of her as depressed, rather than as simply inadequate, however, because of her history. Even her way of earning a living bespeaks a person who can operate at a high level of skill with concentration for hours at a time. And we know what she has been doing for Martha over the years the school has known both of them. Thus a key issue in our thinking concerning potential neglect is the fact that Mrs. M. has had a strong level of functioning. If she were relieved of her present emotional state, she would have something very healthy to go back to. Her prognosis in treatment, then, ought to be far better than that of a person who has never adapted well. Indeed, most people who are essentially normal, as we say, or who have "strong egos" cure themselves of mild depression, even without help from a therapist or physician.

It is conceivable, then, that Mrs. M.'s depression will be, as they say in medicine, self-limiting, and all that is indicated is to offer Martha some extra attention at school for a while until her mother recovers. On the other hand, given the kind of person we know Mrs. M. to be, her symptoms seem more than mild, and she has not been able to shake them off by herself for a period of several months. Meanwhile, one wonders if she has, in the course of the depression, started to set in motion a downward spiral of causation. Have her withdrawal, irritability, and, perhaps, the drop-off of sexual interest that often accompanies depression, contributed to losing her lover? Will she next endanger her job? The way to put a timely end to this incipient soap opera would be to try to get Mrs. M. some treatment. Because of the kind of person she is, once again, we suspect that Mrs. M. is well aware that there are places she can get help. If she has not sought help it is probably because she prefers to solve her own problems, using a pattern that has stood her in good stead over the years. And, besides, she is a proud person. So it is possible that the person in the best position to offer her emotional first-aid for her reactive depression will be the school social worker, under the aegis of discussing ways of helping Martha survive this difficult period in her mother's life.

We believe that all caseworkers should be well acquainted with the dynamics, symptoms, course, and casework treatment of reactive depressions because so many of our clients are more or less depressed. The reason they are is that such dreadful things have often happened, or are happening, to the people who find their way to us. Our effort to summarize this information has been given elsewhere, in a form that evidently has been useful to those dealing with neglect, in the monograph by Polansky, DeSaix, and Sharlin (1972). There were two reasons for introducing the case of Martha M. at this point. It fits a myth we have found to be widespread in this field. The myth is that most instances of child neglect represent situations with readily definable causation, usually in the family's environment, and which can quickly be set to rights, so that the family can take over on its own and thereafter provide the child the level of care he or she needs. There are departments of human resources in at least several states which have promulgated policies to their front-line workers requiring them to identify immediately their specific goals of treatment, and even stipulating that a case may be carried for no more than six months. These policies exist in spite of the fact that caseworkers recognized as expert, from agencies with long experience in protective services, have told us the average severely neglectful family has to be tried in treatment for at least a year even to estimate whether it is likely to be treatable at all. Among the forty-five neglectful women for whom diagnoses were able to be attempted in our Philadelphia study, only two were thought to be neurotic, and a reactive depression is a neurosis. All the rest had long-standing character problems. So, the hopeful prognosis and specifiable treatment for Mrs. M. and Martha are unfortunately very atypical.

The second reason for introducing the case of Martha M. and her mother was to illustrate how important it is that the worker have at least some knowledge of character. Compared to most, this was a relatively uncomplicated instance of marginal child care and potential neglect. But one could not diagnose the family situation, or Mrs. M., or approach a treatment plan without taking into account "the kind of person" Mrs. M. is. And by that we mean the constellation of traits and motivations that she has shown over a period of time which is called her character. Character is the major intervening variable determining response to treatment.

Choosing a Characterology

Anyone with the requisite gift for protective service work comes to it with intuitions about the major ways in which other people are likely to be put together. Yet if the caseworker is not to be at the mercy of common sense, it would be helpful also to make use of the learnings of others, especially of those who have devoted years of their lives to searching out patterns consistently found in humans. The systematic study of character is called characterology.

In clinical practice, traditionally, the diagnosis of a patient is done at two levels. There is a diagnosis of the patient's dynamics, the things currently affecting or bothering him and his changing reactions to them. There is also the character diagnosis, the attitudes, favored defenses, prominent motivations that are relatively unchanging over time. Thus one might describe a man with a hysteric personality as showing a phobic reaction following a heart attack; or a woman with a personality with many obsessive-compulsive elements might be said to be displaying reactive depression following abandonment by her husband—a person like Mrs. M. Both levels of diagnosis contribute to understanding.

Note, however, that what we term dynamics, the changing events and clients' immediate responses to them, tend to be universal. The basic drives are universal; anyone can undergo depression; most people experience anxiety from time to time. Thus the core issue is not so much marking these changing patterns as establishing fixed structures in the personality. One concludes that locating the character type is the differential element in case diagnosis at the level of the personality. From which established characterology should we choose our diagnoses?

To be really useful, a system of character typing should satisfy the requirements of condictive power and of treatment relevance. Otherwise it will add nothing to the work and become merely an exercise in labeling.

Condictive Power

Condiction was a term employed by the late Gordon Allport (1937) to describe a process very like prediction. Whereas prediction involves using things that are known in the present to forecast the future, condiction projects from what one now knows about a person to other aspects of the current personality that "ought to be true" but which one does not know about. For example, once one has some evidence that a person fits the obsessive-compulsive mode, even if one has not observed him in this, one suspects that he is likely to play psychological games in which he "feels forced" by outside occurrences, rather than chooses; he also is likely to use the defense of *undoing,* "one step forward, one step back." The ability to help us project from what we know to things we do not from theory and observations of others, then, is a highly desirable feature of any system for typing people. It is not necessary that the condictive power of the system be perfect, for no method of character typing yet devised seem to meet this criterion. But it *is* necessary that the condictions it implies be highly probable or usually true. Protective services work seldom affords the leisure or opportunity to gather detailed histories on the parents; diagnoses must be attempted from only a few known facts, and rapidly confirmed or revised when the conditions one attempts prove true or untrue.

Treatment Relevance

If one routinely diagnoses a group of parents but offers all of them the same treatment, regardless, then the character diagnosis does amount merely to labeling people. On the other hand, if diagnosis is to make a difference in how one treats the parent or the family as a whole, there must be the possibility of choices among modes of treatment.

Those schools of thought which offer essentially the same treatment to all clients or patients should find character typing irrelevant. Indeed, most of them do so, except for "common sense" appraisals of those they treat. A listing of such treatment approaches uncovers some strange bedfellows: the Rankian approach to casework; behavior modification; brief therapies à la Carkhuff; Rogers' client-centered counseling; psychodrama; the "classical technique" of psychoanalysis; and mass cures for all society's ills. It seems little wonder that character typing has become passé. If a young analyst is going to have every patient lie on his or her back and free associate during the hour, and adhere closely to the standard rules of his trade, what does it matter which term he uses for summarizing the patient's enduring traits? Thus treatment relevance seems crucial in choosing a characterology to adopt for social work.

Mrs. M. was described as a person who had, perhaps, some "obsessive-compulsive" features although there was no evidence, thus far, that they dominated her personality to a crippling degree. In other words, we would not see her as *typifying* the obsessive-compulsive character. Each of us represents some form of character, and it has been remarked that the predominant type among American professionals probably represents a mixture of obsessive-compulsive and hysterical features. As far as we knew, then, until Mrs. M. became depressed to a neurotic degree, or neurotically depressed, she was "essentially normal," a reasonably mature, successfully coping person. Therefore we would be surprised if she were to prove hostile and suspicious when she was approached about her child, or if one were completely unable to talk realistically and sympathetically with her. It would be disappointing to discover her to be unaware that her level of operating had changed, although she might be defensive at first about saying so to her worker. These would be condictions affecting the worker's approach to her. A *prediction* from her character diagnosis would be that her depression was self-limiting, that she might well cure herself or show a "spontaneous remission." Could one be equally hopeful about Mona, in chapter 1?

The characterology being employed in these examples comes from the tradition of dynamic psychiatry, especially the psychoanalytic school. In psychoanalysis, in more modern times, characterology has been regarded as an aspect of ego psychology. This was because in the newer version attention shifted from the primary area of fixation, as in oral character and anal character, to predominant defenses and adaptive styles (Polansky 1971; Shapiro 1965). Even among psychoanalysts there has been reluctance to think in terms of character, as noted. Departures from the "classical technique," or parameters, were condemned as "not psychoanalysis." However, an instance in which such departures were widely adopted is the treatment of borderline personality states. It was decided that exposing a patient with loose ego boundaries to a deliberately unstructured, uncovering form of treatment was dangerous to the patient (Knight 1951).

Our own concern with characterology, then, certainly did not arise from the sense that it was stylish or the "in thing." It will be recalled that it stemmed from our failure to find neatly encapsulated sets of dynamics typifying child neglect. Rather, neglect was associated with a whole parental life-style. It was part of the warp and woof of parental functioning. In choosing a system of character types from which to borrow, we have leaned toward the psychoanalytic tradition. Among the reasons for doing so was the absence of alternatives. We could have separated our clients into pyknic, asthenic and athletic body types, for example, but that did not seem worthwhile. The analytic characterology is not completely satisfactory, but it does provide a language helpful in the diagnosis of neglectful parents.

The Parent as Part of a Family System

There are those committed to the general systems approach who believe that the psychoanalytic framework is antithetical to dealing with the neglectful family as a unit. They believe that a systems approach prescribes treating the total family. To us, it does not seem that the link between the level of theorizing and treatment strategy is that close or that automatic. Exclusive use of the classical technique, popularly associated with psychoanalysis, is not dictated by reliance on the psychoanalytic theory of the personality. Analogously, viewing the family as a system does not preclude working, at times, with only one of a pair of parents.

Many in social work first became aware of the significance of field theoretical conceptions while undertaking to work with individual clients. Others using psychotherapy had similar experiences. For example, when one was working with a husband and his neurosis, when he started to improve there was an upset in the equilibrium that had existed between him and his wife. Both the patient and the marriage were affected by the therapy. Satisfactions the wife had been finding in the marriage, some of which were unconscious, were now missing. For one thing, the man in her life now had an engrossing involvement with someone else. Thus it was entirely possible that the person to whom the patient was closest might become ill. Of course there was another possibility: if wife and husband were locked together in such a fashion that they were making each other neurotic, improvement in the husband might be beneficial for the wife as well. In such fortunate instances, by the way, it was nearly universal for the wife to attribute any gains in her own way of functioning to the fact that the husband was now "easier to live with." The wish to regard one's problems as nearly entirely outside oneself is not confined to infantile personalities.

But one could not count on the probability that an improvement in the wife would parallel her husband's; one could not assume that because of their solid attachment they would work out a new mutual accommodation. Having dealt with only one of the partners, having had only his reports of the wife and the state of the marriage, even after discounting distortions we knew the patient was likely to make, our knowledge of their situation was necessarily limited. Those who have lived through this process, whether as therapist, patient, or spouse can readily color in the kinds of feelings likely to exist in the nude we have been painting. Thoughtful caseworkers, then, had good reason for caustic remarks on why so many instances of supposed cure nevertheless ended with the rupture of long-time loving relationships. It was also common for a marital partner, made anxious or disgusted by changes of which the patient was so proud, to try to interrupt or otherwise defeat the therapy. This, too, could be damaging to the therapy unless, as was also sometimes true, the untreated partner was the one with the more realistic view of what the new set of defenses the patient was utilizing would do to his life adjustment outside the therapeutic hour. For example, it is seldom socially *de rigeur* to discuss one's intimate life history after one cocktail.

It was therefore desirable that, if one member of the pair sought treatment, the other should also get supportive help. At least the wife could better understand some of the changes she was living with. There was a variety of patterns in vogue. Sometimes the marital partner was seen by another caseworker; sometimes one saw both, individually or jointly; and so forth. Needless to say, those who routinely chose joint treatment often became very adept in that mode of treatment. And because their previous psychoanalytic orientation was short on concepts for understanding the behavior of pairs or of total family units, they began to borrow and invent new terminology, new theory, and new ideas for treatment. It was not surprising that the psychoanalytic theorists had few synthetic systems conceptions, for Freud's mode of thought for approaching causation was, of course, analytic. Of the earlier group of related theorists, the only one who comes to mind as having approached his clinical material in field-theoretical or synthetic terms was Harry Stack Sullivan (1947), and he seems to have done so intuitively rather than our of a grounding in the newer logic of science.

A number of those who do only joint treatment or whole-family therapy believe their style is far more effective for most purposes than is individual treatment (Minuchin 1967). Their conviction is like that of Kurt Lewin (1951), the father of group dynamics, who preached that the most efficient way to treat group-anchored attitudes was to try to change the group as a whole. It does seem noteworthy that so many of those practicing family treatment have first been soundly grounded in individual therapy. Perhaps this magnifies their perception of emotions at work within the family. It is easier to learn human psychology by starting with its less complicated units.

Nevertheless, it does not follow from basic psychoanalytic theory that treating clients conjointly or in family groups is never done. Neither does it seem that a general systems approach prescribes treating the whole family simultaneously. If treating only the husband can upset the marriage relationship, it must mean that in a system at a high level of interdependence of parts—Lewin spoke of the degree of *unity* of the system—a change in one has repercussions throughout the whole. The repercussions *may* prove to be in directions that are desired.

In the family of Mona and Frank (chapter 1), the street-wise, manipulative Frank made himself unavailable for meaningful contact. Would a general systems approach dictate that, if we could engage only Mona in social treatment, no attempt ought be made? Quite the opposite. If Mona is our only point of entry into the system, obviously we must begin with Mona. Indeed, the only chance we may have of involving Frank might come from upsetting the equilibrium of his relationship to Mona, one in which he was getting many practical needs met and, one assumes, some emotional needs as well. There are successfully functioning families for which one would deeply regret disturbing their equilibrium, but is this an untenable risk in this household, or does it provide our only opportunity?

For a person trained analytically, it would be no surprise if Frank tried to defeat Mona's treatment. Indeed, also taking into account Mona's own problems and probable resistance to change, the psychoanalytically astute worker would have less reason, not more, to try to undertake individual treatment than would the person with a view of the larger system in mind.

Thus there is no antithesis, really, between the two lines of theory. They can usefully complement each other in plans for treating neglect. The theory being followed does not seem to dictate the intervention; the choice of the form of intervention involves us with issues of efficiency, not with general theory. The way in which a set of attitudes, traits, defenses, and motivations *within* the person are fitted together may also be thought of as a system (Polan-sky 1971), a microsystem. The mezzosystem of the Stay-Brown household (Mona and Frank's) contains five such microsystems. Thinking at both these levels is helpful to understanding what is going on, and may also be helpful to the family. It is a hardship of the work, alas, that while there are, perhaps, some fairly abstract laws governing the behaviors of *all* systems, the content we have to learn for understanding individuals is by no means the same as that we have to learn for assessing whole-family functioning. Indeed, the work of J. C. Flügel (1935) in which he sought to interpret family processes in terms of the Oedipus complex was once familiar to most caseworkers, but is rarely mentioned nowadays.

Treatment Leverage

Finding an entry into the family brings us to the general issue of treatment leverage. By this concept, we mean the basis from which a worker can exert any influence on the system in which he hopes to intervene. Speaking of clients who come voluntarily to family agencies, Ripple, Alexander, and Polemis (1964) summed up moti-vations that held clients in treatment over five interviews as a com-bination of "the push of discomfort and the pull of hope." These are reasonably appropriate motives for treatment which can be taken pretty much for granted with a client who has heard good things about social casework from another client and who is seri-ously concerned to improve his or her marriage. But this happy combination of eagerness and desperation is rare in initial contacts between clients and protective service workers. There exists no need to welcome contact with the worker because of the service which he may offer. Welcoming is among the feelings farthest from the client's mind. Since so little can be taken for granted in the way of the client's readiness, protective services work requires that we think through very realistically the possibilities for treatment leverage.

Leverage for influencing another person ordinarily comes from having control over something that person wants. This point can be dramatized by the power the neglectful parent typically has over the caseworker. Because the worker has, in the first place, a job to do and, even more urgently, a concern for the welfare of the client's children, the worker will accede to the parent's wishes regarding when he or she wants to be seen, about where they might meet, and so forth. On his side, the worker may have little choice among leverages he might use. Indeed, his position sometimes reduces to his applying, or withholding, the threat of more drastic action by courts or police. He may be viewed, immediately, in terms of the threat of removing the children the parent loves or at least wants to keep. For it is known from other cases that keeping the children sometimes has more to do with the parent's concern about his or her reputation than with feelings toward the children. Few of those who do this kind of work are comfortable with threats as their only treatment leverage. It is our observation that such reluctance, by the way, is not confined to social workers. Responses that seem instinctive to threatening situations include flight; they also include fight. Even experienced policemen who, one might think, are inured to the use of threats usually prefer to shift their relationship with an arrested suspect as rapidly as possible to one in which what they are doing is seen as reasonable or at least impersonal. Yet in dealing with parents with severe character disorders who see nothing wrong with their care of their children or in themselves, threats may constitute our only entering leverage. Very few caseworkers have been given training in working with this kind of motivation, that is, personifying a threat, but it may well be their only entering wedge into the neglect situation. It is good to report, therefore, that senior workers like Stone and his colleagues in Boston have been developing an analysis of levels of hostility encountered in protective services, and a method for focusing on client hostility to engage the client in treatment (Stone et al. 1980).

What other means of treatment leverage are possible? If the family has physical needs and the parent feels these acutely, one's ability to offer or withhold access to them becomes the next possibility. The sorts of things our families need make up an enormous list, alas, and we know from research that they are the poorest of the poor. The worker, concerned for the welfare of the children, wants the family to have many things: food, housing, bedclothes, medical and dental care. However, the worker as a potential supplier acquires no treatment leverage unless these are things the *parent* wants. One would think that the offer of fifty dollars per family as an inducement to take part in the research would have amply motivated fathers to participate and to make an effort to have their families complete the study. This was certainly not always the case. As a worker commented about efforts to see one father when the senior author suggested possibly increasing the family fee, "An offer of a couple of beers right after the interview? Maybe. An offer of ten dollars more for the family when the study is over? That's not where he's at."

Nevertheless, one's status as a supplier of concrete helps is another potential source of treatment leverage in most families. In addition to the fact that the needs identified are very real, many experienced workers have told us that this role is essential in a beginning relationship. For the worker to be instrumental in further change within the family, then, it is important that his association with the receipt of other aid be maintained. The connection in the client's mind is obviously weakened when all the worker can do is to make a referral after which the client's service is assumed by someone else. Intelligent collaboration with such a worker would require at least the agency supplying the money or food to reiterate his role in their entering the family.

An unspoken source of leverage in many cases derives from the client's liking for the worker as a person. In dealing with many neglectful parents, this kind of attachment does not come readily, for they have had many previous experiences with people which were disappointing to them. With most clients, whose lives have not been that difficult, repeated contact engenders attachment almost automatically. Attachment cannot be counted on in child protection because of most parents' tendencies to transfer hostile and suspicious feelings to the relationship. Therefore it becomes especially important that the worker's realistic role as a well-meaning, essentially helpful person be emphasized as much as possible. Providing concrete services, then, has a dual purpose: immediate direct help to a family which needs it, and reinforcing the worker's image as helpful. Among people who are distrustful, words are weak vehicles of communicating good intentions, certainly as a beginning. Expression of the desire to help in visible, concrete terms is valuable.

From the parent's liking for the worker we may hope there will emerge desires to stay in contact and to please the worker. And it is from the latter that one gains another possible source of influence or treatment leverage. At a very basic level, liking carries with it the desire to be liked in return, and the worker's needs become relevant to the parent. Of course, most of this transaction remains unspoken. We emphasize its existence, however, because it is true in a high proportion of neglect situations that when there is no realistic threat in the picture, the children are very unlikely to be removed unless their care becomes actually life-threatening. The worker's only leverage becomes what he or she has to offer in the way of wanted services or the ability to give or withhold approval, like a loving parent.

Another outcome of the client's need for the worker's attention and approval may be identification with the worker. The nature of identification is worth spelling out in this connection. It is a defense mechanism. Defense mechanisms are used to ward off anxiety, and while the literal words and actions used in the defense may be fully conscious, the *purpose* of the defense is not. In a relationship with someone we love, there is no reason to use a defense mechanism unless there is anxiety in the picture. The expression, "identification out of love" is really a short-hand way of saying, "identification out of the fear of loss of love" (Polansky 1971). For in this mechanism, it is as if we were saying, "If I make my image of you part of my image of me, I can control you." This is the familiar logic of identification with the aggressor, according to which one identifies in order, symbolically, to keep from being hurt. For identification out of love in treatment, however, the phrasing would be, "As you become part of my image of me, I can keep you from leaving me."

Through identification, the client may take over standards of child care and other values the worker has, in a process that is typically unconscious and certainly unspoken. We know intuitively that it would spoil the process if, for example, the worker were to say, "I see you are now picking up what I believe in." To do such a thing would be socially gauche; it might well provoke an adverse reaction in the client. Speaking technically, it would also amount to interpreting, bringing a defense to consciousness. And the effect of such interpretations, in interview treatment, is usually to dissolve the mechanism. Thus such useful identifications are best left unidentified.

The process of identification enters into treating neglect not only through casework, but also when parents' groups are used to facilitate change. We also hope the clients will identify with the mature and giving women who enter their homes as homemakers, so that teaching can go on both consciously and unconsciously. Mothers brought in to assist in day care may also pick up patterns of disciplining and teaching their children from exposure to trained personnel in those settings.

Thus identification is often much to be desired. Alas, it is unlikely to occur under conditions in which the parent has nothing to lose. She will have no reason to try to keep an image of her worker within her if she develops no need for the worker's approval and affection. And when approval is made completely unconditional, there is no implied threat, so there is no identification, either. This occurred in children spoken of as "spoiled" in an earlier generation. Clients who "do not relate," as we say, who develop no need for the worker may be particularly nettling.

Some Hard-to-reach Clients

Mrs. Farmer is a divorced woman living on AFDC with her four children, born during her nine years of marriage. She comes from a family she describes as demanding "so that nothing you did was ever good enough." She described her own mother as having been a detached person who "warned all of us not to get too attached to anyone." She spoke repeatedly of never having felt loved by her parents; of a rule in the home which said, "do as I say, not what I do"; of having been a bedwetter, "but it was never talked about. They just beat the living shit out of me for being so uncontrolled"; of parents who "only loved you when you did as they wished" and punished by beating her with a strap.

After getting excellent grades in parochial school, Mrs. Farmer arranged to enter a convent. However, on the day she was to go there, she ran away to another state and was married. "I was scared, and whenever I'm scared of new things, I manage to run." Marriage was a burden, with too many babies too close together, and eventually she "signed [herself] into the state hospital leaving the old man with a new baby so as he would get a taste of it all." However, she got out after one day, and found a doctor to prescribe Valium, to which she became addicted for some time.

Following her divorce a couple of years ago, she has had several liaisons, "because I felt like it." For the past month, she has been living with John, a recently released prison inmate and brother of a man she had previously dated. "He makes me feel like a woman. God only knows how long it will last."

When she is home, Mrs. Farmer keeps her home orderly and neat. She suffers from a variety of physical and some psychological complaints; she has emphysema, but continues to smoke. During the period we knew her, she was in and out of difficulty. One weekend, she left for New York with John, leaving her seven-year-old in charge of the others. Neighbors reported her to the social agency. On another occasion she threatened hysterically to "put all these kids away because I can't stand it." She was constantly under pressure from creditors. John gave her money to pay the phone bill, which she spent on new frames for her glasses because "I was tired of the old ones." She was then angry at the phone company for cutting off service. Using the pretext of going on a religious retreat, she tried to manipulate her social worker into staying with the children, but immediately blurted, "If you do, I'll go to the shore with John." In short, she presents a picture of restlessness, intolerance of stress or of routine, craving for excitement, and an almost childlike manipulativeness.

In Mrs. Farmer, we have a fairly good illustration of a person who did not incorporate much of a superego, an automatic set of internalized controls, in her own childhood. She felt her own parents' exhortations were hypocritical, and her conformity was a matter of meeting demands experienced as external. In her adulthood, she behaves like a four-year-old, and we think of her as an impulse-ridden character with some hysterical features. It is obvious her approach to her worker will be primarily manipulative:

"What do I have to do to get you off my back?" We do not anticipate that she will have much ability to form a loving attachment
with her worker, but she may come to respect her, and accept
suggestions when she learns that they lead to more pleasure and less
pain. As a beginning, she said of her protective services worker,
"Mrs. Dodgson is here to help me to learn to think rather than act."
Mrs. Dodgson's treatment leverage will rest, for the near future, on
the threat she represents and on being a possible source of gratifications. If Mrs. Farmer finds her worker has some humor about her
manipulations, she may also enjoy her as a confidant. It is fatal to
take people like her more seriously than they do themselves.

Mrs. Caller reminds us that narcissistic people are, among other
things, crippled in their ability to derive pleasure from the happiness experienced from those they love. Hence they are reduced to
trying to get what satisfaction they can from their own orifices, oral
or sexual, and from trying to create an image of themselves which
they can admire.

Marge Caller is a sexually provocative young woman of
twenty-three who always wears tight blue jeans and a shirt. Her
dark brown hair, brown eyes and olive complexion are cues to
her Italian heritage. Always sitting with feet under her, she
chain smokes to assuage her obvious anxiety. Rings which
adorn every finger accentuate her tobacco-stained hands.

Marge is a "tough spoken" mother of two physically attractive little girls. Alice, age three and Karen, age six, were both
present for every visit and were always being punished, sometimes quite abusively, for the slightest infraction. Mrs. Caller
has "no time" for the children and lets them know her feelings
in her usual loud, curt manner. The family has been receiving
public assistance for three years, since Mr. Caller left prior to
the birth of Alice. Mrs. Caller stated, "this broad ain't got no
time for a job, honey. I got to have my fun with my man." I was
soon to learn that Mrs. Caller has only male friends and "fun"
is the top priority of her life, at any cost.

The Caller family learned of the study through the counselor
at the local elementary school. Their home is located in an area
of Fishtown surrounded by a railroad and numerous factories.
Helping me to gain a knowledge of "my turf," Mrs. Caller explained, "the kids use the vacant lot for a playground, and the
streets for bike paths when the mill closes." This row home has
its bricks painted yellow giving it a "springlike air"; however,
the exterior does not cover up the dilapidation and rat infesta-
tion which exist inside.

Mrs. Caller was quite articulate in telling me about her life
once she presented her "tough" exterior to me. "O.K. baby, this
broad will tell you all about raising kids as soon as I get my
smokes," she announced. She then told me, quite nastily,

"maybe I'll not tell you anything." I accepted all of this, stating that telling what she wanted to volunteer was part of our agreement. Mrs. Caller went nonstop for over two hours during each interview. It took very little time for me to see that the surface brittleness which Mrs. Caller was using served to ward off depression, and that inside she is a hurt, frightened, deeply lonely young woman who is afraid of relationships: "I have been hurt too many times and this broad ain't gonna be nice to no one no more."

Mrs. Caller is the fifth child of eight children born to a promiscuous mother and a father she never knew. She told me, "the old lady married once but God only knows which kid was his." Mrs. Caller stated she received "nothing from the old lady" because "she was for herself and left us to raise ourselves." An older sister was always left to mind the children "but she was only seven years older than me." She could only remember her years around age ten when "I drank and ran around with the wrong crowd." Mrs. Caller had her first sexual experience at age 12 and had several abortions before age sixteen when she conceived and gave birth to Karen. "Nobody cared," she added, "so I got my kicks out of life myself." She married a Puerto Rican man at age eighteen—"not the father of any of my brats." This created conflict with her siblings, and her isolation from them continues. "I never cheated on him but he was a real stud," reported Mrs. Caller, "so I threw him over." Alice was conceived after "I lived with John. I had her, then I got me fixed, honey," Mrs. Caller recollected, " 'cause I like my good times."

Life for the Caller children is tough because their mother goes away with "men friends" or "parties" all night. A male boarder takes care of the children: "Bob's a nice guy but I can't get it on with him," Mrs. Caller explained. So Bob watches the children in exchange for a room in the house.

Mrs. Caller is ambivalent about the children and admits to hitting and "bruising them." She feels "those kids make me look bad to the neighbors and that school" and when they do not do as she wishes she strikes out. Mrs. Caller talked of placing the children—"I hate being a parent"—however, placement with an agency is out of the question as she wants them "with someone who will bring them once a week to see me." At one visit, she had refused to feed the children stating, "I ain't hungry, so you ain't." No one ate breakfast that morning and Mrs. Caller screamed and hit each one stating "get out of my sight. I don't care if all of you starve."

A woman like Mrs. Caller epitomizes the metaphor for narcissism, the deprived child saying, "If nobody loves me, then I will." Everyone and everything around her is viewed in terms of herself. The children are a source of income; perhaps they help a bit with her loneliness, but they are a nuisance because their state makes her look bad in the neighborhood. When they give her work, or fail to gratify her by not responding as she wishes, she gets furious and strikes them. The dynamics, in other words, resemble those often found in families involved in outright child abuse. Giving thought and self-discipline to correcting children in ways that would make them easier to rear is quite beyond her; even farther beyond, of course, are thoughts of the effects of what she is doing on their long-range life adjustments. She lives in the moment, using "fun" to try to get by.

Obviously, one's treatment leverage with this damaged young mother cannot come from recognizing her failures in child rearing, for she will take this as a further insult. The research caseworker saw, however, that there were other bases on which she might be involved. She is a lonely person; she is self-preoccupied. Encouraging her talking about herself and listening attentively fit these needs. Similarly, if one were to determine that, for their own safety, the children must be placed, one would do well to propose that such action was being done on her behalf, too: "All this is just too much for you, you need something for yourself"; or simply giving permission when she says she wants to be rid of them. Occasionally, however, attentiveness to the needs of such an empty mother improves the child care.

Is it not interesting that a household like the Callers was not active with a protective service agency? But the mother arranges for baby-sitting when she is out, she usually feeds and clothes the children, the slaps given the children are not that severe, and verbal abuse not that rare, alas, everywhere. The school counselor was active and regarded the situation as neglectful, and so did we. Thus this is an example of the many families contributing to their children's emotional damage that still elude the grasp of our whole system for protecting children.

Mrs. Farmer and Mrs. Caller remind us forcibly how hard it is in disorganized families to divide the victims from the oppressors. For simplicity of exposition, we described two one-parent families. What about the men who fathered these children and then eloped? If the marriage broke up, they could still have wanted to maintain a protective contact with the children, but they are not in evidence. Still, if they were found, and even if they were made to pay something in child support, the care of the children might not be greatly altered. And one's punitive zeal would flag as it was discovered how lonely and incapable the fathers are, too.

So the search for a treatment leverage has to be made with perceptiveness, with shrewdness. The aim is not simply to outmaneuver a dreadful person who is parent to the child-victims.

Rather, it becomes an issue of trying to rescue the children's lives by working within the symptoms and severe limitations some of their parents show. In the search for treatment leverage, one starts, as a first approximation, with acceptance that the treatment is going to have to fit the case. Diagnosis includes the family situation and the parent's present dynamics; it also includes assessing the parent's character. By condicting from character, a judgment is made about what approach is most likely to fit. Trying to predict one's leverage may fail, but the attempt to predict is always instructive, confirming or discounting one's working diagnosis.

Deliberate Disequilibration

The level of care within a family usually fits Lewin's (1951) model of a quasi-stationary equilibrium. We usually think of an equilibrium as a state of affairs, but there are ongoing processes that act as if they were in equilibrium. One example is a chemical reaction in which acid and alkaline ions are constantly being released or neutralized so that the degree of acidity remains constant. Rates of production in factories also behave as if they were equilibrium. If the Childhood Level of Living Scale were administered to a family on successive days, one would not expect the score to stay the same. The first day it might be 90, then 88, then 91, and so forth, fluctuating around a standard typical for the household. We believe there are probably forces at work making it unlikely the score will suddenly jump to 100; we observe that among families embedded in helping networks, the score is unlikely to drop to 60, because loving relatives will step in to help out.

The state of care in most neglectful families seems to us to be usually in some sort of equilibrium or in a state of slow decline. Sometimes the family is caught in what is called, in general systems theory, a "downward spiral of causation." A girl, lonely and unhappy in her own home, tries to escape into an early marriage in which she soon has several children. However, partly because of the choice she makes of a partner, and partly because of her own troubles in relating, the marriage goes badly. There are periods of fighting, slow estrangement, which certainly does little to make either her or her mate feel loved, and finally a break occurs. The man takes off, and she is left alone to cope with the heavy burden of rearing three children with little support from her family and no solution in sight.

Even when things are not in a decline, the level of equilibrium in most neglectful households is such that the children are being destroyed. Yet one has to keep in mind that any equilibrium usually reflects spontaneous solutions to life problems. We cannot recognize what satisfactions or necessities lie behind the equilibrium when we first enter a situation. Some of the limiting forces at work may be fairly obvious. Sheer lack of money, a father's lack of skills for repairing things around the house, a mother's low intelligence, an overpopulated apartment. But there are other forces which have to be ferreted out.

A parent with a great deal of guilt over repressed hatred of his parents may feel, "I am no good; I don't deserve to live well." Unfortunately, his children may share his carrying out his self-imposed, neurotic abasement. Many of us find life infinitely easier in a somewhat orderly and regulated environment. Indeed, for people with a bit of inner looseness, who lack inner boundaries, a regulated life-style eases anxiety. Yet a number of thoughtful workers have had occasional—fortunately rare—cases in which a mother tried to develop a more scheduled style of housework and child caring, and broke down. It was as if the woman needed to live with external tumult and disorder to distract herself from her internal conflicts. As her environment became more peaceable, her internal commotion was ineluctable. There have been instances of neglectful families on their way to being "cured" in which success was interrupted by a mother's psychotic break or a father's reincarceration.

Such instances are dramatic, but they remind us that the parent, or the whole family, may "need" things to remain as they are. It is a useful exercise, in thinking about a family one knows intimately, to ask oneself what they might be getting out of the status quo, if not consciously, then unconsciously. From such an appraisal, it becomes clear that well-meaning efforts at help also introduce deliberate disequilibration into a system with which the family, itself, has come to terms. A major disequilibration comes from breaking up the family, removing the children, but any intervention that has an impact brings the family to an unknown future. And they often have all they can do to live with the effects of their pasts. As one patient said, "It's an awful way to go, but it's the only way we know."

Clinging to the existing state of affairs, however pathological it may look from the outside, resembles what we call *resistance* in individual therapy. Resistance is expectable in any attempt to alter a state of affairs that has gone on for a period of time, if only because those involved will have found at least some ways to milk what satisfactions they can from the disaster of their lives. Thus any effort at change is always met with mixed emotions. The worker who thinks his good intentions in the face of so much need should at least be rewarded with gratitude has not thought through the logic of treatment resistance. And when it is present, it usually means that one part of the parent may be operating to undermine advances that other parts are trying to very hard to make. This occurs, of course, when the resistance is experienced as conflict within the client. In protective services, it is relatively easy for the parent to externalize the conflict, as we say, and make it a problem between him and the worker. This is what we would encounter in trying to reach Frank in the Mona-Frank household. That pairing, by the way, was in much better equilibrium without the children.

Resistance can be reduced when the intervention includes new gratifications for the client, or things that help to replace what the client would lose if he were to change his way of operating. As a crude but very real example, it would be easier for Mrs. Farmer to give up recurrently abandoning her children if she had a loving mother who would care for them when she wanted to go on a trip. It might even help a person like her, who craves excitement, if she had some arrangement for regular afternoons out, a convenience middle-class women take for granted, since they can afford baby-sitters. It might even help Mrs. Caller if there were someone in her life other than herself, such as a caseworker, who seemed to care what happened to her. Perhaps this would move the balance a bit so that she could spend a little attention on her children, a shift in cathexis. When we notice how few people disengage from patho-logical relationships without support, we are also noting their need to substitute a new object as a buffer against loneliness.

To bring about a necessary change, then, means breaking up the present equilibrium, trying to get the family's life-style to move in a direction more beneficial for the children, and helping them establish a new equilibrium at a more desirable level. Lewin called this sequence unfreezing, moving, and refreezing (1951). Obvi-ously, it is less likely to occur when the worker has little recognition of the family's needs and wants. Moreover, it also cannot be done except by a worker willing to take responsibility for an opinion of what children need, and to engage in intervention in other people's lives.

Much of the problem of neglect, as we have seen it, is involved with parental character. The part of the character which is the surface defense has been called "the character armor." Mrs. Caller's "tough broad" exterior is obviously part of her armor, for she uses it to avoid feeling hurt. Intervention in neglect involves us with the parents' character armor. They have to decide whether to lower their shields; we have to judge whether we must try to pen-etrate them. There is no change without risk.

Fourteen

Treating Loneliness

We have been discussing the treatment of child neglect as if the aim was to make it possible for the children to remain with their parents without being seriously harmed. We do not mean to imply that we believe children ought never be removed, for that is far from our thinking on the issue. It must be borne in mind, nevertheless, that in the great majority of cases, the children do remain in their natural homes, for a variety of reasons: the risks to any youngster entering the foster care system; the cost to the public of placing children; the wish to let the children develop with parental figures who, at least, remain the same even if they are somewhat inadequate (Goldstein, Freud, and Solnit 1973). To these might be added the continuing high valuation placed on the family as an institution, which requires us to have very definite evidence of a present danger to chidren before courts will sever parental rights. And as a technical aspect of treating such difficult situations, our ability to distinguish who will be treatable from who will not is often so poor that the only ethical move is to begin with an effort at treatment. So in this chapter, we shall continue examining the implications of our study for treatment, on the assumption the child may be able to remain at home. Let us start by reviewing one of the concepts guiding the research, the apathy-futility syndrome.

The Apathy-Futility Syndrome

Earlier research on the personalities of neglectful parents in Appalachia made us very conscious of the problem of futility and of associated immobilization. The content of this apathy-futility syndrome was delineated in chapter 4. Based on learnings of the Appalachian study, this character type was seen as one form of severe immaturity or infantilism. That the same trait clusters were significant to understanding urban child neglect was underscored by various findings recounted in chapter 8.

An index, the Reciprocal of Apathy-futility, was constructed from the research caseworkers' ratings of items in the Maternal Characteristics Scale. This index was scored with a positive meaning, so that a higher score meant the *absence* of apathy-futility elements. It correlated (point-biserial r) .58 with the neglect/nonneglect dichotomy. Case judges also rated the parents on a ratio scale for the absence of these elements. Their ratings of mothers correlated (r) .69 with scores given the focal child on the Childhood Level of Living Scale's physical care; the correlation with psychological care was .77. Ratings of fathers also proved highly significant, but were somewhat lower at .45 and .47 respectively. There was some evidence of interobserver reliability in the fact that case readers' and research social workers' ratings of the mothers correlated .78 ($P < .001$). Thus the greater the presence of elements of the syndrome in either parent the poorer the child care.

When diagnostic impressions were done for each parent, the apathy-futility syndrome was thought to be the character type most frequently found among neglectful mothers, including 39% of that sample. Next most frequently cited was another form of infantilism, the impulse-ridden character, for 23%. These character types were found among the control mothers, but much less frequently, making up 13% and 4% of that sample, respectively. Apathy-futility was not prominent among neglect fathers.

The diagnosis was found to have ominous meaning for the care of children. Mothers diagnosed as normal or neurotic averaged a score of .85 on the Childhood Level of Living Scale; those diagnosed as exhibiting the apathy-futility syndrome had a mean of .48. Indeed, the mean of those showing the syndrome was much lower than that for women showing all other forms of character disorder, whose mean was .64. For example, in chapter 13, we described a highly impulsive mother who kept house fairly well—when she stayed home. Results of the replication study, then, strongly reinforced the concern about the apathy-futility syndrome which came out of our initial rural research. The findings, as was earlier remarked, were good for the research but bad for the children. For the mother's reluctance to form relationships limits one possible treatment leverage; her massive affect-inhibition, which dulls her wants and feelings, limits other sources; and it is always harder to negotiate with clients who are immobilized and whose only way of asserting their existence is negativism.

Among those of us who were clinical social workers at the time of the first study, the syndrome bore a resemblance to what was then being called the schizoid personality. Thus the mother with that diagnosis might be said to be "far out on the schizoid spectrum," or to have had "many schizoid elements." Feelings of futility were regarded by many as the characteristic affect of the schizoid personality, just as barely suppressed anger and feelings of disappointed entitlement are looked for in borderline personalities.

For insights into the probable etiology of the apathy-futility pattern in people, we drew heavily on the writings of Fairbairn (1952) and Guntrip (1969). In their image of what has occurred, and what the schizoid person continues to relive, the studious detachment is seen as a kind of reaction-formation against the wishes to devour the mother. Aggressive oral fantasies were thought to stem from severe deprivation in infancy "love made hungry" in Guntrip's apt phrase. The deprivation also accounted for the sense of emptiness so many patients had reported, and that seemed also pervasive among the apathetic-futile mothers.

The schizoid individual, then, was seen as having a fear of intimacy because of the infantile fantasy he would devour the very source of his supplies, the mother. This put him in an insoluble dilemma: if he comes close, he will injure the loved person; if he keeps his distance, he will perish of loneliness (Polansky 1971). Similar expressions of the initial fear of closeness were also readily visible among the women who concerned us—and in their children as well. The writings of Fairbairn and Guntrip, then, were enormously helpful in explicating the common dynamics of detachment, but they were somewhat nonspecific. For example, their theory assumed that the infant "knows" he and the mother are separate individuals. They did not really deal with the perceptual problem, the failure of cognition out of which the threat of losing one's sense of identity derives, in large measure, from not yet having established one's existence as independent of the mother's. The perceptual as well as emotional processes involved in developing the earliest form of identity, "*that* I am," are central to the discussions of Mahler, Pine, and Bergman (1975). Another area of nonspecificity in the Fairbairn-Guntrip model, it seemed, was the lack of ideas about how *much* deprivation must occur for patients to be unable to achieve a good resolution of the schizoid position, as they termed it. Guntrip indicated only that persons reflecting an unresolved schizoid process were more deprived, "hungrier," than those showing the depressive position. Yet we found Guntrip's descriptions of clinical phenomena engaging, at times enlightening, and close to the mark with respect to the treatment of schizoid individuals.

Still, the image of the treatment situation was far removed from the circumstances of work with neglectful parents. The English authors depicted seesions in which one imagined tweed-clad gentlemen and gentlewomen presenting themselves for treatment several times a week and competent or at least organized enough to pay for it. Moreover, the various quotations bespoke a clientele that was reflective and articulate. These images did not fit in with treatment of neglectful parents through interviews carried out in their mountain cabins. The style of treatment, too, was at some distance from the training prevalent among child protection workers with whom we were acquainted.

Thus an effort was made to use the insights gleaned from Fairbairn and Guntrip, but to locate treatment tactics to deal with the parents' problems of intimacy which were more appropriate for child protection work. Accordingly, we wrote about *encouraging* dependency since, if the infantile client relates at all, he or she will relate first at that level (Polansky, DeSaix, and Sharlin 1972). Of course, it was fun to outline a course of action contrary to the widespread injunction against encouraging dependency, which seemed to us to be something of a shibboleth.

An approach that seemed readily transferable from the circumstances of office psychotherapy was taken from the work of Hellmuth Kaiser (Fierman 1965). Kaiser believed that an important key to the treatment of all patients was "helping the patient stand behind his words." The senior author had developed the concept of verbal accessibility to describe this aspect of behavior (see chapter 9). Focusing interviews with schizoid persons around their verbal inaccessibility and refusals to commit themselves regarding important feelings and attitudes had proven helpful in in-patient work. Those neglectful parents with the apathy-futility syndrome were also wary of self-revelation, and verbally inaccessible. Nor were we alone in this observation:

> Our experience indicates that the problems in verbal communication at the affective level not only involve a lack of experience in talking or having the requisite vocabulary, but are also the result of an incapacity to tolerate anxiety. Therefore, anxiety is discharged in a range of activities. [Sullivan, Spasser, and Penner 1977, p. 103]

It is obvious that "helping the patient stand behind his words" can have curative effects at a variety of levels: encouraging the ego's synthetic function; stimulating the use of words to bind impulses and to assist tolerance of anxiety; offering a means to facilitate problem-solving by detours into conceptual thinking; and so forth (Polansky 1971). Thus we tried to describe for protective service workers the rationale and methods one might use for helping clients enhance this critical dimension of personality functioning, and especially clients showing the apathy-futility syndrome (Polansky, Borgman, DeSaix, and Sharlin 1971; Polansky, DeSaix, and Sharlin 1972). Work on verbal accessibility moved in the direction of an initial penetration of detachment.

The present study brought more forcefully to attention another parental trait associated with neglect, namely impulsivity. Not only were impulse-ridden personalities frequently found in the neglect sample of mothers, but when the conception was treated as a personality dimension it correlated substantially with the neglect/nonneglect dichotomy. We have the impression, which of course was not tested formally in the present research, that impulsivity may constitute more of a problem for urban child protection than it did in the rural area originally under study.

Impulsivity as a personality dimension has a fairly high correlation with apathy-futility. At first glance this seems an anomaly, for we associate vivacity and bounciness with being impulse-ridden. But again, this is common sense. Many withdrawn people also live quite planlessly and emerge from their withdrawal to make purchases and more important decisions after little or no reflection. A review of the related index in the Maternal Characteristics Scale in appendix 2 will serve to point at that a number of impulsive behaviors are not mutually exclusive with detachment and futility. Who else would leap before looking? Similar correlations were obtained in the original study, and that is why the two patterns have been regarded as differing modes of infantilism. One may speculate that there are many clients whose craving for excitement is, in fact, a defense against the emptiness and desolation more openly visible in the apathy-futility syndrome, and a way to get around the inability to feel very much or even to feel very much alive (Polansky 1973). There are some clients who appear to alternate between the two positions. One might speculate further that the two syndromes have their roots in similar early deprivations, but that the use of pleasure-seeking and manipulativeness is at least evidence of active attempts at coping by the young ego.

When one looks at the escapades in which these impulsively neglectful mothers become involved, a great many are exercises in falling in love. Even when the woman is deprecating about a relationship, what problem was she trying to solve? Looked at sympathetically, she was trying to deal with a feeling that is much more openly visible in one who is simply apathetic: she was a terribly lonely person.

Sunshine is a remnant of the generation that "tuned in, turned on, and dropped out" in the late 1960s. However, for her this was not an alternative life-style; it was the only game in town. On my first visit to the home, I was greeted with an unusual sight. It was of a young woman covered with grease and in the midst of repairing her motorcycle. The bike was the gift of a former beau, and the family's sole means of transportation. Sunshine is a heavy-set, buxom twenty-five-year-old woman, who is regularly attired in ragged dungarees and a rumpled top. Since coming to the city about five years ago, her pattern has been to move about every nine months to a different place which, in general, coincides with her adopting a new paramour. In this first meeting she assumed a businesslike stance. Rather than resisting entering the study, she identified with it, name-dropping various full professors and graduate students of psychology in local universities.

Her daughter, Marcie, was by an Ivy League law student. At the time Sunshine was admittedly a confirmed, "strung-out" Methadone addict, who continued to use the drug during the first trimester of her pregnancy; not until the seventh month did she get meaningful medical attention. The law student was less than ecstatic when she told him she was pregnant, so Sunshine fled to her home community, where the baby was born five years ago. He reportedly now makes over $40,000 a year, but contributes nothing to the child's support. Sunshine left him because "it's uncool to press yourself on people." The youngest of four, Sunshine comes from a rural township in the East. Her parents' marriage broke up when she was eight because of her father's alcoholism and abusive behavior toward mother and children when he was drunk. Sunshine was reared by her fundamentalist mother, who died suddenly of cranial hemorrhage when the client was twelve. She then was sent to her aging, rigid, and cold grandmother. The client was somewhat in touch with her rage at her abandonment, "I used to tell my grandmother she didn't want me around." She is angry that none of her elder siblings, already married, would take her in. At fifteen she was sent to a boarding school run by a fundamentalist group, but left within the year and struck out on her own.

The next couple of years were a series of crash pads up and down the East Coast. During this time she acquired her nickname, Sunshine, from a type of LSD known on the street by that appellation. Since settling in this city, she has had a series of men in her life who were all bright graduate students and all seemingly absorbed in rescue fantasies involving her. The most significant of the lot has been Craig, who befriended her when she was near termination in her second pregnancy, took her to the hospital, stood by her while she put the baby up for adoption, and took her in with him. This was a high point for her, as she describes it, and while it lasted she was concerned about her appearance and mobilized enough to get through a couple of semesters of a junior college. "He was my God, my world. I was always competing with him, but he could do everything better than I could. But I was too much of a drain, too dependent." At the time I saw her, her home had been burglarized and she immediately found a passive, aging "hippie" who was going to let her and Marcie move into the decrepit house he shared with a group. "We share a bed but don't plan to have an exclusive relationship." He offered me a weak handshake when introduced, and sat obsequiously by while the interview took place. No thought had been given to how the child, Marcie, would fit into the group, and within a couple of days Sunshine moved back to the apartment she had left because the others were unwilling to have a child in the household. On two of three visits I had to talk with her in the yard, as Sunshine was too embarrassed to let me see her apartment, and would not even let me use the bathroom because it was "a mess." When the apartment was finally visited on a "good day," the description proved apt. Marcie usually sleeps on the floor with her mother, unless the latter has a man in, when she moves to a couch elsewhere. Sunshine spends her spare time in one of the city's infamous bars. During the course of the contact, I received a drunken call from her one evening while I was at work at a second job. She wanted me to come to a place she described as the "Low-Life Inn" for a beer. When I begged off, she pressed me, finally asking directly if the reason was my "professionalism or some such shit." I then said it was, and Sunshine remarked that such restraint was why she had abandoned several therapists. She then made a veiled threat to drop out of the study. When I came to see her by appointment the next day, she had a young man in tow, who, it turned out, had been picked up casually the previous evening. Sunshine had the idea that Marcie is not doing very well, but shows no willingness to look at her own contributions to the girl's symptoms.

At the end of the research interviewing, we sat down and asked ourselves this question: leaving out the machinery of research, the standardized interviews, the rating scales and psychometrics and statistics, what do these neglectful parents, especially these neglectful mothers, seem to have in common? The answer was they are such lonely people.

Later, in the course of analyzing the data given in chapter 7 on parental isolation, we found ample statistical support for the subjective impressions of the caseworkers. But, as other practitioners-cum-researchers will attest, only those findings which jibe with one's own innermost sense of what is going on seem real. The loneliness is real; it is ubiquitous; and its recognition may have carried us an important step beyond where we were when the study began.

Learnings from the Bowen Center

In the United States there is a host of admirable people working directly, every day, with the parents we have been discussing in this book. Some of them continue to do so under distressingly discouraging working conditions. The most outstanding project we have encountered, however, was the Bowen Center Project in Chicago. We have come to know those involved in operating the project, and have talked with them at length about its rationale and some of their findings. Predictably, with our system for awarding grants, the project died of financial anemia at about the time it was commencing to bear fruit.

Those leading the project have written a manuscript about it (Sullivan, Spasser, and Penner 1977). They began by recruiting from an area of Chicago a series of families, severely neglectful, on whom other agencies had given up. Over a period of three years they treated a total of thirty-five such families. The project was housed in an unused church. The staff began with casework and a day-care center and added services as it became evident they were needed. Eventually these included special education classes for older children, homemakers, emergency placement service, temporary shelter, parents' groups—all housed and administered in a single structure and accessible through a caseworker. The manner in which they established a tie with the family is instructive:

> Contact with a caseworker was initially established by a caseworker through home visits. Although other staff members eventually provided the necessary services, the social worker remained the constant and primary source of support. Having one person consistently in touch proved particularly vital to helping parents whose life experiences had never afforded them the opportunity for an ongoing and stable relationship.
>
> Initially, the social worker worked with the family to provide tangible help to meet obvious gross needs. Beyond assuring that the children were maintained in the Center's program, the worker helped the parents to obtain food, clothing, shelter, and financial assistance, since meeting such needs of daily living was frequently far beyond what the parents could do for themselves. In the course of such activities as doing the family laundry with their social workers at the Center, the mothers in particular

grew more comfortable in the setting and came to know other staff who could then become involved with the family and provide additional services. Although the parents became the "Bowen Center family" in this process and enjoyed an expanded world of human relationships, the social worker remained for them the primary helping individual, consistently relating to their needs and feelings.

Advice and direction were given as needed. Every effort was also made to help the parents to talk, not on a deep interpretive level, but in relation to who they were, what they felt, and what they wanted.... Couples whose lives were so barren of pleasure were encouraged to share the enjoyable experiences provided through the Center's activities. These ranged from family outing days, birthday parties, and holiday celebrations to bimonthly parents' nights... and their children were cared for by the day care staff....

The first mothers' group provided recreational and educational experiences which might ameliorate the misery of their home situations.... Later, a second concurrent group was established specifically to help the mothers develop and use their capacities for parenting. In both groups, we continually sought ways to provide opportunities for sublimation and to engender belief in their ability to do things. [Sullivan, Spasser and Penner 1977, p. 53–54]

So well integrated a range of services has never existed, before or since, for the treatment of neglectful families. Their content is of especial interest since, as noted, many of them were included in the Center's program only as a need for them became apparent. This sophisticated group did not make the error of starting with a service package and then seeking out families to fit. And their program was very satisfying in a number of respects. An important feature was that they succeeded in maintaining contact with many, many families in a process that was essentially voluntary. The clients' attachment to the workers, and to the Bowen Center as a symbol, became the major source of treatment leverage. And if one looks in detail at the various devices cited, there is a theme that recurs: the Bowen Center was treating loneliness.

They were not just treating loneliness, for this would be a gross oversimplification. For one thing, people who are not particularly lonely can be, nevertheless, quite inadequate parents; the same may also be true of parents who were formerly lonely, but now have a place to turn to. Thus the clients' need for reassurance against this dread feeling was not the only matter at stake. But to reiterate, two things stand out: that the Center became attractive to these neglectful parents because they were, most of them, such lonely people; and that the emotional problem the Center moved most quickly to assuage was their loneliness.

In this respect, it is interesting to go through the Center's services and note how many might be accessible to a more fortunate parent from his or her own parents: financial help, baby-sitting, laundering together, family gatherings and joint recreation, emergency shelter of children or of the whole family, advice, concern—all the many things loving and competent grandparents so often give to their grown children during the early years of the latters' marriages. As a matter of fact, these were the kinds of mutual halping and guarding against loneliness which led many of our nonneglect families to remain in their native neighborhoods near the grandparents and extended kin. At least part of the hostility to invasion of the working-class neighborhood by other ethnic groups stemmed from the desire to keep housing available for extended families already settled there. Which is not to say, of course, that there were no other reasons.

One of the many functions of the Bowen Center, then, and perhaps its most important one, was to provide an artificial extended family for its clientele, the "Bowen Center family." And a general function of this family was to help combat loneliness.

This problem becomes among the first to which one must attend in designing treatment, for it gives rise to a number of other symptoms that hinder parenting. The clients' loneliness, however, may also provide us with our most reliable initial source of treatment leverage. What do we really know about this feeling?

Loneliness

Despite the relative dearth of professional writings about it in our field, loneliness is a problem ubiquitous among the clientele of social work. We encountered its significance in relation to neglectful parents, but of course we were not the first to concern ourselves with it. Writing on loneliness is in some danger of becoming a crowded field, with contributions ranging from the literary and journalistic to papers that are tightly analytical and empirically based. The senior author has recently reviewed the concept's meaning and implications for social work practice in two lectures at the Smith College School for Social Work which have now been published (Polansky 1980).

In a posthumous paper, Frieda Fromm-Reichmann (1959) left us an enlightening discussion of the concept. She distinguishes a variety of other states and circumstances from what she considers "real loneliness." For example "real loneliness" is not the same as the oceanic feelings we get from being on the desert or the ocean;

neither is it the self-induced solitude in which nearly all works of creative originality are conceived (Fromm-Reichmann 1959; Moustakis 1975); nor is it a temporary state, like being confined with a cold or vacationing away from loved ones. Even the feeling engendered by death or other loss of a loved one can be combatted by the ego through processes of identification, fantasy, and the like. True loneliness is truly desolate, beyond the phase of feeling sorry for oneself so that even the "good objects," associations to people who have given pleasure, are more or less forgotten:

> This loneliness, in its quintessential form, is of such a nature that it is incommunicable by one who suffers it . . . it cannot even be shared empathically, perhaps because the other person's empathic abilities are obstructed by the anxiety-arousing quality of the mere emanations of this profound loneliness. . . . [Fromm-Reichmann 1959, p. 5]

Fromm-Reichmann regards true loneliness as very like other serious mental states such as panic, and thinks that it is associated with psychosis. Her writing foreshadowed some of the formulations later made by Mahler, Pine, and Bergman (1975), who spoke of regression from the symbiotic to the autistic state in some children, in which good objects are lost.

There is no doubt that empathizing with severe loneliness is painful, and many of us working with such people have limited capacity for tolerating the feeling, despite our good intentions. We infer from this that loneliness is somewhat like anxiety: it is an affect, but one so hard to bear that just avoiding it becomes a quasi need. Indeed, Fromm-Reichmann speculates that the lack of professional attention to the state may stem from the therapist's dread of encountering it in himself. We have wondered whether the matter has been filed under other headings, such as anaclitic depression, mirasmus, autism, hostile dependency, separation anxiety, or existential *Angst,* not so much to make it easier to think consciously about loneliness as to shield us from it. Blunt confrontation with one's own aloneness—facing the fact that one is born alone and dies alone in a possibly uncaring and meaningless universe—is invariably disturbing.

To be alone is not the same as to feel lonely. The latter is a state of mind; the former a state of affairs (some would say, a lack of them). However, to be chronically alone produces, in most people, feelings of loneliness. They may be well defended, but they are there. And the state of being alone is often not chosen, but is imposed by others. A distinction may be made, therefore, between circumstantial and self-imposed loneliness. Both forces operate on many of our neglectful parents, leaving them both alone and lonely.

The causes of loneliness are innumerable. People are left alone because of the deaths of loved ones or by being abandoned by them. People can find themselves shunned by relative strangers because of such things as race, religion, poverty, deviant opinions or actions, deviant status (such as being in foster care), a physical handicap, obesity or personal unattractiveness, and low-status occupations. There are personality attributes that lead to one's being shunned such as being bored or conceited, or displaying an insensitivity which shows itself in compulsive talking or intrusiveness. Many avoid those they find ridden with free-floating hostility or who are explosive. We have commented that being seen as well-intentioned and helpful is attractive; being unhelpful leads to one's being shunned, even when the cause may lie in one's inadequacy or lack of resources rather than in one's self-centeredness. It is also a sad fact that a too obvious hunger for companionship can put people off. It is unpopular to be unpopular—and to mind being so. These are all interpersonal dynamics that we know exist among average-expectable people from sociometric and other studies of leadership in small groups. Without going into the theory of why there are such determinants of social repulsion, one might wish they did not exist, but they do. And neglectful parents often suffer from several of these social stigmata simultaneously. Many find themselves left out of helping networks, for example, because they establish a record of failing to return favors given. The cause may lie more in inadequacy than in lack of gratitude, but the effect on their standing is equally bad.

Self-imposed loneliness is also a problem. We mentioned above the typical schizoid fear of closeness, "Stay away lest I hurt you." Present in many neglectful parents, very discernibly, is the use, and overuse, of the detachment mechanism. "I have been hurt before, so let's not get involved." Detachment from the love object one has lost is really a good device for coping. Without it we could hardly bear the losses that life brings: falling out of love, the death of a loved person, desertion, moving away. It would be difficult to survive without such a mechanism for self-healing. But the danger of detachment is that one may become addicted to it, pushing people away so that one is protected from losing, but then paying a terrible price because, of course, one never wins.

Among neglectful parents are many who make their circumstances worse by self-imposed aloneness, and who must thus live with dreadful loneliness. One could conclude that, in this sense, they are getting what they ask for, what they "deserve." Which led to another slogan born out of the research: most—not all—people get what they deserve, but that does not make it any easier to bear.

A striking impression gleaned from our study, then, was the high proportion of neglectful parents who are very much alone and lonely, out of a combination of their life circumstances and their own intolerance of closeness. Also striking were the many unable to do anything to alter their condition.

The effects of loneliness on a person are the subject of studies now emerging (Lynch 1977). A study in California, for example, dealt with a nine-year follow-up of a very large cohort from one county. Death rates were two or three times higher among those who were relatively isolated when compared with those who were married, had friends, and were embedded in social networks (Berkman and Syme 1979). Loneliness may be dangerous to one's health.

There is a need for an analytic mapping of the methods people use for coping with chronic loneliness. Some, which are adaptive, could be useful for offering advice to clients in need of such help; others are seriously maladaptive, and knowledge about treating such mechanisms needs to be collected. Narcissism, in an extreme degree, offers an example of maladaptation. A healthy amount of dignity or pride sustains the personality in the face of rebuffs and psychic insults. These useful defenses read, "If no one else loves me, at least I do." A heavy reliance on this mechanism, however, results in withdrawal of interest in others. Instead, there is a fascination with one's own image which, in turn, begets hypersensitivity and extreme dependence on the opinions of others. Narcissism clearly interferes with productive work; it reduces the chances of formation of sublimatory channels. Pleasure-seeking may be reduced to one's erogenous zones and other bodily orifices.

Defensive narcissism makes it more likely a parent will "use" his children, for example as buffers against his own loneliness. Since his investment in them is also narcissistic, he is likely also to experience their inadequacies as slights against his image of himself. In child abuse for example, there are instances of parents dreadfully punishing a child because the youngster is unable to live up to their unreal expectations, e.g., in toilet-training, cleanliness or the like. Such a parent is hardly appealing when we consider his lack of conscience or his vicious behavior. The anxiety that lies behind the action may be disregarded, but it is there.

A parent unable to displace drive-cathexes from herself to her children is cheated. A loving mother can get vicarious pleasure out of her children's enjoyments. Even during a day of household drudgery, if she looks out the window and sees her children laughing and running in the yard, she gets a momentary lift. She gets pleasure out of their liking their food, sleeping with smiles on their faces, winning competitions. But the parent who is caught in a narcissistic defense experiences duties from motherhood but few rewards. She may bind her youngsters to her to provide security against abandonment; she may bask in the admiration she demands from them; but these are negative gains, not pleasures. The example of defensive narcissism reminds us that loneliness may have noxious side-effects destructive to parenting. Alleviating this feeling, then, ought to improve the parenting in at least some cases, even if what is done does not seem to bear directly on the acts of parenting.

We have felt it worthwhile, therefore, to examine some of the means for treating neglect which serve to counter or to ameliorate parental loneliness. Most of these modes of treatment have other ends in view, but because of our interest in loneliness we wish to point up that aspect in particular.

Casework Functions

A social worker is reminded each day of the large number of adults whom nobody loves. Their states are not projections of their own inability to feel; they are literally unloved. Some have no families, no living relatives; others have rejected their families or been rejected by them; many elderly people have lost those who were genuinely fond of them to death or disabilities. It is tolerable to be totally unloved, apparently, if one is strong or can at least persuade himself of his invulnerability. But an infant, for example, would be totally unable to survive unaided for more than a matter of days. To all who are vulnerable, unloveability is dangerous and it may portend death. If, as we believe, loneliness is associated with feelings of being unloveable, it is not surprising such feelings are warded off or totally denied. Indeed, we often find that clients who act as if they were responding to loneliness deny that they feel it, while men and women who have undertaken to sail the Atlantic or around the world single-handed openly speak of the lack of human companionship as among the greatest hazards of such voyages.

The child protection worker, as a caseworker, has a number of interrelated functions in handling child neglect. Among these we listed earlier the *liaison* role as essential to tying the families into other services. The act of being a liaison, however, is a service in itself, simply as expression that someone cares who is competent to put the parent in touch with other forms of help. The assuagement of loneliness, then, may be the most important single service the caseworker offers. It takes skill to offer it, for those being assuaged are often suspicious, detached, slow to form relationships. They require time; they also require patience in the face of rebuffs they will administer to the worker, sometimes out of sheer ignorance of others' feelings, more often out of indifference to them.

The worker helps, as well, by her or his skill as an interviewer.

An interesting, poignant sidelight of our research was the number of people who said, "Nobody ever was interested in my life or my opinions before." If one considers the experience most of our clients have had in trying to pour their hearts out to others, only to be told, "You've got troubles? Let me tell you about my husband . . ." and the like, the worker's discipline of *listening* attentively is an extremely important way to indicate caring. Many have also had trouble putting their feelings into words, so that the part of interviewing skill which involves helping clients find means to express themselves, unobtrusively educating them in a vocabulary of feelings by echoing back, is essential. Should the client's loneliness be brought out by clarification or interpretation? As always with painful material, the intervention must be paced to client readiness. Open expressions of loneliness, however, should be welcomed sympathetically and discussed. For it is healing to the client to talk about these feelings with someone who can empathize; and talking about them is preferable to some of the attempts they have made to cope with their loneliness which have proved disastrous for their children and themselves.

Workers also act to "disconnect the panic button." Parents sometimes are indifferent to real dangers to their children and themselves, but carried away by fears that are groundless. For another adult to help them begin coping by asking, "Well, what if X happens . . . ?" reduces panic and helps them cope realistically. Workers also act as counselors and advice-givers on subjects ranging from sources of financial assistance to medical problems to acceptable modes of disciplining youngsters. When advice is offered with tact, and with respect for the others' capacities, it may also be experienced as a gift.

The role of the worker as a therapist, as someone who helps the client deal directly with sources of anxiety and hostility within himself or herself, is not to be discounted. As we have noted, the practice of intensive casework as part of protective services is a far cry from office treatment on a regular schedule. But there are many clients, probably a majority, who will show readiness at some point in the contact to deal with attitude change and even with self-exploration. To whom are they likely to turn? Given their general reticence with new people and new situations, referral to a family agency or a mental health clinic may well be contraindicated. So it comes to this: if they are to be treated by anyone, it will have to be the caseworker, with whom they already have a relationship. If this reasoning is correct, it tells us that the protective service worker must include among his or her skills the capacity to conduct interview treatment, along with other abilities, for it will be needed at times in almost all cases. There are at least some who will slowly emerge from being oriented toward protective service into what we think of as intensive treatment. If this is not possible because of time pressure, it is helpful to many clients for the worker to be able to offer at least a sample of what interview treatment is like, as well as to deal with fears of talking treatment and to try to resolve initial resistance while making referrals.

The advocacy role is well established in social work. In recent years, Alfred Kahn, among others, has done important work on formalizing our thinking about this aspect of our work and has described how it may be organized (Kahn, Kamerman, and McGowan 1972). But caseworkers have often found themselves speaking on behalf of clients to other agencies, to landlords, to utilities, and so forth. There were clients whose cases would have stirred action on their merits, but who needed our greater articulateness to present them; there were clients who were being treated unjustly, even illegally, for whom our implied threats of publicity and our use of the righteous indignation to which all good hysterics are heir carried the day. But there were many clients who could not rouse indignation, when we had to appeal not for justice but for mercy. One recalls Mona's unpaid heat bills. Even after the worker interceded with the utilities personnel to have the heat turned on, she still spent the money on other things. Thus the advocacy role is often invaluable in obtaining services desperately needed by neglected children. One should not overlook, therefore, that in carrying it out, the worker is also treating loneliness. How much better we feel, when faced with a threatening situation, if we can take a companion along to consult with, to back us up, to help us bear it. There are neglectful parents, particularly women rearing their children without males in the home, who must deal constantly with the world, unaccompanied. Even to go along with the mother to a clinic may be unique in her current way of life. Such an action takes time, but it is not to be too lightly discounted, for it, too, treats loneliness.

There are other phases of the worker's role, some of which become possible only after there is a tie of affection between worker and client. One of the worker's jobs, after all, is to stand for values about child-rearing that fit children's needs, and that the community also supports. These values may be transmitted, if one is lucky, partly by identification with the worker, through the process we described in the last chapter. At times, however, the worker does have to remind the client of the threat involved, that certain kinds of care are unacceptable and if they cannot be altered, the worker may have to take steps she or he would prefer not to take. In line with this, once there is enough of a tie to bear some weight without fear of rupture, the worker can also begin to institute counter-regressive demands, encouraging the parent to assume his or her parental role, in effect to "act your age." Such demands can be experienced as rejecting if they are too burdensome, or hostile; but, they can also be experienced as supportive, as a compliment to the part of the parent that assures him he can do better.

In all interpersonal functions, a worker's effectiveness is increased by the degree to which he or she comes across as a likeable person. Fortunately for all of us who find ourselves less than glamorous, a rather wide assortment of persons has proven capable of carrying on protective services. Of course, as noted, there are clients whose deep-seated problems make it hard for them to like most people. Some are prejudiced along ethnic or racial lines, and it may be necessary to assign cases with this in mind, although this is unusual. The sex of the worker makes a difference, of course, but it does not seem a major determinant of who can do this work.

There are, naturally, characteristics of one's demeanor worth bearing in mind, since they make a difference. These include such habits of speech as speaking reasonably slowly and distinctly, and in a voice that is audible but not strident or which has an edge. Minimizing the use of abstractions is a good idea in all interviewing, and especially with clients who are poorly educated, distracted, or mentally slow. Steadiness and unflappability help, and humor is a *sine qua non*. Being in touch with one's own feelings, and expressing them openly when need be fits in better with protective services work than with intensive treatment. It is important to be able to look at the parent without being intrusive, just as it is necessary not to be put off by people who find it difficult to look at the worker. Decisiveness helps one's impression of personal power and potential usefulness. However, it is not necessary always to come up with an immediate decision. One may give the same impression by saying one understands the issue and will have to think about it, or find out more in order to decide. It is important to be able to tolerate hostility, of course, in this kind of work. Most successful workers develop more and more effective defenses for dealing with it as they gain experience. A useful guide to tactics in initial interviews has been provided by Goldberg (1975).

Marital Counseling

We have written at some length about ways in which the caseworker may operate to assuage or heal feelings of loneliness in clients. But the professional, by the very nature of his limits, offers a substitute object or a temporary one. He is most successful when, in fact, he is a transitional object. By this we mean a person from whom the client learns it is not as dangerous as he thought to involve oneself with others, and in whose companionship he learns to practice ways of dealing with people and of conversing with them which he can use in other relationships.

This is the element of the transitional relationship we think of as the most significant aspect of the experiential component of the treatment. The client may then generalize from changes he has learned in his casework relationship to his dealings with others in his life. Improved relationships with friends represent generalizations from learnings in the professional contact. With any good fortune, they give rise to another "spiral of causation." Unlike the set of character defenses in which they were trapped and which contributed so heavily to their isolation, however, this would be a beneficial spiral. As they open up more to others, others do the same to them, and some of their loneliness may be resolved, which in turn permits the dropping of still other defenses. Something like this is meant when we refer to the fact that the treatment continues outside the office. The important part of this other side of treatment is that it takes place with fellow amateurs, people with whom the client may hope to form ties that are not transitional and limited but potentially lifelong.

It happens not infrequently in contacts with neglectful families that the two parents, both of whom are needful and lonely, have either lost or never found the ability to comfort each other. To whatever internal problems each brought to the marriage is now added the conflict between them. In effect, they are making each other sicker. Yet their loss and deprivation would vanish if only their need for relationship could be met between them. Such a family constellation requires marital counseling. Once again it is desirable if the protective service worker has a reasonable knowledge of what is involved in doing this, and is able to make use of it in contacts with the family. This is not the place in which to set down all that has been learned in our field about this area of work. The gist, in the present connection, is that the worker tries to help open up channels of communication between the parents so that they can go about the business of healing each other.

A common source of the conflict, in our experience, occurs around the issue of who will get to be mothered. It is as if each is saying, "You be mother," and the other is replying, "No, I need you to do that." Each is hurt, each disappointed, and they may become locked in a stubborn match during which neither admits need or makes overtures. The worker constitutes a new element in the situation, sometimes uncomfortably so, for the caseworker's main function is to be an outside enemy they can ally themselves against. Since much of this process goes on outside our observation, it may well be that a role which is so hard on the worker may be proving beneficial to the marriage. Speaking in Kleinian terms, it is as if each needed a "bad mother" in the picture in order to be able to treat the mate as a "good mother." The tendency will be to lock the worker out of the interaction, of course, after which pathology will resume. A more fortunate outcome is when the worker in trying to help plays the good mother to both. The hope is that by feeding each, the level of tension between them will subside to a point at which they can be helped to negotiate their differences. Of course, the hope is also that the introduciton of a person who remains warm, giving, and accepting will also help the general atmosphere.

Closely related to marital counseling, of course, is the practice of family therapy. None of us has had much formal training in this form of treatment, but we are certainly appreciative of its potential in many situations. Few neglectful families, alas, will organize themselves sufficiently to come as a group and cooperate in series of structured sessions, and in that sense the technique has limited applicability for direct treatment. On the other hand, since so many contacts take place in the home, and since the tendency of the family to cluster where the action is is so common, it is usual for a worker to be involved, if not in formal family therapy, at least in conjoint interviewing or family interviewing. (The family may, indeed, include the TV, a more regularly present and more vocal family member than a grandparent.)

While organized family therapy will not often prove possible under the circumstances of this work, the concepts and insights available to us all from that field of practice are certainly applicable. The worker will have opportunities to observe role renunciations by parents, role assignments to particular family members, and the presence of alliances among the children which sometimes substitute for what they are not receiving from their parents. The way in which they deal with the worker's presence will be interesting to observe; no less so will be their patterns of communication or lack thereof.

Mrs. D. was an obese, overwhelmed mother of twelve. On the worker's first visit, she was shunted into a waiting pattern by an aggressive teenager while the adolescents and their mother sought to deal with the rent-collector. Mrs. D. was a woman who was rejected by her own mother and sent to live with her grandparents, in whose care she "somehow" fell down the stairs and received a hip injury from which she still limps. Placed in a succession of foster homes, she eventually became pregnant by and married a man whose "religious convictions" included polygamy (or at least having other women). He left Mrs. D. when she finally had her tubes tied, but she still speaks longingly of his return.

Her children were disorganized, underfed, and referred to

their passive mother as "Stupid." So, this lonely unfortunate was both the disappointment and the scapegoat of her brood. However, the worker found her hungry for relationship, and she was almost surprisingly articulate in recounting her sad life story.

Having taken psychological tests in the course of the research, Mrs. D. was fascinated and pleased that she scored in the normal range. She announced to her children, "Don't you ever call me Stupid again." With support from the research caseworker, she was able to seek help from a local family agency. That worker has been assisting materially, with furniture and clothes, and helping Mrs. D. organize her home. With much praise for each accomplishment made, she was cleaning up the home, doing the cooking, and generally moving toward assuming her place in the family. Her response to some support and much appreciation were all the more remarkable for a person who had a very low opinion of herself and, as she felt, not a single achievement.

Parents' Groups

Given their loneliness and pleasureless existence, it has been natural to try to bring neglectful parents into group treatment. In the Bowen Center, for example, groups were formed, first around participating in the conduct of the day care center, later around discussing common problems of child caring and discipline. We have had frequent encounters with staffs interested in forming such groups and with others who were conducting them.

The difficulty of forming and sustaining parents' groups for dealing with the neglectful has been, in our experience, consistently underestimated. If one takes at all seriously the results in chapter 7, it must be obvious these are not people to be invited, by letter, to a series of twelve sessions of parent education in a local church basement. Few are joiners and many are actually phobic about group situations of all kinds. Thus in the mountains we had heard all sorts of tales about families who believed in snake medicine and who were opposed to doctors. What we found, in at least some homes, were men and women who very much wanted to have their children seen by physicians and nurses, but who could not face visiting the county clinic because there were so many people in the waiting room. Neglectful parents, especially the mothers, have poor self-images, as we have noted. They do not expect to be taken in and liked at a meeting with strangers; they have good reason to believe they will be anxious and uncomfortable. Moreover, needs are not the same as wants. Many, perhaps most, neglectful parents do not think of learning in a group situation, which smacks of school, an arena of some of their earliest miseries. If one adds to this their common lack of organization and inability to get places regularly and on time, the future of a psychoeducational group looks even more dismal. Besides, a lot of these families are extremely pooor. Their budget does not provide for transportation to a group meeting, paying dues, and the like.

We have known of agencies with such groups in operation. Almost always they were in existence because of very active support from the caseworkers who knew the mothers and were trusted by them. A successful device, in fact, was for the worker to pick up the woman and transport her to her first meeting, or even a series of succeeding meetings, staying with her until she felt comfortable by herself. Programs were of a sort that permitted people to interact with others, if they felt able, or to appear engrossed in what they were doing if not. In other words, relationship strains were minimized until the mothers felt more secure and bonds began to form with the group leader and with the other parents. An excellent description of such a program has been done by Ambrose (1975).

The usual outcome of such projects is that, of the parents introduced, mothers are far more likely to come and to adhere to the group. Even so, if one starts, say, with twelve mothers, an expectable yield in the way of regular membership would be six or seven. Yet for those mothers who do continue, such a group may have excellent effects. They may prove more open and verbal than they had been before; they will extend themselves to welcome newcomers to the group. Occasional sessions closely resemble group psychotherapy. Ambrose reports, and others have told us, that among those who attend regularly improved self-esteem, seen in the form of efforts at dressing and grooming, are rewarding to see. These changes seem to extend to their housekeeping and child caring as well.

If no one will love you, anyhow, why try? But what could be more reassuring to a mother that she is, in fact, able to be loved, than her discovery of acceptance and respect among others whose life positions are similar to her own? For suggestions regarding the use of activities and programs to promote social interaction in groups the reader would do well to refer to the classic text by Wilson and Ryland (1949), and such later writings as those by Ganter, Yeakel, and Polansky (1967), or Gump and Sutton-Smith (1955).

The loneliness we encounter in studying child neglect is but a more extreme version of the loneliness that exists throughout our society, and especially among the poor and powerless. Several volunteer messiahs have emerged to offer their persons and their movements as solutions to the unwary. Such persons include

Charles Manson, the murderer from California, and the Reverend Jones, who led his flock in mass suicide in Guiana. There are others who are the more dangerous because they are less self-destructive. They have shown ingenuity and adeptness at devising tactics with which to use people's loneliness to attract them and then to exploit their labor and their bodies. While all mass movements, including the major religions, offer supports in the face of this ubiquitous human emotion, some are, of course, more rewarding in their intentions toward their followers and the world at large. But such movements, too, remind us of the power that can be garnered through offering help with the dread of loneliness.

It has seemed to us, therefore, that the learnings we have been able to put together from the study of neglect have implications for all aspects of social work practice, including those far-removed from child protection services. The woman who said, "Even the social workers did not want me" may have been sending us a message. For it is basic to our tradition and continuing existence as a field that, even if no one else seems to care about the client, we do.

We cannot close this chapter without a final cautionary note. Several modes of treatment and methods possibly useful for the social treatment of child neglect have been described from the standpoint of the etiologies, sequelae, and treatment of loneliness. We have chosen this focus because it was so strongly suggested by facts and impressions from our research. But we are certainly not urging that making these issues the sole bases of one's attempts to help will in and of themselves "cure" all cases of neglect. There is no wish, here, to contribute a new panacea or incite another fad in our field. It is quite possible, for example, to be lonely and inadequate, and, with help, to become less lonely—but still inadequate. Treatment of the human personality, even on those occasions when the course seems clear, is always a complicated business, and single-issue treatment approaches inevitably resemble what Fritz Redl used to call "an insult to the complexity of nature."

What we hope to have done, rather, is to point out the significance of the client's loneliness with regard to the plight and gyrations in which we find him, and to show that at least some of the complexity can be reduced if we follow the thread of loneliness and the need to escape from it, which can exact a terrible cost from both the children and the parent. While we believe insufficient attention has been paid this thread in the past—in part because it is so painful for us to contemplate—it is not the only thread in the miserable garment of neglect.

Fifteen

Parental Prostheses

It must be the feeling of being embattled, along with a touch of vainglory, that leads us to think about the struggle to treat chronic social problems like child neglect in military terms. The circumstances are unfortunately analogous. In approaching neglect it would increase the child's chances of being reared with a consistent set of personal objects if he were able to remain with his parents; it would also be a great convenience to the remainder of society. Arguing against his remaining with them, of course, is the danger that he will become a permanently damaged person, perhaps one who falls below the threshold of social acceptability. So we begin the struggle on his behalf with a maximum objective in mind, the goal of producing enough change in the parents' functioning and their circumstances so that the child can safely be permitted to remain in his family.

The last chapter described some strategies and tactics for bringing about parental changes, if not in basic character structures, at least in their levels of operation. If these methods and others like them succeed, the downward spiral of causation will be halted, the "initial kick" having been administered, and the families will be able to embark on an upward spiral out of which they will emerge free-standing in most respects. The outcome would be that no more treatment, or even surveillance, was needed. Certainly this is a worthwhile mission. It can already be carried out with some families; one hopes their proportion in the total will increase. But what do we do if our assault fails, if in fact we are unable to bring about enough improvement in the family to leave it alone? It becomes necessary to think about fall-back positions, retreat lines we can adopt in order to hold as much territory as possible.

When the parenting does not improve enough to meet the child's growth needs, but conditions in the home do not put him in acute danger, it is time to consider supplementing the quality of his care. Supplement is needed when natural parents, doing what comes naturally, fall short. If the parent's lack were in having an undeveloped leg, he might wear a brace; missing teeth are substituted for with dentures; the lack of capacity for adequate child caring calls for prostheses, too—parental prostheses.

All families use parental prostheses to an extent, but among those better placed in society and more generally competent, their use goes unremarked. The situation is comparable to the very large numbers of Americans who are never counted as unemployed, although they do not work because they are rich enough not to. When a child is sent to public school, to music lessons, to dancing class, his parents are using others to supplement their own efforts. Sunday schools are intended to help strengthen the child's identification with his parents' religious beliefs and moral attitudes. Hence the need in neglectful families for parental prostheses does not differ from the norm in principle so much as in degree.

The need for parental prostheses is greater in neglectful situations, of course, because of the natural parents' incapacities. It is magnified by the fact that their incapacity has, typically, not suddenly arisen but has been there since the child's earliest days. Thus neglected children have not only to keep up, they have to try to catch up with their age-mates. Early in the book, we described the ménage of Mona and Frank, the two former heroin addicts. That family came to attention in the first place when a clinic found the eldest child already a year developmentally retarded at age two. A therapeutic day nursery, supplementing Mona's mothering, was having excellent results.

In planning programmatically for parental prostheses, there are three general principles to be borne in mind: primacy, sufficiency, and quality. The primacy principle reminds us that, in an organism capable of learning, earlier events leave marks that affect how later happenings are experienced. Hence, the earlier the intervention, the greater the impact it may have on the child's developing personality. An important discovery of the past two decades of experimenting with intellectual enrichment programs, such as Headstart, is that six years is already fairly late in a child's intellectual growth, and that stunting which has occurred by that age may be irreversible. Many experts think age three is already far along in the process, that, for instance, the average child will already have acquired two-thirds of the words in his eventual working vocabulary by that age. Thus there is an urgent need to identify the child much in need of supplemental cognitive care well before school entry. Until recently, our main opportunity for some external observation of the children has been compulsory school attendance. Comments parallel to those concerning cognitive maturation may be made concerning the child's physical and emotional care and the emergence of control systems. Thus the principle of primacy reminds us that, in general, the earlier the age of the intervention in the life of a neglected child, the better. It will be recalled that neglect may begin prenatally; in a sense, it may predate conception.

The second principle, sufficiency, reminds us that sometimes to offer too little supplementation is nearly as useless as to do nothing. Scientifically, there is no such thing as an effect without a cause nor a cause without an effect, and one can argue that every effort makes at least some difference. While this is incontrovertible logically, it is also true that in many kinds of treatment there seems to be a critical minimum of quantity below which the treatment fails. This is found, for instance, in the chemotherapy of cancer. We have also observed the principle in psychotherapy in which some patients' only chance of improving has to be in a totally controlled inpatient setting wherein several types of treatment can be simultaneously applied. Regrettably, nearly all programs for treating neglect err on the side of niggardliness. Those who allocate public funds in this society are generous in those expenditures through which roads and their private fortunes may be cemented. But in nearly any program for children that has a hint of extravagance, the funds are bled before they can affect the children's care. The holders of the purse-strings want miracles, very large returns from very small investments. Alas, there are no miracles, nor are there, at the present stage of the art of compensating parental failure, many bargains.

The quality of the supplementation has always to be carefully watched. A child of two can be removed from his uncomfortable, filthy, and disorganized home to spend six hours a day in a nursery school or day care center. But if it is one of those operated so greedily that thirty children are overseen by two adults who require them, for their own convenience, to sit motionless in lined up chairs for hours at a time, the day care is supplementing parental neglect with societal abuse.

A court making the decision as to whether children should or should not be removed from their parents cannot accept programs that exist mostly on paper as viable fall-back arrangements. For example, one might decide the child could remain at home if he were given suitable therapy on an outpatient basis. There are reports in the literature from fine craftswomen like Selma Fraiberg (1971) which provide evidence that such treatment can be done in principle. Few local communities possess such gifted workers, however, and the best among us make no pretensions of doing what we cannot. Many clinics are able to diagnose developmental lag, but personnel trained and gifted at direct work with very young children are relatively rare in this country at this time. There may be no recourse but to utilize the more inclusive psychological nurture provided by a good foster mother.

Those contemplating the use of parental prostheses need also to think about supporting the standing of the family's caseworker with the family. The need becomes greater when it is recognized that the worker may have identified the need for a service, but is of course not an expert on how it can be provided. There is a temptation, under such conditions, to circumvent the protective services worker and deal directly with the parents. When this is done persistently it naturally undermines the worker's treatment prestige and exaggerates the worker's vulnerability to manipulative parents. Every agency thinks of its own contribution as the focus of the treatment and, perhaps, it is well that it does so. But in families with many problems there are many focuses of treatment. The task of the primary caseworker involves, in part, the countering of the loneliness in the parents, which we discussed in the last chapter. Is a mother or father likely to look for protection and assuagement from a worker who turns out to be discounted by her or his fellow professionals, treated as nonessential? Or is the implication to the parent that she is "leaning on a weak reed"?

This eight-year-old girl was referred to child protective services because she came to school with evidences of having been beaten. When her worker visited her mother and the man living with her, they readily admitted the severe punishment. The child had been seduced by a much older boy in the neighborhood, and was exposing herself to other little boys and encouraging advances from older ones. She was both seductive and extremely provocative, tormenting her mother, who had borne her out of wedlock and who supported the child and herself by heavy work in a local factory. They had beaten her because they were at their wit's ends. Eventually the mother accepted the suggestion of a local clinic that inpatient treatment was needed, and cooperated with placing the child in a hospital some distance away. It was hard for her to do this, however, because of her need for the daughter's company and because of the failure the placement symbolized. Although she visited the hospital regularly, there was little direct work with this woman. Meanwhile, her daughter complained bitterly about the discipline and so forth, and when she ran away to her home a second time, the mother refused to bring her back.

At that point the hospital became suddenly active with the worker who had referred the child, demanding that she get the woman to return the child immediately, and blaming her for the failure of the treatment. To the consultant, it seemed that the issue was not who was to blame for the failure to treat this dangerously manipulative little girl, but of what collaborative arrangement would have had a better chance of holding her in treatment. The young worker, confused and appalled by the unfamiliar sexuality of so young a girl, was perhaps all too willing to relinquish the treatment to the hospital, discounting her own potential contribution. The mother felt thoroughly left out. And the hospital, engrossed in its own processes, did not think of preparing fall-back arrangements, should they fail, or even of adequate follow-up arrangements if the child were to be returned. For both of the latter there was a need to support the function of the local children's worker. The side of the mother that was more mature and oriented toward reality recognized that both she and her daughter needed help with this mounting problem. The side of her that was sensitive to her loneliness and pride—which also has something to do with loneliness—simply wanted her daughter returned. But to whom is she going to turn now? Her worker has an uphill task to recover leverage in the family.

In the remainder of this chapter, we will survey a number of services which, according to our understanding, may be used to supplement natural parenting so that children may remain in their homes. In this survey, attention will be given those most frequently called upon and evidently found most useful. We will not attempt a thorough description of each, for that would take us beyond the province of this volume and beyond our expertise. Neither shall we presume to set down how each service ought be conducted as a field of practice in its own right. The concern here is simply to view these services in terms of major themes and requirements emerging from our researches on neglectful parents of neglect. Those wishing more information and other perspectives would do well to avail themselves of standard texts on child welfare by such experts as Kadushin (1974) and Costin (1972).

There is also a very helpful set of publications prepared under the auspices of the National Center on Child Abuse and Neglect, Children's Bureau, Administration for Children, Youth and Families, Department of Health and Welfare, P.O. Box 1182, Washington, D.C. 20013. A series of "user's manuals" prepared by Kirschner Associates is especially germane to the actual implementation of services. There are also annual reviews of research related to neglect and abuse prepared by Herner and Company for the National Center. Single copies of most of these publications are distributed free.

What Needs Correcting?

Nearly two decades ago, Leon Eisenberg (1962) published a paper with the arresting title, "The Sins of the Fathers: Urban Decay and Social Pathology." As a child psychiatrist at the Johns Hopkins University, he was reporting on 140 cases referred for help in foster care decisions by the welfare department of Baltimore County, Maryland. Those referred for psychiatric consultation were compared on several variables with the generality of cases under foster care in the state. Eisenberg also attempted to summarize some outstanding clinical impressions of the children seen. It was noted that the foster children referred were far more likely to have been abandoned by their parents than was the average child in the program. Although their average intelligence was in the normal range, only 10% of those referred were in the age-appropriate grade. Aggressive behavior was the chief reason for referral; the largest single diagnosis, made for 35%, was personality disorder.

Clinically, he found the children inarticulate: "Their reluctance to verbalize and lack of verbal facility reflects a subculture in which feelings are expressed in doing rather than talking" (p. 11). Because of the chaos of their lives, he found they had been unable to learn such basic points of orientation as time, place, and person. They were self-deprecatory, apathetic, and mistrustful, and thus withheld any enthusiasm they might have felt. Many were found to be relatively unsocialized and primitive in their eating and toilet behaviors. He also commented that caseworkers do such youngsters no favor when they encourage them to maintain fantasy relationships with parents who do not really care about them.

Those who work solely on foster care may be slightly insulated from the child's origins. But among those engaged with the homes from which children may have to be removed, Eisenberg's observations provoke no shock. What is more surprising is that many youngsters are not even more damaged than they are. The resiliency displayed by these children is amazing. It requires painstaking carelessness, evidently, to destroy a child. Those who survive reasonably intact speak appreciatively of the occasional adults who softened their lives—a relative, a teacher, a kindly neighbor.

Speaking very generally, what is needed in these homes? Basic physical care, of course, including food, warmth, medical attention, rest, protection. Basic psychological care, including love, attentiveness, talking, teaching, limiting. There is also a need for predictability, that people and things will stay in place, that promises will be kept, that one's own actions will have consequences one can count on. There is a need for organization, so that things get done, and one knows how to help get them done. There is even a need to have it proven that day-to-day living can be pleasurable, if not ecstatic.

Homemaker Service

A good homemaker brings many, if not all, of these things to the family she is assigned to work with. Her task is to help put the home in working order and to train the mother to take over and keep it that way.

Homemakers have been available through family agencies since around World War II. Intelligent, mature, and competent women were trained to enter households and perform many of the functions a mother might. If the mother were suddenly hospitalized, for example, and the father was overwhelmed by the need to care for his children while trying to hold onto his job, a homemaker would be assigned to help hold the family together. It was understood, of course, that the arrangement was temporary, that the mother would resume her role in the family when she recovered, or else some more permanent arrangement would be made. While the homemaker did perform such chores as bedmaking, washing, scrubbing, and cooking, she was regarded as more than a maid; she was a person capable also of shopping for the family and of caring for the children as a substitute mother.

Faced with a large number of neglectful families, the thought occurred to us that homemakers might prove very helpful in these situations. A substantial proportion of neglectful mothers show, among their other problems, ignorance about how to cook, how to clean, and how to shop. A lack of organization in the way household tasks are carried out is very common. These are not women who would start a load in the washing machine (if they owned one) and make the beds while waiting for it to finish its cycle. Because of the need to clean the house and provide the children minimal care a homemaker would be assigned, almost on an emergency basis. In this way, removal of the children might be avoided.

It was soon recognized, however, that the presence of the homemaker might be an important tool in teaching the mother necessary household skills. Very few learn well by listening; the homemaker, however, could teach very concretely, showing the mother how to cook or how to shop, while doing these tasks with her. The hope was that out of the experience of learning-by-doing, and by simple imitation of realistic examples, the mother's own housekeeping and child caring skills would improve. Hence the homemaker in many agencies is regarded as a key participant in the overall social treatment of neglectful families. She is a member of a special staff with its own administration, and she confers regularly with the family's caseworker to share observations and to try to coordinate their efforts.

For the teaching function, it has become common to assign a homemaker a half-day or a day a week for a period of three months or so, by which time it is hoped the mother will have learned how to manage on her own. There has, however, been some experimentation with the service in an effort to see whether providing it more intensively would facilitate changes in severely neglectful families. One agency, Youth Services of Philadelphia, which has done such experimenting, concluded that two days a week was about the maximum the mother—and the homemaker—could stand. At that point they have had enough of each other.

Like all interventions, provision of homemaking has its complications and pitfalls. It is, of course, not unusual for the homemaker to be welcomed into the home and cheerfully permitted to take over all the housework while the mother does none. Some mothers exploit their helplessness to avoid participating in a pattern that often started in dealings with their own mothers, "Oh, I could never do that . . ." Others naturally try coercive anger to avoid the pressures to learn and collaborate. But, on the other hand, many are glad of the opportunity provided to work alongside someone else and to learn while doing. It is very common for the homemaker to become a confidant; some have developed skill in sympathetic listening, but avoid expressing opinions, while encouraging the mother to talk over her problems and decisions with her caseworker. The hours spent together can induce a close tie between the women, so that learning by identification is frequently observable, affecting the mother's way of disciplining children, her style of dress, and so forth.

Thus the homemaker becomes, in effect, a "good mother" to the parent, reassuring her and comforting her loneliness. For those with much anger toward their own mothers, the effect of this close relationship in the household may be to shut the worker out. That is, the mother'e transference onto the homemaker involves the "good mother/bad mother" ambivalence. She handles this by idealizing the homemaker, who "talks my language," repressing her anger in her usual all-or-nothing fashion. The object of the bad-mother feelings, then, becomes the caseworker, who is seen as mean, demanding, untrustworthy. Any time two persons are assigned to treat the same patient, the setting is right for splitting of the object in the transference, and we have found it fascinating to observe in situations so distant from the serene and affluent offices in which such phenomena were discovered.

To a considerable extent, the homemaker's entering a family is like substituting artificially for a loving grandmother or elder sister. As noted above, many average-expectable homes undergoing a crisis have the same need from time to time. But our information on the relative isolation of the neglectful families, including their poor relationships with their extended families, makes the service all the more important to them. As of this writing, homemaker service is almost universally regarded as a temporary expedient, to be introduced for a limited period and withdrawn because the mother has learned to take over—or because she seems unwilling or unable to do so. Our own feeling, however, is that there are numerous families for whom the assignment of the service needs to be thought about as very long-term, that is, as taking place over a period of years rather than weeks or months. If this much service makes a critical difference between leaving the children in the home and removing them, then, on a purely economic basis, it would pay to maintain the family unit with the support of this device. Arguing against this course of action, of course, would be the likelihood that a family as consistently unable to profit from treatment as one needing permanent homemaking service would have other disadvantages as well, such as providing their children with adult models who are helpless and inadequate. Still, if one recalls that most competent housewives learned their skills from their own mothers over a period of ten to fifteen years, and that many neglectful mothers had no such opportunities, six months of this kind of treatment is not really very long for women with learning problems.

Day Care

Social workers and others have been accustomed to the use of day care as a means whereby women with young children may leave them all day in order to work. There is very widespread use of such arrangements in this country, both formally and informally (Emlen 1974). In the North Carolina mountains, for example, we found a number of women whose jobs in sewing plants twenty to thirty miles from home were essential to keeping their families off welfare. Who, then, was chosen to care for the children of several other women while they worked? In several instances the person serving as baby-sitter was the mother all agreed was too incompetent to hold a job at a sewing plant or in other work "outside the holler".

Such an instance reminds the rest of us that the place in which a preschooler spends his days is not just a parking space; its environment will have an impact, good or ill. A number of authors, especially Caldwell (1967), have established criteria for suitable programs.

Given the neglectful parent's self-preoccupation, it is fortunate that day care may quite honestly be interpreted to her as something offered on her own behalf as well as her child's. Here is a secure and appropriate place where she can leave one or more of her children for part of the day, giving her a respite from child caring so she can more easily do her housework or seek entertainment outside her house. To the woman who usually manages well but who becomes frustrated by her routine, the arrangement may help ward off an impulsive escapade. Many others are simply overwhelmed by the results of their having neglected to space their children, as well as other problems, and removing the children part of the day relieves some of this feeling.

For the child, of course, a good nursery school or day care center offers supplementary nurture in many areas of living: a good lunch and snacks to improve nutrition; services of a nurse for minor illnesses; warm adults who talk to the child and with him; an organized, more or less comfortable routine where life is not chaotic; other children to play with; play materials and things to learn with adults patient and skilled at helping the learning. The main baby-sitting service in the majority of neglectful homes we entered, in this day and age, was the ubiquitous television set, turned on at arising and operating until late at night. Day care offers real objects for children who tend heavily to fantasize or observe, and replaces passive looking with active learning and vocabulary building. It is no wonder that several of those working with disorganized families, such as Pavenstedt (1973), have viewed day care as a most important parental prosthetic. Sullivan, Spasser, and Penner (1977) of the Bowen Center, it will be recalled, started their program for treating severely neglectful families around two major services, day care and casework.

From what we have learned, day care is a highly acceptable service to many of the families that concern us. Although those at the Bowen Center found many families so disorganized they had to send out Vista Volunteers to wake the children, dress them, and bring them to the Center, apparently a majority of the mothers will bring the children in, or at least have them ready to be picked up. Many of those dealing with neglectful families also seek parental involvement in the operation of the day care. Parents' groups are formed, for example, to support the service with their work.

Mothers come as volunteers, too, on a rotating basis. There is the opportunity, then, to provide the family with a chance to be with others and to talk about mutual problems through their joint use of the day care center. Mothers volunteering are, of course, also exposed to the staff's way of handling children, and this becomes another opportunity for them to learn child-rearing skills.

This is an excellent parental supplement when it can be instituted. Mothers who are extremely fearful and withdrawn, of course, are unlikely to attend the day care center, or even permit their children to be taken there. Some women will sabotage the child's attendance by inducing fearful reactions in the child in order to allay their own separation anxiety; the dynamics are well known from studies of school phobia.

Volunteers

For nearly a decade, at the time of this writing, there has been publicity devoted to the neglected and abused children of our country. Magazines, newspapers, television, and radio have all carried stories aimed at increasing public awareness of the problem. These efforts have helped to instigate the updating of applicable laws in nearly every American jurisdiction; they have undoubtedly helped, also, to improve the money and facilities available for professionals working on the problem. The increased general awareness of neglect, then, has been useful. Among the most heartening outcomes have been the large numbers of volunteers committed to augmenting the humanpower engaged in the work. Their good will is heartening because so many of those implicated in maltreatment belong to what George Bernard Shaw facetiously labeled "the undeserving poor" in *Pygmalion*. We have encountered groups of volunteers in cities and in rural counties, in Michigan and in Georgia. They are most impressive.

Volunteers may be asked to work one-on-one with an individual family, thus becoming part of an artificial extended family. They provide transportation to clinics or for shopping; they may help the family find furnishings and bed linens; they act as warm foster-aunts and foster-uncles to the children in the home or as Big Brothers and Big Sisters. They take the whole group on family outings. At times the volunteer babysits for the family, to offer the natural mother a respite or to relieve her of concern while she visits her physician. Some of these aids are, of course, reminiscent of the concrete services offered by caseworkers. But in counties with large caseloads the worker cannot offer that much individualized attention to each, and the family's volunteer supplements or substitutes for the worker. The existence of this artificially extended family provides the beleaguered natural parent with another source of security. When an emergency strikes, they have another person to turn to for help. Volunteers, for example, have been known to accompany the parents to court, sitting with them and offering emotional support during a hearing.

Thus the volunteer can do much to buffer the neglectful family against its pervasive sense of loneliness. The volunteer also offers a much-needed bridge to the way life is in average families of the society, for many neglectful families, as they become isolated, lose touch with the ordinary pleasures and pursuits of common daily living. There is another function of the volunteer which is not much emphasized, and perhaps should not be. Along with faulty development in other adaptive spheres, large numbers of neglectful parents have superegos which are spotty or immature. They are aware of values about child-caring, but these values are not fully internalized. Rather, they are still in the stage at which the child controls his impulses mostly to please his mother, rather than himself. The presence of a person who is friendly and accepting, but who is nevertheless a representative of the world outside the family, may help to support the parents' superego. The volunteer, although not wishing to spy, does operate to augment the surveillance function of the caseworker in the service of superego support.

Some knowledge is evolving regarding the recruitment and use of volunteers (Fisher 1979). (A fine program design and training manual has been prepared for the state of Michigan by Kapelle, Scott, and Western [1976].) Despite, or perhaps because of, their fine motivations they are as prone to frustration with neglectful families as are their caseworkers. Each of us, along with his rescue fantasies, harbors the dream that he is especially qualified and gifted at helping people. Others may have failed with a parent after long weeks of tedious effort, But they do not have our magic. It is an important part of the growth experience for caseworkers to learn that parents whom others have found to be hard to work with are very likely to be difficult also for us. Volunteers usually come to the work with their fantasies of therapeutic glory still untested; usually they are not even fully conscious. Helping with the family involved in child maltreatment is greatly useful for puncturing such dreams, but the process is not welcomed at the time. The volunteers also experience the same alternating feelings of being shut out or of being sucked into a bottomless pit of needfulness as do we.

In short, this is no work for people who require instant repayment for the act of giving, or support for their own narcissism in playing lady bountiful. Fortunately, there appears to be a pool of mature and substantial people who are, nevertheless, willing to try. A critical issue in their survival in the role appears to be success of the agency in matching volunteer individual or couple with the neglectful parent or parents. Among the other dimensions, we have been told that similar hobbies or sports interests can prove very useful in establishing initial common grounds.

Emergency Services

That family is lucky which has never had to move its children in the middle of the night to the home of a neighbor or relative because of a parental emergency. Among ordinary families, we think of such events as a sudden severe illness of one of the parents, or injury in an accident, or the death of a parent or other close relative. Neglectful households can add substantially to that list: the father's being arrested for fighting, stealing, or drunkenness; the single mother's involvement in an escapade that keeps her away from home all night; either parent suffering an overdose from a drug or a combination of drugs and alcohol; the apartment catching fire because of overloaded wiring or dousing kerosene on a fire; a brawl between the parents. We are speaking here of people whose shortened time-perspective, inability to plan, immobilization, and impulsivity make them emergency-prone. The parent with no helping network, who is likely to use poor judgment or to panic under pressure, is very apt to make inadequate arrangements for his or her children in an emergency, or no arrangements at all. So the children are left alone, neighbors become concerned, the police are called, and there is a case of child abandonment. And, in fact, they are abandoned. Not only that, but when the police arrive they may well encounter infants who are dirty and uncared for, messy housekeeping, no food in the refrigerator—familiar signs of child care that is chronically marginal or neglectful. So the protective service workers are called, and the children are placed.

Some workers have argued that the removal of the children too often sets in motion a process that is hard to reverse and that is sometimes uncalled for. If there were facilities available to offer the children shelter understood to be temporary, in an arrangement not yet formalized as "removal" of them, support might be offered so that, in a good number of cases, the family might remain intact. At a minimum, if the child care system were equipped to handle emergencies routinely—which seems like a contradiction in terms, but actually is true of most hospitals—all concerned could examine what has been going on in an orderly fashion. Burt and Balyeat (1974) have reported an arrangement in Nashville, Tennessee, wherein twenty-four-hour access to child protection workers, emergency foster care, and other services has reduced the numbers of families brought to court and the number of children placed.

There are other occasions in which a caseworker is engaged in the long process of trying to improve child care. No one would expect such a process to go smoothly. Impulse-ridden parents will give way to their impulses from time to time, those abusing alcohol will backslide, apathetic-futile mothers go through periods of withdrawal and worse immobilization that usual. Access to temporary foster care provides a backup arrangement for continuing the treatment effort. Therefore, a number of protective service agencies, collaborating with the child placement units within or outside their own agencies have found it very useful to maintain temporary foster homes in their communities on an "on call" basis (Paget 1967). For example, these might be foster families who have space available, and who are paid a small retainer for their willingness to accept children on very short notice.

Parents fortunate enough to have warm and competent grandparents or siblings in the community make these arrangements themselves. But we have documented the isolation and estrangement from relatives experienced by many of our neglectful parents. It is psychologically advantageous to the children when there are such foster families, and they are sent to the same one each time a removal becomes necessary. From the standpoint of the young child, it is bad enough to be taken away from home in the middle of the night, without knowing where one's parent is or if she or he will return; it is even worse to have to go to an unfamiliar place, to be cared for and told what to do by people the child has never seen before. The child of an alcoholic affluent family at least always goes to Grandpa's. Failing that, cannot he go, at least, to the known house of Mrs. Brown? A case could be made that even a familiar receiving home or other small institution would be preferable to having the children placed in a succession of short-term arrangements. One is reminded, too, of how important it may be that the caseworker from the agency, whom the child has seen before, accompany him to his new living place if possible, or visit him as soon after placement as possible. Among the many desirable attributes of protective service caseworkers, sheer continuity and constancy as a *perceptual* object ought not to be overlooked. In an alien environment, even familiar enemies are welcomed.

New and often fascinating services are constantly being developed (Lauderdale, Anderson, and Cramer 1978). But the main ingredient of parental prostheses turns out, on consideration, to be the skill and caring of other people. Each of us who reads this book can recall how he benefited while growing up from the interest and attention of adults outside as well as inside the home, craftsmen and mechanics who showed us what they were doing, coaches who inspired our best efforts, compassionate medical personnel.

Institutional Placement and Foster Care

Removal from the home and care by others such as foster parents could, we suppose, be regarded as the ultimate form of parental prosthesis. We have left it for last, after emphasizing other means that might be tried first, because it does, of course, involve a very major rupture in the child's life. Those responsible for taking such action do so with reluctance and sobriety. Our own reluctance is not based on a notion that the family, as such, is somehow sacred, for social institutions are man-made, and hardly any social institution qualifies for such status. The family is valuable as an institution which, if it operates at all well, seems to do the best job we have observed thus far at the large-scale rearing of children. And we take very seriously the writings of colleagues such as Selma Fraiberg (1977) about the child's need for a consistent maternal object, especially early in his development. The concern remains, however, for the child receiving the kind of mothering we have been describing, and the kind of inconstant object he may be experiencing. Many neglectful parents are really not able to be parents, and in various ways they are telling us so. Removal of the child or children is experienced with a feeling of relief.

It has also become *de rigeur* of late to shrug in a deprecating way and say, "Well, you know the foster care system." Social workers are appropriately uncomfortable about abuses which have crept into that system; they are guilty about them because they have something to do with the conduct of the system. Some foster homes are poor; the children under care often have to be moved and removed because, foster parents, after all, do not make a permanent commitment and, like everyone else, changes in their lives sometimes mean they have to give up the work. So we feel the child has been cheated. And he has been. He has been cheated in terms of what foster care *could* be and, fortunately, is for some; but he is rarely cheated in terms of what he had before. It seems quite possible that, following the current fad, too few children are now being placed routinely, just as at one point too many were being placed.

Foster care placement probably works out best when it is done with the agreement of the natural parent or parents. Placement is not always an adversary arrangement, and there are numerous instances in which workers and parents have remained close through the process of removing the children and working toward their eventual return—or even their formal relinquishment for adoption. Much depends on the worker's ability to help the parent see that the placement is also in her or his best interest. Of course, much also depends on the maturity and orientation toward reality of the parent. Our information suggests this cannot always be counted on, to put it mildly.

There is a very large literature on foster care, and it is one area in which social work research has had a very important impact on practice (Kadushin 1978). So we will just make a few observations from the point of view of our own research. For example, the significance of loneliness in the lives of many neglectful parents has been emphasized in this book, as well as the function of attachment to the child as a means of dealing with that loneliness. An important defense against the anxiety associated with breaking such an attachment, and perhaps the only one that really works reasonably well for such a person, is detachment. The latter may be viewed, of course, as a kind of primitive reaction-formation against attachment. As a result, the parent may have a kind of all-or-none relationship with her child. Either the child is treated almost as a part of herself or himself, or the child loses meaning entirely. Fanshel (1975), for example, has observed that many parents not actively encouraged regularly to visit their children in placement withdraw and act, in effect, as if they had forgotten the children, ceasing their efforts to bring them home.

Another observation is that the majority of children in placement because of serious neglect—and it is usually serious if they have been placed—will have been damaged. It seems necessary to specify this because some foster care agencies persist in the attitude that this is their sole function, that they are not "treatment" agencies. How they wish to define themselves is, of course, their own affair, but many of the children coming to them in an era when Social Security coverage is widespread and few children are full orphans are the products of neglectful families. For example, it is common for such children to show learning difficulties and to be retarded in school. For them, placement is but the end of the beginning of treatment.

Finally, for those who treat seriously damaged children in institutions, parents are frequently seen as the causes of their troubles, as the enemy. If the parent is described at all, it is in terms of such descriptive trait-clusters as we erected to facilitate the generalizations in chapter 8. The parents' range of dynamics, the things they have suffered and continue to suffer, remain unknown, in part because of their verbal inaccessibility. Of course this limits ability to work with them, understandingly, or to grasp the full import of the expression, "They did not mean to be this way." The thought occurs that inpatient workers might be better able to work with parents if they have had at least some experience in child protection. At the same time, we recognize that each of us can live only so many professional lives, so we hope our book will help flesh out the images.

Sixteen

Where Do We Go from Here?

In this book, we have sought to bring together our most important learnings about neglectful parents. The effort has included collating the work of others as well as reports of our own researches. Particular attention has been given to a major study involving comparison of a set of neglectful families in Philadelphia with a control group. This study, which was a replication and extension of one previously done in the mountains, had not previously been fully reported. Based on our own experiences and those of others with which we have become familiar through teaching workshops and consulting, a number of implications for practice have been inferred from the results.

There are, of course, important limitations to the state of knowledge in this field. The relevant research consists of a mere handful of studies, each of which has both strengths and faults. Whole areas of interest have not been dealt with systematically at all. What do we know, for instance, about child neglect among the affluent? Do the parents have some of the same character disorders which we have found in low-income groups? Is it possible, as some of us suspect, that one can "buy one's way out of neglect" through hiring a mature housekeeper, or placing one's children in private boarding schools? Individual cases come to light, from time to time, but the overall pattern remains unknown. What, then, would be the form of neglect typically found among the affluent?

Studies of low-income families have been done which were not limited to whites, as were ours. But it has been suggested by colleagues that research similar to our own ought also be conducted with black and Chicano people. It seems likely, for example, that the Childhood Level of Living Scale would be applicable also among the nonwhite segments of America, but that supposition ought to be tested. Earlier we mentioned the desirability of collecting many more cases measured on the Childhood Level of Living Scale from known populations to improve our ability to compare a given case against established standards. Several generations of educated mothers had their anxiety raised by Gesell's infant development scales, not knowing they had been based on around 125 youngsters from the homes of the Yale faculty. As all research students learn, a larger sample is not necessarily a more representative sample, but sheer numbers are helpful.

It would be useful, also, to test the generality of our findings about the character traits of mothers and fathers implicated in neglect. If our research may be taken to show that neglectful parents differ from other white, low-income populations, one might conveniently take the further step of applying the Maternal Characteristics Scale to large samples of families under care in protective agencies. Since the instrument has been developed, such research can be done relatively quickly and cheaply, for example, by training caseworkers already familiar with the parents in its use.

Throughout our research, we have taken the position that if one begins by grouping together abusive and neglectful parents, assuming they are alike, he will never know if they are, indeed, different in their modal personalities. That there are different reactions to offers of therapy is frequently reported from the field, with abusive parents said to be more often open to the idea of seeking treatment. Both groups are thought to consist largely of parents who are grossly immature. The finding of Wolock and Horowitz (1979) that the majority of the abusive mothers on Aid to Families of Dependent Children were also neglectful comes to mind. Yet one has the impression that parents who are simply neglectful are more passive and show fewer areas of competence. While less shocking in the way their pathology affects their children, it seems to us quite conceivable that, on the average, they are the more damaged of the two. This issue, too, could use a combination of statistical and clinical research for its clarification, for programs oriented toward the treatment of the "typical" abusive parent are often ineffective with the neglectful.

There are other ideas one could set forth regarding the next steps needed in programmatic research into child neglect. It can be a very difficult area in which to conduct studies, of course, and its difficulties ought not be underestimated by researchers projecting elaborate study designs and those undertaking to support them. We have met a number of newer investigators starting studies of child maltreatment; each was more or less appalled by the problems of reaching subjects for the research. Research into important social problems also seldom provides opportunity for the exercise of controls with anything like the rigor one associates with laboratory experiments. It becomes necessary to outgrow the tenets of one's own doctoral training, not because they are wrong, but because they may cripple rather than facilitate the effort. Competent researchers will be fully aware of the limitations of the conclusions from their studies; they will be buoyed, however, by a truism for all who seek to help people in the real world through clinical work or investigations: some valid information is better than no information.

The probability that new, major investigations will be launched in the near future is not great. The mobilization to do something about child maltreatment in this country has begun to run its course. Political leaders, and those who operate our great funding establishments, are turning their attentions elsewhere. The wave of funds and interest in the problems of neglect and abuse are starting to recede, for it is typical that we leave off work on a problem not because it has been solved but because it has gone out of fashion. It becomes all the more necessary that social workers set down and preserve, as systematically as possible, the achievements of knowledge at this particular high water mark. Those outside our field are aware of the cyclical nature of interests in it by which similar problems are placed center-stage, albeit under different labels (e.g., the multiproblem family; the delinquogenic family). They ask whether each turn of the wheel finds us essentially at the same place, or whether we seem slowly to inch forward. One has only to turn back to the writings of Charles Loring Brace and other leaders of his time, serious men and women whose observations even now strike us as perceptive. Are we farther along than they? Of that there is no question.

Those of us who have worked at this research, practitioners ourselves in various fields, end it with concern and sympathy for the great majority of parents implicated in neglect. Their lives are not easy, and the damage their own childhoods inflicted on them burdens their days. Yet most make some effort to "do right" by their children and love them in the form and at the level of which they are capable. If they fail as parents, and their children must be protected by removal, such a step is taken in sadness, not in rage.

We end this work with admiration for the many hundreds of protective service workers who spend their days and numerous nights treating, or at least observing, the families involved. Their steadfastness, their increasing competence, and their deep concern for the children merits applause from the rest of us. Their work is, of course, very draining, and turnover rates are high in many agencies. One of the earlier writings on the loss of young workers from this field was that of Wasserman (1970). More recently, the term "burnout" has come into use. Daly (1979) has recently defined this as a reaction to job-related stress. A typical course of burnout would begin with the worker's using increasing amounts of psychic energy to get the same amount of work done; then there is a phase of resistance, in which much energy goes into managing internal conflicts; finally, there is a state characterized by anxiety and fatigue, and—too often—the decision to leave the job altogether. Some of those experiencing this sequence may remain in the work, but at the cost to their clients and themselves of maintaining emotional detachment from it.

Burnout is typically discussed as a kind of aberration, a work-related illness that ought to be cured by better treatment of the front-line workers. Indeed, those able and willing to do the work deserve to be well paid for their efforts. They deserve recognition and solid support from the public and from their agency administrators. As we have tried to show, their requests for a variety of resources are wholly reasonable. But none of this will mitigate the degree to which emotional strain and anxiety are intrinsic to the work itself.

The worker suffering burnout has been described as frustrated and angry, as a response to difficult clients, bumbling administration, the low prestige that goes with having a clientele made up of low-status people. Stereotypes in the media showing protective service workers as insensitive baby-snatchers, or as self-righteous and humorless "do-gooders" certainly do not help. But in discussing what goes on inside the worker, frustration and anger do not begin to describe the complexity involved.

Workers feel drained because many of the clients who *can* relate do so in a famished, demanding manner. After a time, one feels as if he were about to be sucked dry. The same kind of clutching relationship is frightening in another way: the worker begins to feel somehow absorbed, as if his or her own boundaries were becoming blurred by the client's need to fuse with him. It is as if one were being invited to regress to a state of symbiosis. Workers are also depleted by repeated contact with the dreadful loneliness so many neglectful mothers and children experience. Loneliness is, of course, an abhorrent feeling. As with anxiety, most of us are capable of experiencing it, and have experienced it, but have erected a variety of defenses to keep it out of consciousness (Polansky 1980). The effect of dealing with it in clients is to remind ourselves of the same feelings in us. Thus one can start a day of work happy with the way one's own world has been going and end it in sadness from the onslaught of clients' misery.

The point has been made that much of what is termed burnout really is not. A person with little background in the human services who becomes a protective service worker may find out very rapidly that this is not his or her choice of employment and quit. Such resignations do not represent what is meant by burnout, they are simply instances of screening out persons unsuited to the work, which happens in any job. Actually, in our observation it is the worker who enters the field most open to empathizing with clients, most perceptive of their needs, who is the more in danger of a burnout, and this is sad because such workers are the most promising.

Success in working with people requires clinical identification, that is, taking an image of the client into oneself in order to feel what he is feeling, think as he is thinking, even surmise motives of which he is himself not conscious. Such identification is more effective if we open ourselves up not only to the client's feelings, but to our own which respond to his. From identification with the client one may, as a matter of fact, partly continue one's own "cure." For in going over with him his aches and conflicts, we revive memories of similar pains in our own lives; in helping him resolve his problems, we are also taking another step in resolving remnants of our own. But the price for clinical identification is the resurrection of old and painful memories, and stumbling over our own loneliness.

How do we deal with losses, then? One thinks immediately of detachment (Bowlby 1961). Detachment is a merciful mechanism; for it heals the deaths, the rebuffs, the departures of loved ones that life brings. Surely this is a merciful gift. But detachment works so well, one may become addicted to it, like the neglected children we encounter who are determined not to lay themselves open to loving and losing once again. The process described as burnout is a process of detachment. The worker may remain in the work but feel nothing; or the worker may actually quit the agency.

In child protection, then, as in all intensive work with people in misery, the need is to find an optimal blend of clinical identification and detachment. The following lessons may be drawn from the coping devices used by those workers who seem able to succeed in the work and remain in it:

1. It is important to stay in touch with one's own feelings. Not to know one's reactions may be dangerous to the client; it may be even more dangerous to one's own mental health. So, while acting out anger, for example, may be contraindicated by the needs of the case, awareness that one is angry—or frightened or sad—has to be

permitted. Bottling up feelings has a tendency to spread, and if rage is rigorously disavowed, so may pleasure and fun.

2. Having a theory that guides what one is doing is helpful. For one thing, to place oneself in a situation in which success or failure depends on being the sort of person one is puts too much at stake all the time. A worker obviously can be a well-intentioned, generally competent person, and not *know* how to treat a particular client problem. Having a theory behind one's practice lends organization to the effort; a theory may also help the worker predict and deal with reactions expectable in herself or himself. Because of a fear of becoming overintellectualized, several generations of social workers have been warned against too much preoccupation with theory in their practice. But the thought of a person who relies heavily on intellectualization as a defense gravitating to the sights and smells associated with protective service work is really rather funny.

3. It helps if one has worked through, in one's life, many of the kinds of problems likely to be encountered in clients, but it is not absolutely necessary. Fortunately for all, quite good treatment has been, and can be, done by imperfect personnel. Of course, if one becomes very uncomfortable with the opening up of old sores, one might seek therapy for oneself before deciding simply to flee by changing jobs.

4. Consideration has to be given, in a field like this, to the fact that many of those doing good work do so, in part, out of a "need for love." Statements to the effect that the worker needs a happy personal life to do the work are not accurate; there have always been marvelous workers whose home lives were lonesome or tumultuous. No, the need is to build in some solace on the job. Every worker needs some hopeful cases. Indeed, having at least part of one's caseload made up of essentially normal people may be a prerequisite for keeping perspective when a client's behavior is odd or bizarre.

5. To stay with a demanding field, some sense of progress is essential. Workers need to be able to progress in pay as they mature, and in status as well. It is very helpful to feel one has also been able to progress in competence, to be able to do easily what was hard a year or two ago, and to succeed with some cases now with which one formerly failed. Opportunities for training should be graded, so that highly experienced workers do not find themselves forever rehashing first principles, but have an opportunity to interact with others at their own advanced levels. Many more workers could contribute to our knowledge of technique if they would write up their clinical learnings.

6. It is important to bear in mind the importance of the work. There are hundreds of thousands of children involved in neglect

nationally. America is no longer a nation whose strength is so enormous she can afford the loss of productive people and the drain of those who have to be imprisoned and incarcerated. For if the rest of us are part of the ecology of neglected children, they are also part of ours. Their pain and the marks it leaves are also ours. Even though glorious success stories are infrequent, they do happen, and many, many families are helped enough to salvage the lives of their children.

Recently, the senior author taught a workshop on treating loneliness in neglectful families, mentioning what each of us must do to comfort his fellows against the void. One woman, who had not yet talked, spoke up.

> I know what you're talking about, because I was myself neglected, and also beaten and abused. I don't know what would have become of me, if it weren't for the people who were my teachers, and who kept telling me they saw something in me worth developing. Do you know, when I finished high school, I couldn't believe I could get to college, but one of them said, "You're going," and drove me down, got me registered, and got me a scholarship. After a while, I graduated with a degree in journalism, and had a good job. I was proud of myself, happy, thought I had it made. Then, one day as I was walking to the bus, I passed a group of other young black girls. One of them looked at me shyly and said, "Gee, lady. You sure have pretty shoes." It came over me that that was me, that I was that little girl. I said to myself, "What are you doing?" So, I went and got some more training, gave up my fancy job, and I've been doing protective service work for four years now. I wouldn't be doing anything else, because this is where it's at.

What else is there to say? Whom does she owe that we do not?

Appendix One*

Childhood Level of
Living Scale

	Key to Scoring	
Items and Scoring Part A—*Physical Care*	*Yes*	*No*
I. General Positive Child Care. Eigen value 19.54, 53.2% of variance.		
1. Mother plans at least one meal consisting of two courses.	1	
2. Mother uses good judgment about leaving child alone in the house.	1	
3. Mother plans for variety in foods.	1	
4. Mother sometimes leaves child to insufficiently older sibling.		1
5. Mother plans meals with courses that go together.	1	
6. The child receives at least 9 hours of sleep most nights.	1	
7. Child is offered food at fixed time each day.	1	
8. Bedtime for the child is set by the parents for about the same time each night.	1	
9. Mother has evidenced lack of awareness of child's possible dental needs.		1
10. Mother expresses concern about feeding a balanced diet.	1	

245

*Originally published in "Assessing Adequacy of Child Caring: An Urban Scale," *Child Welfare* 57, no. 7 (1978): 439–49. ©1978 by the Child Wealfare League of America, Inc.

11. Mother enforces rules about going into the
street.   1
12. Child has been taught own address.   1
13. Child is taught to swim or mother believes
child should be taught to swim.   1
14. Mother will never leave child alone in the
house.   1
15. Mother uses thermometer with child.   1

II. State of Repair of House. Eigen value 3.83,
10.4% of variance.
16. Storm sashes or equivalent are present.   1
17. Windows are caulked or sealed against
drafts.   1
18. Doors are weatherproofed.   1
19. House is dilapidated.   1
20. There are window screens in good repair
in most windows.   1
21. Wood floors are cracked and splintered.   1
22. There are screen doors properly mounted.   1
23. There is an operating electric sweeper.   1
24. Floor covering presents tripping hazard.   1
25. Living room doubles as a bedroom.   1

III. Negligence (Reciprocal Meaning). Eigen value
3.36, 9.2% of variance.
26. There are food scraps on the floor and furniture.   1
27. Child 5 years or older sleeps in room with
parents.   1
28. At least one of the children sleeps in the
same bed as parents.   1
29. Mother plans special meals for special
occasions.   1
30. Windows have been cracked or broken
over a month without repair.   1
31. Clothing usually appears to be hand-me-
downs.   1
32. Buttons and snaps of child's clothing are
frequently missing and not replaced.   1

IV. Quality of Household Maintenance. Eigen
value 2.81, 7.7% of variance.
33. There are dirty dishes and utensils in
rooms other than the kitchen.   1

	Yes	No
34. There are leaky faucets.		1
35. The roof (or ceiling) leaks.		1
36. The floors of the house appear to be swept each day.	1	
37. Bathroom seems to be cleaned regularly.	1	
38. Mother takes precautions in the storage of medicine.	1	
39. Mattresses are in obviously poor condition.		1
40. Repairs one usually makes oneself are left undone.		1

V. Quality of Health Care and Grooming. Eigen value 2.02, 5.5% of variance.

	Yes	No
41. Mother has encouraged child to wash hands before meals.	1	
42. Ears are usually clean.	1	
43. Mother mentions she makes effort to get child to eat food not preferred because they are important to child's nutrition.	1	
44. Poisonous or dangerous sprays and cleaning fluids are stored out of child's reach.	1	
45. Mother has encouraged child to wash hands after using toilet.	1	
46. Mother cautions child to be careful of flaking paint.	1	
47. It is obvious that mother has given attention to child's grooming at home.	1	

Part B—Emotional/Cognitive Care

VI. Encouraging Competence. Eigen value 17.94, 49.4% of variance (of Part B).

	Yes	No
48. Planned overnight vacation trip has been taken by family.	1	
49. Child has been taken by parents to see some well known historical or cultural building.	1	
50. Child has been taken by parents to see a spectator sport.	1	
51. Mother mentions that in the last year she has: taught the child something about nature; told the child a story; read a story to the child.	1	

52. Family has taken child downtown. 1
53. Child has been taken by parents to see various animals. 1
54. Child has been taken by parents to a carnival. 1
55. Mother is tuned into child's indirect emotional signals. 1
56. Mother mentions that she has played games with the child. 1
57. Mother mentions use of TV to teach child. 1
58. Child has been taken by parents to a parade. 1
59. A prayer is said before some meals. 1
60. Mother comforts the child when he is upset. 1
61. There are magazines available. 1
62. The family owns a camera. 1
63. The child says prayers at bedtime. 1
64. Child has been taken to children's movie. 1
65. Mother mentions that she answers child's questions about how things work. 1
66. Child has been taken by parents to the firehouse. 1
67. Child has been taken fishing. 1

VII. Inconsistency of Discipline and Coldness (Reciprocal Meaning). Eigen value 7.36, 20.3% of variance.
68. Mother seems not to follow through on rewards. 1
69. Mother mentions that she cannot get child to mind. 1
70. Child is often ignored when he tries to tell mother something. 1
71. The child is often pushed aside when he shows need for love. 1
72. Mother seems not to follow through on threatened punishments. 1
73. Spanking is sometimes with an object. 1
74. Mother threatens punishment by imagined or real fright object. 1
75. Very frequently no action is taken when discipline is indicated. 1
76. Mother frequently screams at child. 1

77. Mother is made uncomfortable by
child's demonstration of affection.   1

78. Mother complains a lot about life.   1

79. Mother mandates child's play according
to sex (i.e., girls may only play with
dolls).   1

80. Child is never allowed to make a mess.   1

81. Dolls are available to the child for play.   1

VIII. Encouraging Superego Development. Eigen
value 2.62, 7.2% of variance.

82. Mother expresses to the child her concern for child's safety if there is a real
danger.   1

83. There is a designated area for play.   1

84. Parents guard language in front of children.   1

85. Child is immediately spanked for running into the street.   1

86. Mother mentions child asks questions
showing curiosity about how things
work.   1

87. Child is taught to be respectful of adults.   1

88. Mother puts child to bed.   1

89. Mother mentions that she limits child's
TV watching.   1

90. Child is encouraged to care for own
toys.   1

91. Child is taught to respect property of
others.   1

92. Mother expresses pride in daughter's
femininity or son's masculinity.   1

93. Mother is able to show physical affection to child comfortably.   1

94. There are books for adults in the house.   1

95. An effort is made to provide choices for
the child.   1

IX. Material Giving. Eigen value 2.24, 6.2% of
variance.

96. Crayons are made available to the child.   1

97. A play shovel is available to the child.   1

98. Child is sometimes rewarded for good behavior with a treat.   1

99. The child has a book of his own.   1

Definitions

The following definitions were used in making assessments:
A. Terms generally used
1. Appears—is readily apparent from observation.
2. Complains—expresses discontent with the situation.
3. Expresses—reveals in any manner, as in words, gestures or actions.
4. Mentions—spontaneous reference to.
5. Plans—intentional ordering or arranging to achieve purpose or goal.
6. Routine—conforming to a habitual course of procedure.
7. Seems—apparent from observation.

B. Relative to specific items
1. Item 1—"meal courses"; either meat and one vegetable or two vegetables.
2. Item 3—same as Item 1.
3. Item 4—"insufficiently older sibling"; child less than 12 years old or any person who could not reasonably be expected to provide adequate care.
4. Item 14—"yes" means mother will not do this.
5. Item 16—"equivalent"; a plastic covering.
6. Item 18—"Weatherproofed"; can be with insulating material of any sort.
7. Item 19—"dilapidated"; a house that does not provide a safe and adequate shelter.
8. Item 21—"splintered"; not just one splinter.
9. Item 29—"special occasions"; birthdays, Thanksgiving; Christmas, etc.
10. Item 55—"indirect emotional signals"; mother interprets child's behavior.
11. Item 73—"object"; belt, shoe, switch, etc.
12. Item 81—"dolls"; includes male dolls (e.g., super-hero dolls, etc.)

Scoring

The CLL scale is scored so that a high score reflects a good level of child care. Conversely, a low score indicates a poor level of child care. A one (1) in the appropriate column should be scored as 1. The highest possible score is 99. Total score is the *unweighted* sum of all items credited.

The items, as they appear in the scale, are ordered according to the cluster analyses. In using this scale, one should disassemble the clusters, so that items are randomly listed. This will help prevent coders from introducing unconscious biases, or halo effects, on items of known loadings.

Appendix Two

Maternal Characteristics Scale

Like the Childhood Level of Living Scale, the Maternal Characteristics Scale (MCS) stems from the original work in southern
Appalachia. By asking the research caseworker to partialize and to
specify judgments, the hope was to get reasonably objective ratings
of the mothers involved. Thus, rather than simply rating the mother
on impulsivity, we used a large number of specific behaviors which
were thought to define this trait operationally when added together.
The first study had a very large number of items in the MCS, which
were grouped rationally into three subscales. Subsequently, a factor
analysis was done on the data from the original field study, and
other data from fourteen AFDC workers who used the scale to
describe women from their caseloads. This factor analysis showed a
great deal of intercorrelation among items and few decipherable
factors. However, we did get item loadings on the three scales that
interested us most: apathy-futility, impulsivity, and verbal accessibility. Sixty items were chosen from the original pool in the mountain study in terms of their weightings, twenty from each of these
scales. The sixty items provided the initial pool for the Philadelphia
study.

These items were then placed on a form, in random order, so that
the workers doing ratings would not get an impression of what they
were accumulating as a score for each parent. The workers, in fact,
did not know the dimensions we were seeking to measure. A factor
analysis was then done of data from the present study by Dr.
Samuel Snyder, our statistical and design consultant. His analysis

picked out a total of six factors worthy of further examination. Of these, one simply seemed to divide cases in terms of whether a husband was present in the home, so it was discarded; the other accounted for minimal variance. Hence the scale kept for final analyses consisted of the four factors listed below: (1) relatedness (absence of apathy-withdrawal); (2) impulse-control; (3) confidence (absence of futility); (4) verbal accessibility. Note that all are described in "positive" terms, which meant, in the cases of (1) and (3) defining them also as the "absence of" something. These two factors, (1) and (3) we believed could be combined into a score giving the reciprocal or absence of apathy-futility. Factors (1), (2), and (3) may be combined to represent the absence of infantilism. Combinations are justified on rational grounds and also because the factor scores are intercorrelated.

As with the Childhood Level of Living Scale, each item is a declarative sentence which the worker scores as yes or no, that is, as true or false for the client. A yes on a positive characteristic yields a plus; a no on a positive characteristic a zero. A no on a negative trait yields a plus; and a yes yields a zero. Hence one's degree of "health" on each factor scored represents the proportion of pluses received out of the total number of items scored. Use of a percentage of possible pluses means that if an item or two are missing or proved unscorable, the person's score would still be roughly comparable to that of another with none missing.

The content of the factors, with items retaining their numbers as listed in the original pool for illustrative purposes, are given below. The Eigen values and variance for each are also given. Correlations with the control/neglect dichotomization are in table 8.1 (p. 101).

For future use by others we recommend that the items be rescrambled, of course, and listed on one form, with scoring to be done after the caseworkers or others have used the instrument on their cases. The reader will also note that the thirteen items listed under factor (1) accounted for over half the variance of the total item pool of sixty items, with our particular sample. In other words, a fair estimate of the client's "maturity" or intactness can be derived from the much smaller number of judgments.

Maternal Characteristics Scale

Factor 1. Relatedness (absence of apathy-withdrawal). Eigen value 17.62, 55.5% of variance

Item

10. It is hard for her to consider a new way of looking at the same thing. (loads $-.70$)
26. Can laugh at herself.
36. Frequently and appropriately expresses herself in abstractions.
4. Expresses awareness of complexities in others' decisions; that they have to weigh alternatives.
16. Seems incurious about the inner feelings of others.

50. Evidences sense of humor.
51. Shows interest in, and knowledge of, larger world scene.
11. Says she enjoys living.
17. Discusses her children's behavior as if from the outside.
20. Talks of her situation with practically no outward sign of emotion.
7. Shows warmth in gestures with interviewer.
33. Takes pleasure in her childrens' adventures.
54. In discussing children, client frequently adverts to self.

Factor 2. Impulse-control. Eigen value 3.13, 9.9% of variance
Item
43. Has shown defiance toward authorities in word and deed. (loads −.65)
14. Has engaged in behavior not acceptable in her own community.
27. Sets and maintains control on her own behavior.
24. Apparently married to escape an unpleasant home situation.
23. Plans realistically for herself, children, family.
13. Follows through on plans that have been made for herself, children, family.
34. Shows tolerance of routine.
42. Belongs to a church.
5. Often buys things impulsively.
2. Shows belligerance toward interviewer from time to time.

Factor 3. Confidence (absence of futility). Eigen value 2.43, 7.7% of variance
Item
8. Has a sad expression or holds her body in a dejected or despondent manner. (loads −.71)
58. Evidences (some verbalization) negative or discouraged attitude toward future accomplishments or attainments.
3. Speaks in a faint voice or voice fades away at end of sentence.
30. Keeps virtually the same posture throughout the interview.
52. Speaks with pride of personal achievement or possession.
59. Mentions she is aimless, or getting nowhere.
60. Shows enthusiasm.

Factor 4. Verbal Accessibility. Eigen value 2.03, 6.4% of variance
Item
40. Answers questions with single words or phrases only. (loads −.61)
49. Verbalizes embarrassment.
51. Shows warmth in tone when talking with her children.
57. Shows warmth in tone in discussing her children.
25. Usually states opinion reasonably directly.

References

Alfaro, J. D. 1978. Summary report on the relationship between child abuse and neglect and larger socially deviant behavior. New York: New York State Assembly Select Committee on Child Abuse.

Allport, G. W. 1942. *The use of personal documents in psychological science.* New York: Social Science Research Council.

———. 1954. The historical background of modern social psychology. In Lindzey, ed. *Handbook of social psychology, vol. 1, Theory and method.* Cambridge, Mass.: Addison-Wesley.

Ambrose, B. M. 1975. Parent rehabilitation and enrichment group. Albany, N.Y.: School of Social Work, SUNY at Albany. Photocopied.

America's Children 1976. Washington, D.C.: National Council of Organizations for Children and Youth.

American Psychiatric Association. 1968. *DSM II: Diagnostic and statistical manual of mental disorders.* Washington, D.C.: The Association.

Becker, D. G. 1971. Charles Loring Brace (1826–1890). In Morris, R., ed. *Encyclopedia of social work.* New York: National Association of Social Workers.

Becker, W. C. 1956. A genetic approach to the interpretation and evaluation of the process-reactive distinction in schizophrenia. *Journal of Abnormal and Social Psychology* 53:229–36.

Berkman, L. F., and Syme, S. L. 1979. Social networks, host resistance and mortality: A nine-year follow-up study of Alameda county residents. *American Journal of Epidemiology* 109:186–204.

Bibring, E. 1953. The mechanism of depression. In Greenacre, P. ed. *Affective disorders.* New York: International Universities Press.

Boehm, B. 1964. The community and the social agency define neglect. *Child Welfare* 43:453–64.

Bowen, M. 1975. Family therapy after twenty years. In Arieti, S., ed. *American Handbook of Psychiatry*. 2d ed. New York: Basic Books.

Bowlby, J. 1961. Separation anxiety: A critical review of the literature. *Journal of Child Psychology and Psychiatry* 1:251–69.

Brace, C. L. 1872. *The dangerous classes of New York and twenty years' work among them.* New York: Wynkoop and Hollenbeck. Quoted in Criner.

———. 1886. *Short sermons to newsboys with a history of the formation of the newsboys' lodging-house.* New York: Charles Scribner and Co. Quoted in Criner.

Bronfenbrenner, U. 1958. Socialization and social class through time and space. In Maccoby, E. E., Newcomb, T. M., and Hartley, L., eds. *Readings in social psychology.* New York: Henry Holt.

Brown, G. W., and Harris, T. 1978. *Social origins of depression.* New York: The Free Press.

Bullard, D. M. Jr., Glaser, H. H., Heagarty, M. C., and Pirchik, E. C. 1967. Failure to thrive in the neglected child. *American Journal of Orthopsychiatry* 37:688–90.

Bureau of Labor Statistics. 1961. *Revised equivalence scale for urban families of different size, age, and composition, 1960–61.* Washington, D.C.: U.S. Department of Labor.

———. 1976. *Urban family budgets and comparative indexes for selected urban areas.* Washington, D.C.: U.S. Department of Labor.

Burgess, R. L., and Conger, R. D. 1978. Family interaction in abusive, neglectful, and normal families. *Child Development* 49:1163–73.

Burt, M., and Balyeat, R. 1974. A new system for improving the care of neglected and abused children. *Child Welfare* 53:167–79.

Caldwell, B. M. 1967. What is the optimal learning environment for the young child? *American Journal of Orthopsychiatry* 37:8–21.

Cantor, M. 1975. The formal and informal social support system of older New Yorkers. Paper presented at the Tenth International Congress of Gerontology, Jerusalem.

Child Welfare League of America. 1973. *Standards for child protective services.* New York: The League.

Chrisman, O. 1920. *The historical child.* New York: Badger.

Cohen, J. 1960. A coefficient of agreement for nominal scales. *Educational and Psychological Measurement* 20:37–46.

Committee on Standards for Child Protective Service. 1960. *Standards for child protective service.* New York: Child Welfare League of America.

Costin, L. B. 1972. *Child welfare: Policies and practice.* New York: McGraw-Hill.

Criner, J. 1957. Charles Loring Brace and his dangerous classes. Los Angeles, California. Mimeographed.

Cronback, L. J., and Gleser, G. C. 1953. Assessing similarity between profiles. *Psychological Bulletin* 50:456–73.

Daly, M. R. 1979. "Burnout": Smoldering problem in protective services. *Social Work* 24:375–79.

Davis, A., and Havighurst, R. J. 1946. Social class and color differences in child-rearing. *American Sociological Review* 11:698–710.

Densen-Gerber, J., Hochstedler, R., and Weiner, M. 1973. Pregnancy in the addict. New York: Odyssey House. Mimeographed.

Dollard, J., Doob, L. W., Miller, N. E., Mowrer, O. H., and Sears, R. R. 1939. *Frustration and aggression.* New Haven: Yale University Press.

Dytrych, Z., Matczek, Z., Schuler, V., David, H. P., and Friedman, H. L. 1975. Children born to women denied abortion. *Family Planning Perspectives* 7:165–71.

Edwards, A. L. 1954. *Statistical methods for the behavioral sciences.* New York: Rinehart and Co.

Eisenberg, L. 1962. The sins of the fathers: Urban decay and social pathology. *American Journal of Orthopsychiatry* 32:5–17.

Elmer, E. 1967. *Children in jeopardy.* Pittsburgh, Pa.: University of Pittsburgh Press.

Emlen, A. C. 1974. Day care for whom? In Schorr, A., ed. *Children and decent people.* New York: Basic Books.

Erikson, E. H. 1956. The problem of ego identity. *Journal of the American Psychoanalytic Association* 4:56–121.

———. 1959. Growth and crises of the healthy personality. *Psychological Issues* 1:50–100.

Evans, S. L., Reinhart, J. B., and Succop, R. A. 1972. Failure to thrive—a study of 45 children and their families. *American Academy of Child Psychiatry* 2:440–57.

Fairbairn, W. D. 1952. *An object relations theory of the personality.* New York: Basic Books.

Fanshel, D. 1975. Parental visiting of children in foster care a key to discharge. *Social Service Review* 49:493–514.

Fanshel, D., and Shinn, E. B. 1972. *Dollars and sense in the foster care of children: A look at cost factors.* New York: Child Welfare League of America.

Festinger, L., Schachter, S. S., and Back, K. 1950. *Social pressures in informal groups: A study of human factors in housing.* New York: Harper.

Fierman, L. B. ed. 1965. *Effective psychotherapy: The contribution of Hellmuth Kaiser.* New York: The Free Press.

Fisher, N. 1979. *Reaching out: The volunteer in child abuse and neglect programs.* Washington, D.C.: National Center on Child Abuse and Neglect, Children's Bureau.

Flügel, J. C. 1935. *The psycho-analytic study of the family.* London: Hogarth Press.

Fontana, V. J. 1973. *Somewhere a child is crying.* New York: Macmillan.

Forss, H., and Thuwe, I. 1971. One hundred and twenty children born after application for therapeutic abortion refused. In *Abortion and the unwanted child.* New York: Pringer.

Fraiberg, S. 1971. Intervention in infancy: A program for blind infants. *Journal of the American Academy of Child Psychiatry* 10:381–404.

———. 1977. *Every child's birthright: In defense of mothering.* New York: Basic Books.

Friedman, H. 1953. Perceptual regression in schizophrenia: An hypothesis suggested by the use of the Rorschach test. *Journal of Projective Technique* 59:83–86.

Fromm-Reichmann, F. 1959. Loneliness. *Psychiatry* 22:1–15.

Ganter, G., Yeakel, M., and Polansky, N. A. 1967. *Retrieval from limbo.* New York: Child Welfare League of America.

Garbarino, J., and Crouter, A. 1979. Defining the community context for parent-child relations: The correlates of child maltreatment. Boys Town, Nebraska: Center for the Study of Youth Development. Xerox.

Garbarino, J., and Sherman, D. 1978a. High risk neighborhoods and high-risk families: The human ecology of child maltreatment. Boys Town, Nebraska: Center for the Study of Youth Development. Mimeographed.

————. 1978b. Child maltreatment as a research issue in applied community psychology. Presented at the Annual Convention, American Psychological Association, Toronto, Canada.

Geismar, L. L. 1971. *Family and community functioning.* Metuchen, N.J.: Scarecrow Press.

————. 1973. *555 families: A social psychological study of young families in transition.* New Brunswick, N.J.: Transaction.

Geismar, L. L., and LaSorte, M. A. 1963. Factors associated with family disorganization. *Marriage and Family Living* 25:479–81.

Gil, D. G. 1970. *Violence against children: Physical abuse in the United States.* Cambridge, Mass.: Harvard University Press.

Giovannoni, J. M., and Becerra, R. M. 1979. *Defining child abuse.* New York: The Free Press.

Giovannoni, J. M., and Billingsley, A. 1970. Child neglect among the poor: A study of parental adequacy in families of three ethnic groups. *Child Welfare* 49:196–204.

Glass, H., and Stanley, J. 1970. *Statistical methods in education and psychology.* Engelwood Cliffs, N.J.: Prentice-Hall.

Glass, L. 1974. Narcotic withdrawal in the newborn infant. *Journal of the National Medical Association* 66:117–20.

Goldberg, G. 1975. Breaking the communication barrier: The initial interview with an abusing parent. *Child Welfare* 54:274–82.

Goldfried, M. R. 1962. Some normative data on Rorschach's developmental level "card-pull" in a psychiatric population. *Journal of Projective Techniques* 26:283–87.

Goldstein, J., Freud, A., and Solnit, A. J. 1973. *Beyond the best interests of the child.* New York: The Free Press.

Gump, P., and Sutton-Smith, B. 1955. Activity setting and social interaction: A field study. *American Journal of Orthopsychiatry* 25:755–60.

Gunn, A. D. G. 1970. The neglected child. *Nursing Times* 66:946–47.

Guntrip, H. 1969. *Schizoid phenomena, object relations and the self.* New York: International Universities Press.

Hall, M. 1979. Summary of distinguishing factors between neglecting and abusing families. Dallas, Texas: Children and Youth Project, Department of Pediatrics, Southwestern Medical School.

Hally, C. F., Polansky, N. F., and Polansky, N. A., 1980. Child neglect:

Mobilizing treatment. Washington, D.C.: National Center on Child Abuse and Neglect, Children's Bureau.

Haring, J. 1965. Freedom of communication between parents and adolescents with problems. Unpublished DSW dissertation, Case Western Reserve University.

Harlow, H. F., and Harlow, M. K. 1962. Social deprivation in monkeys. *Scientific American* 207:136–46.

Harlow, H. F., Harlow, M. K., Dodsworth, R. O., and Arling, G. L. 1966. Maternal behavior of rhesus monkeys deprived of mothering and peer associations in infancy. *Proceedings of the American Philosophical Society* 110:58–66.

Harris, D. B. 1963. *Children's drawings as measures of intellectual maturity*. New York: Harcourt, Brace and World.

Hartman, H. 1958. *Ego psychology and the problem of adaptation*. New York: International Universities Press.

Herzog, E., and Sudia, C. E. 1970. *Boys in fatherless families*. Washington, D.C.: Children's Bureau.

Hollingshead, A. B. 1957. Two factor index of social position. New Haven, Conn. Mimeographed.

Hollis, F. 1964. *Casework: A psychosocial therapy*. New York: Random House.

Jacob, T. 1975. Family interaction in disturbed and normal families: A methodological and substantive review. *Psychological Bulletin* 82:33–65.

Jenkins, R. L., and Boyer, A. 1967. Types of delinquent behavior and background factors. *International Journal of Social Psychiatry* 14:65–76.

———. 1970. Effects of inadequate mothering and inadequate fathering on children. *International Journal of Social Psychiatry* 16:72–78.

Jones, M. 1953. *The therapeutic community*. New York: Basic Books.

Kadushin, A. 1974. *Child welfare services*. 2d ed. New York: Macmillan.

———. 1978. Children in foster families and institutions. In Maas, H. S., ed. *Social service research: Studies in the seventies*. Washington, D.C.: National Association of Social Workers.

Kagel, S. A., White, R. M., and Coyne, J. C. 1978. Father-absent and father-present families of disturbed and nondisturbed adolescents. *American Journal of Orthopsychiatry* 48:342–52.

Kahn, A. J., Kamerman, S. B., and McGowan, B. G. 1972. *Child advocacy*. New York: Columbia University School of Social Work.

Kapelle, B., Scott, V., and Western, S. 1976. Model design and training manual for a parent aide program. Division of Protective Services, Michigan State Department of Social Services, Lansing, Michigan.

Kardiner, A. 1945. *The psychological frontiers of society*. New York: Columbia University Press.

Katz, S. N., Howe, R. W., and McGrath, M. 1975. Child neglect laws in America. *Family Law Quarterly* 9:1–373.

Kerlinger, F., and Pedhazer, E. 1973. *Multiple regression in behavior research*. New York: Holt, Rinehart, and Winston.

Kernberg, O. 1966. Structural derivatives of object relationships. *Inter-*

national Journal of Psycho-Analysis 47:236–53.

Kerr, A. D., Bogues, J. L., and Kerr, D. S. 1978. Psychosocial functioning of mothers of malnourished children. *Pediatrics* 62:778–84.

Kissel, S. 1965. A brief note on the relationship between Rorschach developmental level and intelligence. *Journal of Projective Techniques and Personality Assessment* 29:454–55.

Klein, M., Heimann, P., Isaacs, S., and Riviera, J. 1952. *Developments in psychoanalysis.* London: Hogarth.

Knight, R. P. 1951. Management and psychotherapy of the borderline schizophrenic patient. *Bulletin of the Menninger Clinic.* 17:139–50.

Kogan, L. J. 1975. Principles of measurement. In Polansky, N. A., ed. *Social work research.* Chicago: University of Chicago Press.

Kogan, L. J., and Jenkins, S. 1974. Indicators of child health and welfare: Development of the DIPOV Index. New York: Columbia University Press.

Kohn, M. L. 1968. *Class and conformity.* Homewood, Ill.: Dorsey Press.

Koppitz, E. M. 1964. *The Bender Gestalt test for young children.* New York: Grune and Stratton.

Kramer, E., and Francis, P. S. 1965. Errors in intelligence estimate with short forms of the WAIS. *Journal of Consulting and Clinical Psychology* 29:490–94.

Lauderdale, M. L., Anderson, R. N., and Cramer, S. E. 1978. *Child abuse and neglect: Issues of innovation and implementation.* Washington, D.C.: National Center on Child Abuse and Neglect, Children's Bureau.

Levy, D. 1943. *Maternal overprotection.* New York: Columbia University Press.

Lewin, K. 1951. *Field theory in social science.* New York: Harper.

Lewis, H. 1969. Parental and community neglect: Twin responsibilities of protective services. *Children.* 16:114–18.

Lewis, H., Jahn, J., and Bishop, J. A. 1967. Designing more effective services: Intervening in the recurrence cycle of neglect and abuse of children. Philadelphia: University of Pennsylvania School of Social Work. Mimeographed.

Lowenstein, S. 1976. Passions in the lives of women. Boston: Simmons College School of Social Work. Photocopied.

Lynch, J. J. 1977. *The broken heart: Medical consequences of loneliness.* New York: Basic Books.

Maas, H. S., and Engler, R. E. 1959. *Children in need of parents.* New York: Columbia University Press.

Mahler, M. S. 1963. Thoughts about development and individuation. *Psychoanalytic study of the child. Vol. XVIII.* New York: International Universities Press.

Mahler, M. S., Pine, F., and Bergman, A. 1975. *The psychological birth of the human infant.* New York: Basic Books.

Martin, H. P. 1976. *The abused child.* Cambridge, Mass.: Ballinger.

———. 1979. Developmental impact of neglect on children. Paper presented at the Ninth Annual Child Abuse and Neglect Symposium, University of Colorado School of Medicine, Keystone, Col., May 17–19.

Martin, M. P. 1978. *1977 analysis of child abuse and neglect research.*

Washington, D.C.: National Center on Child Abuse and Neglect, Children's Bureau.

Martin, M. P., and Klaus, S. 1978. *1978 annual review of child abuse and neglect research.* Washington, D.C.: National Center on Child Abuse and Neglect, Children's Bureau.

McDougall, W. 1932. *The energies of men: A study of the fundamentals of dynamic psychology.* London: Methuen.

Meier, E. G. 1964. Child neglect. In Cohen, N. E., ed. *Social work and social problems.* New York: National Association of Social Workers.

Miller, R. R. 1977. Disappointment in therapy: A paradox. *Clinical Social Work* 5:17–28.

Minuchin, S., Montalvo, B., Guerney, B. G., Rosman, B. L., and Schumer, F. 1967. *Families of the slums.* New York: Basic Books.

Morris, M. G., and Gould, R. W. 1963. Role-reversal, a necessary concept in dealing with the "battered child" syndrome. In *The neglected/battered child syndrome.* New York: Child Welfare League of America.

Moustakis, C. E. 1975. *The touch of loneliness.* Englewood Cliffs, N.J.: Prentice-Hall.

Nagi, S. 1977. *Child maltreatment in the United States.* New York: Columbia University Press.

Oliver, J. E., and Taylor, A. 1971. Five generations of ill-treated children in one family pedigree. *British Journal of Psychiatry* 119:472–80.

Osgood, C. D., Suci, G. J., and Tannenbaum, P. H. 1957. *The measurement of meaning.* Urbana, Ill.: The University of Illinois Press.

Paget, N. W. 1967. Emergency parent: A protective service to children in crisis. *Child Welfare* 46:403–7.

Pavenstedt, E. 1973. An intervention program for infants from high risk homes. *American Journal of Public Health.* 63:393–95.

Podell, L. 1973. Family planning by mothers on welfare. *Bulletin of the New York Academy of Medicine* 49:931–37.

Polansky, N. A. 1969. Powerlessness among rural Appalachian youth. *Rural Sociology* 34:219–22.

———. 1971. *Ego psychology and communication.* Chicago: Aldine.

———. 1973. Beyond despair. In Kahn, A. J., ed., *Shaping the new social work.* New York: Columbia University Press.

———. 1975. Theory construction and the scientific method. In Polansky, N. A., ed. *Social work research.* Chicago: University of Chicago Press.

———. 1979. Help for the help-less. *Smith College Studies in Social Work* 49:169–91.

———. 1980. On loneliness: A program for social work. Northampton, Mass.: Smith College School for Social Work.

Polansky, N. A., Borgman, R. D., and DeSaix, C. 1972. *Roots of futility.* San Francisco: Jossey-Bass.

Polansky, N. A., Borgman, R. D., DeSaix, C., and Sharlin, S. 1971. Verbal accessibility in the treatment of child neglect. *Child Welfare* 50:349–56.

Polansky, N. A., Borgman, R. D., DeSaix, C., and Smith, B. J. 1970. Two modes of maternal immaturity and their consequences. *Child Welfare* 49:312–23.

Polansky, N. A., Chalmers, M. A., Buttenwieser, E., and Williams, D.

1978. Assessing adequacy of child caring: An urban scale. *Child Welfare* 57:439–49.

Polansky, N. A., DeSaix, C., and Sharlin, S. 1972. *Child neglect: Understanding and reaching the parent.* New York: Child Welfare League of America.

Polansky, N. A., DeSaix, C., Wing, M. L., and Patton, J. D. 1968. Child neglect in a rural community. *Social Casework* 49:467–74.

Polansky, N. A., Doroff, C., Kramer, E., Hess, D. S., and Pollane, L. P. 1978. Public opinion and intervention in child neglect. *Social Work Research and Abstracts* 14:11–15.

Polansky, N. A., Hally, C., and Polansky, N. F. 1975. *Profile of neglect.* Washington, D.C.: Public Services Administration, Department of H.E.W.

Polansky, N. A., and Polansky, N. F. 1968. The current status of child abuse and child neglect in this country. Report to the Joint Commission on the Mental Health of Children.

Polansky, N. A., and Pollane, L. 1975. Measuring adequacy of child caring: Further developments. *Child Welfare* 54:354–59.

Polansky, N. A., and Williams, D. P. 1978. Class orientations to child neglect. *Social Work* 23:397–401.

Powell, G. F., Brasel, J. A., and Blizzard, R.M. 1967. Emotional deprivation and growth retardation simulating idiopathic hypopituitarism: Clinical evaluations of the syndrome. *New England Journal of Medicine* 276:1271–78.

Radin, N., and Glasser, P. H. 1965. The use of parental attitude questionnaires with culturally disadvantaged families. *Journal of Marriage and the Family* 27:373–82.

Rapaport, D. 1951. The autonomy of the ego. *Bulletin of the Menninger Clinic* 15:113–23.

———. 1967. Edward Bibring's theory of depression. In Gill, M. M., ed. *Collected papers of David Rapaport.* New York: Basic Books.

"Reports" February, 1977. National Center on Child Abuse and Neglect. Children's Bureau.

"Reports" October, 1979. National Center on Child Abuse and Neglect. Children's Bureau.

Ripple, L., Alexander, E., and Polemis, B. W. 1964. *Motivation, capacity and opportunity.* Chicago: School of Social Work, University of Chicago.

Rosen, S., and Polansky, N. A. 1975. Observation of social interaction. In Polansky, N. A., ed. *Social work research.* Chicago: University of Chicago Press.

Rubinstein, C., Sharer, P., and Peplau, L. A. 1979. Loneliness. *Human Nature* 2:58–65.

Ruesch, J. 1948. The infantile personality: The core problem of psychosomatic medicine. *Psychosomatic Medicine* 10:134–44.

Sanders, L. F. 1979. Sweden's unique approach to child protection. *Child Abuse and Neglect Reports* 1–4, March.

Sandgrund, A., Gaines, R. W., and Green, A. H. 1974. Child abuse and mental retardation: A problem of cause and effect. *American Journal of Mental Deficiency* 79:327–30.

Schaefer, E. S., and Bell, R. Q. 1958. Development of a parental attitude research instrument. *Child Development* 29:339–61.

Schlesinger, B. 1970. *The multi-problem family.* 3d ed. Toronto: University of Toronto Press.

Schorr, A., ed. 1974. *Children and decent people.* New York: Basic Books.

Scrimshaw, N. S. 1969. Early malnutrition and central nervous system function. *Merrill-Palmer Quarterly* 15:375–87.

Sears, R. R., Maccoby, E. E., and Levin, H. 1957. *Patterns of child rearing.* New York: Harper and Row.

Shapiro, D. 1965. *Neurotic styles.* New York: Basic Books.

Shuford, K. H. 1978. Specific personality attributes of child abusing mothers. Unpublished master's thesis, Department of Psychology, University of North Carolina at Greensboro.

Shyne, A. W., and Schroeder, A. G. 1978. *National study of social services to children and their families.* Washington, D.C.: National Center for Child Advocacy. U.S. Children's Bureau.

Silverstein, A. B. 1970. Reappraisal of the validity of the WAIS, WISC and WPPSI short forms. *Journal of Consulting and Clinical Psychology* 34:12–14.

Skinner, B. F. 1969. *Contingencies of reinforcement: A theoretical analysis.* New York: Appleton-Century Crofts.

Smith, S. M., and Hanson, R. 1972. Failure to thrive and anorexia nervosa. *Postgraduate Medical Journal* 48:382–84.

Smith, S. M., Hanson, R., and Noble, S. 1974. Social aspects of the battered baby syndrome. *British Journal of Psychiatry* 125:568–82.

Spinetta, J. J., and Rigler, D. 1972. The child abusing parent: A psychological review. *Psychological Bulletin* 77:296–304.

Spitz, R. 1945. Hospitalism: An inquiry into the genesis of psychiatric conditions in early childhood. In *The psychoanalytic study of the child, Vol. 1.* New York: International Universities Press.

Srole, L. 1956. Social integration and certain corollaries: An exploratory study. *American Sociological Review* 21:709–16.

Steele, B. 1975. *Working with abusive parents from a psychiatric point of view.* Washington, D.C.: Office of Child Development.

Steele, B. F., and Pollock, C. B. 1974. A psychiatric study of parents who abuse infants and small children. In Kempe, C. H., and Helfer, R. E., eds. *The battered child* 2d ed. Chicago: University of Chicago Press.

Steiner, G. Y. 1976. *The children's cause.* Washington, D.C.: Brookings Institution.

Stone, E., Levant, R. F., Rabinowitz, J. B., and Harrell, B. T. 1980. *Casework focus on hostility shows promise with child abusers.* Dorchester, Mass: Roxbury Children's Service, Inc. Unpublished photocopy.

Sullivan, H. S. 1947. *Conceptions of modern psychiatry.* Washington, D.C.: William A. White Foundation.

Sullivan, M., Spasser, M., and Penner, G. L. 1977. *Bowen center project* for abused and neglected children. Washington, D.C.: Public Services Administration, Office of Human Development.

Tatsuoka, M., 1971. *Multivariate analysis: Techniques for educational and psychological research.* New York: Wiley.

Varon, E. 1964. Communication: Client, community and agency. *Social Work* 9:51–57.

Vore, D. 1973. Prenatal nutrition and postnatal intellectual development. *Merrill-Palmer Quarterly* 19:253–60.

Wald, M. S. 1976. State intervention on behalf of "neglected" children: standards for removal of children from their homes, monitoring the status of children in foster-care, and termination of parental rights. *Stanford Law Review* 28:628–706.

Wardle, M. 1970. The Lordsville project: Experimental group work in a deprived area. *Case Conference* 16:441–46.

Wasserman, H. 1970. Early careers of professional social workers in a public child welfare agency. *Social Work* 15:93–101.

Wasserman, S. L. 1974. Ego psychology. In Turner, F. J., ed. *Social work treatment.* New York: Free Press.

Werner, H. 1948. *Comparative psychology of mental development.* New York: International Universities Press.

Wilensky, H. 1959. Rorschach developmental level and social participation of chronic schizophrenics. *Journal of Projective Techniques* 23:87–92.

Wilson, G., and Ryland, G. 1949. *Social group work practice.* New York: Houghton Mifflin.

Winer, B. J. 1971. *Statistical principles in experimental design.* 2d ed. New York: McGraw-Hill Book Co.

Wolock, I., and Horowitz, B. 1979. Child maltreatment and material deprivation among AFDC-recipient families. *Social Service Review* 53: 175–94.

Young, L. 1964. *Wednesday's children: A study of child neglect and abuse.* New York: McGraw-Hill Book Co.

Subject Index

Abuse: in mothers' histories, 153–155; and parental narcissism, 211

Alienation of neglectful parents, 91; in adolescence, 95

Anomia: related to paternal absence, 141; Srole's scale for, 91

Apathy-futility syndrome, 39–40; correlated with poor child care, 200; etiology of, 43, 201; interobserver reliability of 109; judges' ratings of 103–4, 106; on Maternal Characteristics Scale, 101; and parental isolation, 96; prevalence among parents, 200

Appalachian studies, 31

Bowen Center, 30, 206–8

Burnout, causes of, 241; self-treatment for, 242–44

Case illustration, 3–5, 77–78, 114–25, 150–51, 180–81, 191–92, 193–94, 204–5, 217–18

Casework treatment of neglect, 176–79; functions in, 212–15

Causal theories: economic, 22–23, 33; ecological, 25–29; personalistic, 29–31, 34–36

Character disorder: diagnosis of, 109; prevalence in parents, 110; treatment of, 161

Character structure: in abusive parents, 30–31, 103; among Appalachian parents, 35; significance to treatment of, 179–85

Childhood Level of Living Scale, 245–49; and child's intelligence, 127; construction of, 65–73; and maternal attributes, 114; and maternal intelligence, 128; need for urban revision of, 56–57; and paternal attributes, 116; and poverty, 79–80; and social class values, 80–85; validity of, 73–79

Community attitudes: as affecting child care standards, 27–28; as affecting intervention, 11, 160–69

Community neglect, 28

Day care, 229–31

Detachment: and the child's verbal

Index of Names